The Fiction of Imp

Writing Past Colonialism Series

Edited by Phillip Darby, Margaret Thornton and Patrick Wolfe,
Institute of Postcolonial Studies, Melbourne

The leitmotiv of the series is the idea of difference – differences between culture and politics, as well as differences in ways of seeing and the sources that can be drawn upon. In this sense, it is postcolonial. Yet the space we hope to open up is one resistant to new orthodoxies, one that allows for alternative and contesting formulations. Though grounded in studies relating to the formerly colonized world, the series seeks to extend contemporary global analyses.

THE FICTION OF IMPERIALISM

Reading Between International Relations and Postcolonialism

Phillip Darby

CASSELL

London and Washington

Cassell

Wellington House, 125 Strand, London WC2R 0BB, England

PO Box 605, Herndon, Virginia 20172–0605, USA

First published 1998

British Library Cataloguing in Publication Data
A catalogue record for this book is available from the British Library.

ISBN 0 304 70158 0 Hardback

 0 304 70159 9 Paperback

Library of Congress Cataloging-in-Publication Data

Darby, Phillip.
 The fiction of imperialism : reading between international relations and postcolonialism / Phillip Darby.
  p. cm. — (Writing past colonialism series)
  Includes bibliographical references and index.
  ISBN 0-304-70158-0 (hardcover). — ISBN 0-304-70159-9 (pbk.)
  1. Politics and literature. 2. Imperialism in literature.
 3. Decolonization in literature. 4. Literature, Modern—20th century—History and criticism.
 5. Developing countries—Literatures—History and criticism. I. Title. II. Series.
  PN51.D285 1988
  809.3'9358—dc21   97–27690
                                                              CIP

Typeset by Ben Cracknell Studios

Printed and bound in Great Britain by Biddles Ltd, Guildford and King's Lynn.

Contents

Introduction   1

PART I   **Making Connections**

CHAPTER ONE   **The exclusions of politics**   9

CHAPTER TWO   **The orientations of fiction**   34

CHAPTER THREE   **Rereading dominance**   53

PART II   **Situating Debate**

CHAPTER FOUR   **The Indo-British relationship**   79

CHAPTER FIVE   **African literature and cultural politics**   136

PART III   **Reframing Issues**

CHAPTER SIX   **Fiction's silences and relocations?**   191

CHAPTER SEVEN   **A postcolonial retrospect**   215

Bibliography   236

Index   247

To the memory of
Albert Paolini
1963–1996

Introduction

This book is an attempt to promote dialogue between established approaches to international politics and new formations of knowledge concerned with postcolonialism and culture. To this end, it addresses the contribution of fiction to an understanding of the imperial relationship between the West and Asia and Africa. It does so by tracing the ways in which fictional narratives have depicted the interaction between colonizer and colonized, between North and South. These are referenced, on the one hand, to the conventions of disciplinary international relations, and, on the other, to the understandings which inform postcolonial studies. Throughout, literary texts constitute the primary site of engagement. Their content and meanings are taken to matter in themselves. At the same time, the texts serve to establish connections between different schools of thought which ought to communicate, but mostly do not.

The idea of the project was sparked by my use of imaginative literature in teaching courses on the international politics of the North/South divide. The response of students to the fictional material and the angles that we were led to consider suggested that here was a subject for study in its own right. The question which emerged can be put with deceptive simplicity: what do we learn by reading fiction that is missing from the conventional political and historical sources? By 'we', I had in mind primarily students of North/South and Third World politics. As the book took shape, however, this constituency came to be supplemented by another, a readership comprising those scholars intent on promoting new ways of thinking about the colonial relationship and its aftermath through concentrating on the discursive and the subjective. The book is thus oriented to two very different readerships, neither of which has previously shown much interest in the concerns of the other. It is therefore sensible to set out the way my thinking developed with regard to the scope of the inquiry and how this might relate to the presumptions of prospective readers.

From the outset, it was my conviction that disciplinary international relations needed to engage with the apparently very different world revealed through imaginative literature. The discipline has not been alone in its suspicion about the pertinence of literary narratives to its own particular version of the systematic study of political aggregates. World systems theory, comparative politics and globalization discourse exhibit a similar reluctance to allow fiction anything more than secondary status. Coming from a background in disciplinary international relations, my arguments are mostly developed in relation to that material but there is good reason to think that they have a more general applicability. At various points in the text, reference is made to established scholarship in international and imperial studies but I have tried to avoid the twin pitfalls of assuming this to be a secure anchorage and presenting it simply as orthodoxy that needs to be overturned.

When I first turned to literary narratives the presumption remained strong (certainly in positivist disciplines such as politics) that a more or less clear line could be drawn between fiction and non-fiction. The idea that there exists an essential difference between the two has now been exploded and, at least theoretically, one would be hard-pressed to maintain that literature constitutes a discrete category. This does not mean, however, that there are not significant generic differences between a novelist's approach and that of (say) a political scientist, or that we read all narratives in much the same way. The established conventions remain too strong for that. In other words, the claims of the theorists seem in many respects at variance with disciplinary practice. To argue to the contrary would leave one unable to account for the selectivity about source materials and the silence in significant areas which mark some disciplinary approaches, for example, international relations.

Coming close on the heels of the rejection of literature as a distinctive province is the diminution of its status, at least in certain circles, as a repository of critical and reflective thinking. Not only, we are told, is the author dead but literature is as well. In the words of one critic, literary theory and practice have become the dominant modes of literary expression, and literature itself is 'merely the site for the intersection of various discourses'.[1] It is easy to retort by pointing to the many new writers who keep returning to the old writers and even to the canon – perhaps none more so than our critic's mentor, Edward Said.[2] Yet one can hardly fail to notice that in postcolonial discourse, for instance, fictional narratives have lost their earlier prominence and the essay has been increasingly favoured over the novel. Some of these issues will be taken up in the concluding chapter, but only at its margins is this book concerned to debate questions of literary or other theory. It proceeds on the conviction that imaginative literature has an ideational value which is located in the conversation between text and reader. Literature also has an instrumental value when it is related to its cultural context and to material interests. We need to take account of the way it is implicated in the processes of imperial expansion and how it is used to advance decolonization in a variety of forms. This side of the politics of fiction has often been overlooked but should not be today. But this is not a reason for displacing the text as text. Coming to literature from politics, there was an innocence about my approach. I have learnt a lot while working on this book but I hope I have retained a little of my earlier innocence.

Initially I had proposed to restrict attention to Western literary narratives because these were more familiar to me. The reach of the book would have been curtailed accordingly. It was Ravinder Kumar in Delhi who persuaded me to take account of Third World literature as well, one argument being that this would introduce dialogue in place of monologue. Although I have followed Professor Kumar's advice, in this particular respect I believe his reasoning was mistaken. Despite the stamp of shared culture, Western texts often contend with each other and even in individual works different currents of thought carry the narrative forward. It is scarcely less true that there is a sense of cut and thrust within the various national and regional bodies of Third World literature. The argument will be developed that, in the interests of solidarity and resistance, the tendency has often been for this to be down-played.

The presumption that contestation is the mark of literary engagement across the divide needs to be approached with circumspection. While it is true that imperial texts galvanized nationalist texts, the obvious alterities should not obscure the less obvious commonalities and continuities. It is now more widely recognized that the colonial encounter, by virtue of its very intensity and intrusiveness, had its moments of intimacy (the word derives from Ashis Nandy) and its measure of cultural collusion. There is therefore all the more reason to study the texts of colonizer and colonized concurrently, not simply to amplify the politics of difference but to expose a measure of congruence which arrests the pull of binarism.

Even by this point, it will be apparent that my approach has been influenced by the emergence of colonial discourse analysis and postcolonial theory. These new formations have been responsible for the resurgence of interest in literary texts about imperialism, directed especially to their role as conveyors of the culture and interests of imperialism, on the one hand, and of liberation, on the other. This book connects in part with these concerns but it also stands at a certain distance from them. As with disciplinary international relations, I have resisted being drawn into debates intelligible only to the insider, concentrating instead on identifying areas of congruence and basic divides with other discourses. In some instances I have attempted a kind of translation exercise, suggesting that communication between different formations of knowledge is possible (and desirable) even though, on the face of it, their terms of reference appear quite different.

There is, I believe, much to recommend such an approach to post-colonialism. For a discourse which has invested so heavily in developing a politics of othering, postcolonialism has been remarkably insensitive to recognizing other ways of proceeding or engaging with other knowledge formations. There is hardly a reference to international relations or dependency theory in the literature and many fewer than one would expect to imperial history. Then there are the barriers put in place by the choice of a prose style and vocabulary which work to exclude the uninitiated.[3] In some circumstances, difficult and unfamiliar language has its uses but in a discourse committed to the elevation of the subaltern, such writing practices are inappropriate.

Here, as far as possible, I have tried to avoid disciplinary jargon and write in plain English. My hope is that this will serve as a neutral medium helping to bring together different discourses. At the same time, it should assist in making the book accessible to those people in the Third World who are cut off from recent theoretical debates in the West. As a counter to the colonizing tendencies of much contemporary Western discourse, I have chosen to use the nomenclature of North, South, Third and First Worlds. There are difficulties about such terms.[4] Objections can be raised against their political connotations and historical associations. Alternative formulations in the vocabulary of international politics raise problems of their own – to my mind more serious. The lexicon of postcolonialism has failed to produce satisfactory substitutes and, all too often, analyses in terms of othering give a semblance of sameness to power relations everywhere, irrespective of what is at stake.[5] The terminology used in this book is meant to indicate broad commonalities between some societies and peoples and shadow lines of demarcation between these and others. It is necessary, however, to be attentive to the claims of mobility and to recognize a fluidity which is dependent upon the criteria employed.[6]

The book is divided into three parts. Part I establishes the ground on which the project goes forward. It argues against the positivism and compartment-alization in international relations which has characterized the treatment of North/South relations and, even more, led to their neglect. This is contrasted with the more open and often introspective orientation of the fictional texts and the way we tend to read them. Literary and non-literary approaches are then brought together in a study of dominance which encapsulates the basic themes of the book. Part II situates the general lines of argument and is of a case-study nature. The imperial connection between Britain and India is explored through a reading of both British and Indian texts. The hinge of the analysis is the question of the personal as political. This is paired with an analysis of African literature and its treatment of history, community and modernity. The theme here is the relationship between culture and politics. Part III approaches literature from the outside. The penultimate chapter considers questions about economic interest and power politics that are of foundational importance to the student of international politics and asks about the apparent silence of the fictional texts in these areas. The final chapter reviews the themes of the book in the light of postcolonial discourse. How do the arguments about the utility of fictional narratives stand up when approached from the vantage-point of a discourse which increasingly takes its bearings from theory?

It is a pleasure to acknowledge the help I have received from friends and colleagues in working on this book. In Oxford, where the project took shape, I benefited from the stimulation and encouragement of Max Beloff, Marilyn Butler and Molly Mahood. In Melbourne, in the final stages of the project, Patrick Wolfe suggested ways in which arguments could be sharpened and presentation improved. In several extended visits to India and Africa I was pointed in new directions and introduced to material I would not otherwise have seen. All I can do here is to mention by name some of the people who helped, but this hardly conveys my indebtedness and affection. In Madras there was K. R. Srinivasa Iyengar; in Mysore, C. D. Narasimhaiah and V. R. Anantha Murthy; in Hyderabad, Susie Tharu and Alok Bhalla; in Calcutta,

Nabaneeta Dev Sen, P. Lal, Subir Roy Chaudhuri, Gouranga Chattopadhyay and Partha Chatterjee; in Delhi, Ashis Nandy, Ravinder Kumar and Meenakshi and Sujit Mukherjee; in Accra, Kofi Agovi and George Hagan; in Calabar, Celestine Bassey, Ebele Eko and Ernest Emenyonu; in Ibadan, J. F. A. Ajayi, Femi Osofisan, Isodore Okpewho and Niyi Osundare; in Nairobi, Henry Indangasi, Chris Wanjala, Francis Imbuga, Rosemary Ndegwa and Roger Kurtz; in Kampala, Timothy Wangusa, Arthur Gakwandi and Mahmood Mamdani; in Harare, Anthony Chennells, Hasu Patel, Chenjerai Hove, Flora Veit-Wild and Jonathan Moyo; and in Dar es Salaam, Mwesiga Baregu and Daudi Mukangara.

I am grateful to the Australian Research Council for providing financial support and to Jan Souter, Rita Corelli and Wendy Ruffles for transferring my handwritten script onto computer disk (although on the condition that I come to grips with modernity hereafter).

Most of all I am indebted to my research students who have provoked and cajoled me to rethink. In particular I must mention Albert Paolini, Grant Parsons, Richard Fuller, Edgar Ng, Sekai Nzenza, Kirsty Major and Kosmas Tsokhas. I had hoped to dedicate this book to Albert Paolini, the prime mover in this process. Albert died last year at the age of thirty-three. I now dedicate the book to his memory.

Notes

1. Mustapha Ben T. Marrouchi, 'Literature is dead, long live theory', *Queen's Quarterly*, 98:4 (Winter 1991), 775–801 (pp. 784–5).

2. Significantly, our critic does not discuss this aspect of Said's writing. See Mustapha Ben T. Marrouchi, 'The critic as dis/placed intelligence: the case of Edward Said', *Diacritics*, 21:1 (Spring 1991), 63–74.

3. See here the telling criticisms of Dane Kennedy, 'Imperial history and post-colonial theory', *The Journal of Imperial and Commonwealth History*, 24:3 (September 1996), 345–63 (pp. 349–50).

4. See for instance George Yudice, 'We are *not* the world', *Social Text*, 31/32 (1992), 202–16; Ania Loomba, 'Overworking the "Third World"', *Oxford Literary Review*, 12 (1991), 164–91; and Mark T. Berger, 'The end of the "Third World"?', *Third World Quarterly*, 15:2 (1993), 257–75.

5. For a clipped but penetrating discussion of some of the problems, see Ella Shohat, 'Notes on the "post-colonial"', *Social Text*, 31/32 (1992), 99–113.

6. I have argued the case more fully in Phillip Darby (ed.), *At the Edge of International Relations. Post-colonialism, Gender and Dependency* (Pinter, London, 1997), pp. 8–11.

— Part I —

Making Connections

CHAPTER 1

The exclusions of politics

An inquiry into sources necessarily raises questions about subject matter and disciplinary divides. It is for this reason that in practice there is often much less openness about source materials than tends to be assumed. How, then, are we to understand the politics of North/South relations? What issues and concerns are involved in such relations? Which formations of knowledge can be expected to advance our understanding? In the present climate of intellectual contestation, very different answers are likely to be given to such questions. Until perhaps two decades ago there was a broad consensus. The relationship between Africa and Asia and the West was largely the province of imperial history, except that at a certain stage in the story – around decolonization – international relations took over. During this time, literature maintained a marginal presence through studies of imperial and Commonwealth fiction. Mostly, however, such studies proceeded on a text-by-text basis and disciplinary conventions remained too strong for the politics of fiction to be pursued in any depth. Then interest quickened and approaches diverged. Third World historians claimed a space for stories of their own, as did dependency theory and its associated modes of thinking. Now new discourses follow suit. Colonial discourse analysis and postcolonial theory see themselves as centrally concerned. There is a vigorous body of work in gender studies. Globalization theory maintains at least a nominal interest.

No doubt there is much to recommend a diversity of approach. It is unfortunate, however, that the increasing specialization in the humanities and the emergence of new formations of knowledge have been accompanied in many instances by a lack of contact between old and new discourses and between different schools of thought. Established disciplines jealously guard their orthodoxies and new discourses, each with its own language, methodology and publishing outlets, tend to allow their own distinctive concerns to overrun their explanatory capacities.

Prima facie, disciplinary international relations makes an appropriate point of entry into the study of the relationship between the West and Africa and Asia because of its concern with external politics. In saying this, I advance no proprietary claim for international relations as a discipline nor imply that it occupies some high ground from which to judge the strengths and weaknesses of other approaches. It is in fact my view that, so far as the Third World is concerned, the discipline has not even been a reliable witness. None the less, it is an underlying assumption of this book that the discipline has identified certain systemic features of politics in the global context which must be addressed. More than this, coming as I do from a background in international relations, it is probable that other disciplinary presumptions have found their way into the text without my awareness. Taking account of these considerations, our inquiry begins by addressing the inheritance of the discipline and its weaknesses when it comes to engaging with North/South relations. With the ground thus prepared, we will be in a position to consider the ways in which a reading of fiction can expand our understanding of the politics between North and South. At a later stage – in the penultimate chapter – we will return to disciplinary international relations and its insistence on having uncovered the basic determinants of state action. The question then will be whether fiction disregards international relations' strictures – and at what cost.

Towards a broader conception of international relations

By the logic of its narrative, international relations lays claim to North/South relations. In the matter of politics among nations, the discipline's territory covers the whole world. Its theorizing is of a universalist nature, its precepts making little allowance for cultural difference or admitting subsystems operating along alternative lines. Such are its appeals that it has colonized or won converts in most parts of the world. Hans Morgenthau's classic post-war text is required reading in universities throughout Asia and Africa; PhDs framed in terms of national interest have become almost a global industry. Yet it is increasingly apparent that international relations' writ is confined within the disciplinary domain. Development and democratization discourses at least concede a place for international relations even though they largely exist outside it. Other formations – most notably postcolonialism and Third World studies – strike out in directions of their own, without acknowledging international relations' claims or concerning themselves much with its literature.

Having situated disciplinary international relations within the broader context of scholarship concerned in one way or another with North/South relations, I now want to engage with the adequacy of its terms of reference. The central argument of this part is to assert the need for a broader conception of international relations than that traditionally adopted. Put this way, there may be a suspicion that the subject is being defined to suit the source material. In any case, it might be said, the proposition invites agreement. Who would readily defend 'narrow' disciplinary constructions or suggest that the bounds once set must remain so for all time? These points could be debated, but they scarcely affect my basic contention that there has been remarkable resistance to breaking down the in-built Eurocentrism of the discipline or widening the conception of the political.

Let us consider Eurocentrism first. For a discipline which projects itself as the primary grid of reference for mapping global politics, international relations has directed only limited and episodic attention to North/South relations. It has been even less concerned with the position of the Third World itself. These patterns were established in the era of imperialism. During this period colonial issues intruded very little into international politics. Imperial relations were not international relations and they fell outside the main concerns of the discipline. As a result, international relations distanced itself from the processes that helped to shape the future of more than two-thirds of the world's peoples and the division of its resources. After decolonization, Afro-Asian states fared little better. Overshadowed by the politics of the cold war, their place in international relations was basically determined by their relationship to the principal protagonists. The salient issues were those that were seen to connect with the East/West struggle. We are now entering a new phase in which, supposedly, the global divisions of the past are being swept aside as more and more countries embrace neo-liberal market economics and the pressures for democratization become irresistible. So it may appear on the surface of international relations, but whether the proclaimed world order meshes at all well with what is happening on the ground in many parts of Asia and Africa is quite another thing. There is a strong case to be argued that the order envisaged is nothing more than the latest manifestation of Western universalism.

Much of the ethnocentrism and universalism of disciplinary international relations follows from its fixation with power. In the predominant view – which is textualized in the theories of power politics, realism and neo-realism – the pursuit of power is the defining feature of world politics. In most accounts, power is understood in unproblematic terms as residing essentially in the military and economic spheres and as being constant over time and space. Add to this the way in which the discipline has been implicated in the decision-making processes of the major Western states – above all the United States – and it is no wonder that the South has been accorded so little influence in international affairs. Arguments have been advanced by writers such as Ali Mazrui, Adda Bozeman and Jayantanuja Bandyopadhyaya that the precepts and behavioural patterns of Third World states diverge substantially from those of the older states and that the South may be in the process of challenging the nature of the international system. Ideas of this kind have been dismissed by the mainstream as a romanti-cization of the Third World or as exercises in political manoeuvring. Such has been the statecentric nature of analysis, that there has been no sustained inquiry into whether developments within Third World societies might modify the terms of engagement between North and South and hence affect the workings of the international system generally. It is possible that this may change over the next few years. The emergence of postmodernist analyses has disturbed disciplinary complacency and put representation and knowledge on the power agenda. As yet, however, the debate which has been engendered has failed to unsettle the established lines of thought with respect to the non-European world.

The same basic point holds for culture, although it needs to be elaborated in rather different terms. For most of the discipline's history, the cultural domain has been held to be out of court. Culture has been seen as pertaining to society. International relations' subject is the state. This is pre-eminently the case with power politics which, in this respect also, remains deeply marked by its European background. Until the breakdown of the Concert of Europe in the last decades of the nineteenth century, the gulf between rulers and ruled meant that nationally distinct cultural patterns did not significantly intrude on the diplomacy of the 'civilized world'. Indeed, princes and statesmen shared a community of thought and values which went back to the Enlightenment and which, in large part, separated them from their subjects. Lord Louis Mountbatten, reminiscing in a television documentary some years ago about his childhood visits to the royal houses of Europe, felt no embarrassment in remarking 'world affairs for us have always been very largely family affairs'.[1]

It also appears that the very construction of international relations as a discipline works against a cultural orientation. Partly as a mark of distinction from diplomatic history, the tendency has been to proceed in terms of system and to highlight those features of international life that are shared and assumed to derive from common roots, whether they be in the nature of humankind, states or the international system itself. Traditionally, culture has been tied to place and time and has been most usually associated with difference and diversity. It may therefore be seen as introducing a specificity that disturbs the patterning of international politics and hence the explanatory capacity of the discipline.

Yet it is evident that in this century cultural constraints and pressures have had an increasing impact on the behaviour of states and the nature of the international system. In the West this has stemmed from internal political processes which have made diplomacy more responsive to the views of the electorate. The classic case is the success of the anti-war movement in the United States in ensuring America's withdrawal from Vietnam. In the Third World, where rule is often by presidential or military decree, the ballot-box has had nothing like the same sanction, but even here policy can seldom be formulated in disregard of community sensibilities and aspirations. Élites must be responsive to their ethnic and class constituencies, and developments in communication and transport and the processes of state-building and modernization have enlarged the constituencies of public politics.

One consequence is that the actions of states may become increasingly distinctive, even idiosyncratic, diverging markedly from the established, mostly Western-derived, norms. Such was the case with Iran after the revolution of 1978–9, whose behaviour was unpredictable when viewed through the mono-political lens of conventional Western scholarship. There is clearly some force in the assumption, implicit in power politics thinking, that given similar interests and capabilities, states tend to act alike. There is also some utility in systemic presuppositions put forward by economic theorists about the behaviour of élites. Both approaches, however, leave too much out of account. One of the challenges of international relations is to establish the balance between the systemic influences that promote commonality in the international actions of states, and those forces, mostly within societies, that encourage particularity.

More than this, however, it has become apparent that culture has international significance not simply through its impact on states but more or less directly through its connection with social change and resistance to social change. The concern of the new discourses with identity politics and the internationalization of consumption attests to the significance of culture as a site of global struggle. Increasingly, debate has been conducted in terms of the globalization of modernity. While some pertinent contributions have been made by international relations scholars,[2] this way of proceeding has not found favour in the discipline as a whole. As a result, the discipline has been marginal to the rethinking now taking place and is seldom cited in the literature.

Responding to the need for a broader contemporary relevance, inter-national relations has of late grudgingly conceded some significance to culture. Mostly, however, such gestures have been reactive and situated within the old referential frames. It has been a matter of invoking culture, rather than confronting it in its particularity. The initiatives taken by Ali Mazrui, Peter Worsley and Immanuel Wallerstein are of a different nature, but these writers come from backgrounds outside the discipline and their work has had only a limited impact within it.[3] Something similar can be said of R. B. J. Walker, whose interest in culture is related to his postmodernist bearings.[4] Although his writing is directed to the discipline it remains largely at the margins – as he himself has recognized.[5]

The need to elevate culture as a subject of study in international relations directs attention to people as a neglected dimension of the discipline. Policy-makers are of course there – and have been from the earliest days of diplomatic history. Especially since the 1960s a literature has developed on their belief systems, images and perceptions and use of historical evidence.[6] What has been missing is people outside the circles of official power; people who in some way are expressive of their society and carry its values into other societies and the international arena. Where in international relations are there accounts of Third World people responding to ideas and impositions from overseas? Where are the villagers and traders who have no direct connection with overseas politics but may be materially affected by its ramifications and whose actions, in turn, may have repercussions on global processes? After all, the politics of North/South relations do not take place above the daily life of Africans and Asians; to some degree they are contained within them.

The discipline has been depersonalized largely because that its main building blocks have been aggregates: states, nations; in a minority tradition, classes; more recently, élites and social movements. It is of the nature of aggregation that some attributes are magnified at the expense of others. The significance of distancing the discipline from humankind is perhaps best apprehended by considering the assumptions about the bases of action in international affairs. States and other aggregates are understood to act rationally – or at least this is the presumption. The scholar's task thus becomes one of relating action to real or imagined interests, usually calculated in terms of power or economic advantage. No one would question that rationality – and attendant notions such as calculation and the stress on intended consequences – must be at the core of thinking about international relations. However, when such ideas are extracted from their human context, the tendency is for them to develop a life of their own, to carry all before them.[7] This is especially so because of the urge to generalize and identify recurrent patterns – which, as has been observed, is accentuated by the so-called scientific study of world politics.[8] It follows that the temptation is to pass quickly over apparently irrational elements and to play down unintended consequences.

Much the same has happened with personal emotions or affects. We have been preoccupied with the ideational crust of politics, declares A. F. Davies, and 'emotions constitute a whole missing dimension'.[9] In the case of international politics, while the importance of emotions has been acknowledged with respect to individual policy-makers, affects have failed to dent the systemic presuppositions of thinking. Anger, frustration, attraction and hope are too transient and lacking in solidity to be invested with significant explanatory capacity. More than this, the discipline has been resistant to pursuing questions relating to identity formation and the relation of the unconscious/fantasy world to that of the conscious and the social; in a phrase to move from subject to subjectivity. It is partly for this reason that Christine Sylvester calls for the substitution of 'relations international' for 'international relations'.[10] This would put the emphasis directly on the variety of connections across the world, rather than concentrating only on certain of their forms. In her work on women's co-operatives in Zimbabwe she shows how the shifting identities of local women have international repercussions and hence are worthy of disciplinary attention.[11]

It can be confidently asserted that since the Second World War ordinary people, assuming new identities in their everyday lives, have more directly affected international relations than formerly. Inevitably the discipline has taken some account of this development, even if it has not had much impact on models and theory. One illustration is the recognition that conquest and the occupation of foreign territory have lost much of their earlier utility because of the difficulty of controlling an alien population and bending it to the will of the dominator. Another is the rethinking in some disciplinary quarters about the problems and status of refugees. Traditionally, refugees were viewed largely in humanitarian terms. The emphasis was on individual persecution, which was perceived to be peripheral to the central processes of international politics. Recent perspectives, however, have questioned both the established framework of thinking and the international arrangements for dealing with refugee movements.[12] The issue of refugees may be seen, therefore, as a case study of the way in which over time the personal can be reinterpreted as political. It is significant, however, that reappraisal within the discipline falls far short of the reconceptualizations undertaken in postcolonial discourse in relation to exile and displacement, which emphasize the subjective and the spatial.

The neglect of culture and the depersonalization of the discipline are aspects of a more general shortcoming of much writing in international relations: the delimitation of the subject matter to the formally political. The point applies with particular force to realist writing and less to approaches such as dependency theory which challenge the dominant paradigm. At its most extreme, politics is seen 'as an autonomous sphere of action and understanding apart from other spheres';[13] more usually it is a matter of restricting attention to material directly related to the supposed core issues. Because these are judged to be mostly conflictual, there is an ingrained tendency to downgrade activities or possibilities which are co-operative or integrative. The narrowness of this restricted focus is brought home by considering the significance of the activities of explorers, travellers or humanitarian and educational organizations. Think also of processes such as the movement of peoples across borders or the spread of European languages in Africa and Asia. The literature of international relations passes quickly over the way ideas and values pass from one society to another, take root and, perhaps in a hybridized form, affect self-conceptions, material expectations and external orientation. With respect to the Third World, key categories here are modernity, consumerism and Christianity.

So often the separation of the political from other aspects of life tends to mask the possibilities of change. At the very least, what is needed is some notion of the 'becoming political' which directs attention to developments outside the formal processes of policies which are potentially transformative. Consider, for example, the expansion of Europe into Africa and Asia in the 1870s and 1880s. With the advantage of hindsight, the activities of missionaries and the decisions taken by colonial authorities about education seem far more consequential to colonial peoples than the diplomatic jostling between the powers or the ground rules for orderly settlement laid down at the Berlin Conference of 1884–5. There is also the problem of reckoning with inter-cultural difference. One lesson to be drawn from the imperial experience is that ideas about what is political are not easily translated from one cultural context to another. In M. G. Vassanji's *The Book of Secrets*, some villagers in south-eastern Kenya discuss the significance of the border between Kenya and Tanzania after the outbreak of the First World War.

> Since when is the Chagga tribe our enemy? And if a Taita lives across the border – eti, where is the border? – is he my enemy, bwana?
> – You ask where is this border, eti heeeh!
> – Do you know?
> – Nobody knows, my brother. See that mountain – the mountain knows. The British gave it to the Germans.
> – How?
> – They draw a line in the grass, then they rub it out and draw another one.
> – One day all their lines will be rubbed out.
> – Or their fingers cut. Some lines they draw are deep.[14]

These illustrations of the limitations of approaching politics as a domain of its own help explain why disciplinary international relations is so out of step with trends in other formations of thought concerned with processes of international exchange. A deference to the established agenda of international politics, an absorption with the well-recognized, more formal patterns of interaction, may actually stand in the way of recognizing dislocations or considering alternative conceptualizations. The political prism highlights certain (admittedly crucial) planes – states, norms of international behaviour, interests – but diverts attention from others – identity, values and aspirations, insecurity. In this way it forecloses lines of inquiry which might open up debate. It is instructive here to quote Raymond Williams: 'There is a kind of politics whose local tactical modes positively prevent people from seeing what is happening in society.'[15] Challenged that an earlier book he had written deprecated politics, he went on to say:

> by drawing back I was able to reintroduce certain themes and issues which have seemed to me the crucial stuff of action to this day, but which were absent from what I knew then and often know now as politics.[16]

There is no reason to think that international politics is different in kind from domestic politics but it has yet to find its Raymond Williams.

When compared with the new discourses, what stands out about the way of thinking in international relations is its positivism. The categories of reference are clear-cut; there is a fixed, almost dogmatic, quality about many of the judgements regarding outcomes. Positivism is part of the scholarly tradition of the discipline and it is intimately related to the dominance of realism. It may be that this aspect of realist thought is a legacy of its battles with utopianism and idealism after the First and Second World Wars. Certainly it was boosted by realism's subsequent encounter with behaviourism. Positivism is not, however, confined to the realist school. Dependency theory, which presents a very different world-view, is marked by many of the same characteristics. In a variety of formulations there is a similar tendency to shy away from the indeterminate and the evolving, and an even greater propensity to lock the relationship of the constituent parts by turning a systemic key.

Two aspects of this cast of mind need specific mention. First, there is the assumption that power and influence flow along clearly defined channels, between more or less well-recognized actors, and that for the most part the traffic is one way. International politics is not necessarily seen as a zero-sum game, but there is an expectation that there will be winners and losers. In short, mainstream analysis proceeds along the lines: A has power over B; X wins this round over Y. Yet much of international relations is not like this at all. Power is more fluid and multi-layered.[17] Seldom can outcomes be summed up simply in terms of one party winning and the other losing. A striking feature of contemporary international politics is the erosion of the capacity of great powers to control lesser powers and regulate the course of world affairs. Even when it is exercised, dominance may prove hollow; guns cannot of themselves keep the oil flowing. We are increasingly being brought to realize that, in some situations, dependence or exploitation provides opportunities for leverage. Third World debt is a case in point. If the sum owing is substantial, the debtor has influence as well as the debtee.

Second, the assumption that realism (or for that matter dependency) has uncovered something hard, that it provides a map with which to chart the waters of international politics (or international economics) is belied by change over time. Explanation and analysis in international relations are at their strongest, I would argue, when the focus is short-term. The categories and presumptions of the discipline are much less attuned to taking a longer view and reflecting on differences between one historical period and another. Developments which make an impact only slowly and indirectly are not easily caught by a mesh made up of nation-states, calculations of power and the idea of national interest. Moreover, it is apparent that as the time-span is extended, events can take on a very different complexion. Ambiguities inherent in a situation come to the surface. Tensions within societies cause eruptions at the international level. What gave an impression of being settled is revealed as nothing of the kind. Thus in the late 1970s the situation in Angola – the victory of the MPLA, the rise of Soviet influence and the presence of Cuban troops – appeared to represent a round to the Soviet Union and a setback for the United States. But a decade later, from almost any perspective, interpretation was very different. Another illustration is provided by the record of Western involvement in the Third World during the period of the cold war. Mainstream analysis consistently exaggerated the significance of Western political and military dominance because attention was concentrated on governments, formal diplomatic processes and conventional military power. In the light of America's defeat in Vietnam, the fall of the Shah of Iran, the fading of hopes for rapid development and the failure of the Westminster model, who would now doubt that the levers of Western influence were more short-term and their reach within Third World societies more limited than was supposed at the time?

These criticisms of conventional scholarship make apparent the extent to which international relations has evolved within a specific cocoon of thought. The problem has not been an absence of debate but the degree to which debate has been an 'in-house' affair, mostly restricted to an established agenda. Only in a limited way has inquiry and contention reached out to material in other bodies of knowledge. Belatedly, mainstream international relations came to engage with dependency theory, but only after several years during which the two schools of thought passed like ships in the night. Rather later, feminist approaches forced an entry into disciplinary debates and there seemed a possibility that they might stimulate rethinking about the hard core of international relations.[18] It would be difficult to claim that any such thing has occurred. Writing in 1993, Christine Sylvester complained of the way feminist thought continued to be marginalized, even on the part of those committed to fundamental change.[19] I would agree but at the same time argue that some streams of feminism have come to be domesticated within the discipline, accommodating themselves too easily to existing reference points such as the state and security. Something similar might be said of the initiatives taken to draw on cultural anthropology. For the most part, their frame of reference has been tied to only one aspect of world politics, namely analyses of international security.[20] The reluctance to tap other bodies of thought may well be related to the relative youth of the discipline and the associated desire to maintain the distinctiveness of its subject matter. That international relations has for so long been intent on safeguarding the walls which separate it from other fields of inquiry suggests that it is a good deal less secure about its *raison d'être* than the texts would have us believe. Account should also be taken of the discipline's proximity to established power-centres in the West, which reinforces orthodoxy and conservatism. This is especially marked in the area of security studies, most of all in the United States. Consultancies, an orientation to governmental agendas, even the practice of being a sounding-board for officialdom are hardly conducive to radical rethinking. What is certain is that the relative insulation of international relations from developments in social theory, literary studies or even history has contributed to the failure of the discipline to be self-reflective about its methods and presuppositions.

This situation has come under challenge over the past few years with the emergence of the so-called 'third debate', in which writers influenced by postmodern or post-structural theory (Baudrillard, Derrida, Foucault, Lyotard) have struck out at disciplinary traditionalism. Arising from within or at the edges of international relations, this 'post-positivist' movement[21] has attempted to interrogate both the politics and postulates of mainstream approaches and to advance new ways of thinking. Thus, as one participant put it, the enterprise constitutes a 'discipline-defining debate'.[22] The writings of scholars such as R. B. J. Walker, Richard Ashley, Michael Shapiro, James Der Derian, Robert Cox and Simon Dalby have encouraged a deliberate shift to the epistemological premises of the discipline, with the result that in some quarters attention has turned to issues of representation, discourse, textuality/narrative and culture. What is at issue, therefore, is the very manner in which international relations as a discipline, and international relations as a subject matter, have been constructed. Undoubtedly this represents a break with orthodoxy and, compared with earlier challenges, its radicalism is less likely to be blunted through accommodation and appropriation. Yet for this reason it may well remain a school of dissenting thought, increasingly directing its energies to more particularized concerns and making alliances with other, more compatible, discourses. It is suggestive that theorists use words such as 'exile' and 'dissidence' to position their work in relation to the main body of the discipline.[23] Writing about territoriality, John Gerard Ruggie had this to say:

> We are not very good as a discipline at studying the possibility of fundamental discontinuity in the international system; that is, at addressing the question of whether the modern system of states may be yielding in some instances to

postmodern forms of configuring political space. We lack even an adequate vocabulary: and what we cannot describe, we cannot explain.[24]

There are also questions regarding the utility of postmodernist approaches when applied to the configurations of North/South politics. As yet there has not been much debate on this score – a fact of some significance in itself – but there is considerable scepticism on the part of international relations scholars in Asia and Africa. Some of the emphases of postmodernist thought – for example, its critique of modernity and its elevation of the marginal – appear a corrective to established disciplinary approaches. In other respects, however, the pattern of thought seems likely to compromise the enunciation of oppositional politics. The fact remains that so far postmodernist writings have not engaged very much with what might be considered distinctively Third World problems or paid much heed to Third World sensibilities.[25] Imperialism has not been addressed in any substantial manner and orientalism is conspicuous by its absence.[26] The problem, in the words of a contemporary reviewer, is that 'many postmodernist writings commence from a remarkably self-contained and self-referential view of the West'.[27]

Re-establishing the links between politics and literature

My object in this section is to show that imaginative literature and analysis in international relations do not inhabit different worlds; they overlap and even intertwine – or at least they should. That for the most part and certainly until very recently the two have been kept apart has made scholarship on both sides the poorer. International relations has not had the assurance to reach out and allow the subjectivity of fiction to disturb its stable structures. The study of literature, or more particularly literary theory, has had such confidence in bursting out of its one-time seams that it has often not bothered to reckon with the stock-in-trade of other fields it has colonized.

Our initial concern is to take account of developments in theory – particularly narratology – which over the past two decades or so have laid siege to the walls between different disciplines. From this quarter comes the challenge that the commonalities of approach are of greater import than the differences in content which previously commanded attention. In the first instance the debate can most usefully be pursued with respect to history. Politics has been much less involved and, until its contemporary encounter with post-structuralism, international relations scarcely at all. Next, it is relevant to consider the worldly connection (to use Said's phrase) between the spheres of literature and politics. Fiction has frequently engaged directly in politics, with novels serving both to underwrite the existing order and to act as instruments of change. Finally, and with respect to learning, I will argue that fiction can play a special role in engaging interest and changing apprehensions. This serves to introduce chapter 2 which identifies specific areas in which fiction contributes to our understanding of international relations.

The idea that there is some easy or absolute distinction between fiction and non-fiction has become less and less tenable. Although it has been part of the furniture of our minds for so long, over the past quarter of a century it has been subjected to scrutiny and indirectly assailed by developments in literary theory. As a result, the barriers which kept the world of the storyteller separate from the world of the scholar have worn thin and there is increasing leakage between the two. Structuralism in the sixties, followed by deconstruction theory, cut a new path with their emphasis on language as a signifying practice as distinct from a mere representation of either the real or the imagined. Narrative theory went further, highlighting the shared forms and structures of the story. At the same time social scientists questioned many of the old assumptions about methodological differences. Within particular disciplines, especially anthropology and history, researchers turned to new areas and challenged established conventions about what was important and how it should be presented.

As Foucault has shown, literature and politics are recent categories which can be applied to medieval culture, or even classical culture, only by a retrospective hypothesis.[28] The point is made in the course of a larger argument that the field of discourse cannot be articulated through specific genres such as religion, history and fiction. Unquestionably the hold of the categories is powerful, yet it also tends to hide the extent of change within. Let us for a moment consider the case of history. It has been asserted often enough that until a little more than a century ago history was regarded as a branch of literature. How far this was so is arguable,[29] but there can be no doubt that in the latter part of the nineteenth century the belief developed that history had taken a quantum leap by becoming hard-nosed, scientific and objective. We think of Marx uncovering the 'iron laws of history' or of Lord Acton's letter in 1898 to contributors to the *Cambridge Modern History*: 'we approach the final stage in the conditions of historical learning'.[30] Since then the trend has been to favour some relativism, a degree of experimentation, more openness about what constitutes evidence and a less sacrosanct approach to what has been called a 'documentary model of knowledge'. The process has been uneven, concentrated in certain areas – most notably social history – and it has been accompanied by deep divisions within the discipline about the status of its findings. On occasions the Third World commitment to rewriting the received account from Europe has led to the canonization of revisionist history. The eight-volume UNESCO *General History of Africa*, for example, is introduced in terms of the 'true history', and the drafting procedures are presented as providing 'the best possible guarantee of the scientific objectivity of the General History of Africa'.[31] A further caveat might be added. In the opinion of critics such as the cultural historians Hayden White and Dominick LaCapra, the process of rethinking has barely begun.[32]

Such a view appears less persuasive when the case of history is put alongside that of politics. White and LaCapra take their cue from social and literary theory, and their complaint is that too many historians have either resisted or been unaware of the challenges posed by recent developments in narratology. Perhaps so, although the freedom to pursue issues about the nature of discourse (meaning the uses of language, conceptions of rhetoric and the conventions of the story) is always likely to be more constrained when the object of a discipline is applied rather than self-revelatory. When we look at politics, and most of all at international relations, however, the issue until the emergence of postmodernism was not about restraints but about barriers to almost any examination of the significance of discourse to the apprehension of the field of study. This is perhaps because international relations has not had the same success as history in securing its field of study – which, paradoxically, may be related to the absence of a 'documentary model'. It is probably in part because the concentration on the claims and counter-claims of rival schools within the discipline inhibits a broader questioning process. Whatever the reasons, it is not possible to trace over time a comparable movement of thought towards greater relativism and a sensitivity to social construction in international relations as in history.

Comparing history with fiction, the pattern is reversed. Starting from a not dissimilar position, while history has moved hesitantly towards change, the novel has embraced it. In the nineteenth century there was a fixity about the novel; more or less agreed conventions established its form, its authority and its sense of objectivity. The movement away from realism was an implicit rejection of the idea of one reality. It was a movement which admitted uncertainty, subjectivity, different points of view and different modes of presentation. LaCapra writes of a 'tremendous explosion of exploratory approaches to narrative'.[33] Scholes and Kellogg draw particular attention to the trend away from authorial omniscience.[34] The driving force, in their view, has been the growing consciousness of a gap between the apprehendable and the true,[35] and here the novelist has captured the whole movement of mind from the Renaissance to the present.

At this point we come to the work within narratology that draws heavily on the novel itself. In essence the argument is that narrative involves the telling of a story, and so far as the form of the story is concerned there is not much to distinguish fiction from non-fiction. Reality is not 'out there' and somehow discovered. The past is not 'back there' and simply retrieved. What is 'out there' or 'back there' is constructed or created in a regulated way. Thus narrative itself has a patterning role: it helps to determine what is used and how it is used and what is excluded or foreshortened. Put another way, stories are shaped by conventions and these conventions directly impinge on accounts of events and the meaning imposed upon them. To move beyond these broad propositions is to enter zones of contention between different theoretical approaches and it would not be useful here to attempt to summarize the debate.[36] Instead, and perhaps in magpie fashion, I want to draw attention to certain lines of argument which bear directly on the purposes and presuppositions of this book.

One consideration which has worked to erode clear-cut distinctions between fiction and non-fiction is the recognition that many texts are mixtures of different kinds of writing. As a first step, we may note the narratologists' view that story elements and non-story elements are often found in the same text. A novel, for example, may include description as well as narrative. In the judgement of Scholes and Kellogg, the novel is of its nature an 'unstable compound',[37] which means it cannot be set apart from other texts on the basis of some essential quality – or at least none that emerges from traditional poetics. This may not necessarily end the matter. Shlomith Rimmon-Kenan concludes his study of the similarities between fiction and other types of narrative with the suggestion that poetics must pose again the question of the distinctiveness of narrative fiction.[38]

Taking another step, consider a particular form of narrative, the auto-biography, which by general agreement defies clear categorization as fiction, history or psychology. We might plump for labelling it fiction because it imposes on an unformed past a coherent pattern derived from the present (but in what way is this different from history?), or because at the very least some things will be repressed or obfuscated (but in politics is not public testament as likely to conceal as to reveal?). We might take the same decision on the basis that 'the truth of facts is subordinate to the truth of the man'.[39] If forced to decide, most scholars of the genre would come down on the side of fiction. Many would argue, however, that the dichotomy between fiction and non-fiction is a false one.[40] In a sense this is so, but it remains of great significance in determining which texts are relevant to which disciplines and how they are to be read, i.e., for 'facts' or for 'feel'. The case of autobiography is instructive because of the considerable and increasing reliance on the genre in African studies and race relations, and, on a rather different basis, in international relations. Once the appropriateness of autobiography as source material is conceded, the case for shutting the door on fiction (or fiction generally) is much weakened.

Turning to non-fictional narrative, the argument of the theorists is that it is precisely the narrative impulse which distances an account from the evidentiary material upon which it draws. The point is well taken. Hayden White puts it this way: 'it is this self-conscious fashioning activity . . . that decreases [a work's] "objectivity" as a *historical* account'.[41] It is of the essence of our way of understanding the world, of making sense of real events, that we look for connections, patterns of causality, some kind of starting-point and some sort of closure. It is obvious that events in the real world do not of themselves admit any such patterning; they do not offer up a ready-made story. Our need for coherence, to see continuity and so on, translates itself into rules or conventions about form and these in turn order our arrangement of the raw material. The finished product is thus a discourse about how we imagine the real world. Moreover, scholarly conventions are such that a narrative in, say, politics or history is likely to be crafted so as to emphasize certain values, for example relevance and structure, at the expense of others such as human interest and emotional impact. Consider successive drafts of an essay. The first draft is combed for inconsistency, the central themes are made to stand out boldly; the argument in some respects takes over and awkward facts or what appear to be extraneous details are deleted.

The same broad arguments apply to narratives about the inner world as to those about the outer world. Psychoanalytic theorists, like historians or political scientists, approach and present their material through the medium of narrative; it is not simply a matter of extracting the reality 'in there'. Roy Schafer observes: 'One may say that *psychoanalytic interpretation tells about a second reality.'*[42] According to Erik Erikson, when psychoanalysts '"take a history" with the intention of illuminating it, we enter another's life, we "make history"'.[43] Only recently have scholars and clinicians begun to explore the significance of such an understanding of the psychoanalytic process. The problem goes back to Freud. Donald Spence has pointed to what might be called an implicit tension in Freud's legacy. On the one hand, there is his insistence on free association on the part of the patient, and 'evenly-hovering attention' on the part of the analyst. On the other, his case histories are of such persuasiveness and literary style that both patient and analyst are impelled to search for coherence, continuity and other narrative virtues.[44] In short, the appeal of the story can easily overrun or submerge actual episodes in a life history. Spence goes on to argue that making contact with the actual past may be less important than constructing an acceptable version of the past.[45] In some circumstances, narrative truth may have a greater utility than historical truth.

Spence is concerned with the clinical process but his argument has a broader applicability. Occasionally reformers or radical social movements attempt to cleave a new path not on the basis of an understanding of history and politics derived from rational analysis but from inner conviction. In other words, the way forward draws its sustenance not from historical truth but from a truth derived from or related to the self. Gandhi and his concept of satyagraha is an exemplary case. For Gandhi the past, however interesting, held no key to the future. It could not provide answers to his questions or guidance as to how he should act. Indeed too much attention to the historical record could inhibit the search for truth and hold back a commitment to action. In *Hind Swaraj* he declares: 'To believe that what has not occurred in history will not occur at all is to argue disbelief in the dignity of man.'[46] The truth can only be found 'within', and there is some symbiotic process whereby 'within' catches the strength and moral values of humankind. It has been said that Gandhi, when he listened to his inner voice, heard the clamour of the people.[47] Also that 'his thought took on many of the basic qualities of life itself'.[48] Erik Erikson offers a fascinating insight when he presents *satyagraha* as a counterpart to psychoanalysis. Using the convention of a letter to the Mahatma, he writes:

> In studying your method of Satyagraha, I have become increasingly convinced that psychoanalysis . . . amounts to a *truth method*, with all the implications which the word truth has in Satyagraha. This, I submit, is more than a vague analogy; it is a correspondence in method and a convergence in human values which may well be of historical, if not evolutionary, significance.[49]

The rejection of the idea of a single truth has profound implications for how we should approach fiction and our expectations about the kind of benefits that might ensue. Our instinct would most likely be to regard texts in international relations as having established the landmarks in the area and thus fiction would be left to vary the emphases or provide illustrative detail. Yet the challenge from narratology is that fiction should not be seen as subordinate to non-fiction; accounts in politics and history may be as problematic as those in literature. Hayden White makes the point clearly when he rejects the presupposition of much interdisciplinary research that one field of study is effectively secured.[50] LaCapra argues to the same effect when he rails against the practice of according literature second-class status in historical research. In his view, if the novel is read at all in history, it is typically as a source of facts.[51] We thus reach the conclusion that novels should be approached with a receptivity to the possibility that they may offer alternative ways of presenting and understanding aspects of international relations to those established within the discipline. Needless to say, this is easier to accept in theory than to observe in practice.

Thus far we have been concerned with the divide between literature and politics which is a consequence of disciplinary boundaries and the conventions of scholarship. There has been a good deal more interaction when account is taken of lived experience. Novels have played a part in the political process; politics has contributed to the evolution of the novel. The case for studying literature in international relations is therefore underlined by the recognition that it is mostly in the world of formal learning that the two have been kept apart. It is not so much a matter of bringing an outside source into international relations, as of drawing on material which is already involved. The crucial reference-point here is the power of representation and signification as encoded in narratives of all kinds. For reasons which will be elaborated in later chapters, I am critical of the extravagance of much postmodernist thought which attributes the meaning and reality of social relations solely to representational practices. None the less I take it as manifest that the relationship between North and South was and is inseparable from the systems of representations which served and serve as mechanisms of control and challenge.

Here tribute must be paid to Edward Said, whose work took as its starting-point the role of literary narratives in a construction of the European self and its other, and broadened into a critique of the culture of imperialism.[52] It was Said's achievement to transpose key elements of post-structuralist thought to the phenomenon of imperialism (a subject which has been largely ignored by theorists such as Foucault and, arguably, Bourdieu), to spell out the systemic significance of representations and knowledge for North and South, and, especially in his later work, to clear a space for political agency.[53] Yet it needs to be pointed out, and it hardly detracts from the originality of Said's orientalist project, that many of the ideas drawn upon were by no means new. The self/other conceptualization of the East/West encounter, for instance, had been rehearsed much earlier.[54] What Said did was to invest it with a new significance.

I now want to indicate some of the ways in which literary narratives have been implicated in the international politics of the North/South encounter. At this stage my concern is simply to direct attention to the politics of literature; we can return in chapters 6 and 7 to address some of the problems of literary politics.

It is almost a truism to observe that the work of late-Victorian authors shored up and pushed forward the imperial enterprise. Haggard, Buchan and, more ambiguously, Kipling and Conrad rendered the expansive spirit of upper- and middle-class English society, magnified some of its constituent elements and projected the whole to a far wider audience. In substantial measure the fiction of the period meshed with accounts of soldiers, explorers and missionaries in a discourse which elevated the rulers and ennobled their purposes and in tandem downgraded subject races. This discourse constituted part of the very basis of imperial power. Its mechanisms are now familiar to us: the Manichean categories of reference, the valorization of imperialism's mission as the pursuit of progress and enlightenment, the representation of non-European cultures in terms of a litany of horrors ranging from despotism and backwardness to cannibalism and sexual aberration. In addition, there was the revival of old myths and legends about the heroic and the romantic and the celebration of values associated with masculinity and adventure.

Fiction's constructions and apprehensions cannot be seen as merely incidental to the processes of imperial expansion. On the contrary, they were fundamental to the existence of empire itself. The project could never have gone forward without ideological justification; domination had necessarily to be interpreted as dominion. More than this, the ideas about moral responsibility were an extension of the character and values of those who promoted them. In this sense, imperialism was both a state of mind and a way of life. So also the denigration of other cultures had its function within the larger imperial discourse. As Philip Curtin observes: 'The darker the picture of African barbarism, the more necessary the work of the missionaries.'[55] The preference shown by writers like Kipling or Cary for the 'real' Indian or the 'primitive' over those who had received some sort of Western education served to widen the gap between ruler and ruled and to extend the period of colonial tutelage.

Although it is probable that we will never be able to assess in any hard-edged way the extent to which imperial writers shaped opinion and thereby influenced action, it can scarcely be doubted that in some measure they did. One thinks of the public sensation created by the publication of *King Solomon's Mines*, the heady praise the book received from critics and the fact that it became an immediate best seller. Then there is the testimony of so many Anglo-Indians to the influence of Kipling's writings both in kindling their interest to serve in India and as a guide to the code of conduct that regulated life on the subcontinent.[56] Benita Parry has argued with respect to Conrad that the subversive implications of his fiction were not apparent to contemporary reviewers.[57] The point stands for other imperial writers also, and it can be extended to include the general readership as well as the critics.

It is, I think, significant that metropolitan fictional narratives concerned with the contraction of empire have not been approached with the same eye to their direct involvement in imperial politics. As we shall see in Part II, novels by E. M. Forster, George Orwell, Edward Thompson and Edmund Candler convey a pessimism about the accomplishments and prospects of British rule in India. There are doubts about the benefits supposedly conferred by the Raj on its subjects and a growing concern about the effects of the moral dislocation of the system on the British. A character in one of Thompson's novels catches the literary sentiment of the period when he observes: 'The days of our pride are nearly finished and our race is about to come to judgement.'[58] Unquestionably such ideas reflected something of the disillusionment with empire already existing in liberal circles in Britain, but they also presented a challenge in their own right to the hold of imperial thinking and contributed to the changing temper of opinion. The extended controversy which followed the publication of E. M. Forster's *A Passage to India* attests to the contemporary belief that the novel was politically significant. Writing much later, Nirad Chaudhuri ventured the opinion that *A Passage to India* was possibly an even greater influence in British imperial politics than in English literature. He went on to argue that the novel 'became a powerful weapon in the hands of the anti-imperialists, and was made to contribute its share to the disappearance of British rule in India'.[59]

In the case of America's involvement in Asia, for perhaps half a century novels set in Asia were an intrinsic part of the political debate and provided a stock of ideas and assumptions which informed and nourished policy. Indeed, it may be that fiction played a larger part in shaping the contours of involvement than was true of Britain, because firsthand contact was more limited and politics more attuned to popular culture. The influence of Pearl Buck's writing on China has been widely recognized. During the 1930s she became the key interpreter of China to the American public, and in her later career one of the few authorities on Asian matters generally. For many Americans her novels constituted the major part, if not the entirety, of their knowledge about China. 'It can almost be said', Harold Isaacs observes, 'that for a whole generation of Americans she "created" the Chinese, in the same sense that Dickens "created" for so many of us the people who lived in the slums of Victorian England.'[60] For the 'professionals' in academe, business and government also, Buck's novels were often a point of departure which remained influential in their later careers.[61]

During the cold war era three best-selling novels articulated what were taken to be the crucial issues and framed discussion about the nature of America's commitment. Graham Greene's *The Quiet American*[62] stung both the literary and political establishments. Widely criticized as an anti-

American polemic, none the less the book could not simply be dismissed. What happened was that the content of the novel was submerged by a wave of national indignation. Taking exception to a review by Philip Rahv which lacked the required severity, Diana Trilling used her own review to launch an attack on American liberals, accusing them of capitulating to the clever Europeans.[63] Most other critics were even less focused upon the issues Greene raised than Trilling, and damned the novel as much for its impertinence as for its political misjudgements. Another response was for novelists and commentators to draw upon the novel without acknowledgement to sustain their own analyses of the shortcomings of American foreign policy. In doing so, however, the novel was stripped of its radical critique and the abstracted fragments were made to support positions quite different from that of *The Quiet American*.

The key work in this respect was Lederer and Burdick's *The Ugly American*,[64] which undertook the task of reaffirmation. It carried the message that America's problems in Asia were about means and not ends. The novel was a remarkable popular success on its release and had an immediate political impact. Four well-known public figures – including Senator John F. Kennedy – sent copies to each member of the United States Senate.[65] Senator William Fulbright delivered a lengthy critique from the floor of the Senate. Richard Nixon made use of the novel in a major speech prior to his nomination as the Republican presidential candidate. The State Department produced a pamphlet for those considering joining the service, correcting what it alleged were errors of fact.

By 1965 *The Ugly American* had lost its persuasiveness and a new orthodoxy was proclaimed by *The Green Berets*.[66] Because of its 'comic-book' simplicity, this novel was not well received by the political and literary establishments. Yet it both expressed and for a time consolidated popular support for the Vietnam War. Reportedly the book induced 'so many enlistments that the Selective Service was able to suspend draft calls during the first four months of 1966'.[67] Even on the most restrictive conception of politics, there can be no argument that texts such as these became directly involved in the political process. Given a broader understanding of the political, virtually the whole corpus of fiction set in Asia during these years can be understood to be implicated in the cold war struggle.

The politics of Third World literary narratives will be considered in Parts II and III and only a few remarks are needed at this stage to indicate their significance. Whereas in English literature until a few decades ago the dominant tradition disparaged writing that was overtly political, there was much more recognition in Afro-Asian thought that politics could not be dissociated from literature. In part this drew on the dissenting Western tradition, Marxism. But it also followed directly from the colonial negation of indigenous cultures and histories which was so intimately linked with the politics of imperialism. That novels should be imbued with a political purpose was not therefore seen as aberrant in some way and indeed was more likely to be a cause of celebration. Hence the category 'resistance literature' emerged to describe texts of cultural affirmation and national liberation, and to denote the recognition that literature itself had become a medium of struggle.[68] Then, after independence, resistance entered a new phase with literature mostly directed against the new élites and characteristically taking the form of political allegory.

The view that the colonial and postcolonial situation has imposed special responsibilities on the novelist has been held particularly strongly in black Africa. Chinua Achebe has written of his commitment 'to help [his] society regain its belief in itself and put away the complexes of the years of denigration and self-denigration'.[69] Nuruddin Farah began writing, he once explained, 'in the hope of enabling the Somali child at least to characterize his otherness'.[70] According to Ngugi wa Thiong'o, literature is 'a very important weapon . . . in the struggle for communal and individual self-definition', and for him this involves taking a stand against the imperialist tradition.[71] Each of these writers has been seen as entering the political arena through fiction. Ngugi and Farah live in exile. Achebe's status has given him some protection from official persecution despite his commitment to change. Through his fiction and other writings, Ngugi has mobilized opinion internationally and become a celebrated figure among students all over Africa. It is too early to know whether African writers will play a substantial part in recasting the political order but the potential exists for them to do so in a way which is unthinkable in Western societies.

Yet there is another side. As I will argue in later sections of this book, resistance has often been over-emphasized, including its expression in literary narratives. We should not neglect the ways fiction has worked to familiarize and to legitimize postcolonial structures and attitudes of mind. The politics of some novels are unquestionably conservative – one thinks immediately of Manohar Malgonkah. The writing of V. S. Naipaul, however sensitive and agonized, may be profoundly disabling to those working for change in the Third World. Rallying behind the national cause, a characteristic of some African texts until very recently, almost certainly held back the process of reconsidering the appropriateness of the nation-state to African circumstances. In short, Third World fiction operates to uphold the politics of the status quo as well as to undermine them.

To conclude this chapter and to introduce the next, I want to consider the argument that fiction often excites interest and engages the emotions more than disciplinary political analysis. The editors of a source book on the political imagination in literature lament the fact that works in conventional political studies often 'fail to touch the imagination': the material remains 'distant, uninteresting, in no way personally compelling'.[72] While the generality of this claim is troubling, it brings out the need for connection between text and reader which is seldom raised in politics. Associated with what I have called the exclusions of politics is the sense of detachment from the phenomena being analysed. Detachment is obviously a by-product of the commitment to objectivity or scientific method but it also follows from the 'aesthetics' of language, structure and argument. In other words, the sense of distance from what is being discussed is partly a function of the form of the text which is shaped by scholarly conventions. It is probable that in this respect the new approaches at the margins of politics or outside the discipline do rather better.

Unlike politics, the relationship between text and reader has long been on the agenda in 'English' or literature as an academic discipline. According to one tradition of thought, the novel tends to bring issues alive and encourage a sense of involvement on the part of the reader. Of late such thinking has been eclipsed by developments in literary and social theory and the movement of disciplinary English into cultural studies. But the question of the power of the compact between reader and literary text has not been dealt with because of the emergence of new interests and different perspectives.

It is a working proposition of this book that literature has the propensity to engage because ideas and processes are realized in the behaviour of individuals and groups. Readers are drawn in by literature's social orientation and the way in which the political is embedded in the personal. Readers relate more easily because feelings and emotions nestle alongside power and interest. Irving Howe catches another side when he says that the novel tries to confront experience in its immediacy and closeness.[73] Engagement is also, of course, a matter of the expectations we bring to bear as readers. Writing more than a century and a half ago, Alessandro Manzoni contrasted the reader's approach to the historical novel with that to history. 'To believe, to believe swiftly, readily, fully, is the wish of every reader' of the historical novel.[74] History, on the other hand, 'makes you doubt because it intends to have you doubt'.[75] We can no longer deal in such clear-cut distinctions between different categories. It is a matter of which readers and how they choose to read. If we read contrapuntally (in accordance with our values not the author's, by today's standards not yesterday's), we will not be wishing to believe. But the turn to representations, and the argument about how deeply literature is implicated in politics presuppose that there are or were other readers who wish or wished to believe. Why otherwise would we bother with Henty and Buchan? If this is not so, what is resistance literature for?

Enough is in place to lay the basis for arguing that imaginative literature is potentially a powerful educative force, especially with respect to politics. The novel has a focus of sympathy. The reader is encouraged to take up positions subliminally. The likelihood is that the reader will identify with one or more of the protagonists. There is thus a sense of participation; the reader shares something of the read experience. On one view, the art of writing narrative fiction includes coaxing the reader into the story.[76] Once so involved, the chances are that our guard against particular positions will be lowered; the psychological mechanisms which screen unwanted messages will be bypassed. We may therefore be led into attitudes that we would not normally have countenanced. To cite one case among many, Mary McCarthy records how at the age of twenty her politics were transformed by reading a novel – *The 42nd Parallel* by Dos Passos.[77]

Mary McCarthy remarks that she cannot explicate the process and believes there is something accidental in these things.[78] The distinguished classicist Gilbert Murray expressed something of the same idea when nearly seven decades earlier he drew attention to what he termed the power of revelation in literature. As he explained it, revelations in literature are never statements of fact; they are never accurately measured; 'their value lies in their power of suddenly directing your attention, and the whole focus of your will and imagination, towards a particular part of life'.[79]

Notes

1. Mountbatten was a great-grandchild of Queen Victoria. John Terraine, *The Life and Times of Lord Mountbatten* (Hutchinson, London, 1968), p. 2.

2. For an excellent discussion see Richard Devetak, 'The project of modernity and international relations theory', *Millennium*, 24:1 (1995), 27–51.

3. Key publications by these writers are: Ali A. Mazrui, *Cultural Forces in World Politics* (James Currey, London, 1990; Heinemann, Kenya and Portsmouth, 1990); Peter Worsley, *The Three Worlds. Culture and the World Development* (Weidenfeld & Nicolson, London, 1984); Immanuel Wallerstein, 'Culture as the ideological battleground of the modern world-system' in Mike Featherstone (ed.), *Global Culture. Nationalism, Globalization and Modernity* (Sage, London, Newbury Park and New Delhi, 1990).

4. See R. B. J. Walker, 'Culture, discourse, insecurity', *Alternatives*, 11:4 (October 1986), 495.

5. R. B. J. Walker, 'The concept of culture in the theory of international relations' in Jongsuk Chay (ed.), *Culture and International Relations* (Praeger, New York, 1990), p. 8.

6. For an overview of some of this material see Richard Little and Steve Smith (eds), *Belief Systems and International Relations* (Blackwell in association with the British International Studies Association, Oxford, 1988).

7. It is significant that Hans J. Morgenthau commends his concept of interest defined in terms of power on the basis that it 'infuses rational order into the subject matter of politics'. *Politics Among Nations* (Alfred A. Knopf, New York, 3rd edition 1963), p. 6.

8. Ralph Pettman, *Human Behaviour and World Politics. A Transdisciplinary Introduction* (Macmillan, London, 1975), p. 73.

9. A. F. Davies, *Skills, Outlooks and Passions. A Psychoanalytic Contribution to the Study of Politics* (Cambridge University Press, 1980), p. 293.

10. Christine Sylvester, *Feminist Theory and International Relations in a Postmodern Era* (Cambridge University Press, Cambridge, 1993), p. 219.

11. See Christine Sylvester, *Zimbabwe: The Terrain of Contradictory Development* (Westview Press, Boulder CO, San Francisco and Oxford, 1991); and 'Urban women's cooperatives, "progress", and "African feminism" in Zimbabwe', *Differences*, 3:1 (1991), 29–62.

12. See, for example, G. Loescher and L. Monahan (eds), *Refugees and International Relations* (Oxford University Press, London, 1989).

13. Morgenthau, op. cit., p. 5.

14. M. G. Vassanji, *The Book of Secrets* (Macmillan, London, 1995; first published 1994), p. 114.

15. Raymond Williams, *Politics and Letters. Interviews with New Left Review* (Verso, London, 1981, 1st edition 1979), p. 103.

16. Ibid., p. 106. The book under discussion was Raymond Williams, *Culture and Society 1780–1950* (Chatto & Windus, London, 1958).

17. For a Foucaultian analysis see Albert Paolini, 'Foucault, realism and the power discourse in international relations', *Australian Journal of Political Science*, 28:1 (March 1993), 98–117.

18. For an introduction to recent feminist critiques see Rebecca Grant and Kathleen Newlands (eds), *Gender and International Relations* (Oxford University Press, London, 1991); V. Spike

Peterson (ed.), *Gendered States: Feminist (Re)Visions of International Relations Theory* (Lynne Rienner, Boulder CO, 1992); Anne Sisson Runyan and V. Spike Peterson, 'The radical future of realism: feminist subversions of international relations theory', *Alternatives*, 16:1 (Winter 1991), 67–106; and Sylvester, *Feminist Theory and International Relations*.

19. Sylvester, *Feminist Theory and International Relations*, pp. 209–11.

20. For an introduction to some of the work in this area see Robert A. Rothstein and Mary LeCron Foster (eds), *The Social Dynamics of Peace and Conflict. Culture in International Security* (Westview Press, Boulder CO and London, 1988).

21 See Mark Hoffman, 'Restructuring, reconstruction, reinscription, rearticulation: four voices in critical international theory', *Millennium*, 20:2 (Summer 1991), 169–85 (p. 169).

22. Yosef Lapid, 'The third debate: on the prospects of international theory in a post-positivist era', *International Studies Quarterly*, 33:3 (September 1989), 235–54 (pp. 236–7).

23. See, for example, Richard Ashley and R. B. J. Walker, 'Introduction: speaking the language of exile: dissident thought in international studies', *International Studies Quarterly*, 34:3 (1990), 259–68; and Richard Ashley and R. B. J. Walker, 'Conclusion: reading dissidence/writing the discipline: crisis and the question of sovereignty in international studies', *International Studies Quarterly*, 34:3 (1990), 367–416.

24. John Gerard Ruggie, 'Territoriality and beyond: problematizing modernity in international relations', *International Organization*, 47:1 (Winter 1993), 139–74.

25. Refer here to Arif Dirlik's criticisms in 'The postcolonial aura: Third World criticism in the age of global capitalism', *Critical Inquiry*, 20 (Winter 1994), 328–56.

26. It is revealing that there is no citation of Said's *Orientalism* in James Der Derian and Michael Shapiro (eds), *International/Intertextual Relations: Postmodern Readings of World Politics* (Lexington Books, Lexington MA, 1989).

27. Sankaran Krishna, 'The importance of being ironic: a postcolonial view of critical international relations theory', *Alternatives*, 18 (1993), 385–417 (p. 388).

28. Michel Foucault, *The Archaeology of Knowledge and the Discourse of Language* (Pantheon Books, New York, 1982; first published 1971), p. 22.

29. See Herbert Butterfield, *History and Human Relations* (Collins, London, 1951), ch. 8, 'History as a branch of literature'.

30. Lord Acton, *Essays in the Liberal Interpretation of History*, edited and with an introduction by William H. McNeill (University of Chicago Press, Chicago and London, 1967), p. 396.

31. The words are those of Professor B. A. Ogot, President of the International Scientific Committee for the drafting of a General History of Africa. See J. Ki-Zerbo, editor, *General History of Africa*, Vol. I (UNESCO; Heinemann Educational Books, London, University of California Press, Berkeley, 1981), p. xxiv.

32. See Hayden White, *The Content of the Form: Narrative Discourse and Historical Representation* (Johns Hopkins University Press, Baltimore, 1987); Dominick LaCapra, *History and Criticism* (Cornell University Press, Ithaca NY and London, 1985).

33. LaCapra, op. cit., p. 123.

34. Robert Scholes and Robert Kellogg, *The Nature of Narrative* (Oxford University Press, London, 1966; reprinted 1978), pp. 274–6.

35. Ibid., p. 203.

36. An excellent overview is to be found in the introduction to Wallace Martin, *Recent Theories of Narrative* (Cornell University Press, Ithaca NY, 1986).

37. Scholes and Kellogg, op. cit., p. 15.

38. Shlomith Rimmon-Kenan, *Narrative Fiction: Contemporary Poetics* (Methuen, London, 1983), p. 131.

39. I appropriate the formulation from Georges Gusdorf, 'Conditions and limits of autobiography', pp. 28–48 (p. 43) in James Olney (ed.), *Autobiography: Essays Theoretical and Critical* (Princeton University Press, Princeton NJ, 1980).

40. See, for example, Barett J. Mandel, 'Full of life now' in Olney (ed.), op. cit., pp. 49–72 (p. 56).

41. Hayden White, 'The value of narrativity in the representation of reality', 1–24 (p. 17) in W. J. T. Mitchell (ed.), *On Narrative* (University of Chicago Press, Chicago and London, 1981).

42. Roy Schafer, 'Narration in the psychoanalytic dialogue', in Mitchell (ed.), op. cit., 25–49 (p. 46).

43. Erik H. Erikson, *Life History and the Historical Moment* (W. W. Norton & Co., New York, 1975), p. 114.

44. Donald P. Spence, *Narrative Truth and Historical Truth. Meaning and Interpretation in Psychoanalysis* (Norton, New York, 1982).

45. Ibid., p. 28. The idea is developed more fully in chapters 5 and 6 below.

46. Quoted in Partha Chatterjee, *Nationalist Thought and the Colonial World – A Derivative Discourse* (Zed Books for The United Nations University, Bath Press, Avon, 1986), p. 93.

47. Erik H. Erikson, *Gandhi's Truth. On the Origins of Militant Nonviolence* (Faber & Faber, London, 1970), p. 397.

48. Bhikhu Parekh, *Gandhi's Political Philosophy: A Critical Examination* (Macmillan, London, 1989), p. 223.

49. Erikson, *Gandhi's Truth*, op. cit., pp. 244–5.

50. Hayden White, 'Historical pluralism', *Critical Inquiry*, 12 (Spring 1986), 480–93 (p. 484).

51. LaCapra, op. cit., pp. 125–6.

52. Said's seminal works are *Orientalism* (Routledge & Kegan Paul, London, 1980; first published 1978) and *Culture and Imperialism* (Chatto & Windus, London, 1993). In a recent interview, Said observes that the heroes of *Orientalism* are basically the novelists. See 'Orientalism and after: an interview with Edward Said', *Radical Philosophy*, 63 (Spring 1993), 22–32 (p. 23).

53. On the influence of post-structuralist thought see 'Orientalism and after', pp. 24–6 and *Culture and Imperialism*, pp. 29–30. On the need for activism see Edward Said, 'Identity, negation and violence', *New Left Review*, 171 (1988), 46–60 (p. 59).

54. See, for example, the discussion between Arnold Toynbee and Raghavan Iyer in a UNESCO radio programme in April 1959 reproduced in Raghavan Iyer (ed.), *The Glass Curtain Between Asia and Europe* (Oxford University Press, London, 1965), pp. 329–49.

55. Philip D. Curtin, *The Image of Africa. British Ideas and Actions, 1780–1850* (Macmillan, London, 1965), p. 326.

56. Philip Mason, for example, declared: 'The answer to why I went to India is Kipling.' See Charles Allen (ed.), *Plain Tales from the Raj* (Futura, London, 1976; first published 1975), p. 39.

57. Benita Parry, *Conrad and Imperialism. Ideological Boundaries and Visionary Frontiers* (Macmillan, London, 1983), p. 1.

58. John McCormick in Edward Thompson, *An End of the Hours* (Macmillan, London, 1938), p. 125.

59. Nirad C. Chaudhuri, 'Passage to and from India', *Encounter*, 2:6 (June 1954), 19–24 (p. 19).

60. Harold R. Isaacs, *Scratches on Our Minds. American Views of China and India* (M. E. Sharpe, Inc., White Plains NY, 1980; first published 1958), p. 155.

61. Ibid., pp. 155–8.

62. *The Quiet American* is a fictional indictment of America's belief in the transferability of its own experience and ideology to Asia. Written in the tradition of exploring the political through the personal. Alden Pyle, the quiet American, embodies the warped innocence of his country's world-view. Graham Greene, *The Quiet American* (Penguin, Harmondsworth, 1971; first published 1955).

63. Diana Trilling's and Philip Rahv's contributions in the pages of *Commentary* in 1956 were the most interesting but also the most ideologically blinkered of the reviews of *The Quiet American*. See *Commentary*, 21:5, 488–90, and 22:1, 66–71.

64 In this novel, which is really a series of loosely linked short stories, Asians and Americans are shown to think, act, and even look alike. Homer Atkins, the ugly American, is as at home in an Asian village building and marketing his water pump as in America. The novel thus depoliticizes America's problems in Asia by dissolving cultural difference. William J. Lederer and Eugene Burdick, *The Ugly American* (Corgi Books, London, 1960; first published 1958).

65. For this and other accounts of the book's reception see Joseph Buttinger, 'Fact and fiction on foreign aid. A critique of *The Ugly American*', *Dissent*, 6 (1959), 317–67; John Hellman, *American Myth and the Legacy of Vietnam* (Columbia University Press, New York, 1986), pp. 17

and 18; and Donn V. Hart, 'Overseas Americans in Southeast Asia: fact in fiction', *Far Eastern Survey*, 30:1 (January 1961), 1–15.

66. Robin Moore, *The Green Berets* (Avon Books, New York, 1965).

67. Hellmann, op. cit., p. 53.

68. See Barbara Harlow, *Resistance Literature* (Methuen, New York and London, 1987), esp. ch. 1.

69. Chinua Achebe, 'The novelist as teacher', reprinted in William Walsh (ed.), *Readings in Commonwealth Literature* (Clarendon Press, Oxford 1973), pp. 181–5 (p. 184).

70. Naruddin Farah, 'Childhood of my schizophrenia', *Times Literary Supplement*, 23–29 November 1990, p. 1264.

71. Ngugi wa Thiong'o interviewed by Hansel Nolumbe Eyoh, *Journal of Commonwealth Literature*, xxi:1 (1986), 162–6 (p. 162). See also his *Decolonising the Mind. The Politics of Language in African Literature* (James Currey, London, 1986).

72. Philip Green and Michael Walzer (eds), *The Political Imagination in Literature: A Reader* (The Free Press, New York, 1969), p. v.

73. Irving Howe, *Politics and the Novel* (Books for Libraries Press, Freeport NY, 1970; Essay Index Reprint Series), p. 20.

74. Alessandro Manzoni, *On the Historical Novel*, translated with an introduction by Sandra Berman (University of Nebraska Press, Lincoln NB and London, 1984), p. 71.

75. Ibid., p. 74.

76. Joan Rockwell, *Fact in Fiction. The Use of Literature in the Systematic Study of Society* (Routledge & Kegan Paul, London, 1974), p. 43.

77. Mary McCarthy, 'The lasting power of the political novel', *New York Times Book Review*, 1 January 1984, pp. 1, 27 and 29 (pp. 1 and 27).

78. Ibid., p. 1.

79. Gilbert Murray, *Humanist Essays* (Unwin Books, London, 1964), p. 98.

CHAPTER 2

The orientations of fiction

In his essay on literature as revelation, Gilbert Murray is concerned to record the wonder and probe the nature of revelation. My concern in this book is broader in that it relates not simply to those exceptional fragments of literature, those rare moments of revelation. It is also more directed because it attempts to indicate those spheres of thought most likely to be affected. The purpose of this chapter is to consider the particular ways in which fiction can advance our understanding of the politics of imperialism. What is it that could give literary narratives a different slant on imperial processes from narratives in international relations and imperial history? Are some facets of the interaction between North and South more likely to be brought into view than others? Can anything be said about what we might expect to gain from different kinds of fictional narratives? Essentially I will be presenting a series of hypotheses which can be re-examined in particular contexts in later chapters.

It is apparent that the qualities and emphases of literature with which we are concerned are not fixed or invariable; on the contrary they need to be seen as tendencies, recurrent patterns, or perhaps simply possibilities. In some of the traditional writing on the role of fiction in historical studies and the social sciences there has been an interest in characterizing the approach of the novelist and contrasting it with that of the scholar. Often enough we read that fiction's contribution to historical or political understanding flows from the novelist's insight, intuition, and above all, creative imagination. At least by inference, we are given to understand that these are qualities usually lacking in academic analyses. Because of the very nature of the inquiry, there is a tendency to slide into essentialism of this kind[1] – and we need to guard against it. For one thing, it must be remembered that the enclosure of bodies of narrative in terms of fiction or politics or history is itself an artificial exercise. In the previous chapter we noted the variety of fictional forms. Although there has been no comparable experimentation within politics or history, it would be foolhardy to attempt to draw up a model of narrative in these disciplines. Even in disciplinary international relations there is simply too much that is contestable, and plurality is increasing markedly.

But there is a more fundamental point. In the search for the kind of strengths that fiction can bring to the study of politics and history there can be no clear-cut distinction between the different bodies of writing, no definitive contrast in terms of approach and method. Writing well before the theoretical perspectives of narratology, James Davidson observed: 'The writer of fiction does not do something so utterly different from the writer of the treatise that there is no possible comparison.'[2] Today this would seem an understatement on almost any count. The argument can be developed by considering the role of imagination which has always been seen as intrinsic to the domain of literature. It cannot be said that imagination is somehow the preserve of the novelist, to which the writer of the treatise has no access because of the need for fidelity to source material, even-handed coverage or similar constraints. In history, as in politics, material does not simply await its chronicler; it must be selected, at times drawn from new or unexpected quarters, in some respects created. It must then be given voice; rarely does it speak for itself. Reflecting on the work of writers such as Ranke or Tocqueville, Hayden White comments:

> It is to the power of the constructive imagination of such classic writers that we pay tribute when we honor their works as models of the historian's craft long after we have ceased to credit their learning or the specific explanations that they offered for the 'facts' they had sought to account for.[3]

The same basic point holds, I believe, when we look at the history of empire and at contemporary North/South relations. Robinson and Gallagher's thesis about the nature and causes of Victorian imperialism made extensive use of the archival material, but it drew its sustenance from the authors' conviction that the grand theories and modern myths of imperialism were in need of overhaul.[4] Its power and the controversy it engendered[5] owed comparatively little to a reading or rereading of the documents; what counted was the boldness of the ideas about the pessimism and strategic neuroses of the late-Victorian statesman. *Africa and the Victorians* spawned new ways of thinking not only about the expansion of empire, but also about the nature of nationalism and the causes of imperial contraction. Could empire have gone forward without collaborators? Was not nationalism more a matter of specific interests than of a broadly based ideological consciousness? In the process of imperial contraction, did not the directors of empire act from a position of strength, rather than weakness? Because of their breadth and the implicit assumptions which underlay them, none of these questions could be settled simply by appealing to the documentary evidence.

In view of their relevance to the subject matter of this book, let us consider for a moment the work of the revisionist historians and the dependency theorists. In the 1960s and early 1970s the revisionist historians, led by Gabriel Kolko and William Appleman Williams, recast thinking about the bases of America's world role with their radical critique of traditional scholarship and their assertion of the primacy of economic interest. Their scholarship relied on statistics on overseas trade and investment and analyses of policy and policy-making. But their thesis that American capitalism was a system which organically exerted itself overseas was an exercise of creative thought – a 'beyond' diplomacy or economics. At least as far as Asia and Africa were concerned during the cold war period, the revisionist themes no longer carry conviction.[6] Notwithstanding the eclipse of this part of the argument, however, few would deny that the revisionist challenge pierced the ideological casings of historiographical orthodoxy and pushed debate in new and fruitful directions.

The case of dependency theory is perhaps even more salutary. Although others had rehearsed the arguments before, the central figure in the development of the dependency paradigm in the late 1960s was André Gunder Frank. Breaking decisively with Marxism and paying little systematic attention to the nature of capitalism or imperialism, Frank argued that the effect of capitalist penetration was to generate underdevelopment. In short, 'the development of underdevelopment' was tied to a ubiquitous capitalism. Very few scholars today would accept Frank's thesis in the terms in which he put it, yet his influence has been enormous. A critic at the time commented that Frank is 'so great *and* so awful'.[7] The one is related to the other. It was precisely the extravagance of his conception, the crudity of some of his arguments, and the radicalism of his departure from orthodoxy which accounts for his extraordinary impact. In the 1970s Frank was taken up by the participants in the North/South debate – I remember Sonny Ramphal, when Secretary-General of the Commonwealth, saying that it does not matter whether dependency is true, it is its moral message which counts. In terms of theory, Frank's approach spawned a school of thought about development capable of self-criticism and conceptual sophistication.[8] In addition, it stimulated and informed other streams of radical thinking, for example on food production and distribution, ecology and pollution, and technology transfer and Third World debt.

In these last paragraphs I have been attempting to indicate the part imagination can play in writing about international politics. One might go further and suggest that imagination is potentially of greater importance in international politics than in history or politics generally because the field is more open to diverse conceptualization and the 'facts' are less determining. There is, of course, no such thing as international politics in any positivist sense. Nothing of the kind lurks behind the diplomatic records, ready to be uncovered by diligent researchers. Rather, international politics is a way of describing how we apprehend certain transnational phenomena, guided by a set of scholarly traditions and a body of what were once generally accepted conventions about the regulation of international life. We have never been able to separate clearly what is international from what is domestic. In any case our understanding changes over time – witness interpretations of Article 2 (10) of the United Nations Charter. There have always been different views of what is political and what is not. What the discipline has done is to outline and set limits to the field which have met with a fair measure of agreement until the present moment. In other words, we have constructed an understanding of what is international politics but forgotten the extent to which it is contrived. In the end, I think it must be admitted that international relations itself is a fiction.

It now becomes necessary to say a little about how we read fiction and what we might expect to gain from different kinds of fictional narratives.

Without engaging in debates on literary theory, what is required are some guidelines for this particular project about what literature can communicate and how we may choose to use it. The reader is entitled to know something about how I have approached the literary texts and what assumptions I have made with respect to the value of texts which might be put in the category we have traditionally called 'literature', as compared with those we label 'popular fiction' or some such title.

It follows from the very nature of the undertaking that I will be reading with a political eye, which has moreover been focused (and blinkered) by my disciplinary background. In construing meaning, I will be influenced to some degree by a politics outside the text as well as that within it. Now that so much attention is directed to the reader, presumably no one would argue that the text contains within it everything that is needed to interpret it. Part of the critical process must necessarily involve taking account of other materials, most obviously non-fictional narratives – remember Hayden White's injunction that no one field of study can be regarded as secure. It is a basic argument of this book that much writing in the new discourses shows a decided reluctance to draw on knowledge in established disciplinary fields such as history or politics. Certainly there are exceptions – the New Historicism, for instance, or, in the United Kingdom, cultural materialism – but so often assurance of thought tends to be associated with a cavalier approach to what went before. Now there are good reasons for being wary about becoming ensnared by the repressions and enclosures of existing knowledges,[9] but they hardly amount to a warrant for non-communication. With respect to many of the issues examined in this book, I have been struck by how few references are made in literary critiques to material in other discourses. Whether it be the economics of empire or Third World politics, in so many instances argument proceeds on the basis of reconceptualizations which reflect prevailing moral sensibilities but pay little heed to specialized scholarship in the area. This has been seen as a major shortcoming of much contemporary postcolonial analysis.[10] One critic, well aware of the insularity and conservatism of imperial history, has called for a dialogue between imperial history and literary studies for their mutual benefit. The methodologies of the historians could be broadened, while the 'theoretical excesses' of literary scholars 'could be checked by the sober scrutiny of the historians'.[11]

All this serves to underline the point that the orientations of fiction are not simply there, innate in the texts. The tendencies which I am concerned to spell out catch something of my own cast of mind and the nature of the inquiry we have embarked upon. Much the same must be said of our approach to particular texts, both when we follow the story and take it on its surface terms and even more when we read beyond the story – as often we do. For a start, not everything in the text will be directed to the progressive unfolding of the plot; there will be extraneous material which needs to be considered in its own right. Frequently this is the kind of overt authorial commentary on politics or morality to be found in political or philosophical narratives. Then there are those occasions when we read into the text messages or disclosures which run counter to its manifest theme. Frank Kermode has highlighted the tension within a text between narrative sequence and what he calls 'secrets'. His counsel is to be alert for suppression and distortion so that secrets can take their place alongside the apparent, manifest message as conveyed by the story.[12] A much more radical opening-up of the text is involved if, as some theorists insist, we foreground the gaps, flaws and fissures which reveal alternative possibilities that negate or subvert the text's apparent meaning. This is also true if we 'read against the grain' or 'contrapuntally' as we are often required to do. It is, I think, obvious that we read texts in each of these ways; when and how much of each is heavily influenced by the relationship between the text's politics and our own.

We must now take a half-turn and revisit our purposes in looking at literature. Although not our primary concern, in some parts of the book we will be interested in the literary texts for their representations and significations. That is to say, we will want to know what they tell us about the culture in which they are embedded. Often the value of a text will lie in it being so integrated into the dominant culture that it reproduces society's perceptions and prejudices in literary form. Let me give an illustration. It has been argued that over a 75-year period Rhodesian novels perpetuated a series of settler myths about the incapacity of Africans to be creative and to order their lives, the savagery and military prowess of the Ndebele, and the emptiness and inhospitality of the land. These and other myths were resurrected during the liberation war and helped to fuel misunderstanding about the nature of the nationalists and the course of the fighting.[13] Anthony Chennells concludes:

> What the novels show more clearly than Smith's speeches ever did were the reasons for this fatal lack of understanding. The novelists' world was shaped by particular myths which sustained them. Rather than discard the myths as no longer having any bearing on their world, the new world which the war had created was shaped to give the myths themselves a continuing vitality.[14]

Our major purpose in turning to literary texts, however, is not for their representations but for their ideas and moral sensibility which might expand understanding and stimulate rethinking. By this, I do not mean to suggest that such ideas and values are outside the culture in which the text was produced, but rather that we read them not for what they tell us about that culture but for what they may tell us about our own, our way of thinking, our historiography. It needs to be recognized that a text is not exhausted by the singularity of its use. And it should be stated that this approach gives the text a more positive role than accords with contemporary practice in literary studies.

The question thus arises as to how we are to know when to follow the lead of a text and when not. Are some texts more likely than others to give new bearings? Are some categories of fiction more prone than others to mislead? Clearly there is no simple or single answer. I do not think the problem is different in kind from that involved in making judgements about non-literary texts. I have already observed that part of the process of evaluation must include reference to non-fictional sources. So far as the text itself is concerned, there are strong presumptions against pressing back into service some notion of great literature as opposed to popular fiction. Great literature is a much more difficult category than was earlier supposed. As has been shown, it was often tied to culture and class. Yet the concept has a utility when we compare (say) *The Quiet American* with *The Ugly American*. And it has a way of reappearing in other guises. It is suggestive that Frank Kermode advances the proposition that secrets will tend to increase as respect for propriety decreases. He writes:

> In the kinds of narrative upon which we conventionally place a higher value, the case against propriety is much stronger: there is much more material that is less manifestly under the control of authority, less easily subordinated to 'clearness and effect', more palpably the enemy of order, of interpretative consensus, of message.[15]

It is also significant that these same texts are less likely to be enclosed by prevailing cultural orthodoxies. In one way or another, they stand at a distance from popular conceptions or they reflect critically on conventional wisdom. Kipling is 'knowing'; V. S. Naipaul 'anticipates the obsolescence of his own discourse'; Achebe 'creates a space' for a different social order. To paraphrase Lionel Trilling, writing of this kind contains the yes and the no of the culture.[16]

For those reasons and others, it seems to me that some working distinction between serious literature and popular fiction is both apt and useful – notwithstanding that it goes against the grain of much contemporary literary study. So far as making judgements is concerned, I see no fundamental difference between the problems in literature and those in the social sciences.[17] In any case judgements of this kind are often made implicitly, as evidenced by the concentration of writing in postcolonial discourse on serious texts rather than ephemera. In this respect, Edward Said was perhaps simply more forthright than out of step with contemporary practice when he said in a recent interview: 'There are good books, and there are less good books.'[18]

We are now in a position to consider literature's particular utilities. If any proposition in the literature and politics exchange can command general assent, it is that literature's orientation in personal. Fiction focuses on people: the way they behave, the question of their motivations and the nature of their relationships, both to each other and to society. In so far as the novel offers a broader social or political commentary, it usually does so by working outwards from the lives of the characters, which are presented in some detail and in a way that generates a sense of emotional involvement. Mostly, attention is directed to individuals but this is a matter which is historically and culturally conditioned. As Lukács has shown, the centrality of the individual in the realist novel was related to changing economic and social conditions in Europe in the late eighteenth and nineteenth centuries.[19] The movement to capitalism and the emergence of new areas of personal freedom found expression in changing conventions with respect to character. In earlier literary forms the treatment of human individuality was circumscribed by a kind of societal determinism and an absorption in the visible life.[20] However, as a result of the growth of tension between the individual and the collective, and between the private and the public spheres of life, the behaviour of individuals, their specific traits of character and their inner consciousness, came to be literature's prime concern.

The evolution of characterization does not, of course, stop with the realist novel, any more than the development of human individuality stopped with the industrial and agrarian revolutions. We should not, therefore, hobble our approach to literature with preconceptions derived from nineteenth-century fiction about what is required of character and how this informs political understanding. Lukács's insistence that characters evince a historical consciousness – that they are able to comprehend the nature of their times – has been criticized on this count. His implicit attempt to freeze the novel at a particular point in socio-economic development makes him an unreliable critic of modernist works – and runs counter to his own recognition of 'the concrete possibilities for men to comprehend their own existence as something historically conditioned'.[21] One of the distinctive features of the modernist novel is characters who are unable to direct their lives, who cannot comprehend their own situation, much less the social forces which have contributed to their alienation or 'selflessness'. Jeremy Hawthorn has argued that such characterization 'often illuminates (because, in complex ways, it reflects) aspects of the development of human individuality in our society'.[22] He concludes: 'At its best the modernist portrayal of character allows us to see things in art that habit conceals from us in life.'[23]

The extent to which the individual is accented and the way in which character is delineated also bear a cultural stamp. Because so much of our thinking about the novel has been shaped in the West, there is a danger of universalizing literary conventions and critical standards which are specific to only part of the world. The fact that the novel is a Western literary form should not lead us to overlook the degree to which it has been adapted to the often different circumstances of the Third World, and at times to the distinctive purposes of Third World writers. In many parts of Asia and Africa the primary unit has been the collective – caste, religious movement, ethnic group or tribe – and the identity and role of the individual has been defined in relation to it. At least in some spheres, therefore, the boundaries of personal choice have been tightly drawn. The openings for love and friendship, for example, may be substantially limited by the joint family system and customary practices such as arranged marriages. The voice of authority and tradition within the community may also speak with such force that the individual has less of that inner turmoil which so often accompanies the making of one's own decisions.

This rootedness of the individual within his or her community leaves its mark on many Asian and African novels in that characterization is less personal and psychological than we have come to expect. Moreover, the concrete, 'here and now' aspects of personality are often infused with some spirit of a mythic past or of the collective will of the community. We may note also that in some instances the writer has an interest in emphasizing the extent to which the community as a whole is implicated in the action, and thus a particular character is presented as representative of the collective outlook and aspirations. This is characteristic of much Gandhian literature.

I observed earlier that the literary focus on the individual was historically and culturally conditioned, but history and culture are not separate and self-contained worlds. Clearly, over time socio-economic developments intersect with culture. The emergence of the novel in Asia and Africa was itself the result of developments in education and technology and changing social relationships. It has been argued that the conditions associated with the development of the novel in India 'show a striking similarity to the socio-economic changes and re-orientations which brought about the rise of the novel in England in the eighteenth century'.[24] This seems an overstatement because the turn to the novel was also culturally derivative. But it is certainly true that the evolution of the novel in the Third World was responsive to the processes of social and economic change that had taken root. As a result, for example, of the spread of the cash economy, the movement of people to the cities and the wider circulation of ideas about modernity and development, Third World novels have come increasingly to reckon with the individual. Instead of characters being the embodiment of their societies, we see them moving between different social worlds, usually struggling to arrive at some accommodation between them. Obi Okonkwo, the main protagonist in Chinua Achebe's *No Longer At Ease*, is representative of this dilemma.[25] Unlike his grandfather, the hero of *Things Fall Apart*, whose strength (and weakness) lay in his commitment to traditional society, Obi is situated in the space between the old and the new orders. He is torn between his personal morality and material needs and his financial obligations to his family, village, and the Umuofia Progressive Union which paid for his overseas education. He is also caught between his belief that he should be able to marry the woman of his choice and the opposition of his parents and local community to marrying a social outcast.

What, then, can be said about the significance of literature's personal orientation for broadening the canvas of international studies? Building on the arguments developed in chapter 1, many facets of the relations between societies can be related to lived experience. Literature brings to our attention individuals situated in the cross-fire of cultural exchange and hence emplaces debates about the negotiation of difference. I am thinking, for instance, of the European 'on the spot' whose outlook was often different from that of people at home and whose actions were by no means always directed from the metropole. He, and occasionally she, is a familiar figure in imperial history but fiction widens the range of actors and introduces new angles for consideration. Susan Blake asks with regard to travel writing what difference gender makes.[26] Does a woman respond to Africa and Africans differently from a man? The question can equally productively be applied to fiction. Similarly, we might ask what difference sexuality makes. Do homosexuality and the rejection of a dominant masculinity contribute to different ways of seeing other peoples and other societies?[27]

In Third World narratives there is frequently an emphasis on people whose actions we would not usually understand to be political. A character in one of Nuruddin Farah's novels reflects that:

> history was as much about the movements of tribal peoples with no technological know-how as it was about the conquest of territories, of 'protections', of 'pacificatory' methods and of created famines whether in Vietnam or in the Ogaden.[28]

Especially in female-authored texts, it is notable that women are often portrayed as being resourceful in difficult circumstances, their everyday behaviour changing the terrain of public life. The question is thus raised of whether women have coped with the turbulence associated with imperial and global intervention better than men. Approached along such lines, fictional texts can contribute to an understanding of the ways in which identity is constructed and fragmented through contact with other cultures.

There is a strong presumption, therefore, that literature's concentration on the personal can be a corrective to international relations' preoccupation with aggregates, its mechanistic presumptions about international processes and its positivist approach to outcomes. To take one illustration, the depiction (although by no means always the recognition) of the multiple identities of the characters works to problematize the absolutist claims of nation and state. We know, of course, that so much of the discipline's way of proceeding is removed from everyday life. The point at issue is whether it should be.

It must, I think, be conceded that in large part international life is different from personal life; the behaviour of the aggregate diverges substantially from the behaviour of the individual. In this respect, the realists have the better of the argument with the idealists, international lawyers and latter-day progressives. But there is more leakage from the personal to the political, more linkage between the individual and the aggregate, than the discipline has admitted. It is instructive that scholars have no qualms in writing about the significance of France's *humiliation* in the Franco-Prussian war (its consequence being said to extend from the expansion of the French Empire to the counter-insurgency campaigns in Indo-China and Algeria after the Second World War and to the pursuit of the French nuclear deterrent). Who would doubt that the theories about sanctions and deterrence – or more recently about rewards and inducements – derive some of their nourishment from ideas about the behaviour of individuals? In other words, although international relations has depersonalized so much of its stock-in-trade, notions drawn from everyday life inform and give meaning to its accounts of politics between states, even if this is seldom openly acknowledged.

Where the discipline has had unqualified success with depersonalization is with respect to the fate of human beings in international politics. The categories of reference and conventions of argument have ensured that in key areas the human consequences of the action of states are not a subject for consideration. The pre-eminent case is the study of war. Indeed, in strategic studies it is as if the concepts and terminology have been screened so that we do not think of people as being involved at all. It is much the same with respect to poverty. If it even appears on the agenda, poverty is likely to be presented as a structural condition rather than a human tragedy. This is where literature with its focus on people in their ordinary lives can provide an important corrective. It is partly a matter of the level of analysis, which brings different aspects of a subject into focus. It is also a function of particularizing an issue by presenting it as a problem in someone's life. We are thus encouraged to think and to feel differently than before and to make connections which might otherwise have escaped us.

These contentions are well illustrated by Bhabani Bhattacharya's novel, *So Many Hungers*.[29] Set in wartime Bengal, the novel tells of the suffering caused by the famine, which itself was a result of the war. The destruction of the fishermen's boats because of the fear of a Japanese invasion adds a layer of meaning to our understanding of the war which has to be confronted. What is, according to customary perspective, the execution of grand strategy is for the fishermen concerned – who know nothing of the war and still believe, in fact, that they are ruled by the East India Company – an incomprehensible and very personal tragedy. We are also made aware that what is personal at one point in time becomes political at another. The exigencies of the war cause the state authorities to take harsh action across the board and so fuel the rise of the nationalist movement.

In the course of fleshing out the argument, I have moved away from our starting-point which was the relationship between the individual and the collective. A basic question should now be posed, although it will be pursued in Part II in relation to the North/South engagement. It is this: to what extent can political and social processes be explored through the lives of individuals? In studying an episode or aspect of an individual life, are we not often brought face to face with much broader impulses which are rooted in the political culture? For now I will confine illustration to non-fiction works, although this means that the individuals singled out are historical figures of note. In his history of the Russian Revolution, Trotsky draws attention to the passivity and indecisiveness of the Czar and he reflects on the similiarities between Nicholas II, Louis XVI, Charles I and their respective queens. While he concedes that some elements of similarity are accidental, he places much more importance on 'those traits of character which have been grafted, or more directly imposed, on a person by the mighty force of conditions, and which throw a sharp light on the interrelation of personality and the objective factors of history'.[30] Writing from the perspective of a political psychologist, Ashis Nandy examines the relationship between personality and social forces in Gandhi's assassination by Godse in 1948. Here also the importance of accidental elements is minimized. According to Nandy, to some degree Gandhi and his political heirs colluded with the assassins. 'Every political assassination is a joint communique.'[31] More than this, Godse was representative of – in a sense his 'hand was forced by' – dominant sections of Indian society to which Gandhi posed a threat. In killing Gandhi, Nandy concludes, Godse revealed 'a surprisingly acute sensitivity to the changing political–psychological climate in India'.[32]

So often in political studies the focus has been on the leadership, on those who supposedly set change in motion. It is evident that fiction inclines the other way; novelists have usually taken as their main protagonists individuals some way down the social scale. It has been the district officer, the missionary or someone from the village who has caught attention, not the statesperson, high official or merchant prince. Lukács pays tribute to Sir Walter Scott on this score. His heroes are 'middling' figures – correct, average, more or less mediocre English gentlemen – and therefore representative of social trends and historical forces.[33] Third World writers have gone even further – think of Farah's Ebla who flees from the village to the city or Mulk Raj Anand's coolie or untouchable. As we shall see, there can be problems about such representations, but it is I think clear that the novel provides a counter to the élitism of so much writing in international relations which has been preoccupied with those at the apex of the power structure. As a result, the novel has often been more prescient than conventional analysis.

This is all the more so since novels tend to make us aware of the subjectivity of experience. Without at this stage entering the debate about whether the subaltern can speak,[34] novels usually present a range of viewpoints through the speech and thoughts of the characters. Very often, as in Conrad and Kipling, the narrator introduces another interpretative dimension through undermining or going beyond the surface appearance of the received account. It has been argued that realism was and is predicated on the assumption of rationality and good sense, and that it gives little recognition to extremes of action and feeling. As such, it is a form inextricable from liberalism, which explains its persistence in Britain and America.[35] While there is certainly some force in this line of thought, it is not very helpful when applied to, say, Conrad or Kipling and it runs into major difficulties when attempting to account for realism's success in Asia and Africa where it is, after all, the predominant form. It does, however, enable us to see why some writers – for example, G. V. Desani, Salman Rushdie, Bessie Head, Dambudzo Marechera – have chosen other fictional forms in their attempt to show how often in the Third World it is the ordinary that is extraordinary. This theme is not unique to fiction. It finds a parallel in Michael Taussig's work on violence and Achille Mbembe's essay on the banality of power in the postcolony.[36] In various ways, writing of this kind draws attention to the subjectivity not only of political phenomena but of the manner in which they are recorded. A celebrated instance is Rushdie's *Midnight's Children*, where the narrative consciously engages with other schools of writing and draws attention to its own fallibility through the use of an unreliable narrator and by its preference for 'remembered truth' over 'literal truth'.

On several occasions in our discussion of the importance of the individual in literature we moved into the realm of culture, pointing, for example, to the significance of group values and customary practices. This is as it should be, because an individual cannot be considered apart from his or her community. Even when it is the inner life which commands attention, it does not exist in isolation from outside experiences and circumstances; in some respects the psychological is an inversion of the sociological. I now turn to look directly at culture, the idea being to establish the relevance of fictional texts and specify some of the issues and questions to be kept in mind. In view of the variety of approaches to culture and its changing connotations over time, it should be said that here the concept is used to embrace a whole way of life – which includes values, custom, art and social organization – but always with a recognition that this way of life may not necessarily be conterminous with what we normally understand to be a society, much less a nation-state. It is accepted that there are no absolute boundaries between different cultures, and depending on our purposes we may pursue the idea of Bengali culture, peasant culture or imperial culture, as well as the more obvious category of national culture.

It is apparent that the novel has always had a cultural orientation. What once went under the heading of manners was essentially the social values and conventions which informed the sensibilities and shaped the behaviour of people in a particular stratum of a given society. In the late eighteenth and early nineteenth centuries 'manners and morals' was a frequent couplet meaning, basically, way of life. Hence the novel of manners is a story set within the confines of (say) English upper middle-class life and it is understood to be a depiction of that culture at work. Almost as a matter of course, novels set in Asia or Africa have more overtly displayed their concern with culture than many others. In novels by Western authors, this is because of the particular fascination with a foreign way of life. One thinks, for example, of the tradition of writing about the exotic East or the portrayal of 'primitive' peoples as enmeshed in a network of spirits, ritual and sacrifice. Especially from the 1870s onwards, the 'ethnographic novel' became popular – partly, as has been suggested, because it was 'estranged in time and space from the claustrophobic Victorian drawing-room'.[37] In novels written by Asians and Africans, it is mainly because of the perceived need to assert the dignity and complexity of their cultures after years of Western denigration.

It is no less apparent that a basic fictional technique, the utilization of conflict to heighten dramatic interest and bring out more of the character of the protagonists, has had a special importance in colonial and postcolonial literature. It was standard fare for novels of empire to emphasize the gulf between European and non-European cultures. In Kipling's writing there is an almost metaphysical conception of cultural difference. Because the English and the Indians think in different ways and brood over different matters, they 'stare at each other hopelessly across great gulfs of miscomprehension'.[38] Joyce Cary has a more sociological approach to cultural barriers. In his African novels he sets out aspects of Nigerian and, to a lesser extent, British custom and social structure and uses this material to elucidate the behaviour of his protagonists. Even E. M. Forster, for all his liberalism and his love of India, plays up the contrasts between Indian and English ways. His depiction of Indian life highlights mystery and muddle – and in the view of some Indian critics reeks of cultural condescension.[39]

There has been a similar tendency to focus on the conflictual side of the East/West encounter on the part of Third World writers. This is especially marked in the case of African literature. Indeed, the collision of values and customs is so deeply etched on the first generation of African novels that they have been categorized in terms of the culture-conflict theme. *Things Fall Apart* sets the pattern. To some degree, the explanation must run along functional lines. Just as the accentuation of cultural differences by European writers served to provide a justification for imperial rule, so in the hands of Third World writers it carries a message about the damage wrought by imperialism and puts on record the worth and history of their own cultures.

If much fiction has been drawn to accentuate the conflictual aspects of the North/South encounter, some has veered in the opposite direction. There are those narratives in which culture is not seen as divisive and the impression is given that people are much the same everywhere. What mostly occurs here is that the novelist in effect projects elements of the culture of his or her society on to an alien society. In such instances the presumption of common values or behavioural patterns is in fact ethnocentrism taking the form of mono-culturalism. This is true of much of Pearl Buck's work, and it is most clearly expressed in her extraordinarily successful *The Good Earth*. The novel is a family saga and it drew upon what were essentially American values and aspirations, clothing them in Asian garb. The same can be said of Lederer and Burdick's *The Ugly American*. Indeed, the pattern of projecting upon, rather than drawing from, Asian culture has been characteristic of nearly all American fiction set in the Asian region.

I have pointed to some of the ways in which fictional narratives have used cultural characterizations as a means of addressing the relationship between aggregations of people – colonizer and colonized, East and West, the liberal capitalist world and the non-aligned underdeveloped world. However, whatever broader signification is invested in culture, it is usually presented as having a rootedness in place and time. Fiction's depiction of culture in some particularity contrasts with how it has been taken up in much recent academic discourse. Its sudden elevation to prominence has been accompanied by a pronounced tendency to decontextualize and to globalize. This has been a feature of much recent writing in postcolonialism. In chapter 7 we will consider the significance of what has been called 'the globalizing gesture' of the postcolonial condition or postcoloniality,[40] and compare it with the treatment of culture in fiction. Similar problems of universalizing are endemic to globalization approaches. Echoing Roland Robertson's famous remark about the world being a 'single place', the emphasis has been on the system rather than its parts. Frank Lechner, for example, has insisted that we are now living in a truly global society, and this focus is mirrored throughout the collection of essays entitled *Global Culture*, which were originally published in a special issue of the journal *Theory, Culture and Society*.[41] In international relations, after such a long period of neglect, Samuel Huntington has at a single stroke turned culture into a new paradigm within which the traditional working of power politics can continue much as before.[42]

The informing hypothesis of this book is that very often fiction provides a better window through which to view the cultural engagement of the local, the civilizational and the global. This is partly because culture is seldom left to float freely without societal moorings and yet it is often presented in ways which challenge or qualify ideas about the processes of international standardization. In Thomas Akare's novel of Nairobi life, for example, Islamization is used by some migrants to the city as a means of establishing a private space. In such circumstances, conversion to Islam represents a strategy for survival rather than a surrender of local identity.[43] Taking a very different text, Shashi Tharoor's *Show Business*, which satirizes the Bombay film culture, may be read as a refutation of the idea that Bollywood is nothing more than an extension of Hollywood and that arguments about the globalization of the cinema need to take more account of local initiative and adaptation.[44]

Intertwined at various points with culture are ideas about race or ethnicity. Even in the late nineteenth and early twentieth centuries, when pseudo-scientific theories buttressed racial typologies which postulated permanent differences between peoples of different colour, thinking about race seldom stood on its own. Assumptions and assertions drew on cultural stereotypes and generalized notions about a people's religion, politics and history. Although race has long been stripped of respectability as a category of classification and categorization, in popular usage it continues to serve as a way of organizing thinking about human collectivities and the differences between people. Race has thus become a trope for cultural criteria which set people apart, and colour is understood to be a badge of difference.

From its earliest days the novel set in the Third World has been concerned with race and especially with its cultural underpinnings which sustain the lines of demarcation between different peoples. The most favoured approach has been to explore personal relationships which cross the racial divide, paying particular attention to marriage, sexuality and 'miscegenation'. Such material can be of value not only for its representations of race but because it depicts the connections between race and politics – a clear instance being the maintenance of social distance between ruler and ruled. In some cases, it may even be said that fictional treatment of the racial issue provides a study in small compass of the social patterns and tensions of the colonial experience. More recently, novelists have been drawn to write about the problems posed by immigrant ethnic communities and the challenge of bicultural development in postcolonial societies. Such material needs to be brought into the study of international relations, where there has been little systematic scholarly inquiry into race.[45] While it is true that race failed to transform the workings of the international system, almost certainly it has been more important than the discipline has recognized and it might yet severely jostle established precepts and practices.

In summary, and to pitch the arguments of the last few pages at their most expansive, the claim is that literature's cultural orientation makes the novel a repository of political understanding because politics draws its meaning from culture. Two questions are thus put on the agenda to be wrestled with throughout this book. First, to what extent and in which ways are a country's politics derived from or mediated by its culture? Novelists have only occasionally spelt out the nature of the linkage – perhaps the clearest case being the Somali writer, Nuruddin Farah. More usually the relationship between politics and culture has to be teased from the treatment in the text of areas such as family life, the role of tradition or attitudes to sexuality, science and the spiritual. Second, what bearing does any such material have on international politics? It is not so difficult to establish that internal cultural phenomena have external political repercussions. The course of America's involvement in Vietnam and the Iranian revolution are case studies to this effect – although obviously there will be disagreement about particular lines of thought. Consider, for example, Norman Mailer's suggestion that Vietnam 'was where the small town had gone to get its kicks'.[46] The real difficulty, however, lies in unpicking the relationship between cultural factors arising within particular societies and political or economic considerations which are tied to the international system, or which at least appear to be characteristic of the international actions of states. But this is not a problem that derives specifically from the use of literature as a source material. It is intrinsic to the nature of international studies itself.

Drawing on the arguments I have advanced about literature's personal and cultural orientation, it can be said that literature contextualizes politics in life. For instance, many aspects of India's post-independence course are mirrored in such novels of Indian family life as Anita Desai's *Clear Light of Day* and Vikram Seth's *A Suitable Boy*.[47] In much scholarly writing there is a propensity to extract what is being considered from its setting; inquiry is so directed that the subject is not treated *in situ*. Fiction, by contrast, tends to be inclusive and one facet of life is viewed in relation to others. Seldom, if ever, is politics depicted as an autonomous realm of thought and action. For the most part the experiences of individuals are recounted alongside those of the group. Usually the outer world is seen in relation to the inner world – indeed in some modernist works the two merge almost indistinguishably.

It follows, of course, that the reader is led to reflect more broadly; he or she is required to do more of the patterning, making judgements about connections, closures and so on. But the picture which emerges may be richer as a result. In short, the argument is that our understanding of politics is heightened when politics is integrated with life, when the political connects with people's ordinary experiences rather than being a world apart. The proposition is well illustrated by an Indian novel published in 1940, Ahmed Ali's *Twilight in Delhi*.[48]

Set in Delhi in the first two decades of this century, the novel tells the story of Mir Nihal, the head of a traditional Muslim joint family, and records his response to imperial rule, the spread of alien values and the rise of the nationalist movement. The political and social material is so intertwined that an Indian critic raises the issue of whether the story of the family is background to the political motif or vice versa.[49] In truth the two are inseparable, each providing context for the other. One of the strengths of the novel is the way the political elements emerge naturally from the description of everyday life.

Thus the quite long accounts of Mir Nihal flying pigeons over the rooftops of Delhi or going about his day-to-day affairs situate the politics of the novel in his total life-experience. The way in which Mir Nihal clings to the customs and observances of the traditional society is part and parcel of the cast of mind which laments the passing of the Muslim era and rejects the emerging hybrid culture. 'His world had fallen.' 'The glory had gone, and only dreariness remained.'[50] Mir Nihal believed in fighting with naked swords and hence he would have no part in the agitation of the 'chicken-hearted' or the Home Rule Movement, but retreated into his own private world. His hatred of the rulers found expression, not in public declamation, but in rejection of his son's English shoes and shirts and his refusal to allow his son a higher education. In such ways, Ahmed Ali depicts the passing of a culture, a phase in the independence struggle, and its replacement by another.

There is one final observation to be made about literature's orientation which gives sharper point to much of the argument of this chapter and also goes beyond it. It is that literature can focus our attention on moral issues and encourage us to integrate the moral and the political. One of the traditional justifications for the teaching of English was its role in moral education, and this line of thought was basic to Leavisian criticism. It has not found much favour with some contemporary critics, their argument being that reading literary narratives (or pursuing other forms of 'high culture') failed to stop the rise of the Nazis, and in any case the moral lessons were all too often tied to class, race and nation.[51] I do not see that such arguments invalidate the claim that literature can change our thinking for the better. Because preferred conclusions are by no means always drawn from literary (or any other) narratives, and because moral appreciations are not necessarily acted upon, does not discount the role that literature can play in the transformation of thought. Earlier in this chapter I cited Bhabani Bhattacharya's *So Many Hungers* as one such instance and others will be given in later chapters.

I would argue that literature's moral agency, its capacity to induce us to reappraise our values and sensibilities, follows from its personalization of issues and the models of behaviour it offers for our contemplation – many of them beyond our direct experience. We are encouraged to reflect not only because of our emotional engagement but also because, as readers, we are required to pursue possibilities and contingencies – the whole is never there, simply for the taking. This also involves us in wrestling with those aspects of a work which seem false. Iris Murdoch observes that stories 'are almost always a bit or very false'.[52] Mario Vargas Llosa goes further and claims that novels lie – 'they cannot help doing so'. But through lying, 'they express a curious truth'.[53] His point is that through fiction we are able to go beyond ourselves and our concrete situation; we are able to explore our dreams, desires and ideals. Thus fiction both assuages dissatisfaction and incites it.

A powerful contemporary endorsement of the ethical possibilities of the novel is furnished by Iris Murdoch in *Metaphysics as a Guide to Morals*. Discounting structuralist and post-structuralist theory, she asserts that literature enlarges and refines our capacity for moral judgement. In the following passage she articulates in philosophical terms the relationship of artistic to moral experience which she has in different ways written into many of her novels.

> It may be that the best model for all thought is the creative imagination. We cannot exactly say that novelists are unaware or unconscious of these problems, since they have constantly to invent methods of conveying states of mind or to choose between different styles of doing so. Novels moreover exhibit the ubiquity of moral quality inherent in consciousness. We may rightly criticise novels in which characters' thoughts (as well as actions) exhibit a lack of moral sensibility which seems called for by the story. This is an important kind of literary criticism. Indeed the judgment passed upon the moral sensibility of the artist is a primary kind of aesthetic judgment. . . [T]he novelist's problem (the traditional novelist's problem), solved intuitively or otherwise, is precisely a unification of fact and value, the exhibiting of personal morality in a non-abstract manner as the stuff of consciousness.[54]

Notes

1. At one time or another most writers fall into the trap; I will simply cite my own case. See Phillip Darby and Richard Fuller, 'Western domination and Western literature', *Melbourne Journal of Politics*, 14 (1982–3), 5–18.

2. James F. Davidson, 'Political science and political fiction', *American Political Science Review*, 55:4 (December 1961), 851–60 (p. 859).

3. Hayden White, *Tropics of Discourse* (Johns Hopkins University Press, Baltimore, 1978), p. 118.

4. Ronald Robinson and John Gallagher with Alice Denny, *Africa and the Victorians: The Official Mind of Imperialism* (Macmillan, London, 1961).

5. See William Roger Louis (ed.), *Imperialism: The Robinson and Gallagher Controversy* (New Viewpoints, New York, 1976).

6. I have argued this in some detail in Phillip Darby, *Three Faces of Imperialism. British and American Approaches to Asia and Africa* (Yale University Press, New Haven and London, 1987), ch. 9.

7. Aidan Foster-Carter, 'From Rostow to Gunder Frank: conflicting paradigms in the analysis of underdevelopment', *World Development*, 4:3 (March 1976), 167–80 (p. 175).

8. See Tony Smith, 'Requiem or new agenda for Third World studies?', *World Politics*, 37:4 (July 1985), 532–61.

9. Compare Homi K. Bhabha, 'How newness enters the world: postmodern space, postcolonial times and the trials of cultural translation', ch. 11 in *The Location of Culture* (Routledge, London and New York, 1994).

10. See for instance Aijaz Ahmad, 'The politics of literary postcoloniality', *Race + Class*, 36:3 (1995),1–20; Russell Jacoby, 'Marginal returns: the trouble with post-colonial theory', *Linguafranca*, (Sept./Oct. 1995), 30–7.

11. Dane Kennedy, 'Imperial history and post-colonial theory', *The Journal of Imperial and Commonwealth History*, 24:3 (September 1996), 346.

12. Frank Kermode, 'Secrets and narrative sequence' in W. J. T. Mitchell (ed.), *On Narrative* (University of Chicago Press, Chicago and London, 1981), pp. 79–97.

13. Anthony John Chennells, 'Settler myths and the Southern Rhodesian novel' (unpublished PhD thesis, University of Zimbabwe, Harare, August 1982).

14. Ibid., p. 422.

15. Kermode, op. cit., p. 83.

16. Lionel Trilling, *The Liberal Imagination. Essays on Literature and Society* (Secker & Warburg, London, 1951), p. 9.

17. For a discussion of some of the problems and possibilities of articulating the aesthetic qualities of literary texts, see Martin Ryle, 'Long live literature? Englit, radical criticism and cultural studies', *Radical Philosophy*, 67 (Summer 1994), 21–7.

18. Edward Said, 'Orientalism and after', *Radical Philosophy*, 63 (Spring 1993), 24.

19. See Georg Lukács, *The Historical Novel*, translated by Hannah and Stanley Mitchell (Penguin, Harmondsworth, 1969; first published in Russian 1938).

20. For a classic comparison of the epic with the novel see Georg Lukács, *The Theory of the Novel* (Merlin Press, London, 1971; first published 1920), ch. 3.

21. Lukács, *The Historical Novel*, p. 22.

22. Jeremy Hawthorn, 'Individuality and characterization in the modernist novel' in Douglas Jefferson and Graham Martin, *The Uses of Fiction. Essays on the Modern Novel in Honour of Arnold Kettle* (Open University Press, Milton Keynes, 1982), 41–58 (p. 53).

23. Ibid., p. 56.

24. K. S. Ramamurti, *Rise of the Indian Novel in English* (Sterling Publishers Private Ltd, New Delhi, 1987), p. 267.

25. Chinua Achebe, *No Longer at Ease* (Heinemann Educational Books, London, 1963; first published 1960).

26. Susan Blake 'A woman's trek. What difference does gender make?' in N. Chaudhuri and M. Strobel (eds), *Western Women and Imperialism. Complicity and Resistance* (Indiana University Press, Bloomington, 1992), pp. 19–34.

27. See Grant Parsons, 'Another India: imagining escape from the masculine self', ch. 8 in Phillip Darby (ed.), *At the Edge of International Relations. Postcolonialism, Gender and Dependency* (Pinter, London, 1996).

28. The character is Deeriye and the novel is *Close Sesame* (Allison & Busby, London and New York, 1983). The extract comes from p. 86.

29. Bhabani Bhattacharya, *So Many Hungers* (Orient Paperbacks, Delhi, 1984; first published 1947).

30. Leon Trotsky, *The History of the Russian Revolution Vol. 1: The Overthrow of Czarism*, translated from the Russian by Max Eastman (Victor Gollancz, London, 1932), p. 111.

31. Ashis Nandy, 'Final encounter: the politics of the assassination of Gandhi' in *At the Edge of Psychology. Essay in Politics and Culture* (Oxford University Press, Delhi, 1980), 70–98 (p. 70).

32. Ibid., p. 87.

33. Lukács, *The Historical Novel*, pp. 32 and 33.

34. The foundational essay is Gayatri Chakravorty Spivak, 'Can the subaltern speak?' in Cary Nelson and Lawrence Grossberg (eds), *Marxism and the Interpretation of Culture* (University of Illinois Press, Chicago, 1988).

35. See George Levine, *The Realistic Imagination* (University of Chicago Press, Chicago and London, 1981), and the note by Michael Gorra in 'Laughter and bloodshed', *Hudson Review*, 37 (Spring 1984), 151–64 (p. 164).

36. See Michael Taussig, *Shamanism, Colonialism and the Wild Man. A Study in Terror and Healing* (University of Chicago Press, Chicago and London, 1987), and 'Terror as usual: Walter Benjamin's theory of history as a state of siege', *Social Text*, 23 (Fall/Winter 1989), 3–20. Also Achille Mbembe, 'The banality of power and the aesthetics of vulgarity in the postcolony', *Public Culture*, 4:2 (Spring 1992), 1–30.

37. Brian V. Street, *The Savage in Literature. Representations of 'Primitive' Society in English Fiction 1858–1920* (Routledge & Kegan Paul, London and Boston, 1975), p. 4.

38. From the preface, Rudyard Kipling, *Life's Handicap* (Macmillan, London, 1982; first published 1891), p. ix.

39. See, for example, C. D. Narasimhaiah, Introduction, pp. xxi–xxv in C. D. Narasimhaiah (ed.), *Awakened Conscience. Studies in Commonwealth Literature* (Sterling Publishers, New Delhi, 1978).

40. Ella Shohat, 'Notes on the "post-colonial"', *Social Text*, 31/32 (1992), 99–113 (p. 104).

41. Frank J. Lechner, 'Cultural aspects of the modern world system' in William H. Swatos Jr. (ed.), *Religious Politics in Global and Comparative Perspective* (Greenwood Press, Westport CT, 1989), p. 11. The latter reference is to Mike Featherstone (ed.), *Global Culture. Nationalism, Globalisation and Modernity* (Sage Publications, London, Newbury Park and New Delhi, 1990).

42. Samuel P. Huntington, 'The clash of civilizations?', *Foreign Affairs*, 72:3 (Summer 1993), 22–49.

43. Thomas Akare, *The Slums* (Heinemann, London, 1981); and see Bodil Folke Frederiksen, 'City life and city texts: popular knowledge and articulation in the slums of Nairobi' in Preben Kaarsholm (ed.), *Cultural Struggle and Development in Southern Africa* (Baobab Books, Harare; James Currey, London; Heinemann, Portsmouth NH, 1991).

44. Shashi Tharoor, *Show Business* (Picador, London, 1994; first published 1992).

45. I have argued the latter point in *Three Faces of Imperialism*, pp. 84–5, with some supplementary material at pp. 45–8 and 86–7.

46. Norman Mailer, *The Armies of the Night* (Penguin, Harmondsworth, 1968), p. 164.

47. Anita Desai, *Clear Light of Day* (Penguin, Harmondsworth, 1980) and Vikram Seth, *A Suitable Boy* (Phoenix House, London, 1993).

48. Ahmed Ali, *Twilight in Delhi* (Oxford University Press, Bombay, 1966; first published 1940).

49. Gobinda Prasad Sarma, *Nationalism in Indo-Anglian Fiction* (Sterling Publishers, New Delhi, 1978), pp. 129–30.

50. Ahmed Ali, op. cit., pp. 250–1.

51. See, for example, Terry Eagleton, *Literary Theory. An Introduction* (Blackwell, Oxford, 1983), pp. 35–57.

52. Iris Murdoch, *Metaphysics as a Guide to Morals* (Chatto & Windus, London, 1992), p. 105.

53. Mario Vargas Llosa, 'Is fiction the art of lying?', *New York Times Book Review*, 7 October 1984, pp. 1 and 40.

54. Murdoch, op. cit., p. 169.

CHAPTER 3

Rereading dominance

Questions about dominance lie at the heart of the meaning of imperialism and the nature of the contemporary North/South relationship. In his masterful survey of Asia and the West, K. M. Panikkar writes that the arrival of Vasco da Gama in Calicut in 1498 marked the beginning of the epoch of Western domination.[1] Historians who came after Panikkar have taken the century from about 1870 as the decisive period in which Asia and Africa were subordinated to the West. The ascendancy first of Britain, and then of the United States, deeply marked the life of the two continents and transformed their relationships with the outside world. During the imperial era the metropoles took title to and tribute from their colonial 'possessions'. The flow of ideas and values was largely outward from Europe. Within Asia and Africa significant changes took place in the distribution of power and the balance of social forces. The processes thus set in motion brought Afro-Asia into the global economy and the international political system on terms which were indisputably disadvantageous or dependent. In many respects these processes have continued beyond formal decolonization, in ways which have been traced by dependency, globalization and postcolonial theorists.

Situated in this way, it is evident that domination is a multifaceted phenomenon and that no single approach can engage with all its meanings. It is therefore important to set out clearly the object of this chapter, the limits of its inquiry and its relationship to other scholarly approaches. Its starting-point is the need to address and redress the understanding of dominance in international relations which variously informs, or corresponds with, much interpretation in history and globalization theory. In short, the argument is that domination has been understood unduly expansively; too much has been assumed on the basis of too narrow an inquiry.

To suggest that the idea of domination has had too easy a scholarly passage in these circles may appear almost glib. In international relations the notion of domination has a long pedigree and its continuing importance is illustrated by the reception of Paul Kennedy's *The Rise and Fall of the Great Powers*[2] and the critical debate which the book engendered. Yet, surveying the literature, it is apparent that a good deal more has been written on where dominance is to be found and how it can be shored up or overturned than on what it actually signifies. It also appears that the preoccupation with the material attributes of dominance and their external manifestations – that is, in the arena designated international and inhabited by states – has skewed analyses of what is at stake or at least has produced a one-dimensional view of the processes involved. It is a matter of the areas to which attention is directed and the kind of 'evidence' which is admitted. These points can be illustrated by reference to the two texts already cited. It is notable that Panikkar's study, which attributes such power to the West, proceeds on the basis of a geopolitical reading of the relationship between the West and Asia which 'may be briefly stated as the dominance of maritime power over the land masses of Asia'.[3] Kennedy's book is about the passage of dominance from one power to another and hence its concerns are different from ours. He himself concedes its Eurocentrism and its neglect of small powers.[4] What is revealing, however, is that his story is told very largely in terms of economic growth, military effectiveness and the relationship between the two. No one should doubt the relevance of these considerations, though a reading of the new discourses would suggest that many do. What is contended here is that the influence wielded on such a basis has been overdrawn and that fictional narratives provide a salutary corrective.

The informing idea of this chapter is that domination involves much more than the message it flags: that the meaning of overlordship cannot be considered apart from the patterns of thought and behaviour of those who exercise it and those who experience it. This means we must reckon, on the one hand, with the excesses, constraints and inhibitions of those who rule, and, on the other, with the adaption, deflection and desire to impropriate on the part of those who are ruled. The central argument can be put quite simply: the dominion of force is by no means always enabling and in some respects it hobbles those who hold it.

Thus stated, some caveats should be entered lest the contribution of fiction and hence the claims of this chapter appear to be pitched too high. Cutting domination down to size is after all not a novel exercise. Hegel's treatment of the master/slave relationship has a continuing influence, extending presumably even to those who have not read his work.[5] Then there is Foucault's insistence that power exists in a network of relations and that its exercise calls forth an inevitable resistance.[6] James Scott's study of peasant resistance in rural Malaysia provides a case study of challenges to domination which traditionally had not been seen in such terms.[7] Here a reminder is appropriate that there can be no hard-and-fast separation of literary and non-literary sources. Moreover, it is often difficult to tie an idea to a specific source. We should therefore be chary of any insistence that a particular line of thinking derives from fiction or that a contrary position follows from a reading of non-fictional texts. The presumption is that the ideas developed in this chapter were sparked by the reading of fiction, but in some instances it may be that all that can be claimed is that fiction drives home the message more powerfully or illustrates it more vividly. The fiction herein addressed is Western, or at least it is written by Europeans and Americans. What emerges, therefore, are perspectives on dominance drawn from the empowered side of the divide. Of course within this body of work specific narratives are directed to the cause of change.

In certain respects my treatment of dominance is uneven. No emphasis is placed on the magnitude of the West's impact on Africa and Asia; it is the limits of effective influence which are of primary concern. In outlining the way in which fiction brings out the constraints on imperial power, I have not taken up the agency of subjugated peoples as an issue in its own right. That it is one cannot be doubted. Agency has become a major concern in postcolonial inquiry as well as in feminist and historical studies. However, to pursue the matter here would overload the narrative, not least because agency has become a highly contested notion in the struggle to find an accommodation between action and oppression. A consideration of some of the issues relating to agency will therefore be deferred until chapter 5.

Our inquiry begins with the idea that the exercise of power is tinged with insecurity. The public face of dominance is about the capacity to determine, but dominance has another face, more often glimpsed than seen in full view, which expresses anxiety, inner uncertainty and doubt. It may even be that a sense of incapacity is an invariable companion to the possession of capability and is part of the very drive to acquire, to go out, to shape events. Mostly our gaze has been fixed on the public face, with the result that we have exaggerated the degree to which the powerful get their way and we have been hard-pressed to explain the processes of change. The idea of imperial insecurity is by no means new. It arose very largely from imaginative literature and it was literary scholars who were responsible for bringing it to notice and spelling out some of its implications. In the high noon of empire Kipling's 'Recessional' testified to elements of misgiving – even if Kipling himself had to be prodded to retrieve the poem from his waste-paper basket. It was not until much later, however, that its challenge to imperial grandiosity came to be widely appreciated.[8] 'Recessional' was in fact part of a broader literary questioning of the assurance about empire and what it could accomplish. Nor was literature alone in detecting or reflecting currents of strain and insecurity. Lamenting Britain's occupation of Egypt in 1882, Gladstone shrewdly observed that 'with a great Empire in each of the four corners of the world we may be territorially content, but less than ever at our ease'.[9] Historians have tended to confirm his judgement, pointing to signs of displacement or areas of disjunction. In the view of Philip Mason, growing doubt and unease lay behind the racial intolerance and the shrill, arrogant tone of European imperialism in the years from 1880 to 1914.[10] Others have argued that sexual repression and latent homosexuality permeated the imperial venture, so that the surface calm belied an inner turbulence.[11]

None the less, it was fiction which brought insecurity to notice. It was in novels and short stories that the limits of dominion were most fully canvassed. Over many years it was writers, sensitive to the pretensions and vulnerabilities of empire, who proved more acute than their contemporaries in other vocations. A little later I will attempt to explain why this was so, but first it is necessary to set out some of the ideas and themes as they emerge in the literature. We might note as a preliminary that certain lines of thinking, relating for example to the cultural impenetrability of supposedly weaker societies, recur over a period of several decades. The utility of a chronological approach is therefore open to question. One writer – Allen Greenberger – surveying British novels about India, has detected significant shifts in the approach of novelists in different periods. According to his schema, 1880–1910 was the era of confidence while 1910–33 was the era of doubt.[12] While it is evident that over time there were growing apprehensions about the solidity of empire, a sense of insecurity existed from very early days. Greenberger implicitly acknowledges as much when he observes of the era of confidence that the things authors did not discuss, such as race relations and the rise of Indian nationalism, are as interesting (perhaps meaning revealing) as the things they did.[13] To say that the novelists' consciousness was historically conditioned is to state the obvious; what needs to be added is that the best writing had a searching quality about it which ranged beyond the particular in time and place.

Kipling provides a fine illustration in that, for all his immersion in the imperial here and now, not for a moment does he exaggerate its impact on India or imagine that the daily work would shape outcomes over time. In some areas of Indian life things can be achieved and they are worth achieving, but in others imperialism has no purchase, for the ways of India are too deeply rooted in the land, the culture and age-old habits of thought. In the face of such odds, military power or even industrialism and technology mostly scratch the surface, and even then their imprint is likely to be transient. Compared with Marx or Curzon, Kipling's is a sobering assessment of the potentialities of empire. Two pieces of dialogue from his short stories illustrate the gulf between his appreciation and the prevailing orthodoxies. The first, taken from 'The Education of Otis Yeere', is almost incidental to the story. The setting is Simla and Mrs Hauksbee has the idea of establishing a *salon*. Her friend, Mrs Mallow, more experienced in the ways of India, dismisses the idea out of hand because a *salon*, to be any good at all, must be permanent. The fact is, Mrs Mallow explains, 'We are only little bits of dirt on the hillsides – here one day and blown down the *khud* the next.'[14]

The same thought is more powerfully developed in 'The Bridge-Builders' and there, interestingly enough, its most graphic expression is again with reference to dirt. The story has several layers of meaning but the one which concerns us in this chapter addresses the impact of British rule on India. Findlayson, an English engineer, is responsible for the construction of the Kashi Bridge over the Ganges. In many practical matters he relies heavily on Peroo, an Indian who had spent years sailing on British India boats, and who has made the project his own. Shortly before the bridge's completion, it is threatened by an unseasonably early flood. Emergency measures are taken in the short time available and then there is nothing the two men can do except watch the rising waters. After swallowing pellets of opium, they are swept down the river in a small boat, washed up on an island, and find themselves present at an assembly of gods, meeting to decide whether the Ganges should be allowed to sweep away the bridge.

Already, to this point, the imperial edifice has been questioned and British power scaled to size. The bridge is a symbol of Britain's achievement in India; it was to be opened by the Viceroy, blessed by an archbishop, and a trainload of soldiers would cross it. It was 'pukka – permanent – to endure when all memory of the builder . . . had perished'.[15] Yet it is now at the mercy of the elements – which after 25 years in India Findlayson doesn't pretend to understand. Peroo does rather better because his Indian self has resisted the influence of the West. He may have gained his knowledge of tackle and the handling of heavy weights overseas, but he remained unaffected by port missions or Western creeds. Back in India he believed in Mother Gunga, and she had been put 'in irons'. Hence Peroo knew Mother Gunga would speak well before the telegraph gave warning. The narrator goes on to tell us that when nothing more could be done to secure the bridge, Findlayson 'went over it in his head, plate by plate, span by span, brick by brick, pier by pier, remembering, comparing, estimating, and recalculating, lest there should be any mistake His side of the sum was beyond question; but what man knew Mother Gunga's arithmetic?'[16]

The debate between the Hindu gods provides the occasion for a more thoroughgoing examination of the significance of the British presence in India. Assembled on the island are Shiva the Bull, Ganesha the Elephant, Hanuman the Ape, Kali the Tigress, Bhairon the Buck, Sitala the Ass and Gunga the Crocodile (or Mugger). The different gods declaim on what should be done about the bridge in the light of their particular provenances and taking into account whether or not those who follow them have benefited from the changes introduced by British rule. We are thus presented with an interlocution which draws its philosophical meaning from Hindu mythology but which takes cognizance of the role of specific material interests – the latter in some ways akin to the approach of Robinson and Gallagher. The gods who toiled against the bridge – and the British impact – have their say. Those who stand to gain, state their case. In the end the bridge holds against the flood, but what rings in the mind are the voices declaring the ephemeral nature of Britain's intervention. '"What should their Gods know? They were born yesterday, and those that made them are scarcely yet cold", said the Mugger. "Tomorrow their Gods will die".'[17] The debate continues:

> 'They have changed the face of the land – which is my land. They have killed and made new towns on my banks,' said the Mugger.
> 'It is but the shifting of a little dirt. Let the dirt dig in the dirt if it pleases the dirt,' answered the Elephant.[18]

Even with respect to the short-term, the novelists of empire convey a scepticism about how far external intervention can shape the course of affairs in Asia and Africa. Compared with the high hopes which punctuate official rhetoric, writers were much more likely to be cynical about what could be realized through imperialism, and often enough their fiction can be read as a critical commentary on the suppositions of the ruling discourse. Reflecting especially on the British material leads to the observation that the literary and non-literary narratives bring out different aspects of the imperial undertaking. The texts do not, of course, arrange themselves neatly around interpretative poles but there is a sense in which we are offered a macro and a micro view of British dominance: imperialism approached from the perspective of geopolitical power, which carries with it an aura of capability and confidence; and imperialism seen from within, which is marked by uncertainty, miscomprehension and elements of pretence.

What I have characterized as the view from within has a number of rather different angles, though it is also a matter of overall tone or mood. There is the feeling that it is not possible to understand what is happening in the mind of the other or to come to grips with the forces at work in the colonized society. In some cases the realization follows that changes effected in the public domain may not extend to the private sphere. Generally, there is a concern that the imperial writ is restricted to the surface of life; that the authority of the Raj does not extend far into society. Let us consider some of these aspects of thought as they emerge in the texts themselves.

The first statement comes from Kipling. It is made in a story which begins with the visit of a Russian officer, Dirkovitch, to a British regiment, the White Hussars, in Peshawar. Dirkovitch was 'distressingly European' and would speak by the hour of the great mission of civilizing Asia which awaited England and Russia. The narrator presents Kipling's view of the matter in down-to-earth terms:

> That was unsatisfactory, because Asia is not going to be civilised after the methods of the West. There is too much Asia and she is too old. You cannot reform a lady of many lovers, and Asia has been insatiable in her flirtations aforetime. She will never attend Sunday school or learn to vote save with swords for tickets.[19]

Leonard Woolf approaches the same issue from a different vantage-point in *The Village in the Jungle*. There is no direct statement of position in the novel and it is not until the reader is well into the book that the issues relating to imperialism emerge. However, the emotional impact of Woolf's critique of the civilizing mission is the greater as a result. Set in Ceylon, where Woolf spent seven years in the civil service,[20] the first part of the story tells of a village community deep in the jungle which lives continuously on the edge of disaster, threatened by drought, disease and money-lenders. The focus of attention is on a hunter, Silindu, and his family, who are regarded with contempt by the village because they belong to the lowest Sinhalese caste. The village, and especially Silindu and his family, live according to traditional rhythms which make little sense to the world outside. In the second part of the story Silindu's son-in-law, Babun, suffers at the hands of the village headman and his confederate, the money-lender. Babun attempts to petition the British Assistant Agent, some three days' journey away, but meets with resistance from the clerks and peons attached to the office. Framed by the headman and the money-lender, Babun is tried and convicted in a British court for a theft he did not commit. He is given a 'lenient' sentence but, as is the way of people from the jungle, dies in gaol. Influenced by his jungle lore,

Silindu kills the headman and the money-lender, and is in turn convicted in a British court and sentenced to life imprisonment. Disease and death hit the village, huts are abandoned, and the jungle reclaims its own. The closing scene sees Babun's wife, the last member of Silindu's family, on her deathbed with a great boar gliding towards her.

There is little in the novel to suggest that Woolf is attracted to the traditional village system and nothing at all to commend its primitive justice. Yet at least the villagers had an understanding – or believed they had – of how their society was regulated, and to some degree they were able to influence outcomes. The imposition of British rule and legal processes, however, produces incomprehension on the part of most, manipulation at the hands of a few, and the net effect is to perpetrate much greater injustice than occurred before. Babun and Silindu have no understanding of the procedures of the courts and, so far as they are able to cope at all, they simply speak within their own cultural constructs. On the other side are those such as the money-lender who know the ways of the courts and are able to exploit the system for their private advantage. In the middle are the British magistrate and the British judge who formally preside but, because of their ignorance and innocence, are in reality instruments of the very forces of corruption that the system is ostensibly directed against. Woolf strengthens his case against the efficacy of imperial rule by showing that those who administer the system have doubts about its workings. The magistrate who sentences Babun begins his judgment by observing: 'There is almost certainly something behind this case which has not come out.'[21] Later, when Silindu is brought to him, the magistrate contradicts the view of the chief headman that it seems to be a simple case. The magistrate continues:

> I don't think that you know, any more than I do, Ratemahatmaya, what goes on up there in the jungle. He was a quiet man in the village, I believe that. He only wanted to be left alone. It must take a lot of cornering and torturing and shooting to rouse a man like that.[22]

The trial judge evidently held a similar view. According to the narrator, the summing up of the judge 'showed that he was not one of those who regarded it as a simple case'.[23] Enclosed within the structure of the legal system, however, the doubts of the two judges cannot address the root of the problem.

The notion of imperialism as a project of controlled modernization was derided by many later novelists on the ground that it made light of the cultural differences between Europe and the non-European world. Often in the background one can detect a fascination with the pre-modern and a resistance to disturbing the traditional order. In this respect, as Martin Green has argued, Kipling cast a long shadow.[24] The absurdity of the very notion that European ideas would of themselves lead to a modern future was satirized by Evelyn Waugh in *Black Mischief*. Native soldiers, issued with boots for the first time, hold a special feast and eat the lot as extra rations. According to the Minister for the Interior, the message of the New Age is that 'we must be Modern, we must be refined in our Cruelty to Animals'.[25] A sharper note is struck in *Burmese Days*, by Flory who expresses George Orwell's cynicism. He concedes to Dr Veraswami that Britain modernizes Burma in certain ways. Then comes the rub: 'before we've finished we'll have wrecked the whole Burmese national culture. But we're not civilizing them, we're only rubbing our dirt on to them.'[26] His concern, however, is not simply for Burma, and Flory is honest enough to admit that he would 'rather see things a little bit septic. Burma in the days of Thibaw would have suited me better, I think.'[27]

Anthony Burgess writes in the same tradition, although closer to Waugh than to Orwell in both technique and content. *The Long Day Wanes*,[28] a trilogy set in Malaya in the fifties, reflects on the record of empire through the life of its ineffectual anti-hero, Victor Crabbe, a middle-aged schoolteacher. Crabbe went out to Malaya to be useful but found he was neither needed nor wanted. His inconsequential death symbolizes the end of an equally inconsequential colonialism – a shadow-play which did little good but perhaps not much harm because it was so easily used by the locals and changed so little on the ground. *Devil of a State*[29] presents a bleaker picture of the colonial intrusion and its legacy. Set in a fictional island-state off the coast of east Africa, it depicts the failure of colonial modernization and the way that the idea of the modern is cynically manipulated by the successor state.

In Burgess's novels there are suggestions that in its early days imperialism had a certain vigour and perhaps even promise. John Updike's *The Coup* harbours no such illusions. Foreign rule never held prospects of significant change because it had so little substance. *The Coup* is set in the fictitious African state of Kush. Formerly a French colony, Kush is now independent and is ruled by Colonel Hakim Felix Ellellou. Speaking to his first wife, Ellellou reflects on the French impact:

> When we effected the Revolution, we discovered a strange thing. There was nothing to revolutionize. Our Minister of Industry looked for factories to nationalize, and there were none. The Minister of Agriculture sought out the large land holdings to seize and subdivide, and found that most of the land was in a legal sense unowned . . . We sought to restore autonomy to the people, in the form of citizens' councils and elections with pictographic ballots, but they had never surrendered autonomy in their minds. The French had been an apparition, a bright passing parade. The French had educated a few *assimilés*, given them jobs, paid them in francs, and taxed them. They were taxing themselves, to govern themselves. It was exquisitely circular, like their famous logic, like their villanelles.[30]

Ellellou gets carried away with his rhetoric when he says that the French experience was 'exquisitely circular', but his description of French colonialism as 'a bright passing parade' draws some support from post-dependency historiographical revisionism. Compared with earlier historical analyses – certainly of the time *The Coup* was written – the tendency now is to emphasize precolonial continuities, areas of resistance and, to paraphrase Ellellou, the autonomy of the mind. Indeed, according to some formulations, the problem about imperialism was not that it changed so much but that it changed so little.

There is another side to the novelist's critique of dominance. It is not only that the exercise of power may accomplish less than appearances suggest but that it involves costs and risks that can easily prove disabling to its principals. This may be because of the nature of the adversary; it may follow from the fact that the capabilities of the two parties are of different kinds; or it may be a function of the very possession of power. One line of thought is that the imperial actor may not be a free agent. Another is that the directors or representatives of empire may be ensnared in a situation which they cannot control. Let us consider some of the various possibilities as they are elaborated in the fiction of empire.

Both Conrad and Kipling develop the idea that the non-European world threatens in some way those from the outside who attempt to control it. The suggestion is that it has some age-old power that the West can neither grasp nor effectively counter. It is therefore necessary to recognize that there are limits to intervention. Failure to do so puts the intruder at peril. This, I would argue, is one way of reading *Heart of Darkness*. Marlow's account of his experiences is studded with illustrations of how the instruments of Western power cannot find a target or achieve their purposes. There is the French man-of-war anchored off the coast, 'incomprehensible, firing into a continent'.[31] At the Company's station a railway is being built and Marlow observes the 'objectless blasting' of a cliff which was not in the way of anything.[32] All around is dumped the paraphernalia of industrialism, abandoned or ravaged by the elements – 'a boiler wallowing in the grass', 'an undersized railway truck lying there on its back with its wheels in the air', 'more pieces of decaying machinery, a stack of rusty nails'.[33] And then, upriver, 'there wasn't one rivet to be found where it was wanted'.[34]

The most telling of Marlow's recollections is the scene when he comes upon the wreck of his steamer, 'hauled up on the slope like a carcass of some big river animal'. He describes the smell of mud, the stillness of the primeval forest, the moonlight over the rank grass, the matted vegetation and the river itself. 'All this was great, expectant, mute', but Marlow wonders whether the stillness was meant as an appeal or as a menace.

> What were we who had strayed in here? Could we handle that dumb thing or would it handle us?[35]

The imagery in this paragraph is of a vegetation and landscape which are invested with qualities which Marlow finds forbidding – primal, silent, impenetrable. This accords with descriptions in other parts of the novella of the wilderness of Africa, its emptiness and its silence, which convey a sense of mystery and hidden knowledge, invincibility and vengeance.

But it is clear that the continent only takes on a forbidding countenance when it is disturbed by an alien; this is the face that Africa shows to the intruder. And confronted by a continent and a people that cannot be comprehended, much less controlled, the intruder succumbs to fear, frustration and a loss of self-control. The desire is to hit out and to hurt. This is not, however, an exercise of power but an expression of powerlessness. It is the sense of impotence which produces the impetus for mindless action. 'There was a touch of insanity', we are told, about the French man-of-war firing its tiny projectiles into the continent.[36] When Marlow's fevered companion is abandoned by the porters who had been carrying him, the man is very anxious for Marlow to kill somebody. Marlow remembers the old doctor in Brussels speaking of 'the mental changes of individuals on the spot'.[37] Kurtz is a parallel case. His eloquent manuscript about what could be accomplished in Africa, written apparently 'before his – let us say – nerves, went wrong', ended with a note evidently written much later: 'Exterminate all the brutes!'[38]

In some of his early Indian stories Kipling is similarly concerned to show that the imperialist is imperilled by the society or the territory over which he rules. As he tells it, the landscape, the climate and the fact of physical isolation compound the sense of vulnerability and the fear of ineffectiveness which come from presiding over an alien culture. The risk of personal disintegration is therefore very real and must be guarded against by absorption in the work – 'work'll keep our wits together'. If a breakdown occurs it must be concealed, lest it threaten the authority and assurance of the Raj. This is the lesson of 'At the End of the Passage'. Kipling depicts the terror of Hummil's last weeks in terms reminiscent of Conrad in *Heart of Darkness*. There is, however, the difference that Kipling's protagonist does not displace his inner turmoil by hitting out blindly at the native people. Under the influence of morphia, Hummil speaks of his nightmare vision: 'A place, – a place down there.'[39] After Hummil's suicide, his personal servant, Chuma, uses the same imagery to account for what happened: 'this that was my master has descended into the Dark Places, and there has been caught because he was not able to escape with sufficient speed.'[40]

In another story, 'The Strange Ride of Morrowbie Jukes', the protagonist makes an unlikely escape from the 'place down there' but we are given a version of what the place means and how it relates to the precariousness of British paramountcy. Jukes rides into a sand crater inhabited by Indians thought to be dead but whose appearance changes when brought to the burning ghats. As outcasts they live in a wretched state of nature, observing none of the conventions and proprieties of social life, whether deriving from Hindu custom or British imperial culture. Jukes quickly finds that he can no longer rely on his accustomed supports, such as civility from inferiors, and he is brought face to face with the vulnerability of his position: 'Here was a Sahib, a representative of the dominant race, helpless as a child and completely at the mercy of his native neighbours.'[41] Harangued by a former Brahmin government servant on the hopelessness of his situation, Jukes was 'powerless to protest or answer'.[42] The account which follows brings out the debilitating effects of Jukes' terror and his exposure to elemental forces. All the signs point in the direction of immobility and despair, but Kipling cannot bring himself to strip Jukes of the Englishman's capacity for action and calm thought.

Conrad and Kipling are pre-eminent among writers in showing how power can disable those who exercise it, but they hold no monopoly of this motif. The idea that the ruler may become a victim of, or at least be used by, those who are ruled emerges repeatedly in the novels of empire – so much so, that a survey of its treatment in fiction would require a full-length study. How useful this would be for our purposes is doubtful, because what matters is the applicability of the theme to political issues of a less personalized nature, rather than how often it recurs in fiction. Accordingly, I will now restrict attention to works by three other writers which engage in distinctive ways with the politics of domination. These writers are George Orwell, J. M. Coetzee and Doris Lessing.

Among other things, Orwell's *Burmese Days* is a study of how an indigenous collaborator or client can manipulate his/her patron so as to subvert the mechanisms of control and influence. U Po Kyin bought his way into a government clerkship and through bribery, cunning and slander rose steadily in the imperial service. By the end of his career he had been admitted to the Club, officiated as Deputy Commissioner for a whole year (during which he made 20,000 rupees in bribes) and, as a final triumph, was presented with an award for 'long and loyal service' at a durbar in Rangoon. Flory, the major character in the novel, uses his mistress, Ma Hla May, according to custom – though '[s]he was allowed to come to tea, as a special privilege, but not to other meals, nor to wear her sandals in her master's presence'.[43] He has no hesitation in dismissing her on a pretext because of his interest in Elizabeth Lackersteen. For her part, Ma Hla May felt nothing for Flory: '[i]t was the idle concubine's life that she loved'.[44] Deprived of her position of privilege, however, she had enough understanding of the culture of the rulers to exact vengeance. Through her scene at the church, she wrecks Flory's chances of marrying Elizabeth. The end result is Flory's suicide and, as a side-effect, the disgrace of his friend Dr Veraswami.

Two years after the publication of *Burmese Days*, Orwell returned to his critique of imperial dominance, this time to depict a situation in which the colonial subjects determine the way things work out, not through any intent or action on their part, but simply through their presence and expectations. In 'Shooting an Elephant' Orwell tells of his experience as a police officer in Burma, called to deal with an elephant that had gone wild.[45] The events are graphic enough but the real experience is internal, the moment of consciousness when Orwell grasps the insecurity of those who rule, and hence 'the hollowness, the futility of the white man's dominion in the East'.[46] By the time Orwell arrived at the scene the animal was harmless. But an immense crowd had gathered and Orwell felt compelled to shoot the elephant because the people expected it of him.

> I could feel their two thousand wills pressing me forward, irresistibly . . . Here was I, the white man with his gun, standing in front of the unarmed native crowd – seemingly the leading actor of the piece; but in reality I was only an absurd puppet pushed to and fro by the will of those yellow faces behind.[47]

There are points of similarity between Orwell's treatment of imperialism in 'Shooting an Elephant' and J. M. Coetzee's depiction of the bankruptcy of imperial power in *Waiting for the Barbarians*. Here also the key experiences are internal and the difficulties that beset the empire are seen to flow from the nature of dominance itself. As the magistrate puts it to the warrant officer of the Third Bureau: 'We have no enemies.' Confronted by silence, he adds: 'Unless I make a mistake . . . Unless we are the enemy.'[48] The story is set in a remote outpost of empire believed to be endangered by barbarian tribes. In fact, however, the barbarians are not a threat at all. The magistrate observes that once in every generation there is an episode of hysteria about the barbarians. As he sees it, the fears and fantasies of the people living along the frontier are a consequence of too much ease. The significance of the barbarians is that they provide empire with a purpose and a rationale for its exercise of power. What is more, it is the attempt to establish the barbarians as a threat and to wipe them out that brings the empire to ruin.

Colonel Joll and his men from the Third Bureau employ torture in their attempt to uncover a barbarian battle-plan but they hear only what they want to hear. 'Pain is truth; all else is subject to doubt' – this is the message the magistrate takes away from his conversation with Colonel Joll.[49] The soldiers ride out to engage the barbarians but most are lost, the stragglers picked off, others caught by the elements. The barbarians engaged on their own terms by luring the force on and on. A survivor voices the orthodoxy of empire: 'We were not beaten – they led us out into the desert and then they vanished!'[50] The magistrate shares his bed with a barbarian woman and indulges in a ritual of oiling and rubbing her body. He wants to know her, but not for herself; rather for her story, and because she bears the scars of empire. For this reason he fails to learn her inner secrets or to move her: 'it is as if there is no interior, only a surface across which I hunt back and forth seeking entry'.[51] The magistrate confesses to himself: 'It is I who am seducing myself.'[52]

In these different ways Coetzee elaborates the moral of his story. Those who dominate are dependent upon those who are dominated. Yet obsessed with themselves and their power, absorbed in their own knowledge and history, those who dominate cannot make contact with the other. Even when they are deceived, it is a form of self-deception. The end they fear is thus inevitable. And so the outpost of empire decays. The soldiers retreat. The townsfolk flee. The magistrate is left carrying the marks of his humiliation, saved from disintegration because at least he made some attempt to move outside the orbit of domination and grapple with the meaning of it all.

Doris Lessing's *The Grass is Singing* is also a study of the dependence implicit in domination, but its psychological probing is deeper and sexuality is given a significance in its own right. The novel portrays how Mary Turner's initial and outward mastery over her black servant, Moses, is transformed into a state of extreme reliance upon him which leads to her disintegration and eventual murder at his hands. Lessing has other concerns in the novel, such as patriarchy and poverty, which connect with and extend her central theme, but these are less immediately relevant here.

Although Mary's direct experience of natives had been limited, by the time she marries Dick and moves to his farm she is locked into the ideology of colonial racism which denies the humanity of the native. When Dick is genuinely grieved by the departure of his old servant, Samson, Mary is filled with wonder and even repulsion. The narrator tells us: '[s]he could not understand any white person feeling anything personal about a native'.[53] Significantly her first contact with Moses was when she struck him across the face with her whip. It is when she unexpectedly sees Moses taking his bath under the trees that the relationship between the two individuals begins to take on a different character. 'What had happened was that the formal pattern of black-and-white, mistress-and-servant, had been broken by the personal relation.'[54] What mattered was not that Mary had seen Moses rubbing his neck with soap but that it had disturbed her emotional equanimity. Clearly there was a sexual aspect to the experience and it marks the beginning of a growing sexual fascination – though we are never sure how physical it becomes.

Mary attempts to restore her poise by asserting her authority over Moses in a harsh and peremptory manner, but she is checked by Dick's insistence that the boy be kept. Unable to escape from her predicament, she is equally unable to confront the problem. Progressively Mary becomes more and more obsessed with Moses. She fears and hates him, yet she is drawn to him and dependent upon his almost fatherly attention. A new stage in the relationship develops when Moses gives notice. Intimidated by the prospect of another confrontation with Dick, Mary sobs and implores Moses not to go. This creates an intimacy between them. And it is this forbidden intimacy, involving physical touch, that destroys her hold over Moses as well as her grasp of reality. 'It was as though the act of weeping before him had been an act of resignation – resignation of her authority; and he had refused to hand it back.'[55] Thereafter the power relations between Mary and Moses are unalterably changed. He is easy, confident, insolent – and it shows in the way he moves and speaks. She is undermined with fear and senses that the end is coming.

At this point the drama widens, with the result that societal as well as personal factors contribute to the making of the tragedy. Once the inversion of the master–servant relationship impinges on the outside world, Moses and Mary are left with much less space within which to manoeuvre. First there is the intervention of Charlie Slatter, who owns the neighbouring farm, and then of Tony Marston, fresh out from England. Appalled by the intimacy of tone between Mary and Moses, Charlie Slatter forces Dick to sell him the farm and take Mary to the coast for six months. In doing so, he acts not out of self-interest or even pity for Dick: '[h]e was obeying the dictate of the first law of white South Africa'.[56] Three days before Mary's impending departure, there is a further development. Tony Marston, who is to manage the farm in the Turners' absence, orders Moses to get out. Although we are not told what

Moses thinks about these abrupt changes in his situation, it is clear from the narrative that the actions taken by Charlie Slatter and Tony Marston make Mary's murder inevitable.

It is through the character and actions of Charlie Slatter, who is presented as the personification of white Rhodesian society, that Doris Lessing establishes the link between the private affair of two individuals and the nature of the colonial order. Slatter's attempt to get Mary off the farm, recounted in the penultimate chapter, meshes with his determination to maintain appearances after her death, described in the opening chapter. From his perspective, and that of white society, Mary herself did not matter. What Slatter understood instinctively was that Mary threatened the existing order through her relationship with Moses. Their relationship was itself facilitated by aspects of the Turners' life such as their poverty and seclusion and, further back again, by Mary's difficulty in playing the part that society assigned to her. Mary's vulnerability was therefore not simply a personal problem but a running political sore because it exposed the vulnerability of the colonial regime. It was for this reason that Slatter was so troubled by the whole affair and why there was a tacit agreement among people in the district that Mary's murder should not be discussed.

The relationships between Mary and Moses, the magistrate and the barbarian woman and Flory and Ma Hla May point to the final area to be examined – gender and sexuality. Before turning to the texts, I should set out the presuppositions of my argument. Gender is a means of shaping and signifying relationships of power internationally as well as in the domestic sphere. It has thus played a major part in the construction and deconstruction of the relationship between ruler and ruled. Fiction is a key site of gender representations and it is important both discursively and for the complex and often contradictory ways in which gender as metaphor is deployed. By working along these lines we come to see that running through much of imperial and post-imperial fiction is the idea that dominance exploits and at the same time is circumscribed by gender and sexuality.

It is evident that drawing on literary sources and reading them in this way has not been characteristic of approaches in either international relations or history. For some time this situation has been changing and new lines of inquiry are now being pursued. These developments cannot be surveyed here.[57] It is, however, useful to refer to one study – Ronald Hyam's *Empire and Sexuality: the British Experience* – because it is so much at variance with what follows. In his introduction, Hyam cautions against relying unduly on literary evidence. Novels, he asserts, 'seldom tell true stories . . . They may be ways of conveying a truth, but they are not the truth as it actually happened. Their insights are not easily converted into strictly historical evidence.'[58] Leaving aside the virtual separation of history and literature, Hyam's work disappoints in that remarkably little in the way of general interpretative themes emerges from the colourful mosaic of individual sex lives.[59] Moreover, his approach to sexuality is extremely narrow. It is the sexual act itself which is central, not what it signifies or the relationship between sexuality and other traits of character. It is almost as if it is enough to record the sexual harvest of the nineteenth century, recognizing that 'harmless pleasures' seldom compromised 'public duties'.

Fiction can be seen to proceed quite differently. Sexuality is depicted in association with gender, and together they are taken to express elements of the culture in which the text was produced. Part of the appeal of sexuality to the novelist is that it lies at the intersection of personal motivation and the social construction of appropriate and responsible behaviour. It has a broader significance for us because it has been employed by writers, and analysed by critics and theorists, as a symbol of both the urge to dominate and the fear and insecurity which so often lie at the heart of domination. I will elaborate this contention thematically, drawing on a body of literature, in preference to selecting individual works for close textual analysis. This is desirable because particular novels have been so carefully combed for their sexual and gender implications – and have yielded so much – that there is a danger of holding them up as exemplars when they are actually *in extremis*. One such case is Rider Haggard's *King Solomon's Mines*.

Surveying the texts as a whole, what is immediately striking is the current of masculinity that swirls around the treatment of metropolitan intervention in Asia and Africa. It is most evident in the novel of empire but in a less overt way it marks much of the literature of American involvement in the cold war. Characteristically there is a boyishness about the conception of self and the world, but masculinity is also associated with romantic vision, and in the novels of John Buchan it is even endowed with a sense of religious fulfilment. In almost all versions, work, action, toughness and a rugged independence are seen as primary and deep-rooted values. The heroes are invariably men who are doers rather than thinkers, engrossed in the tasks before them. They live by the code of the job or the game, cut off from the hearth and revelling in the challenges beyond domesticity. These qualities of character and the yearning to break free from the civilized world are powerfully magnified by the adventure motif as exemplified in the novels of Henty, Buchan, Masters and Mailer. But the values traditionally associated with masculinity and the fascination with the primitive and the past are also brought out by generic forms of a somewhat different nature, as for instance Joyce Cary's African romances and the satiric or ironic treatment of adventure by Evelyn Waugh and Graham Greene. One thinks of Rudbeck's passion for road building in Cary's *Mr Johnson* or the anti-heroes – Waugh's Basil Seal in *Black Mischief* and Greene's Scobie in *The Heart of the Matter* – who, against the grain of the text, draw us back into the masculinity of empire and the spirit of adventure.[60]

Against this background, let us now consider certain motifs relating to sexuality and gender that are associated with the masculine bias of the texts. These are homoeroticism, the threatening nature of women, and the feminization of the other. It is by working along these lines, I want to argue, that we gain an understanding of the way that gender and sexuality erode the foundations on which domination is partly built.

Although seldom perceived at the time of writing, the homoeroticism of the depiction of the imperial project is now glaringly apparent. The exclusion or marginalization of women provides a space within which male bonding can develop freely. It is characteristic of the texts that intense relationships and those that endure are between men; it is common that male physical attributes and bodily features are stressed; it is not unusual for the idea of romantic love between males to be openly expressed. The homoerotic threads which run through the novels of G. A. Henty – the emphasis of mateship in the field, the code of behaviour between friends, and the bonds between the young man of empire and his mentor – relate structurally to the formulaic pattern of his writing. Henty wrote 82 long books for boys and the storyline is broadly the same: a young hero who goes overseas on the death or impoverishment of his father; rapid upward mobility because of his manly qualities and the presence of an older role-model; a world of men except for a brief meeting with, or rescue of, a young girl whom he marries on his return to England.

In Haggard's case the subconscious is much closer to the surface and the homoeroticism more explicit. His three classic novels of imperial adventure are constructed around the exploits of a close-knit trio of white males. Many of the perils they encounter are challenges to their relationship with each other and much of their will to win derives from the shared feelings between them. In *Nada the Lily* male bonding is also shown to be a feature of Zulu culture. The narrator likens the friendship between Galazi and Umslopogaas to twin trees that have grown side by side. Before going into battle, Umslopogaas declares: 'Perchance I did ill, Galazi . . . and suffered woman to come between us. May we find one day a land where there are no women, and war only, for in that land we shall grow great.'[61] What is of particular interest in Haggard's writing is that the kinship between males is assumed to be so much part of the natural order that it bridges the gulf between the civilized and the savage. In *Allan Quartermain* Umslopogaas tells Quartermain that he loves him 'for we have grown grey together, and there is that between us that cannot be seen, and yet is too strong for breaking'.[62] With some emotion Quartermain takes a pinch of snuff from the Zulu warrior's box and concedes he was 'much attached to the bloodthirsty old ruffian'. Unable to pinpoint Umslopogaas's charm – except that he 'had a tender heart' – Quartermain contents himself with the thought: 'Anyway, I was very fond of him, though I should never have thought of telling him so.'[63]

Here we might pause to underline the significance of the material considered thus far. Our understanding of dominance, I would argue, needs to take account of the hyper-masculine and homoerotic aspects of the imperial venture brought out in the novel of empire. On the one hand, they sharpened the power drive and stiffened the mind-set of imperialism. The concentration of energy, the accent on action and space, the sense of a band of boys – which echoes Milner's 'kindergarten', Wolseley's 'ring', Kitchener's 'cubs' – are sources of strength and reassurance. Further, to the extent that they take root in the consciousness of the colonized élite, they work to extend and prolong imperial domination. On the other hand, homoeroticism and the cult of masculinity constitute areas of weakness; they indicate points of vulnerability. Here I have in mind the significance of psychological self-denial, the necessarily distorted understanding of the colonial other, the fragility of an overseas presence based on role-playing and the growing divergence in values between those overseas and the society at home.

This twin-edged significance of an insecure masculinity to the politics of dominance is not restricted to Victorian imperialism, though clearly cultural differences change the form of its expression. A brief reference to two novels published after the Second World War will illustrate the generality of our theme. David Caute's *At Fever Pitch* tells the story of a British subaltern serving in a West African country on the eve of independence. Michael Glyn, a repressed homosexual, in effect forces his black servant, Sully, to sleep with him. As a result Sully becomes emotionally dependent upon Glyn, asking for more of that 'bed palaver thing, sah'. Unable to cope with his own sexuality, Glyn rejects Sully who, robbed of his identity, declines and eventually dies of fever. Glyn, for his part, is emasculated by the experience. Desperately attempting to find his sexuality, his final act is to be responsible for the shooting of 25 Africans in a political riot in the north. Glyn flies out of Africa a defeated man; Africa is left to its fate; the British record is in tatters.[64]

The interconnectedness of sexuality, violence and domination is also a central concern of Norman Mailer's *Why Are We In Vietnam?* In this novel, however, individual behaviour is emblazoned with a societal stamp and the main protagonists are explicitly drawn to articulate the neuroses of their culture – masculine, corporate America. Although Vietnam is not mentioned until the last page, the bear hunt in Alaska contains within it all the elements that propelled the United States into its imbroglio of violence in Indo-China. We are meant to understand that there was nothing special about Vietnam, nothing exceptional about what America did there: the lust for power, the machismo, the violence, all flowed naturally from the troubled American psyche and above all from the need to shore up male sexual identity. In their last night in the Alaskan wilderness Tex and D.J. lie together under the blankets, struggling with their love/hate relationship and their homosexual desires:

> and they hung there each of them on the knife of the divide in all conflict of lust to own the other yet in fear of being killed by the other and as the hour went by and the lights shifted, something in the radiance of the North went into them, and owned their fear, some communion of telepathies and new powers, and they were twins, never to be near as lovers again, but killer brothers, owned by something, prince of darkness, lord of light, they did not know. . . [65]

Various possibilities suggest themselves and have been taken up by critics. Tex and D.J. have seen through the falsities of contemporary America so there is a chance of a fresh start. Had the boys made love, the hatred and the violence might have been exorcised. But the text admits no such optimism. Tex and D.J. had become 'killer brothers', for God had said 'Go out and kill – fulfill my will, go and kill.' And on the last page, D.J. reveals that 'tomorrow Tex and me, we're off to see the wizard in Vietnam . . . This is D.J., Disc Jockey to America turning off. Vietnam, hot damn.'[66]

I want now to consider the way in which women are treated in the texts. The argument here is restricted to imperial romances and essentially it is that women as women are mainly kept to the sidelines because they represent a threat to masculinity and hence endanger the overseas project itself. It may be that elements of a similar narrative schema are to be found in other forms of overseas fiction in which adventure is less central and which incorporate aspects of the domestic novel, but the material is too diverse for consideration here. Imperial romances conform closely to type, however, and the patterning is clear. For the most part, women are either absent, marginalized or neutered, but at times lusts are ascribed to strategically placed women which give them an other-worldly power. White women fare better than black women in that they appear more often and are more likely to be given a voice. Mainly, however, they are kept out of the plot, very often they remain in the home (if not in the home country), and the qualities that are emphasized are non-sexual and pertaining to the hearth. One thinks of 'the Intended' in *Heart of Darkness*: 'she was not very young – I mean not girlish. She had a mature capacity for fidelity, for belief, for suffering.'[67] The logic is that character and role are so constructed that such women do not interfere in the world of men. Indeed, as in the novels by Flora Annie Steel and Maud Diver, women may consciously seek to maintain the autonomy of that world. The politics of the process are virtually spelt out in John Buchan's *A Lodge in the Wilderness* – an unusual imperial novel in that women are significant actors, but their whole energies are directed to promoting the creed of empire. The hero, Francis Carey – whose 'amazing energy annihilated space' – organizes a gathering of friends in East Africa and lays down one rule as inviolable: there are to be no husbands and wives. He explains: 'We must all be unattached, for domesticity . . . is the foe of friendship.'[68] Later, and more enigmatically, he is said to have observed: 'Every man should be lonely at heart.'[69]

When black women appear in the text, they usually serve a symbolic purpose. It may be as wives, to emphasize the centrality of their husbands' relationship with Europe or a European, as Bamu does in *Mr Johnson* or Sully's two wives in *At Fever Pitch*. It may be as the personification of evil in the form of an old hag, such as Gagool in *King Solomon's Mines*. Most commonly, however, black women serve both as a temptation to the European heroes to cut free from their moorings and also as a warning not to do so. Accordingly, the accent is on their sexuality and seductive power. Remember the description of the woman associated with Kurtz in *Heart of Darkness*: 'a wild and gorgeous apparition of a woman. She was savage and superb, wild-eyed and magnificent.' Yet there was something 'ominous' about her progress, and the man of patches said, 'If she had offered to come aboard I really think I would have tried to shoot her.'[70]

Conrad conveys the threatening aspect of the woman, and that she expressed something threatening about the land and life of Africa, without spelling out its exact nature. Other novelists have not been so reticent. What is most feared is unbridled passion and sexuality, which is assumed to be the natural condition of Asia and Africa. In the words of one of Flora Annie Steel's characters, Eastern passion is a love which 'sears and burns . . . scorches and shrivels'.[71] Edgar Rice Burroughs' evil queen, La – 'a pulsing, throbbing volcano of desire' – is representative of African temptresses.[72] The idea of sexual abandon is often associated with religious perversion – the depravity of Hinduism, the bloodthirsty worship of Kali, the hypnotic hold of ju-ju. There is also a recurrent association of the seductive or powerful female with the ideal of self-sacrifice and elements of witchcraft. Aissa, the religious convert who sacrifices her child in Joyce Cary's *Aissa Saved,* and the 'witch', Elizabeth in his *The African Witch* are interesting variations on these themes. The sense of sexual menace which runs through the literature has obvious implications for conceptions of masculinity but, even more significantly, it challenges ideas about politics and power. In short, dominance is conditioned by, and vulnerable to, gender and sexuality. This argument will be developed in chapter 7.

The presence of exceptional women of great seductive power disturbs the settled lines of the imperial romance and calls for remedial action. Generally this takes one of two forms. The offending woman meets an untimely end and the narrative is able to resume its accustomed course. This is the solution usually favoured by Haggard. Foulatta is stabbed to death by Gagool in *King Solomon's Mines.* In *She* Ustane is shot by Horace Holly and 'She-who-must-be-obeyed' shrivels into a hideous monkey-like form in the 'pillar of fire' and then dies. The other solution is to ensure that any serious liaison between a white hero and a black female brings disaster in its trail. This came naturally to Conrad and is illustrated by Almayer's nemesis in *Almayer's Folly*, Willems' disintegration in *Outcast of the Islands* and the 'hollow sham' of Kurtz in *Heart of Darkness*. It is also, of course, standard fare for British novelists writing about India.[73]

The final motif to be considered is the feminization of the other. What we are concerned with here is the practice in many European texts of transposing the female form or female attributes to other lands and peoples. With respect to Africa, there is the feminization of the continent itself. As recent critical studies have reminded us, anthropomorphism deeply marked the imperial novel set in Africa.[74] One formula employed in the literature was to present geographical features in a way that reproduced or was reminiscent of the female body. The classic expression of the feminized landscape is found in *King Solomon's Mines*. There is the map showing the route to the mines, which resembles the figure of a naked woman, and Allan Quartermain's subsequent description of Sheba's breasts, Solomon's Road and the treasure chamber. In Conrad's narrative – and in the narrative of those who followed him such as

Graham Greene – the female presence is invoked through the very spirit of
the land; it emanates from the earth, from the vegetation, from the figures in
the landscape. For Conrad there is a sexuality, a fecundity, a sense of mystery;
for Greene, a suggestion of innocence and virginity. This association of Africa
with the feminine is not restricted to fiction. It is there in Freud and Jung's
references to female psychology as a dark continent, and it is infixed in the
vocabulary of exploration and the phraseology of imperial history – witness
the 'penetration' of the continent and the 'laying open' of Africa. Nor is it
confined to the classic period of annexation and partition. Consider the
following passage in Marguerite Steen's *The Sun is My Undoing*, a historical
novel set in the eighteenth century and published in 1941:

> Africa . . . Africa's a woman. A dark, devastating witch of a woman: coiling herself
> round you like a snake, making you forget everything but her burning breasts.
> Listen to the drums of Africa . . . reminding every man of things he forgot when –
> when he left his mother's womb.[75]

When it comes to Asia, feminization takes a rather different form. It is not
the place – meaning the landscape – but the culture and even more the people
that are seen in womanly terms. The imputation of femininity had, of course,
to jostle with quite different images, depending on the politics of the time,
and it was by no means always on the surface of the texts. None the less, in
much of the literature there is a generalized sense of the Orient as feminine.
This draws sustenance from the trope of the erotic East, from the practice of
counterposing subject peoples to an imperial masculinity, and from the
passivity and fatalism which supposedly characterized Asian societies and
cultures. The feminization of the Orient is most sharply etched with respect
to India – a point of some significance because, for the British, India
represented the hub of Asia. In one of Maud Diver's novels India is actually
referred to as a 'woman-country': like Italy, '"loved of male lands" and
exercising the same irresistible magnetism, the same dominion over the hearts
of men'.[76] But as Greenberger and others have made clear, it is specifically
the Hindus who are seen as effeminate, above all the Bengalis. There are two
aspects here: the idea of weakness or cowardice which expresses itself in the
absence of a direct challenge to imperial authority, and the notion of craftiness
which supposedly represents female guile. Similar notions informed thinking
about China in the period before the Second World War and in some instances
modernization was presented as a way of introducing manly vigour. In Alice
Tisdale Hobart's novel *Yang and Yin* a young American doctor, Peter Fraser,
trains a Chinese youth named Lo Shih in medical technology. Under Fraser's
tutelage, a transformation occurs in Lo Shih which is not limited to his
scientific skills but affects his whole consciousness. The change is reflected
in his appearance and dress. Peter 'liked to watch his pupil in the laboratory,
his delicate hands so fitted to the delicate technique. There seemed to him,
too, a growing masculinity about Lo Shih, of which he had never before been
conscious.'[77] Rey Chow has noted a very different appreciation in
representations of modern China. She criticizes Julia Kristeva's *About Chinese*

Women and Bernardo Bertolucci's film *The Last Emperor* for idealizing China through the category of the feminine.[78]

In the course of our analysis of gender and sexuality in the texts I have indicated some of the broader implications of the various motifs, but it remains to relate the material directly to the politics of dominance. Overlordship in imperial relations – and I would argue in international relations generally – rests on a construction of power which is essentially masculine. It involves self-denial (of the feminine within), the denial of the action and speech of others (the non-masculine) and, by extension, a narrow self-referential understanding of what constitutes power and how it is exercised. Certain actors and modes of behaviour are privileged: the male adventurer, work and action, the declaratory voice, a fair and open fight; others, associated with the feminine, are displaced or marginalized. That which is feminized is that which is most feared. In Africa it is the continent; in Asia, the people.

This last proposition requires elaboration. As is well recognized, the mystique of the African continent mirrors the fears and fascinations of the imperial mind. Thus what is threatening is not so much 'out there' as the impact of 'out there' on the contrived imperial self. That the other is conceived as threateningly female does not directly empower the other; indeed it may be argued that it deprives the other of self-directed action.[79] The point I am making is that it disempowers the imperial self. At the level of sexual metaphor, penetration is the mark of the masculinity of the exercise, but penetration must not be pushed too far for fear of being swallowed up, of becoming a spent force. Hence the significance of the temptress who might suck imperial virility or the African witch who signifies the threat to male potency. Lying behind the sexual symbolism is what is really at stake, namely the values and self-understanding which underpin the imperial enterprise itself – the bonding of brothers, the celebration of action and vitality, and the construction of power in terms of domination and violence.

With regard to Asia, the argument must be developed somewhat differently. The feminization of Asian peoples catches the unease about cultural difference and attempts to deflect its political consequences. The female attributes – the passivity of the Hindus, the cunning of the Bengalis – represented a challenge not only to the imperial self but also and directly to the structure of imperial power. That the feminine was so derided because of its weakness is the mark of how much it threatened. And it threatened precisely because it operated outside the rules of engagement laid down by the dominant. That is to say, it subverted, compromised, spoke with a different voice; what it would not do was to stand up and fight. Understood in this way, gender and sexuality widen the arena of the power struggle and open up the discourse about dominance.

Notes

1. K. M. Panikkar, *Asia and Western Dominance. A Survey of the Vasco Da Gama Epoch of Asian History 1498–1945* (Allen & Unwin, London, 1953), p. 13.

2 . Paul Kennedy, *The Rise and Fall of the Great Powers. Economic Change and Military Conflict from 1500 to 2000* (Fontana Press, London, 1989; first published 1988).

3. Panikkar, op. cit.

4. Kennedy, op. cit., p. xxiii.

5. See G. W. F. Hegel, *The Phenomenology of Mind*, translated with an introduction and notes by J. B. Baillie (Harper Colophon Books, Harper & Row, New York, 1967), pp. 229–40. For a brief interpretative summation see Charles Taylor, *Hegel* (Cambridge University Press, Cambridge, 1975), pp. 153–7.

6. Michel Foucault, *The History of Sexuality, Vol. 1; An Introduction* (Penguin, Harmondsworth, 1990), pp. 92–7.

7. James Scott, *Weapons of the Weak. Everyday Forms of Peasant Resistance* (Yale University Press, New Haven CT and London, 1985).

8. George Orwell wrote in 1942: 'The whole poem, conventionally thought of as an orgy of boasting, is a denunciation of power-politics, British as well as German.' Quoted in Lord Birkenhead, *Rudyard Kipling* (Star, London, 1980; first published 1978), p. 188.

9. W. E. Gladstone, 'Aggression on Egypt and freedom in the East', *Nineteenth Century* (London), 2 (Aug.–Dec. 1877), 149–66 (p. 159).

10. Philip Mason, *Patterns of Dominance* (Institute of Race Relations, Oxford University Press, London, 1970), pp. 33–5; and *Prospero's Magic* (Oxford University Press, London, 1962), ch. 2.

11. See, for example, Wayland Young, *Eros Denied* (Weidenfeld & Nicolson, London, 1965); Ronald Hyam, *Britain's Imperial Century 1815–1914: A Study of Empire and Expansionism* (Batsford, London, 1976), ch. 5; and *Empire and Sexuality: the British Experience* (Manchester University Press, Manchester and New York, 1990); Ashis Nandy, *The Intimate Enemy. Loss and Recovery of Self Under Colonialism* (Oxford University Press, London, 1983), part 1.

12. Allen J. Greenberger, *The British Image of India. A Study in the Literature of Imperialism* (Oxford University Press, London, 1969), pp. 5 and 6.

13. Ibid., p. 5.

14. Rudyard Kipling, 'The Education of Otis Yeere' in *Wee Willie Winkie* (Macmillan, London, centenary edn, 1982; first published 1895), pp. 3–15 (p. 9).

15. The bridge was a favoured metaphor in the late nineteenth century for British rule in India. In a letter to *The Times* in 1878, Fitzjames Stephen pictured the British power in India as a vast bridge over which Indians passed from a dreary, violent land to one that was orderly, peaceful and industrious. See Eric Stokes, *The English Utilitarians and India* (Clarendon Press, Oxford, 1959), p. 300.

16. Rudyard Kipling, 'The Bridge-Builders' in *The Day's Work* (Macmillan, London, centenary edn, 1982; first published 1898), pp. 1–47 (p. 20).

17. Ibid., p. 31.

18. Ibid., p. 32.

19. Rudyard Kipling, 'The Man Who Was' in *Life's Handicap* (Macmillan, London, centenary edn, 1982; first published 1891), pp. 97–116 (p. 99).

20. Woolf's experiences and feelings in Ceylon from 1904 to 1911 are recounted in the second volume of his autobiographphy, *Growing* (Hogarth Press, London, 1961). For an account of the writing and revision of the novel see Yasmine Gooneratne, 'A novelist at work: the manuscript of Leonard Woolf's *The Village in the Jungle*', *Journal of Commonwealth Literature*, XVIII:1 (1983), 91–104.

21. Leonard Woolf, *The Village in the Jungle* (Hogarth Press, London, 1931; first published 1913), p. 209.

22. Ibid., p. 248.

23. Ibid., p. 277.

24. This is a recurring theme in Martin Green, *The English Novel in the Twentieth Century* (Routledge & Kegan Paul, London, 1984).

25. Evelyn Waugh, *Black Mischief* (The Folio Society, London, 1980; first published 1932), p. 152.

26. George Orwell, *Burmese Days* (Penguin, Harmondsworth, 1967; first published 1934), p. 40.

27. Ibid., p. 41.

28. Anthony Burgess, *The Long Day Wanes. A Malayan Trilogy* (Penguin, Harmondsworth, 1972). The trilogy consists of: *Time for a Tiger* (1956), *The Enemy in the Blanket* (1958) and *Beds in the East* (1959).

29. Anthony Burgess, *Devil of a State* (Heinemann, London, 1961).

30. John Updike, *The Coup* (University of Queensland Press, St. Lucia, Queensland, 1979; first published 1978), pp. 97–8.

31. Joseph Conrad, *Heart of Darkness* (Penguin, Harmondsworth, 1983; first published 1902), p. 41.

32. Ibid., p. 42.

33. Idem.

34. Ibid., p. 58.

35. Ibid., p. 56.

36. Ibid., p. 41.

37. Ibid., p. 49.

38. Ibid., pp. 86–7.

39. Rudyard Kipling, 'At the End of the Passage' in *Life's Handicap*, pp. 183–212 (p. 202).

40. Ibid., p. 208.

41. Rudyard Kipling, 'The Strange Ride of Morrowbie Jukes' in *Wee Willie Winkie*, pp. 168–99 (p. 182).

42. Ibid.

43. Orwell, *Burmese Days*, pp. 49–50.

44. Ibid., p. 51.

45. Although written as a first-person account, the story is probably partly based on fact. In Bernard Crick's view, it is 'a compound of fact and fiction, honest in intent, true to experience, but not necessarily truthful in detail' (Bernard Crick, *George Orwell: A Life* (Secker & Warburg, London, 1980), p. 211; see also the note on p. 96). Raymond Williams stresses the unity of Orwell's 'documentary' and 'imaginative' writing, and observes that Orwell 'got past the conventional division, if only in practice'; Raymond Williams, 'Observation and imagination in Orwell' in Raymond Williams (ed.), *George Orwell. A Collection of Critical Essays* (Prentice-Hall Inc., Englewood Cliffs NJ, 1974), pp. 52–61 (p. 53), reprinted from Raymond Williams, *Orwell* (Fontana Books, London, The Viking Press, New York, 1971).

46. 'Shooting an Elephant' in Sonia Orwell and Ian Angus (eds), *The Collected Essays, Journalism and Letters of George Orwell Vol. 1, An Age Like This* (Secker & Warburg, London, 1968), pp. 235–42 (p. 239).

47. Ibid.

48. J. M. Coetzee, *Waiting for the Barbarians* (King Penguin, Harmondsworth, 1982; first published 1980), p. 77.

49. Ibid., p. 5.

50. Ibid., p. 147.

51. Ibid., p. 43.

52. Ibid., p. 44.

53. Doris Lessing, *The Grass is Singing* (Heinemann, London, Ibadan, Nairobi, 1973; first published 1950), p. 78.

54. Ibid., pp. 177–8.

55. Ibid., p. 190.

56. Ibid., p. 221.

57. For an introduction to recent feminist critiques of international relations, see note 18 in chapter 1. For an indication of rethinking in imperial history see Claudia Knapman, *White Women in Fiji 1835–1930: The Ruin of Empire?* (Allen & Unwin, Sydney, 1986); Helen Callaway,

Gender, Culture and Empire: European Women in Colonial Nigeria (Macmillan in association with St. Antony's College, Oxford, Basingstoke, 1987); Ann Stoler, 'Rethinking colonial categories: European communities and the boundaries of rule', *Comparative Studies in Society and History*, 31:1 (1989), 134–61.

58. Ronald Hyam, *Empire and Sexuality: The British Experience*, pp. 18 and 19.

59. In my view the book fails to live up to the promise of his earlier and much briefer comments in Ronald Hyam, *Britain's Imperial Century 1815–1914: A Study of Empire and Expansionism*, p. 134 and following.

60. On the latter point see Martin Green, *The English Novel in the Twentieth Century*, ch. 5.

61. H. Rider Haggard, *Nada the Lily* (Macdonald, London, 1932; first published 1892), pp. 285–6.

62. H. Rider Haggard, *King Solomon's Mines, She, Allan Quartermain* (Octopus Books, London, 1979), p. 585.

63. Ibid., p. 586.

64. David Caute, *At Fever Pitch* (André Deutsch, London 1959). It must be said that the way the novel ends is not very satisfactory. The withdrawal of the prosecution against Glyn and the Brigadier's ultimatum both lack credibility. For further comments on the novel along the above lines, see Abena P. A. Busia, 'Miscegenation as metonymy: sexuality and power in the colonial novel', *Ethnic and Racial Studies*, 9:3 (3 July 1986), 360–72 (pp. 368–9).

65. Norman Mailer, *Why Are We In Vietnam?* (Oxford University Press, London, 1988; first published 1967), pp. 203–4.

66. Ibid., p. 208.

67. Conrad, *Heart of Darkness*, p. 117.

68. John Buchan, *A Lodge in the Wilderness* (Wm. Blackwood & Sons, Edinburgh and London, 1906), p. 7.

69. Ibid., p. 262.

70. Conrad, *Heart of Darkness*, pp. 100–1.

71. In *The Law of the Threshold*, quoted in Benita Parry, *Delusions and Discoveries. Studies on India in the British Imagination* (University of California Press, Berkeley and Los Angeles, 1972), p. 112.

72. In *Tarzan and the Jewels of Opar*, quoted in Richard F. Patteson, 'Manhood and misogyny in the imperialist romance', *Rocky Mountain Review of Language and Literature*, 31:1 (1981), 3–12 (p. 11).

73. See further chapter 4, pp. 92, 94–5.

74. See, for example, Bette London, 'Reading race and gender in Conrad's Dark Continent', *Criticism*, XXXI:3 (Summer 1989), 235–52; Rebecca Stott, 'The Dark Continent: Africa as female body in Haggard's adventure fiction', *Feminist Review*, 32 (Summer 1989), 69–89.

75. Marguerite Steen, *The Sun is My Undoing* (Collins, London, 1941), pp. 247–8.

76. *Desmond's Daughter*, quoted in Parry, op. cit., p. 97.

77. A. T. Hobart, *Yang and Yin: A Novel of a Doctor in China* (Cassell, London, Toronto, Melbourne, Sydney, 1937), p. 267.

78. Rey Chow, *Women and Chinese Modernity. The Politics of Reading Between West and East* (Theory and History of Literature, Vol. 75, University of Minnesota Press, Minnesota and Oxford, 1991), ch. 1.

79. Along these lines feminist critics have attacked the Mother Africa trope in African fiction, arguing that it operates against the interests of women and denies them agency. See, for example, Florence Stratton, *Contemporary African Literature and the Politics of Gender* (Routledge, London and New York, 1994), ch. 2.

— Part II —

Situating Debate

CHAPTER 4

The Indo-British relationship

In a provocative passage that reveals much about his own approach as a writer, V. S. Naipaul asserts:

> politics have to do with the nature of human association, the contract of men with men. The politics of a country can only be an extension of its idea of human relationships.[1]

The claim excites because of its pithiness, yet its expansiveness invites challenge. Even if the categories of the individual and the collective, and with them, the domains of the private and the public, have customarily been too rigidly separated, is it not going too far to run them together? In hypothesizing that public politics follow the pattern of personal behaviour, must not allowance be made for impersonal processes which work to disconnect the two spheres? To what extent can political and social processes be telescoped into the lives of individuals? Do not the kind of personal relationships which develop within a society echo the nature of its political system? Then there is the question of whether Naipaul's proposition can be extended to cover the situation of two countries, rather than simply one. Can it be said that personal relationships between members of different communities set the tone of the relationship between the two polities?

These questions inform our inquiry into the treatment in fiction of British imperialism in India. No subject in the imperial and post-imperial encounter has had a greater fascination for novelists than that of British rule in India. Indeed, taking into account the number of works tackling the subject, the fact that several have become classics and the extent of cross-referencing between texts and over time, British writing in the area may be said to constitute a sub-genre of the literature of imperialism. Overwhelmingly this body of writing takes personal relationships as its point of reference – which is to say that political issues are broached through the depiction of personal feelings and behaviour. This is not, however, an innocent move on the part of the novelists; it is not by chance that fiction's focus on private affairs happens to address vexatious issues in the public domain. Most of the narratives of British India are intensely political and they are knowingly so. When there are silences about politics, when the linkages remain hidden, this is usually by design. Sara Suleri is correct to point out that these narratives are a 'mode of cultural tale-telling that is neurotically conscious of its own self-censoring apparatus'.[2]

When we come to Indian writing about British imperialism there is a difference in degree but not in kind. Here also we are confronted by a body of literature in which the personal is an allegory of the political, but often the politics are more visible and are not solely concerned with the fact of British rule. During the Gandhian era, for example, Indian novelists shied away from personalizing the imperial presence. The politics of the texts were directed elsewhere – to the possibilities of a Gandhian revolution in Indian life. The Raj was thus a distraction from the task at hand and it was better left in the background with English characters kept at one remove. In what he concedes is a sweeping hypothesis, Fredric Jameson has argued that all Third World texts are necessarily allegorical and must be read as telling the story of the national collectivity.[3] Jameson's theory would seem to hold for Indian fiction in English, though, as we will shortly see, it is highly dubious when applied to Indian texts generally. His associated claim that on this basis Third World texts can be distinguished radically from Western texts is, in the present context, plainly mistaken. Contrary to Jameson's dictum, British narratives set in India seldom split the private from the public. Nor are their allegorical structures unconscious – at least not to such a degree as to require deciphering 'by interpretative mechanisms that necessarily entail a whole social and historical critique of our current first-world situation'.[4]

My analysis of British and Indian fiction proceeds loosely along chronological lines. Three broad periods have been identified: the decade before and the decade after the turn of the century when British paramountcy appeared secure; the inter-war years when most novelists took the foundations of imperial power to be crumbling; and the years after independence when writers looked back on Britain's withdrawal from the subcontinent and reflected on its causes and consequences. The changing personal metaphors employed by writers and the way they were understood broadly correspond with the periods identified. Periodization has its pitfalls but, to make a point so obvious it is often overlooked, a well-chosen time-frame should convey a sense of the cultural climate and political constraints of the era. In some contemporary writing that comes under the rubric of postcolonialism the commitment to creating a space for political agency and to disrupting dominant discourses leads to a disregard of the political and imaginative possibilities at a particular historical juncture.

In large part, the selection of texts has proceeded along familiar lines. In the case of British novels there is unlikely to be much disagreement about choices guided by a text's established status or representative nature. There is more room for argument about Indian novels and there is also the question of language. In line with the parameters of this book, inquiry has been restricted – with one or two exceptions – to works written in English. There has been some debate about how far this body of literature is representative of the totality of Indian fiction, and also about whether it is less 'authentic' than novels written in Bengali, Tamil or other indigenous languages. While these issues cannot be pursued here, it appears that fiction written in the regional languages seldom addresses Indo-British relations directly and that it is uncommon for such novels to have British protagonists.[5]

As far as possible I have endeavoured in this section to approach the literary texts in terms of their own particularity rather than through the established paradigms of history and politics. Extraordinarily enough, there is no international relations paradigm because imperial relations were seen to fall outside the proper concerns of the discipline. My aim is to give the texts some space of their own so that we can observe what, if anything, is distinctive about them. In doing so, we have not given up an agreed interpretive schema. It is apparent that the Indo-British encounter encapsulates two major historical processes: the hold and subsequent decline of imperialism, and the challenge and eventual rise of nationalism. Both are sharply contested subjects. Nationalism has buckled under the weight of meanings and range of explanations placed upon it.[6] Imperial contraction has been understood in very different ways and seen to proceed on very different bases. One line of argument is about Britain's weakness and hence her inability to contain the forces of nationalism; according to another, British policy-makers acted from strength, confident that the cultural, economic and strategic ties established between Britain and India would enable them to stage-manage the move from formal rule to informal influence.[7] Then there is the general challenge mounted by subaltern studies to what is termed traditional élitist history. Given such conjecture and disagreement, it can hardly be said that established scholarship offers some high ground from which to approach the literary narratives.

This contention becomes the stronger given the rejection here of the traditional closure of the discourses about imperialism and nationalism to the personal and the private. Simply to pose two related questions of concern indicates the need to read more openly. How far can it be said that during the years of imperial rule the private sphere was a site of resistance? Yet, after independence, could it be that it was in the private sphere that imperial values were most deeply embedded? In another respect our concerns here cut across the usual lines of closure of mainstream discourse. The dreams, fears and fantasies which emerge in the fictional narratives are taken to be intrinsic to the imperial experience. The assumption is that this imaginative realm better enables us to understand approaches to concrete issues of the day, the 'here and now' of ordinary politics.

In much mainstream writing, evaluation of early attempts to wrestle with problems about the form and nature of community at the macro-level is often predicated on what happens afterwards. To some degree, of course, it is inevitable that all readings are informed by political presuppositions and historical hindsight. Yet it appears that the tendency is to read fiction more openly than, say, history – by which I mean that we are less constrained by accepted categories of analysis or established organizing principles, and less inhibited about exploring the 'dead-ends' and 'might-have-beens' of history.[8] If this is so, to tie fiction to the coat-tails of disciplinary orthodoxy would be to devalue it for our purposes.

Yet, at the same time, I have attempted to resist imposing the reconceptualizations of postcolonialism directly on the literary narratives. Although, as I will argue in the final chapter, the imaginative recasting of approaches to Third World issues is a welcome development, it is often accompanied by an insensitivity to why people acted as they did and to other points of view. In its anxiety to liberate the Third World from the oppressions of the past, the tendency is to dehistoricize and reckon too lightly with material and ideological obstacles to change. If literature is to be taken seriously as a source material, it cannot be allowed to serve simply as a slate upon which to inscribe contemporary politics.[9]

At this stage, therefore, I propose to put to one side both the traditional debates and the postcolonial material and turn directly to the literary narratives. It is accepted that novels cannot be disentangled from other discourses, but for the moment we will privilege the domain of fiction. Attempting to read in historical context, we will simply ask: what pictures emerge in the novels of personal relations between English and Indians? From there we will examine their allegorical significance. At times, fictional characters stand as representations of Britain or India or reflect aspects of the national culture. Equally, personal behaviour, motivations and affects may be suggestive of the politics between the collectivities. In some instances categories derived from interpersonal behaviour are used as devices to probe the nature of the Indo-British relationship, determine what has gone wrong or indicate how things might be put right. The love or marriage partnership, the foundling child and the rape incident are classic cases. Often it will be necessary to situate the personal in the context of the novel as a whole or even to examine the general lines of the narrative to explain why the personal is absent. Sometimes overt political statements intrude into the narrative and these must be taken into account, although not necessarily at their face value.

Dreams and denials

In that crucial period – the last decades of the nineteenth century and up to the First World War – when hopes were high about the possibilities of imperialism, British and Indians failed to come to terms with each other. The picture-books of empire provide part of the explanation with their representations of British power – durbars and regimental messes, princes in resplendent uniforms, ordinary Indians as sepoys, bearers and ayahs. The novelists take it further. For Indians the apparent indestructibility, the unyielding nature of British power, provided an incentive to imagine and to dream. For the British there was a sense of vulnerability and a determination to shore up the foundations of power, and hence strict limits to the extent the two peoples could relate.

To begin with the Indian narratives, the fact of British overlordship meant that two issues had to be addressed: who the Indians were or had once been; and what accommodation could be struck with the British. In its essentials the question of self was now linked with the problem and attraction of the other. And so writers were to wander in their imagination down different paths in an attempt to understand the predicament in which India was placed. One path led into the past, where consolation and hope could be taken from cultural achievements, military victories and a sense of the community of Hindustan. Another was anchored in the present and was concerned to affirm the worth of Indian civilization by chronicling patterns of ordinary life and showing the richness of Hindu culture and religion. A few challenged the idea of British rule more or less directly by showing exploitation and injustice. Others carried the mark of British reformism, grappling with issues such as the position of women or the problem of caste. A characteristic feature of much early writing was its ambivalence towards the British connection and British influence – which goes to show how deep-rooted is the contemporary theoretical concern with notions of hybridity.

At the same time as writers wrestled with the subjection and yet release of British imperialism, they were experimenting with a new form of writing and doing so in a foreign – or at least second – language. The Indian novel in English, born in the 1860s and 1870s, had a patchy beginning. Often an admixture of the political essay, autobiography and epic, it took two or three decades for the alien narrative form to be adapted to the circumstances of the Indian middle-class and a different literary sensibility and tradition.

It is against this background of writers casting in several directions and trying a variety of techniques, that we will now focus on one particular approach to India's imperial dilemma. I want to take three novels, all published at the end of the first decade of the twentieth century, which attempt to comprehend India's relationship with Britain in terms of a marriage or love partnership. The three novels are S. M. Mitra's *Hindupore* (1909), S. K. Ghosh's *The Prince of Destiny* (1909), and K. E. Ghamat's *My Friend the Barrister* (1908). As the novels are not well known or easily obtained, I will give an account of each before addressing their similarities and significance.

The subtitles of S. M. Mitra's *Hindupore* outline the novel's twin concerns. The first part reads *A Peep Behind the Indian Unrest*; the second, *An Anglo-Indian Romance*. We are given diagnosis and prescription and they accord neatly – too much so to make for either good fiction or sound politics. While it can scarcely be denied that the text exudes a sense of political purpose, the novel is much more than an exercise in 'propaganda'.[10] Nor should it be denigrated on the ground that the history in the novel is 'entirely romantic with no basis in actual facts'.[11] Like its politics, the novel's history is largely internal: not an analysis of the public record, but impressions and recollections drawn from the private consciousness.

The story is a good deal less interesting than the novel's themes and the assumptions they embody. An Irish member of parliament, Lord Tara, visits India to gain firsthand experiences of the political situation there. On the ship travelling to India Tara meets Raja Man Singh, the ruler of Hindupore and a man well-disposed to the British connection. The two men strike up a friendship, which leads Tara to visit Hindupore as the state guest of the raja. There he meets and falls in love with Man Singh's niece, Princess Kamala. A marriage proposal is welcomed by the Raja and it is decided that the ceremony will take place at the temple of Jagannath in Puri, south of Calcutta, during a festival commemorating Krishna. The journey of the party to and from Puri, the Hindu festival, and the interracial marriage solemnized by both Hindu and Christian priests provide a framework within which the problems and possibilities of the Indo-British relationship can be explored through minor incidents, conversations and the behaviour of the characters.

It is apparent that the assumptions of the novel are decidedly élitist. The Indo-British relationship is essentially between the upper echelons of the two societies. Its cultivation is a matter for the well born and the well educated – as can be seen from the fact that the task is entrusted to a raja, a princess, a lord and an Oxford-educated ICS officer who 'learnt manners' at Eton. Its disrepair is in large part laid at the door of people who are not 'gentlemen'; there is the racial prejudice of Mr Toddy, the manager of a distillery, and the bigotry and insularity of Colonel Ironside, the political agent, who is the son of an army tailor who rose in the world through lending money to young officers at about 150 per cent interest.

This élitism informs the author's treatment of historical and political issues. In earlier days the Indo-British relationship had been a happier one. When there were no 'P. and O. Company's ocean greyhounds' running between Bombay and London, the British spent their short holidays in India mixing and playing sport with Indian gentlemen. At that time few Indians received an English education, and hence the British learnt the native languages and misunderstandings were prevented. But then the relationship deteriorated as it broadened out. The problem is seen to lie in British arrogance, racial prejudice and lack of trust in the native rulers. Even so, Indian unrest is often a matter of minor grievances. At one stage we are told that it is 'pinpricks' like the Arms Act depriving Indians of the right to use firearms which make the Hindus disloyal.[12] What is required is a new era of trust and understanding, symbolized by the marriage of Lord Tara and Princess Kamala. According to the Raja's Dewan 'a marriage like this would do more than fifty treaties to bring the two races into closer touch with each other'.[13]

There is one issue which does not fit as easily into the personal as into the political schema of the novel. This is the rise of Japan. Japan's emergence as a power and its racial assertiveness are presented as a significant development which hangs in the background almost as a threat. It is partially deployed in support of the author's central argument, but there is an evident reluctance to pursue its full implications for India's future. Well into the novel it is asserted in conversation that the unrest in India is in part due to the rise of Japan but the discussion then turns in a different direction. Towards the end of the novel a Japanese pilgrim speaks of the religious ties between India and Japan, and he goes on to predict that a day will come when the two countries, together with China, will be united in a great empire to challenge the West. We are left with the thought that British statesmen unwittingly assist the unification of Asia by encouraging anti-Asiatic legislation. The attempt to harness the rise of Japan to the cause of strengthening the Indo-British relationship indicates a recognition that there are limits to the efficacy of the personal to affect political change. Resistance has its place alongside collaboration but this can neither be openly admitted nor fully incorporated into the narrative design.

The Prince of Destiny, by S. K. Ghosh, has much in common with *Hindupore*.[14] It addresses essentially the same issues; the perspective is similar; there are many shared themes. Yet *The Prince of Destiny* is an altogether more accomplished novel. Its dramatic interest is sustained and action and characterization are less contrived. At the same time, the linkages between Britain and India are understood at least partly in terms of processes of social change. As in *Hindupore*, the novel looks back to earlier years to establish the touchstone of the relationship, but it is bolder about looking ahead to a different era and taking account of developments in other parts of the globe. It is also less narrowly political in that cultural forces emerge as significant in their own right, and at times the understanding of the political drifts into the realm of myth and dreams.

The Prince of Destiny is the story of Barath, the son of the Rajput ruler of a princely state. Born in 1877, his early education is at the hands of Vashista, the traditionalist high priest to the ruler, who believes the young prince is destined to drive the British from the land. But Barath is of a different temperament, recoiling from narrow orthodoxy and confrontation. This side of his nature is further developed during his years of study in England. There he is influenced by several people who become very close to him, all of whom approach Britain's role in India with great understanding. There is Colonel Wingate, a retired Indian Army officer; his niece, Lady Ellen, who is almost a mother to Barath; Lord Melnor, a progressive Conservative peer; and Francis Thompson, the romantic poet who is fictionalized in the novel.[15] Barath's most significant relationship is with Lady Ellen's niece, Nora, with whom he falls in love. By the time of his departure, Barath feels deeply committed to England and passionately concerned to find some way of reconciling East and West.

Returning to India, Barath finds his father dead and he succeeds to the crown. Vashista, now Dewan, is committed to expelling the British and for this purpose has raised a clandestine army. Princess Suvona, a childhood infatuation, waits to be taken as Barath's bride. Barath's initial doubts about the role assigned to him grow very much stronger after the arrival of Lord Melnor at the palace. Melnor is soon appointed British Resident and in this capacity is joined by his niece, Nora. Barath now comes to reject the old order and proclaim his belief in the British connection. His political vision is complemented by his personal commitment. Barath decides to marry Nora, and this expression of their love for each other will be a symbol of the union of East and West. As the marriage is about to be solemnized, a revolt engineered by Vashista begins. Through force of argument and personality, Barath manages to avert the armed struggle but he has lost the support of his people. Nora renounces Barath because of her love for India. Barath marries Suvona but the marriage is not consummated, and after the ceremony he goes 'out of the palace, into the world' to await the coming of a new teacher of peace and unity.

In many respects a conservative consciousness permeates the novel and there is a sense of nostalgia for a bygone era. Change must come but it should be selective and gradual. Reviewing the procession at the Durbar celebrating Queen Victoria's proclamation as Empress, we are told that the adherence of the princes to the domestic customs of their forefathers constitutes the last hope of India's regeneration. The priesthood is too narrow and inflexible to play a constructive role in the process. Yet it will not do to be ostentatiously modern after the style of some princes, unduly influenced by their English or anglicized Indian friends. But if the princes are the true keepers of India's traditions, they cannot move forward on their own; only by an alliance with the British and by opening the door to reform and modernization along Western lines can India's regeneration be achieved. The task had been begun by Lord Beaconsfield in Queen Victoria's time, when treaty-rights were extended to the 'Sovereign Princes' in an attempt to create bonds of affection and patriotism between India and Britain. But after Beaconsfield's death statesmanship gave way to political expediency and racial arrogance, and a gulf was created between India and Britain. Misunderstanding and conflict were fanned by Kipling – 'a mere youth', 'this banjo-poet' – and his writing contributed to the rise of sedition in India.

This particular indictment of Kipling relates to the contempt he expressed for the Bengalis as the prime movers in the political agitation, but Ghosh's main concern is to rebut Kipling's conception of a great divide between East and West. In conversation with Colonel Wingate, Barath rejects the view that the ways of Hindus are mysterious, their motives inscrutable and their actions unpredictable. It is all a matter of understanding the teachings and hold of Hinduism. There is no attempt here or elsewhere in the novel to gloss over the differences between East and West; rather, these are explored, even celebrated. The crucial difference, we are told, is that reasoning in the East is intuitive whereas in the West it is dialectical. But this is not absolute and a number of Ghosh's Western characters are shown at times to think and speak like Easterners – Barath's professor at Cambridge, Francis Thompson and, most importantly, Nora. The burden of the novel is that East and West can meet. Barath tells Vashista, 'There is no gulf between England and India that cannot be bridged'; to Nora he says, 'East and West are but one.' What is required is greater understanding; it is as if what we would now term hybridity can be achieved through personal relations. At one stage, for example, the author directly addresses the English reader on the need for friendship to be extended to Indian students in London. At another, Barath begs Francis Thompson to complete his poetic translation of an Indian epic into English, reflecting that this would be 'worth the whole British army in India'.

If 'East and West are but one' and Barath's decision to marry Nora is taken partly to symbolize this unity, why, we must ask, does the marriage not take place? The issue is crucial, I believe, to understanding the novel's purpose and vision. During the crisis at the palace when Barath calls on Nora to marry him, he cries 'you are my destiny . . . fulfil your mission'; 'Come, beloved, together let us be immortal.' But this is not realistic because Barath cannot carry his people with him. Nor, we are meant to understand, is some kind of political union between England and India conceivable. Lord Melnor declaims 'no earthly tie can be permanent'; Barath tells his people that some-day there will be a United States of India, committed to the cause of international peace. It is accepted that independence will come but India is not yet ready for it. For the present, and in India's interest, England and India must stay together on the basis of understanding and friendship.

Nora's true destiny, we are told at the end of the novel, was to save England's cause in India, which she did through renouncing Barath and encouraging his marriage to Suvona. She thus wins Suvona's love – 'in this life be my sister' – and Suvona's commitment to England.

> Henceforth, I too am thy country's friend. When the peril comes to England, a million of our sons will hasten to her rescue. I shall labour to that end.[16]

Alongside the treatment of the Indo-British relationship almost as a domestic crisis within a family, the novel takes account of two developments outside the empire which are seen as of far-reaching importance: the defeat of the Italians at Adowa in 1896 and Japan's victory over Russia in 1905. The writing here is more hard-headed; the author draws on contemporary currents of geopolitical thinking and an attempt is made – remarkably prescient in many respects – to discern the changing constellation of international politics in the years ahead. The author's purpose is clearly to reinforce the plea for greater understanding by pointing out the dangers involved in alienating Indian opinion and ignoring the possibility of new power configurations. Inevitably there are suggestions of strain about inserting such overt political commentary into the novel, but overall Ghosh has managed to integrate the material with considerable skill.

K. E. Ghamat's *My Friend the Barrister* is much inferior as a novel to the other two works. Published in Bombay in 1908, it tells the story of a Parsi youth, Rustim, who travels to England to study law. During the voyage he wins the friendship of some passengers who have a love of India and are of a liberal cast of mind, and he is rebuffed by others because of their prejudice and narrow-mindedness. In London he continues to see many of his fellow-passengers but inevitably his circle widens. He mixes easily because of his charm and sincerity, and because the arrogance of Anglo-India has not taken root in English soil. A meeting in Westminster Hall, called to denounce the Indian National Congress, provides the occasion for a rehearsal of arguments about the state of British India and the growth of Indian nationalism. Rustim skilfully presents the moderate Indian viewpoint, though the whole episode reads like a political tract rather than a novel.

While in London Rustim falls in love with an English girl, Maud Osborne, who comes from a family with a background of involvement in India. The two become engaged. Rustim returns to India and the engagement is broken off in an exchange of letters. In fact the letters were forged by Rustim's friend, the barrister Mr Bagla Bhagat, who believes that mixed marriage is a sin. Years later Rustim learns that the letters were forgeries and he returns to England to marry Maud.

The message of the book is a simple one. Political disaffection in India is a result of the arrogance of the English, but once personal relations are established across the racial divide the situation is transformed. Rustim befriends the amorous Major Flapdoodle Spooney, who is being blackmailed by his ill-chosen wife. The Major thus comes to recognize the extent of his prejudice against Indians and resolves to mend his ways. The marriage between Rustim and Maud opens the eyes of English die-hards to the possibility of a permanent union between England and India based on respect and understanding. Echoing the ideas Rustim advanced earlier at the meeting in Westminster Hall, the representatives of English reaction accept the need for administrative reform in India and even the desirability of co-operation with the Indian National Congress.

As in the novels by Mitra and Ghosh, we are given to understand that in earlier years the Indo-British relationship had been less troubled. Sir Augustus Goodfellow, Maud's uncle and himself an old India hand, declares that 'English statesmanship is deteriorating fast in India'. This he attributes to the opening of the Suez Canal and the greater ease of travelling. Whereas once the English stayed in the country for years and tried to know the people, 'nowadays Englishmen seem to have no heart in India'.[17]

In another respect, however, it is made clear that it will not do simply to cling to the pattern of the past. In contrast to the position taken in the two novels considered earlier, we are told that the Raj must work with the educated Indians rather than rely on the princes. In the view of Sir Augustus, 'The Native Princes are but birds in gilded cages.' They are dependent upon the goodwill of the bureaucracy and out of touch with the people. 'The educated Indians alone represent the masses.'[18] A former die-hard expresses much the same sentiment when he argues:

> The Legislative Councils must be reformed, but the reform must not be rendered a mockery by stocking them with titled noodles and brainless popinjays of rich families.[19]

The three novels we have discussed are part of a sub-genre which constitutes a literary expression of the moderate phase of Indian nationalism, ascendant in the last decades of the nineteenth century and remaining powerful until the end of the First World War. For Congress leaders such as Surendranath Banerjea and Gopal Krishna Gokhale, nationalism could be reconciled with imperialism; what was required was a partnership to forge a new social order. The nationalist plea was for constitutional reform over time, leading to some measures of self-government within the empire. Condemnation of the absolutist and racist nature of British overlordship was combined with an acceptance of the essential goodness of the British and a belief that British rule was a dispensation from on high.[20] It is apparent that the approach taken to the Indo-British relationship in these three novels derives from – and reflects in romanticized form – the liberal nationalist creed. The faith in the right intentions of the rulers, the belief that discord was the result of minor grievances rather than incompatible interests, the assumption that individuals of vision could set matters right – all these carry the distinctive stamp of a generation for which idealism had to substitute for action.

Yet it would be mistaken to assume that these texts are nothing more than a literary elaboration of moderate nationalism and are useful only in relation to a particular historical moment and a specific political agenda. They signify a connection with the other which I will argue is an intrinsic part of the Indian imperial experience and extends over time. What stands out is the openness towards external linkages, a spirit of receptive inquiry with respect to an alien society and culture, and a positive approach to personal relations between Indians and English. It is an openness which cannot be understood simply in terms of pragmatism – telling the rulers what they want to hear. As has been pointed out, many novels published before independence contain sharp criticisms of British rule and condemn acts of exploitation and tyranny.[21] Moreover, this openness was not restricted to the late Victorian and early Edwardian period. As we shall see, a similar reaching-out is apparent in post-independence writing.

Following Albert Memmi, Octave Mannoni and Erik Erikson, a fruitful – though partial – explanation might focus on the psychology of dependence produced by the colonial situation, with its attendant ambivalence towards the ruler/father. This line of thought has long been influential and for good reason. Yet it is fundamental to such approaches that drawing close to and adopting the values of the colonizer is understood to be the result of some disorder. Memmi, for example, uses the metaphors of disease and cure; he writes about the colonized subject 'tearing himself away from his true self' and describes the rejection of the colonizer as 'the indispensable prelude to self-discovery'.[22] In the colonial or postcolonial situation, then, the belief is that self-fulfilment can be found only within one's own ethno-cultural community.

But in such a situation the ethno-cultural community may be a construction based on very rickety foundations. Even if it is not, there is the question of what is the 'natural' form of community, and whether this matters anyway. Is there any reason to suppose that pigmentation or religious heritage count for more than the allegiance of ideas and values? In their enthusiasm to promote the Indo-British linkage, our writers perhaps pass through this minefield with too little awareness of the risks. What they do demonstrate, however, is that the nature of the colonial encounter had been such that the conception of self had necessarily to be pursued in relation to the other.

Here two aspects are worthy of note. First, although our texts give a strong sense of India's philosophical and cultural heritage – as signified in *Hindupore*, for example, by the treatment of Jagannath Temple in Puri – this is seen as embracive and outward looking. Second, sectional ties and interests are juxtaposed with Indianness. At least by implication, the texts suggest that education, social position and the response to modernity create subcultures with strong points of tension between them. It is possible to develop both points so that they mesh with the broader arguments that foreign invaders have been internalized in the Indian mind and that the mental boundaries between indigenous groups are narrow and closed.[23] A case can thus be advanced that India's search for selfhood is distinctive. Whether or not this is so, the readiness to countenance new forms of community needs to be recognized for what it is in this period when nationalism had not yet put its steel rim around the kind of connectedness deemed appropriate or natural, nor set its seal on a construction of history which could sustain a self-identity rooted in the indigenous culture. It may even be useful to read these novels as proffering, by way of an alternative scenario, an early commentary on some of the difficulties of relating the modern nation-state to India's circumstances.

The use of marriage as the symbol of a union between Britain and India catches some of the idealism then associated with imperialism and is thus time-bound. In any case, as employed in *Hindupore* and *My Friend the Barrister*, it is too simple. Instead of being a way of exploring how to overcome the difficulties which beset the relationship, it serves as an instant means of resolution. Stripped as it is of any problematic quality, its use is akin to the selective remembrance of the recent past which exaggerates the ease with which British and Indians related to each other before the Mutiny. Notwithstanding that marriage signals the need for a dramatic initiative, it operates fundamentally as an instrument of closure. In this respect only Ghosh succeeds in bringing out both the promise and the strain of the personal as a symbol of the political.

There is also the consideration that neither in *Hindupore* nor *The Prince of Destiny* is sole reliance placed on the union of the principal protagonists. In both novels the case for a closer Indo-British relationship is shored up by pointing to the threatening nature of developments in international politics. It is as if both authors acknowledge that added weight must be given to the personal by resorting to the politics of sanction.

The concern, almost anxiety, to understand the Indo-British connection evident in much Indian writing finds few parallels in British writing until after the First World War. What in the Indian narratives was a disquisition on the bonds between Britain and India through the metaphor of the personal, became in the British texts an exposition of the difficulties and responsibilities of exercising imperial power. We thus have a discourse of a different kind, strictly enclosed and declaratory in nature. The requirements of rule set the parameters of discussion. What was at issue were considerations of order, authority and justice, not affinity or understanding between Indians and English. This was particularly the case towards the end of the nineteenth century when a sterner cast of mind emphasized the need for stability before reform, and social distance between ruler and ruled.[24]

Following as it did the terms of reference of imperial politics, the fiction of the period marginalized and depersonalized the colonial subject. Often enough Indians are absent from the texts, except as part of an ill-determined background. When they do appear, they are seldom depicted in a way with which the English characters – or for that matter the reader – can empathize. As individuals they are mostly stock figures such as the dutiful ayah or the faithful servant, or they are 'types' whose motivations and behaviour are controlled by the political requirements of the text – as, for example, Siri Ram in Edmund Candler's *Siri Ram: Revolutionist.* Collectively, Indians are represented not as a people or peoples, but as chaotic sectarian groups. The depiction of crowd scenes, reference to 'the masses', and the choice of the word 'revolt' over 'mutiny' serve to indicate the lack of cohesion, the absence of social bonds such as existed in Europe.

Kipling aside, it follows that British authors made little use of categories of interpersonal behaviour between British and Indians. Fundamentally the texts were concerned with the position of the British in India, their role as leaders, and the personal and racial qualities which fitted them for rule. We thus find that British heroes were pitted not against Indians as such but against abstractions of the subcontinent and its peoples such as irrational violence, a culture of depravity and decadence, or an inert, stagnant land. The one exception – and it is partial – to the avoidance of interpersonal metaphors is that of parent and child. In many of the novels, as in non-fictional narratives of the time, the British are presented as akin to a parent and the Indians as children. The point is invariably to show the need for parental authority lest the children run riot and their emotions go unchecked. But such references, however useful as ideological reinforcement, cannot be developed at length in the texts because of the inconsistencies and closures of the metaphor. The fact is that the relationship was frozen in time since it was seen in the context of an unchanging East. As J. A. Spender pointed out, in what he dubbed the Peter Pan theory of India, this led to the conclusion that the children would never grow up.[25] Moreover, the British understanding of the parent/child relationship was skewed in that the emphasis was always on teaching and training at the expense of loving. Indeed, in some cases the commitment to authority was so pronounced as to undercut the metaphor itself. In Flora Annie Steel's *On the Face of the Waters,* a British officer insists that governance in India depends on recognizing that the Indians 'are really children – simple, ignorant, obstinate', yet throughout the novel the British are presented not as the parent but as 'the Master' and 'the Master Race'.

In his pioneering study of British literary images of India, Allen Greenberger writes that in the period from 1880 to 1910 the line drawn between the English and Indian communities is such that 'by and large there simply are no relations'.[26] Benita Parry reaches much the same conclusion. Examining the novels of Flora Annie Steel (1847–1929), she asserts that Mrs Steel's most striking achievement 'is in communicating the antipathy and fear possessing the British and their consciousness of an abyss separating them from their human environment'.[27] Interestingly, both Allen Greenberger and Benita Parry clinch their arguments by quoting a passage from Flora Annie Steel's novel *The Hosts of the Lord,* in which an English doctor exclaims:

Understand! Of course you don't. I don't though I've been here two years. And what's more, I don't want to . . . So long as we don't understand them . . . and they don't understand us, we jog along the same path amicably . . . It is when we begin to have glimmerings that the deuce and all comes in.[28]

This depiction of a British community which sealed itself from personal connection or social contact with Indian people must broadly stand. The images which dominate British fiction in these years are of physical separation and cultural distance, and they accord with what we know of Anglo-Indian life. Yet the picture is in need of minor qualification. Very occasionally novelists openly ventured across the divide and speculated on the problems and possibilities of interracial union. Flora Annie Steel undertakes such an excursion in her otherwise strictly orthodox novel of the mutiny. In *On the Face of the Waters* the hero, James Greyman, has an Indian mistress, Zora, and 'the glow and the glamour' between them sustained their life together for eight years. An unforeseen by-product of the relationship was that Greyman gained an understanding of natives denied to other Englishmen, which leads a military man 'to think that perhaps there is something to be said for a greater laxity'.[29] There was more to be said against it, of course, but the text is relieved of this obligation by the death first of the child of the union and then of Zora herself. Despite the narrative closure, the author's doubts about the initiative she has taken in depicting Greyman's love for Zora are evidenced by the attempts to qualify and contain it. These are encapsulated by the line 'even in death a great gulf lay between him and the woman he had loved'.[30]

A decade and a half later Maud Diver strikes out in a similar direction and beats a similar retreat. *Lilamani*[31] portrays the marriage of an English aristocrat with a well-born Indian women which proves to be a happy union, despite initial opposition and Lilamani's attempted suicide during her courtship. The relationship is patently symbolic, however, and is politically inspired. This is apparent from the remarks of Lilamani's uncle, Sir Lakshman, who sees the marriage as a pointer to the future relationship between England and India – a relationship which is specifically presented as reflective of the West as masculine and the East as feminine. The latter aspect is more fully developed in the second novel of the trilogy, *Far to Seek* (1924), where we are told that Lilamani's 'poetic brain saw England always as "husband of India" . . . Long ago her father had told her that nations had always been renewed by individuals . . . For [India] it must always be the *man* – ruler, soldier or saint.'[32] In *Lilamani* Mrs Diver restricts the human meaning of the marriage at almost every point; it is a relationship of love but there is a sense of pre-arranged emotions; it is possible only because the parties are of high caste and is in no sense representative. By the end of the novel – and even more in *Far to Seek* – the significance of the marriage has come to the reside in its exceptionalism.

Kipling is in a class of his own. It is evident that he had much in common with his fellow British writers and it is easy to see why he was taken as the mouthpiece of Anglo-India. Yet in certain, more guarded, respects his approach and receptivity to the other was much closer to our Indian authors – which perhaps helps to explain why his standing in India remained high, even when it plummeted in the world outside. Certainly he expressed himself starkly on the distinctive character of races and the gulf between cultures, and he could be contemptuous of Indian values and customs. Yet at other times he cut through the conventions of British India and wrote approvingly of Indian qualities. Drawing especially on Kipling's use of language, Janet Montefiore has observed how frequently in his stories white men are shown to be inarticulate and lacking in insight, and it is the Indian characters who comprehend more and show greater understanding.[33] My argument here is that when the personal could be detached from the political, Kipling's narratives reach out to Indians and to cultural difference. But they also make plain how little personal space imperialism could allow to remain unpoliticized.

In several of his short stories he explores the problem of understanding Indians and Indian society, using the device of disguise. Understanding cannot be achieved from afar or learnt from books; it can only come through living as a native. Hence Strickland of the Police, who 'held the extraordinary theory that a Policeman in India should try to know as much about the natives as the natives themselves'.[34] But even Strickland, who had 'educated himself in this peculiar way for seven years', had not succeeded in overmatching the natives with their own weapons – though 'in fifteen or twenty years he will have made some small progress'.[35] To go further one would have to cut many of the ties with one's own society. Kipling recounts the case of McIntosh Jellaludin, a drunkard who had reached 'the uttermost depths of degradation', and who 'used actually to laugh at Strickland as an ignorant man – "ignorant West and East"– he said.'[36] The costs of under-standing, then, are very high.[37] Even 'foolish' Strickland was held by his own kind to be 'a doubtful sort of man', and people passed by on the other side. Kipling caps the point by telling us that one of these days Strickland will write a little book on his experiences. 'That book will be worth buying, and even more worth suppressing.'[38]

In Kipling's view, it needs to be said, understanding does not necessarily go hand in hand with personal feeling. Natives hated Strickland, we are told, and they were afraid of him.[39] As for Strickland, we get the impression that what attracted was not native life but the detective work. Presumably in the case of McIntosh Jellaludin there is a genuine closeness but Kipling does not make this plain.

There is an alternative reading which subordinates cultural fascination and its attendant taboos to the purposes of imperial politics. On Gail Ching-Liang Low's account, the role of disguise – cultural cross-dressing as she puts it – is essentially a technique of surveillance which represents yet another attempt at control of subaltern peoples.[40] From Strickland to Kim the white protagonist plays a role, however problematical, in reinforcing the power hierarchies of empire. The personal pleasures – the thrill of penetration – in the end accord with metropolitan interest. But I would argue that this is to read into the narratives the functionality of later theorizing and to read out the cultural warnings. In the case of Strickland, Kipling's emphasis is on the limits of his understanding and the costs involved.

Where children are involved, affinity supposedly comes naturally and overrides the barriers of race and culture. I say 'supposedly' because there is the question of the adolescence of imperialism which we will address when we turn to *Kim*. Kipling's empathy for the world of the child is expressed in tales like 'Little Tobrah' and 'The Story of Muhammad Din'. His line that 'in the hearts of children there is neither East nor West' is not entirely apt because in 'The Story of Muhammad Din', for example, it is the Sahib narrator who is less concerned with the conventional distinctions than the little Muslim child.[41] What is special about children is their social freedom. This is illustrated by 'Tods'Amendment'. Tods, a lively six-year-old, is completely at home with Indians of every description and talk flows freely. Through passing on the objections of tenants to an aspect of proposed legislation on land tenure, he is instrumental in the administration redrafting the bill. The child's access to others and his openness of mind are given added point because in the story Kipling reiterates two of his perennial concerns: the ignorance of English officialdom – 'As if any Englishman legislating for natives knows enough to know which are the minor and which are the major points, from the native point of view, of any measure!' – and the self-interestedness of the educated Indian.[42]

Several of Kipling's stories tell of liaisons across the racial boundary and they are written with sympathy and understanding. Kipling even satirizes 'respectability'. In 'Georgie Porgie' the newly married couple come out on to the verandah after dinner, 'in order that the smoke of Georgie Porgie's cheroots might not hang in the new drawing-room curtains.' Georgina, the abandoned Burmese girl, for all her strength of character was 'crying, all by herself, down the hillside'.[43] In 'Yoked with an Unbeliever', Kipling's concern is that the weak-minded Englishman who stayed with his duly married Hill-girl instead of going back to his English sweetheart, was not worth the attention he received. The Hill-girl's training will save him from perdition, Kipling comments; but he adds, 'Which is manifestly unfair.'[44] Kipling, then, was not unmoved by the claims of interracial love but he was sceptical and apprehensive. His scepticism was directed to individuals. Except for a few singular characters, he doubted that men and women had the self-possession to stand on their own, to be at odds with their kin. As Ameera tells Holden in 'Without Benefit of Clergy', 'kind calls to kind'.[45] Kipling's apprehension concerned the collective. The ties which hold together a community are cultural, ethnic and religious and they should not lightly be put at risk. Social solidarity was a pre-condition of good order, and Kipling could not allow it to be threatened by anything so insubstantial as romantic love. Hence the tragedy that Kipling visits on the relation between Ameera and Holden in 'Without Benefit of Clergy', and between Bisesa and Trejago in 'Beyond the Pale'. 'Without Benefit of Clergy' is the more subtle and moving of the two stories but Kipling alerts us early to what he sees as the social realities. Ameera 'was all but all in his eyes. By every rule and law she should have been otherwise.'[46] The months of absolute happiness for Holden and Ameera were 'happiness withdrawn from the world'.[47]

Making allowance for the twists and turns in Kipling's writings, we are left with the thought that Kipling's heart and mind were of different persuasions. His heart was receptive to an Indo-British relationship of real closeness and understanding; his mind ruled out the possibility because the constraints on the collective were so much more compelling than the constraints on the individual. Once the disjunction came to the surface, it was the collective and the culture which counted for most. The personal had then to be brought into line with the societal and the possibilities earlier canvassed of the self reaching out and identifying with the other, abandoned. Noel Annan is surely correct in seeing Kipling as a social theorist akin to Durkheim, for whom the first concern was the social order and the norms which maintained it.[48] Thus he was not prepared to generalize about societies or break the barriers which separated them on the basis of the encounters of particular individuals. India for the British had to remain a world apart, except for occasional forays in disguise, a few risky liaisons (usually of short duration), and the fact that children had a special pass.

There was one strategy which enabled a fuller exploration than was otherwise acceptable of the possibility of much common ground between English and Indians. This was to trace the early years of a foundling of empire – a boy of European parentage brought up by Indians as an Indian, who did not know the truth of his parentage. Consciously or unconsciously employed, the strategy, which freed its principal subject from the inhibitions and constraints of British India, at the same time freed the writer. The usual taboos and sanctions did not operate in such a situation because the actions and feelings of the characters were not seen to breach the racial and cultural barrier. The writer was thus able to conjecture relationships between Indians and English without weighing up the social consequences, and in a way which ordinarily would be ruled firmly out of court.

Of course often enough the foundling story had a blatant racial purpose; the narrative was so controlled as to drive home a moral about the superiority of British blood. We find that the foundling had more energy, resourcefulness or daring than his Indian companions. In one of Kipling's foundling stories, the narrator observes: 'The blood-instinct of the race held true.'[49] Such racial declarations do not necessarily invalidate the argument I have been advancing. Writers are responsive to a range of impulses, sometimes inconsistent, even contradictory. A theme may feed upon – indeed owe its very existence to – another of an opposite persuasion. All that is being maintained here is that the foundling story provided a context in which the political constraints could be distanced and emotional possibilities opened up to probe understanding and affinity across the divide.

In 1894, when Kipling was making his first attempt at a novel about the orphan son of an Irish soldier – the genesis of *Kim* – *The Story of Sonny Sahib* was published.[50] Its author was Mrs Everard Cotes (née Sara Jeanette Duncan, 1861–1922), a Canadian writer who married an Englishman and spent many years in India. *The Story of Sonny Sahib* has obvious parallels with *Kim*, published seven years later, but it is an altogether slighter work. Cotes has been described as non-racist and anti-colonial.[51] This may be so, but the tenor of her novel is much more in tune with the imperial sensibilities of the era than is *Kim*.

Sonny Sahib was born in Cawnpore at the time of the mutiny. His mother dies of fever but his father, an army captain, believes that both his wife and child have been killed by the sepoys. Sonny is brought up by the ayah and her husband, the table-waiter. Although he is aware of his British parentage, Sonny's early life is essentially that of any young Muslim lad until the Maharajah of Lalpur requires him to live in the palace as a playmate for his son, Moti. The two boys become firm friends. Fortuitously, Sonny saves Moti from being poisoned in a palace intrigue, thus earning the Maharajah's gratitude. An English medical missionary arrives in the kingdom and Sonny is strangely drawn to him – though of course we are meant to understand that it is not strange at all because it is a matter of blood. The missionary is killed because his reforms are resented by Hindu traditionalists. Sonny decides it is time to join his own kin. He escapes from the palace but is captured by a British Army detachment which is about to attack the city. Sonny refuses to divulge information about the Maharajah's defences to the colonel in command. At the eleventh hour the Maharajah capitulates and it is discovered that Sonny is in fact the colonel's son.

An Indian critic, comparing *The Story of Sonny Sahib* favourably with *Kim*, has observed that Sonny was 'quite at home' in his adopted environment and that he became very attached to the people in his immediate circle.[52] Certainly in many respects Sonny responds to the rhythm of Indian life. He relates closely to his foster-parents. He has a genuine friendship with Moti, the Maharajah's son. He refuses to betray the Maharajah, explaining to the colonel: 'I am English, but the Maharajah is my father and my mother.'[53] Yet throughout the book we are made aware that Sonny is different from his Indian fellows; he doesn't quite fit. And the fact of difference counts for more than the common ground. There is an intensity, a more heartfelt quality about the pull of blood than the hold of the environment. At the age of six Sonny began to find the other boys unsatisfactory because he liked to pretend – 'It was his birthright to pretend, in a large active way' – and they didn't. He was also more venturesome: 'On the whole he began to prefer the society of Abdul's black and white goats . . . which had more of the spirit of adventure.'[54] Later, differences with Moti emerge. Moti grew tired of talking about Dr Roberts, the missionary, whereas Sonny 'could talk of him for nine moons'.[55] Hearing the English bugles half a mile outside the city, Sonny was immediately attracted by the beauty of the sound and it stayed with him all day. Moti thought it horrible – 'It screams and it rushes. How can they be able to make it?' he cries.[56]

Clearly this is a story about relationships which cross the self/other divide, but somehow they are never fully developed. For all the ease with which Sonny relates to Indians and adjusts to Rajput culture, there is a sense of something missing. It is not so much Sonny's recognition that he is different nor, for that matter, the recognition of others – as, for example, when the Maharajah, falsely believing Sonny has betrayed him, says 'He is not of our blood.'[57] Rather, race becomes a background force that guides Sonny's destiny and acts as a brake on his ability to be of and at one with his life in Lalpur. It is almost as if Sonny is an actor unable to depart from his script.

With *Kim* it is the opposite. One can hardly fail to have the sense that Kim writes his own lines. He lives the life of his choice, and that life is in largest part an Indian life. Mark Kinkead-Weekes makes the suggestive claim that Kim embodies the urge to become the 'other'.[58] Kim prefers to speak in the vernacular rather than in English and his manner of speach has an earthiness that intimates belonging. At the outset we are told that Kim 'learned to avoid missionaries and white men of serious aspect who asked who he was, and what he did'.[59] There can be no doubt that his outlook on the world was shaped in the bazaar and on the Grand Trunk Road. His formal schooling was decidedly secondary. His short stint at the barrack-school was 'torment'; at St. Xavier's he appears to have been interested only in mathematics, map-making and surveying.

Although critical studies are now more prepared than earlier to see Kim as an exceptional figure in imperial fiction, there remains a tendency to contain him behind the colour line by deduction from the mainstream of imperial culture. Low, in the article already referred to, considers Kim along with white protagonists drawn from John Buchan to John Masters who disguise themselves as natives, and she introduces her commentary by referring to representations of 'the native urban underworld as dark, alien, polluted, diseased and chaotic'.[60] I would argue that disguise is a relatively minor aspect of *Kim* and for the most part we are presented with a character who revels in what he is. Moreover, India as seen through the eyes of Kim could hardly be more removed from the depiction of the 'City of Dreadful Night'. S. P. Mohanty, although more alert to the sensibility of the novel, in the end invests Kim with a racial identity and embeds him within the imperial culture, at least partly on the bases of British responses to the Mutiny and the subsequent writing of Baden-Powell.[61] To my mind, this is to privilege the politics of situation over the cultural exceptionalism both of the protagonist and of the novel.

Kim is certainly aware of caste, rank and race and when it suits his purpose he uses them to advantage. That is of the nature of things. But essentially he is open to all people and he is not constrained by considerations of social distance. His relationships grow naturally from the kind of person he is, and they reflect his background and his sense of belonging to the land. It is of the essence of the story that his closest relationships are with Indians. Kipling's depiction of the love Kim has for the Lama, the almost filial bonds which tie him to Mahbub Ali, the Pathan horse-trader and British agent, or even his rapport with that 'Eye of Beauty', the old woman of Kalu, cut across the body of British fiction about India, including much of Kipling's own writing. It is as if we are transported to another land because we are scarcely conscious that the habitual bounds have been swept aside. When Mahbub asks 'And who are thy people, Friend of all the World?', there can be no doubting Kim's reply: 'This great and beautiful land.'[62] We get the same sense from the evocative line: 'India was awake, and Kim was in the middle of it.'[63]

In contrast to many of Kipling's short stories where the emphasis is on the heat and harshness of India, in *Kim* the landscape is one of beauty and the elements are kinder. The descriptions are inviting: 'the rich Punjab . . . in the splendour of the keen sun'; 'the green-arched, shade-flecked length' of the Grand Trunk Road; 'the cool air and the smell of the pines' in the hills. *Kim* presents an Indian perspective, not a British one tied to the difficulties that officials and soldiers experienced working in alien surroundings – that is the difference. Nirad Chaudhuri pays tribute to Kipling's vision of India which he sees as the real theme of *Kim*. Kipling, he declares, 'had arrived at a true and moving sense of that India which is almost timeless, and had come to love it'.[64]

On the other side, there is of course Kim's slowly awakening sense that he is a sahib and his involvement in the Great Game, the purpose of which is the maintenance of British imperialism in India. In the view of some critics, the hold of this other world undermines Kim's identification with India and scars, if not destroys, his Indian self. According to Jeffrey Myers, in the end 'color conquers culture'.[65] More guardedly, Benita Parry suggests that Kim's Indian world is 'mocked' by that of the Great Game.[66] Proceeding on the assumption that Kim is delivering his adopted people into British bondage, Edmund Wilson argues that 'the alternating attractions felt by Kim never give rise to a genuine struggle', and this is a fundamental weakness in the novel.[67] Such criticisms, based on the premiss that the two worlds are irreconcilable, run counter to my appreciation of the spirit of the novel. Kim, with 'the Irish and the Oriental in his soul', responds to both; he agonizes when from time to time he has to decide on which course he will take, but he is not required to deny his bifurcated nature. The epigraph to chapter 8 tells of the thankfulness of the man with two separate sides to his head. When the Lama meditates on the fact that Kim is a sahib, Kim is vexed and he quotes the Lama's own words: 'there is neither black nor white'.[68] More than this, so far as Kim and the Lama are concerned, the bonds of love establish a deeper receptivity on each side to the world of the other.

But however intense and perhaps homoerotic the relationship between the two, it cannot last and in this respect it is expressive of empire as well as being exceptional to it. In what is the most provocative recent study of *Kim*, Sara Suleri characterizes the narrative in terms of an atrophic adolescence, and in her view the Lama and Kim represent opposite poles of cultural adolescence.[69] That there is no conflict between Kim's relationship with the Lama and his participation in the Great Game thus becomes a recognition that there can be no transition into the phase of adulthood. Kim, like empire itself, has necessarily to be cut short.

There is one other foundling story which bears upon the theme I have been developing – Tagore's *Gora*. First published in Bengali in 1910, it was translated into English fourteen years later and widely compared with *Kim*. 'The book is a Bengali Kim', wrote Edward Thompson, Tagore's first biographer.[70] There are indeed similarities in approach, though the design of the two works is very different. Gora was the son of an Irishman killed in the Mutiny. His mother took refuge in a Hindu home and died on the night of Gora's birth. Brought up as a Brahmin by Indian foster-parents, the fact that he is a foundling is concealed from him until early adulthood. The story is not directly concerned with the Indo-British relationship but turns on the impact of European liberal values on middle-class Bengali society. The main characters are Indian and the conflict takes place between Indians at the level of ideas. Gora is passionately committed to a narrow traditional Hinduism and he resists all attempts to rethink the established conventions, in particular about caste and the place of women. Ranged on the other side are Gora's friend, Benoy, whose openness of mind leads him to probe and question; Gora's foster-mother, Anandamoyi, who rejects the orthodoxies of caste and custom; and the members of a Brahmo Samaj family who live according to the dictates of their sect, committed to the reform of Hindu society.

The foundling device serves the same essential purpose in *Gora* as in *Kim* – to demonstrate the hollowness of the taboos and conventions which prevent individuals from responding to others on a basis of empathy and love. In *Kim* the ideal held out is an almost instinctive zest for life which embraces all humankind and is at one with the physical environment. In *Gora* the informing ideal is a powerful liberalism. The novel presents a carefully reasoned articulation of humanist values expressed in a manner which Tagore believed was consonant with India's history and traditions. The way in which the foundling device is employed is of course quite different. In *Kim* we, the readers, are made aware of the true situation at the outset. We knowingly follow Kim's gradual realization of the significance of his parentage, which challenges his Indianness but, as I have argued, does not destroy it. With *Gora* the truth is not revealed until almost the last pages of the book. Its impact is therefore dramatic; the world that Gora has built for himself is in an instant shown to be illusory. Long before Gora learns that he is a foundling, he begins to doubt his idealization of Hinduism. His visits to a village outside Calcutta make clear that he is neither accepted by the villagers nor can he accept the pattern of their lives. Gora saw, we are told, 'How divided, how narrow, how weak was this vast expanse of rural India – how supinely unconscious of its own power, how ignorant and indifferent as to its own welfare!'[71] Gora stays within the cocoon he has woven for himself, however, until it is stripped from him and he is able to say 'To-day I am free'.[72]

I would further argue that *Gora* is an overtly political novel in that it charts the social consciousness and intellectual conflicts of the Bengali élite, and wrestles with the balance to be struck between individual and social claims and between the national tradition and Western values. Tagore writes with a clear message: orthodox Hinduism had become encrusted with prejudice. His handling of Gora's foundling background is carefully controlled to further this purpose. With *Kim*, on the other hand, there is much less impression of deliberative writing. That Kim is a foundling is a piece of crafting crucial to the story and it is shored up by Kim's boyhood and the Lama's absence of adulthood. Thus the politics of imperialism are for the most part distanced, and Kipling is able to indulge his own love of India,[73] and suspend his belief that the worlds of the modern West and ancient India needed to be kept apart.

Relating these comments on the foundling device to the lines of argument advanced earlier in this chapter, the novelists' resort to the personal does not somehow naturalize politics – as Naipaul's passage quoted at the outset might seem to infer. The personal is not a given simply to be taken up ready-made; whether and how it is deployed is extremely political. The significance of the personal in the fictional narratives we have considered is that it is a way of thinking differently about the politics of imperialism or of escaping from them. It is for this reason that British authors resisted personalizing the interactive aspects of the imperial encounter, and why race, rule and masculinity were written into the make-up of British characters as a way of preventing them from reaching out to Indians. In this way the narratives of empire could shore up the structures of empire and screen its vulnerability. The impossibility of understanding or relating to Indians was patronizing, but it was also politically self-protecting. For Indian writers, on the other hand, the fact of India's subjugation provided an incentive to change the frame of reference. The resort to the personal was a challenge to the structures of empire and a way (within class limits) of envisaging Indian involvement. Hence marriage as a symbol of political partnership. In *Gora*, Tagore was not concerned with empire as such but with the values it had spawned. Hence it was these values that were personalized because the object was to contest orthodox Hinduism, not British rule. The fascination of Kipling is that he used the personal both as a means of closure to safeguard the empire as it was and, less frequently but more memorably, as a way of leaving it behind for an imagined land.

Changing courses

In the years between the wars, the political and fictional narratives approach Indo-British relations in different terms and in large part tell a different story. Reading from the policies and power structures, there is little to suggest any early or substantial recasting of the imperial relationship. The custodians of empire displayed a surprising confidence in their ability to stave off new challenges and hold firm to the old structures of power. The nationalists envisaged a long haul and few were sanguine that opposition and unrest could be made to yield short-term political dividends. By way of contrast, in the fiction of the period British and, more hesitantly, Indian writers portray the crumbling of one order and the emergence of another; this body of writing manifests a post-imperial sensibility. It catches the currents beneath the political surface: on the British side, doubt, anxiety and a pessimism about accomplishments and prospects; on the Indian, an excitement about possibilities, a sense of striking out in new directions. Thus in retrospect the novels of the inter-war years have a prescience about them; the view from within the culture of British India, where the representatives of different societies collided and misunderstood or exploited each other, is more telling than perspectives about geopolitical power or the calculations of policy-makers.[74]

Of course, well-established themes were carried forward into these years and the concerns of the time can be seen to figure in less developed form in earlier texts. But what stands out is the collective sense of a different era and the extent to which literary politics conformed to distinctive patterns. It was now the British writers who puzzled about the links between Britain and India, and with some openness of mind. It was not, however, an openness born of hope – such as typified an earlier generation of Indian writers – but an openness produced by impending loss. Friendship is the predominant metaphor taken up in the texts, but what is dwelt on is the difficulty, even the impossibility, of realizing it and the misunderstandings along the way. Indian writing is of a different tone and has a different focus – on India itself and on future possibilities. In this section we will concentrate on British fiction because it was these texts which were preoccupied with the Indo-British relationship and personalized it in new and revealing ways. First, however, I will briefly sketch the changing course of Indian writing, which *inter alia* will give a sense of the climate that influenced the British narratives.

It is indicative of the times that in the Indian texts published between the wars there is seldom much intensity in the relations between Indian and British characters. The love or marriage motif which we examined in the preceding section all but disappears in these years, signifying the abandonment of any interest in negotiating a new association between Britain and India. A. Madhaviah's *Clarinda* is an exception in this regard because it tells of a close relationship between a Mahratta Brahmin woman, Clavirunda, and an English officer, Lyttleton. Twice saved by the Englishman, first from snake bite and later from the burning pyre of her husband, Clavirunda's feelings for Lyttleton grow from affection to love, and the two live together as husband and wife. Despite the modernism of the depiction of the relationship, the novel is best grouped with those of Mitra, Ghosh and Ghamat as it was published in 1915 and is set in the latter half of the eighteenth century.[75]

More surprisingly, hatred between Indians and British only occasionally features in the texts and it is used sparingly as a device to explore Britain's failure in India and expose the exploitative nature of British rule. Of course there are brutal and vindictive Englishmen; taking the novels of Mulk Raj Anand for example, one thinks of Jimmie Thomas, the drunken foreman at the Sir George White Cotton Mills, in *Coolie*, and Reggie Hunt, the assistant planter, in *Two Leaves and a Bud*. And there is the contempt shown for the former by Ratan, the wrestler from the North, and the fear and panic evoked by the latter in the coolies working on the Macpherson Tea Estate. For the most part, however, when hatred is shown it is set in an institutional framework and is not something that bespeaks an engagement between two individuals. Nor is friendship between Indians and English much in evidence in the texts – at least not in the sense of involving some genuine reaching out on the basis of the nature and personality of the people concerned. In *Coolie*, for instance, Munoo initially contemplated Mrs Mainwaring 'with a restrained wonder', he then hated her for a time, and finally felt 'docile and good and kind' towards her.[76] In Mulk Raj Anand's earlier novel, *Untouchable*, Bakha was drawn to the Salvation Army officer, Colonel Hutchinson, because he was a sahib and wore European clothes, but he was 'baffled and bored' by his proselytizing and hymn singing.[77]

The crux of the matter is that British characters play a much less significant part in the Indian narratives of the inter-war years than they did previously. The British presence is mainly in the background, represented through collectives such as the army or the police, or it is on the sidelines, as the Skeffington Coffee Estate is to the village of Kanthapura in the novel of that name by Raja Rao. When English men and women are depicted in the novels, they are usually minor characters of the cardboard cut-out variety. They do not so much interact with Indian characters as serve as foils against which Indians redefine themselves and rethink the future of Indian society. Perhaps the most notable exception is *Two Leaves and a Bud*, where the English characters are more sharply etched than the Indian and it is they who determine the action – but not the sympathetic focus – of the novel.

In so far as British imperialism is personalized in the texts, this is increasingly done through Indian characters. In the first instance, therefore, our attention is directed not so much to the relationship between Britain and India as to that between different generations and classes of Indians – who are themselves influenced by where they stand with respect to imperial rule. The various tendencies and pressures are explored between father and son, between male and female characters, between those carrying the stamp of the city and those rooted in the village, and within the make-up and life experience of a single character. The extent of change over time and between generations is depicted in K. S. Venkataramani's *Murugan the Tiller* (1927), K. Nagarajan's *Anthawar House* (1939), which recounts the story of a South Indian extended family in the 1920s and 1930s, and Bhabani Bhattacharya's *So Many Hungers* (1947). *Murugan the Tiller* is also significant for the way in which it counterpoises the politics of village and city and expresses the Gandhian rural ideal which was so influential at the time. In several of the novels the Indian Civil Service serves as the point of linkage between the imperial system and Indian life. Thus in K. S. Venkataramani's *Kandan the Patriot* the central protagonist relinquishes his position in the ICS shortly after gaining it in order to further the independence struggle, while his friend, Rangan, only does so much later and prompted by a career setback which was a direct result of his nationalist sympathies.

The pattern which emerges in the literature is that many of the issues arising from British intervention in the subcontinent have now been internalized, at least within the life of the élites. Processes and values once tied to imperial penetration are seen to have taken root, and they are treated with little reference to British action and motives. Despite the immediacy of the nationalist struggle, the narratives are less concerned with the Raj as such than with modernization and Westernization; the challenges which have to be faced relate to materialism, urbanization and the relationship of the individual to the collective. The advent of Gandhism brought these issues to the foreground of the narratives. K. R. Srinivasa Iyengar has argued that Gandhian thought produced a revolution in Indian writing,[78] and it certainly led to a change of focus (most importantly to and in favour of the village), a new sense of moral intensity, and a more distinctively Indian style. It received its classic expression in Raja Rao's *Kanthapura*, which tells in mythic terms how Gandhism transformed the life of a village in Mysore.[79]

Partly because of the Gandhian influence, the narratives of the inter-war years give a strong sense of the cultural interaction of East and West and the accompanying tensions and tendencies toward accommodation. In some texts East and West are represented as more or less enclosed cultural systems: the one characterized by a metaphysical consciousness drawing heavily on the past which too easily translates, in the idiom of some critics, into a 'distinctive Indian sensibility'; the other signified by the materialistic city and modern education and industry. *Kanthapura* falls into this category, as does *Murugan the Tiller* in which Ramachandran (before his conversion) and his friend Kadari (before his ruin) stand for the ways of the West while Murugan, the faithful tiller of the soil, is a Gandhian incarnation of the traditional East. In other texts East and West are never sharply delineated and the engagement between them is not articulated in a patterned way. This is characteristic of a number of South Indian novels where East and West collide and merge within the lived experience of an individual character, a family or a small town. I have in mind novels by A. Madhaviah and K. Nagarajan, but it is R. K. Narayan who is the exemplar of this approach. In the day-to-day life of Malgudi, East blends with West, the modern grows out of the traditional, and the reader is given the impression that this is the natural order of things.

Then there is the case of Mulk Raj Anand, whose narratives address many of the issues between East and West but do not hinge on them. Anand shows little inclination to romanticize the East after the style of some South Indian writers and in many respects his depiction of India emphasizes the way in which the past and social custom condemn the lower castes to humiliating deprivation. Whether he can be seen as implicitly projecting a Western vision, or whether, in the words of Susie Tharo, 'the future belongs more to the career of the Raj than to Dalit freedom',[80] is another matter. Granted the individualism of his characters and the frequent intrusion of Anand's faith in progress, the critical portrayal of industrialism, the elements of uncertainty and helplessness in many of his heroes and the apparent preference for non-violent social change show another side. I would argue that just as Anand's humanism draws on Gandhism as well as Marxism and Western liberalism, so his fiction is of a more hybrid nature than much contemporary criticism would acknowledge.

To take stock of what for us are the main issues, Britain recedes as a significant presence in the narratives of these years. Its influence in the sub-continent is increasingly portrayed indirectly and in the more general terms of Westernization. Stephen Hemenway has observed that Anand sees Britain's role as almost *passé*,[81] and there is a sense in which this is true of other writers as well. The novelist has turned to face change or the need for change within Indian society and the present is approached with an eye to the future. Yet it is notable that when the British presence is depicted, Indian novelists are less derogatory than might have been expected. Indeed, British characters are given an easier passage than is the rule with British authors of the time. It may well be that the note of philosophical acceptance which is conveyed is related to the fact that in these years the centre of gravity of the Indian novel in English was moving south from Bengal to Madras and Mysore.

For British novelists the imperial project in India retained something of its old fascination but it was cast in radically new terms. Whereas before the Great War British narratives were constructed around the solitary respons-ibilities of rule, it was now accepted that it was necessary to bridge the distance between ruler and ruled. What this meant was that representations of the Raj as aloof and unbending gave way to the idea that the Raj had to stoop and make contact. It was now the British who resorted to the sphere of personal relations to find metaphors with which to understand the Indo-British connection and why it was coming apart.

The main lines of the revised narrative design were widely shared and sharply etched. The foundational assumption was a sense of failure or at least disillusionment produced by the realization that the days of the Raj were numbered. Britain's hopes had not been realized and her Indian subjects showed little of the gratitude that had supposedly been evident in the earlier period. The unthinkable had become the inevitable: the knot that tied India to England was giving way and the most that could be done was to generate some continuing sense of purpose for the short-term, anchored in the idea of commonwealth rather than dominion. With the qualified exception of Maud Diver, every major British novelist of the period spelt out in unmistakable terms that the Indian Empire was close to its end, though often this became apparent only well into the text. In this respect Edmund Candler led the way for his fellow writers when he entitled his 1922 novel *Abdication*. Riley, the main protagonist, in effect elaborates on the choice of title when he decries the practice of eleventh-hour conciliation and minor concessions. The fact is, he declares, '[t]he Home Government has abdicated. Why cannot the Government of India recognise it and let the people see that we are really handing over?'[82]

Yet however clear it was that empire had no future, the narrative structure took a more oblique tack. In nearly all the novels two moves had still to be made to sustain interest and to represent the actual situation of the time. Both revolved around friendship as the metaphor chosen to probe the Indo-British condition. First there was an opening up of possibilities: what was required was a new era of friendship between Indians and British, and gestures were made which previously would have been rejected out of hand. Then the possibilities were cut off or cut short: the difficulties and barriers were simply too great for easy personal relationships to develop. It is one of the main objects of this section to investigate how and why. At this point it becomes apparent that the narrative strategy is not directed to the future of empire but to its past; the texts play out what is happening in this transitional period, not so much with an eye to what might be done to put things right but with the intention of establishing what went wrong much earlier. In this way the fictional exercise becomes a post-imperial lament about mistaken turnings and lost opportunities.

The opening up – the sense of promise or expectancy which in fact represents an inquiry into a historical 'might-have-been' – receives classic expression in E. M. Forster's *A Passage To India*.[83] There is Adela wanting to see the real India, wanting to see Indians. ('How new that sounds!') The Collector follows up with the proposal for a Bridge Party – 'a party to bridge the gulf between East and West'. Then Mrs Moore inquires whether she and Adela might call on Mrs Bhattacharya, and Fielding sends a note to Aziz inviting him to come to tea. All is thus set for working through the potentialities of personal friendship across the divide – although from the very first chapter the narrative presages a larger and more philosophical agenda about the place of humankind in the totality of the universe.[84]

A broadly similar strategy to that of Forster is adopted by other British novelists, except that the political intent tends to be more overt. In *Abdication*, for instance, Riley, the liberal editor of the *Thompsonpur Gazette*, greatly admires Chatterji, the editor of the *Gopalpura Standard*, whom he considers fair-minded as well as fiercely nationalist. Lacking other ways of getting to know Chatterji, Riley calls on him in his office in the hope that he can establish some sort of friendship. Even the traditionalist Maud Diver felt it necessary to open the door to a friendship between her hero, Sir Roy Sinclair, and a young Rajput, Suraj, by making them travelling companions in *The Singer Passes*, the last novel in her Indian triology.

In this respect George Orwell's *Burmese Days* is unusual in that the friendship between Flory and Dr Veraswami is well established when the narrative begins. Moreover the two men take genuine pleasure in each other's company, especially through their game of pretending that the empire is an aged female patient of the doctor. Orwell's distinctive narrative strategy serves his political purpose, which is more uncompromising than that of other writers – namely, to condemn the workings of imperialism without reservation. As he sees it, imperialism has corrupted not only the British but the Burmese as well. It is thus a condition of survival for the British to maintain that social distance which other writers are anxious to diminish, so as to avoid being drawn into the mire of native politics. This emerges clearly when Flory receives an anonymous letter (emanating from U Po Kyin) and has to decide what action to take. The decent course would be to give the letter to Dr Veraswami:

> And yet – it was safer to keep out of this business altogether. It is so important (perhaps the most important of all the Ten Precepts of the pukka sahib) not to entangle oneself in 'native'quarrels. With Indians there must be no loyalty, no real friendship. Affection, even love – yes . . . Even intimacy is allowable, at the right moments. But alliance, partisanship, never![85]

While we might question Flory's clear-cut categories, there can be no mistaking Orwell's purpose in this passage. Imperial prudence prohibits friendship. It is Flory's violation of this precept which ultimately ensures his destruction.

Without wanting to suggest that we are dealing with a more or less mechanically applied formula, there is a patterning about the texts which reflects the situational constraints of the imperial culture. It is noticeable that the characters who reach out to Indians are not representative of the British as a whole; indeed, they are distinguished from their compatriots because their thinking and action do not conform to type. Characteristically they are misfits, eccentrics, new arrivals – individuals who are not at home in the club, who do not mix easily, who are seen by their fellows as outsiders, loners, 'new chums'. At times it is even necessary to bolster their position by giving them a badge of orthodoxy such as distinguished military service, as is the case with Candler's Riley and Edward Thompson's Vincent Hamer (in *An Indian Day*). The fact remains, however, that they are at the margin and therefore strategically placed to break new ground; in a way they are the imperial predecessors of postcolonialism's marginalized heroes, but just as they do not suffer at the hands of history, so they also fail to make their mark.

More than this, it is notable that towards the close of the narrative so many of the British characters who were open to the possibilities of friendship with Indians either meet unhappy ends or drift into ineffectiveness. Flory commits suicide. Edward Holme, in Dennis Kincaid's *Their Ways Divide*, is murdered by an accomplice of his Indian friend Naru. Riley goes to Tibet, where he thinks he might be useful and wanted. Maud Diver's Roy retreats into a barren mysticism. Alden, of Edward Thompson's trilogy, fades from the picture sunk in gloom and remembrance. Only Fielding settles for an orthodox life but it is conceded that he is a less impressive individual than before.

To complete the opening-up process, one crucial step had still to be taken – Indians needed to be in a position to respond. Hence for the first time Indians appear as characters in the text. Many of them, it is true, have a one-dimensional quality and they are essentially props to convey themes about Indian political aspirations, however shallow and confused these are seen to be. Candler's Siri Ram serves as a case study of the weakness and confusion of the educated Indian who turns to politics. Then there is Thompson's Sadhu who, as one of the three characters who collectively represent the author's opinion on Indian thinking, is a model of moderate, responsible nationalism.

Even those characters which are fleshed out, namely Aziz and Dr Veraswami, are shown to have foibles and a kind of flightiness which disempower them from wresting the action from the British and detract from their seriousness of purpose. As Lionel Trilling remarked of Aziz, a weightier Indian is required if he is to impose himself sufficiently on the working out of the story.[86] Trilling's observation applies with no less force to other fictional Indian protagonists of the time. There is a further point to be made here: Indian characters are depicted in a way which shows them as naturally open to the possibilities of friendship with the British, if not actually craving it. The in-built assumption appears to be that all that is needed is for the British to reach out.

Yet for all these shortcomings, Indian characters are now in the texts when they seldom were before and they represent an acknowledgement that what Indians think matters. Characterization was thus part of a broader imperative to provide some points of entry into an Indian cultural consciousness. This was manifested in the texts in various ways: through dialogue (Forster, Orwell, Diver), through reflection and theorizing (Thompson) and by tracing the thoughts of a principal protagonist (Candler). To give a thumb-nail sketch of the picture that emerged – and we will follow up particular aspects a little later – Indians who had to be encountered were taken to share something of the culture and values of their British counterparts, but in the end it was the sense of otherness which counted for more. Earlier, Indians were taken to be different – unknowingly in some accounts – and the fact of difference furnished the justification of empire. Now, however, a simple binarism hardly accorded with the revised understanding of empire along the lines of commonwealth or collaboration. It was necessary, in other words, to find points of contact, a degree of commonality. This was done, not by predicating that the Indians were naturally like the British, but by assuming that through education and social change imperialism had produced some correspondence in ideas and values. Westernization, the bane of an earlier generation of British novelists, became for their successors an instrument for reworking the idea of empire. But as it was turned over in the novels, it proved either more troublesome or less well-rooted than might have been hoped.

We thus came to the second move characteristically made in the literature – the closing up of the possibilities of friendship between Indians and British. Opportunities fail to materialize: Mr and Mrs Bhattacharya's carriage never came to collect Mrs Moore and Adela. Social functions produce personal awkwardness: the Bridge Party was not a success. Other novelists follow Forster's lead: gestures are misinterpreted; written communications are misread; openness is seen as intrusive.

Hence friendships remain stilted, fall apart, or are shown to be beside the point. The gulf between British and Indians is simply too wide; the personal is thwarted by the collective or the national; there is no place or space for individuals to relate. How might the various strands of thought be related or separated? Which are major themes and which are subsidiary? Broadly, two lines of thought can be seen to run through the literature, though they are seldom separate and distinct. We might call them structural and cultural. The logic of the structural approach is that the root of the problem lies in empire itself and hence responsibility for the failure of friendship rests ultimately with the British. The other line of approach looks to culture and personality to determine what went wrong and, so far as the texts are concerned, this tends to shift the onus on to Indians and Indianness. Orwell is clearly a structuralist. At the other end of the spectrum, Maud Diver opts for cultural explanations whenever she can.

Nearly all the novelists provide illustrations of the way that the power relations of empire constrain and eventually proscribe the personal relations between Indians and British. It is a condition of foreign rule, we quickly learn, that Europeans band together and make a show of social solidarity. If we take Forster, for example, very early in the text we are introduced to the idea that the constraints of rule rob the English of their individuality. As Hamidullah puts it, they all become exactly the same: 'I give any Englishman two years . . . And I give any Englishwoman six months'(p. 6).[87] Later Forster is at pains to point out that his exceptional Englishman, Fielding, only narrowly escaped the herd instinct – had he been either ten years younger or ten years longer in India he would have conformed, and after his marriage he acquired some of the limitations of Anglo-India and 'already felt surprise at his own past heroism' (p. 309).

Then there is the geography of empire which ensures that Indians and British are given little space in which friendship can develop naturally. One of the first things Aziz says to Fielding is 'where is one to meet in a wretched hole like Chandrapore?' (p. 57). One of Fielding's last reflections about his friendship with Aziz is that 'socially they had no meeting-place' (p. 309). The club and other social and sporting venues are out of bounds to Indians. Home is the place where the British take refuge from India and for Indians it is the sanctum of their Indianness. It is a little different in *Burmese Days* because Flory sees Dr Versawami's house as an escape from the club, but even so it gives their meetings an illicit undertone. 'When I come to your house', Flory says, 'I feel like a Nonconformist minister dodging up to town and going home with a tart'(p. 36). In *Abdication*, Riley has to resort to visiting Chatterji at his office and the atmosphere is naturally constrained. In his Indian trilogy, Edward Thompson contrives a clearing in the forest as the meeting-place for the friendship to develop between Alden, Findlay and the Sadhu. In this way the Sadhu is protected from the rigours and ridicule of ordinary life, but the artificiality of both the situation and the relationship between the characters is apparent.

In virtually all the British narratives it is easy enough to find passages which appear to diagnose the problem as structural. Let us take the case of Forster. On the last page of *A Passage to India*, Aziz locates empire as the lock on friendship when he cries to Fielding: 'We shall drive every blasted Englishman into the sea, and then . . . you and I shall be friends'(p. 312). But for Forster the problem is not as straightforward as this. After Fielding's rejoinder about wanting to be friends now, the narrative closes with the observation that the horses and the earth and the sky didn't want it. This movement from the personal and the political to the anthropomorphic and the metaphysical occurs repeatedly throughout the novel. The significance of the Collector's decision to give a Bridge Party is diminished by the thought: 'All invitations must proceed from heaven perhaps; perhaps it is futile for men to initiate their own unity, they do but widen the gulfs between them by the attempt' (p. 32). The difficulties of Fielding's tea-party, which we understand as flowing from the segregations of empire, are put in another light by the authorial comment 'It was as if irritation exuded from the very soil' and Fielding's reflection that '[t]here seemed no reserve of tranquillity to draw upon in India'(p. 71).

The way that *A Passage to India* slides away from pursuing the implications of its diagnosis that friendship founders on imperialism can of course be explained by the particularity of Forster's narrative vision. It has often enough been remarked that the political was not Forster's main concern; closing off possibilities – disappointment and withdrawal – expresses his understanding of the limits of human agency and is a distinguishing feature of all his fiction. Even so, there is more to be said, especially since a not dissimilar pattern of identification of the source of the problem, followed by a redirection of focus, is evident in the writing of other British novelists of the period.

The tension between disclosure and diversion is, I would argue, characteristic of British narratives of this time. It suggests that the post-imperial realization had still to do battle with a sensibility which remained imperial. British conceptions of self had not yet broken with the traditions and practices of a century and more. Nor had deeply ingrained orientalist habits of mind been overturned by the political revelation that an era was at an end. It is with these thoughts in mind that I now want to examine those strands in the texts which relate the failure of friendship to Indian culture and character.

What is significant here is the way that cultural difference is elaborated in the texts so that Indian customs and values are often presented in a negative light and Indians themselves are seen as possessing certain deficiencies of character. From this perspective, the practice of nearly all British inter-war novelists of drawing – at least occasionally – on familiar orientalist stereotypes serves to shift some of the responsibility for the failure of connection away from empire and Englishmen. Even Forster is by no means innocent in this regard and it is instructive to note that whereas his celebrated depiction of India as muddle and mystery has been given an easy passage by critics in the West, in India itself it has often been seen as embodying a strong sense of cultural condescension.

Much more overt is the tendency to attribute the difficulties in personal relations to assumed weaknesses in the Indian character. With some exceptions, Indians are portrayed as highly emotional and unstable. Their extreme sensitivity and their penchant for abrupt changes in feeling make friendship with them more difficult and precarious than with one's own kind.

This was accentuated by the belief that all too often personal relations were exploited for material or social betterment. Candler's Banarsi Das follows the lines of his earlier character, Siri Ram – 'a youth of the same kidney, the prey of chance influences, equally impressionable, gullible and unstable'. [88] Kincaid's Naru, although in many ways an attractive individual, is so sensitive that he is forever feeling insulted or humiliated, with the result that the friendship becomes impossible. In Maud Diver's texts there is also a scarcely concealed sense of racism. In *The Singer Passes*, Roy Sinclair reflects on his friendship with the Rajput Suraj:

> differences crept in to prove the colour of their minds as diverse as their skins. It was a fact overlooked by those who saw race prejudice as mere odium attaching to colour . . . With the best will on earth he could not fully accept that given assurance from Suraj as he would have from Jerry or Derek or Lance. Too well he knew that, for Indians, truth was apt to be a matter of convenience rather than principle: a difference in the grain.[89]

Even when no fault is found with moral fibre, the very appearance of Indians may at times prove inhibiting to the Englishman. Riley thinks very highly of Chatterji, yet as he is preparing for a chess game he observes details about Chatterji's body and dress with misgiving:

> He saw a frail little man in a dhoti; bareheaded with bare calves. The casual Englishman in the street would probably have looked first at the calves, the white socks, black shoes and incongruous black suspenders, covering a portion of the nakedness beneath the garment which is responsible, more than anything else, for the stranger's lack of sympathy with the Bengali.[90]

This disquiet about the exposure of the Indian body is echoed in Winston Churchill's description of the 'spectacle' of Gandhi 'striding half-naked up the steps of the vice-regal palace', which he used to such powerful effect nearly ten years later.[91]

Observations about the Indian body draw attention not only to the culture of Indianness but also to the culture of those who gaze upon it – or apparently would prefer not to. Taking up certain lines of postcolonial thinking, it may well be that the intimacy of the colonial encounter produced some semblance of a shared culture which involved both attraction and recoil between colonizer and colonized. I want to close our discussion of British inter-war narratives by directing attention to two silhouettes of friendship in the texts which depart from the norm but in opposite ways. These are the friendship which embraces the homoerotic and the friendship which is drained of flesh and blood. Interestingly, both are taken up by Paul Scott, whose work we will consider in the next section.

Drawing on *A Passage to India* and Dennis Kincaid's *Their Ways Divide*,[92] the homoerotic friendship can be invested with a quite different significance from friendship as we have considered it thus far, and it can be used to recast, at least momentarily, the categories of the colonial encounter. *A Passage to India* has long been seen as tinged with homoeroticism and Sara Suleri has taken this much further in her study of Forster's imperial erotic.[93] Kincaid's text has not, to my knowledge, been interrogated from this angle. Clearly much work needs to be done before we can plot the intersections between male sexuality, friendship and imperialism with any confidence, but the following schema may offer a start. The homoerotic impulse is a by-product of the masculinity of imperialism and it is not restricted to relationships within the imperial camp. Indeed, in certain circumstances its pull is more compelling when directed outside. In the narratives of empire it is common – perhaps even characteristic – for the most intense relationships to be between males on opposite sides of the racial divide. Before us there are the friendships between Fielding and Aziz and Edward and Naru – but one is reminded of Kim and the Lama, Rudbeck and Mr Johnson, Glyn and Sully. The homoerotic impulse is vested in the colonizer, but at least in the narratives, it is visited upon the colonized. It is Aziz who is more expressive both in words and action than Fielding: 'I say, Mr Fielding, is the stud going to go in?' (p. 65); Aziz 'rode against him furiously . . . half kissing him'(p. 312). It is Naru, not Edward, who is consumed by emotion and thrown off-course by the limitations of their friendship.[94] Racial and cultural difference triggers sexual attraction. The movement is from the political to the sexual and it is this movement which has within it the capacity to transform the nature of the imperial relationship. Once again we observe that it is those at the margin, those who do not conform to orthodoxy, who carry with them the possibility of change. But sexuality, especially when it is unrecognized by the parties, produces its own difficulties and misunderstandings. The geography of empire allows no space for the development of intimacy – hence the movement from Fielding's tea-party to the Malabar Caves, from hope to disaster. The contact between colonizer and colonized involves a measure of connection but a larger measure of misunderstanding which leads to rejection. From the time of Edward's return to India until the parting of the ways, Naru feels hurt, humiliated, betrayed. The escape route opened up by the homoerotic becomes a dead-end. The enclosures of empire are reasserted and the protagonists punished.

At the other extreme is friendship as depicted by Edward Thompson. In his trilogy, friendship emerges as a theoretical good, consistent with liberal sensibilities, but lacking in human connection. It is as though Thompson responded to the inter-war impulse to make friendship the hinge of narrative, but at the same time recognized that it contained within it the potential to betray the high-minded and reflective nature of his exposition.

In the friendship between the Sadhu, Findlay and Alden, Thompson presents relationships which are both artificial and static. The jungle clearing in which the three meet is a rarefied space, depersonalized even for the Sadhu inasmuch as it comes with his position and for the period of his incumbency. Its remoteness insulates the parties from the kind of social interactions described in other inter-war narratives, which expose the eagerness and hypersensitivity of Indians and the obtuseness of the English and strain the relationship between the principal protagonists. The friendship itself emerges full-blown. There is no sudden leap of sympathy as in Forster; no disappointment as in Diver or Candler. Feelings neither deepen nor develop over time.

The purpose of the friendship is to provide a way of reflecting on empire that does not jar with the fictional format. In this Thompson cannot be said to have had much success because the discussion is too abstract, and minor characters give the impression of having 'walk-on' roles simply to introduce different points of view. The fact is that the friendship between the central characters is incidental to the play of ideas in the novel. There is perhaps another rationale for the prominence of friendship in Thompson's narratives and it relates to the bifurcated nature of his approach to Indians and Indianness. Thompson's love of and respect for India and his commitment to a reconciliation between East and West needed to be personalized in his texts. For this he required an estimable Indian. In the Sadhu he has one: a man of gentleness, compassion, vision; a thinker who had given the 'intellectual heat' to the anti-Partition agitation.[95] And Thompson keeps him that way by protecting him from worldly contamination and the testing of real friendship. But the very purity of the Sadhu freed Thompson to project negative views of other aspects of India and those Indians who did not step into the magic clearing in the forest. The idealized friendship which exists under the banyan tree diverts Thompson's residual orientalism into subsidiary channels and screens the traditionalism that was part of his vision. The result is a curious political and emotional dualism which, although different in form from other inter-war narratives, shares the temper of the time.

Withdrawal and retrospection

Britain's withdrawal from India has held a special fascination for novelists and scholars alike. The first point of reference is 15 August 1947, because it contains within it a multiplicity of stories. It excites inasmuch as it is tied to the idea of fundamental change: the transfer of power, the dislocation of a subcontinent in the name of partition, the end of Britain's role as a great imperial power. On another account, it signifies deception: 'that inescapable date is no more than one fleeting instant in the Age of Darkness'.[96] But if 1947 was the crucial year, it was so at least partly in an expressive sense. Even in immediate terms, it reached back to the developments of the early war years and it encapsulated the drama of the first years of independence. As one of Paul Scott's characters observes, 'a specific historical event has no definite beginning, no satisfactory end'. Sister Ludmila continues: 'As if time were telescoped and space dovetailed?'[97] For perhaps the majority in Britain the die had been cast more than a quarter of a century earlier. For many Indians, on the other hand, there was a time-lag. The meaning of independence was only realized later, or at least different feelings came to the surface and events took on a different complexion. It is apparent, then, that in considering the circumstances and significance of Britain's withdrawal from India we are not dealing with an episode with well-defined boundaries and clear-cut features that the historian can map and lay before us. Rather, it is a matter of perspective – like the view of a landscape – and as such the novelist is at least as likely to produce an insightful picture.

This applies with particular force in the realm of the psycho-social, one aspect of which is plumbed by the metaphor of the Indo-British relationship. In the years after 1947, British writers were drawn to explore the parting of the ways in terms of a rupturing of the emotional entanglement between Britain and India. Indian writers have been less directly concerned with Britain's withdrawal as a subject in its own right. Rather, the focus of their attention has been on its legacies such as neo-colonialism, the horror of partition or the predicament of the princes. None the less, in their treatment of the consequences of British rule, they have been drawn to reflect on the strength of feeling, the emotional affinities and sense of outrage which were part of the imperial experience. For nearly all writers the 1940s provided an incentive to take a longer perspective and re-examine thinking about the earlier state of the Indo-British connection in the light of withdrawal. Was the edifice of a special relationship between the two peoples built on sand? Was it always the case that sentiment counted for little when weighed against cultural difference and political advantage? Could affinity ever have had much meaning in a situation of structured inequality?

In *The Raj Quartet* Paul Scott wrestles with such questions leading us first in one direction and then in another, so that by the end of the *Quartet* very little ground is left uncovered. The four novels are therefore a source of primary importance for our purposes and will provide the frame of our inquiry. Despite belated recognition and some sharp dissent,[98] the position taken here is that Scott's work is a major contribution to the literary study of the psychology of imperialism. That his novels, and even more the television series which followed, won a popular audience and that they resonate with the contemporary nostalgia for empire in some quarters in no way gainsays their seriousness of purpose or imaginative reach. Scott's work is especially relevant to us in that he attempts to catch the measure of Indo-British politics and the culture of imperialism in the lives of his characters. More than this, Scott's interest in the demise of the Raj leads him to reflect on its heyday – to probe its meaning and content when the surface appearance was very different. This he does by presenting his characters as embodying certain traditions – such as that of the regiment or the evangelical ideal – and imbuing many of them with a sense of history so that the past is seldom out of view. In this way *The Raj Quartet* is an inquiry into the whole experience of the Raj, not simply its final chapter. A parallel may be drawn with Anthony Burgess's Malayan trilogy, *The Long Day Wanes*.

In the *Quartet* Scott writes within the tradition of portraying Britain's involvement in India as a relationship of the kind that exists between individuals. The narrator sets the scene on the very first page; the two nations were:

locked in an imperial embrace of such long standing and subtlety it was no longer possible for them to know whether they hated or loved one another, or what it was that held them together and seemed to have confused the image of their separate destinies.[99]

This is a crucial sentence not only about the relationship between the two nations but also because it provides the first clue to Scott's approach to historical interpretation. Before there can be any detached commentary, we must be exposed to the raw experience and especially to the emotions involved. Three volumes later Scott puts his position tautly. Guy Perron, himself an historian, warns against 'that liberal instinct which is so dear to historians that they lay it out like a guideline through the unmapped forests of prejudice and self-interest as though this line, and not the forest, is our history'.[100]

Having begun with the idea of a relationship involving love, and with the text punctuated with reminders either directly by the characters or by the authorial voice about the emotional bonds between Britain and India, we are confronted with a paradox. In the story itself there is much less than we might expect about relationships involving love between English and Indians. Indeed, for the most part there is little personal engagement or even open communication. The relationship between Daphne and Kumar, upon which so much hinges, falls into a category of its own because Kumar is Indian only by birth. 'He is an English boy with a dark brown skin', declared Mr Gopal, who assisted at the inquiry reviewing Kumar's detention.[101] Several of the English characters felt the same, though it was something they could not admit even to themselves. At one stage Connie White, the wife of the Deputy Commissioner, observes to Daphne that she could have understood Kumar's silence better had he been an Englishman. Daphne laughed, yet she longed to be able to say 'But Harry is an Englishman.'

Except for this one deliberately ambiguous case, only rarely do characters in the *Quartet* manage to express or respond to feelings across the racial and cultural boundary. One instance is the growth of understanding between Sarah Layton and Ahmed Kassim which is heartfelt if circumscribed. Another is when Deputy Commissioner White felt he had been given back his humanity by an unknown middle-aged Indian woman who fed him curds when he was ill and disillusioned with India. Alongside the few illustrations of spontaneous feeling are the accounts of individuals who wished or attempted to reach out but failed. Edwina Crane was only able to trust and relate naturally to Mr Chaudhuri, her Indian subordinate, at the eleventh hour when it was too late. Barbie Batchelor develops a genuine affection for an eight-year-old lad in the bazaar who runs her messages, yet she realizes that on neither side do the feelings run deep. Knowing Ashok will not be able to understand, she says in English:

I clasp you to my breast but you conceive of this in terms of an authority unbending. I offer my love. You accept it as a sign of fortune smiling. Your heart beats with gratitude, excitement, expectation of rupees. And mine scarcely beats at all.[102]

So far as the English are concerned, Scott makes plain his view that ideas about race and rule together constitute the lock on the community's ability to respond and that the key has been turned by history. The English in India are required to play a role. Even Miss Crane, who until the war 'had not gone out much in European society' and who was thought by the ladies of Mayapore to be 'cranky about the natives', had curbed her tongue. This made her feel unnatural: 'When you chose your words the spontaneity went out of the things you wanted to say.'[103] Mabel Layton explains to Barbie Batchelor that she has become 'something of a recluse but of course that's not possible in India, for *us*. Even when we are alone we're on show, aren't we, representing something?'[104] Scott is more hesitant about pronouncing on the reasons for Indian role-playing but he gives the impression that this is something which flowed from the colonial situation – partly a matter of fear, but also of living up to expectations. In addition, there is a suggestion that the sense of *'pre-arranged* emotions and reactions' owed something to Indians' use of a foreign language.[105]

The question arises of how we are to understand the regimental tie between officer and soldier. The notion of 'man-bap' – I am your father and your mother – has a wider application than simply within the army. Indeed it can be seen as expressing the essence of the relationship of the Raj to India. But in the *Quartet* it is considered primarily with respect to the regiment. Believing in the old code, Teddy Bingham meets his death attempting to win back former Muzzafir Guides who collaborated with the Japanese after being taken prisoner of war. We understand that man-bap no longer meant to Indian soldiers what apparently it had meant before. We ponder, along with Sarah, whether Merrick himself was not in love with the legend despite his professional rejection of it as a myth. What we have to accept is that the Raj proper clung to the old faith because it had no alternative. Yet the man-bap creed was about duty rather than love; it was the institution that mattered more than the parties. Merrick is right when he says of Teddy's action in Burma: 'He wasn't doing it for himself or for them [the former Muzzie Guides]. He did it for the regiment.'[106]

A more fundamental question concerns the understanding and significance of rape. In the first page of the *Quartet*, immediately before the passage already quoted, we are told 'This is the story of a rape.' In part this is so, but in much larger part it is not. Above all, the *Quartet* is a story of a love that was never realized. Scott could have given more weight to the violation side by broadening out the character of Ronald Merrick or by narrowing his presentation of the Raj so that the two came together, or even by giving Brigadier Reid a larger role. But he did none of these things for the very good reason that they would have run counter to his larger vision. On the evidence of his notebook entries, Scott's first thought was to use rape or imagined rape as a device to explode pent-up fear.[107] There are elements of this in the *Quartet*, but essentially rape is seen in its own terms as a deformity of mind and spirit.

Much of the difficulty about rape as a political symbol in the novels lies in its separation from the other side of the Raj, which holds up the ideal of love. This is compounded by the reversal of racial roles in the rape in the gardens of the Bibighar[108] (the site, incidentally, indicating again the difficulties about place that imperialism puts in the way of relationships across the colour line). The symbolism here is of an Indian assault in response to the British conquest – a reference back to Cawnpore. However, the 'rape' which carries real political significance for Scott's purposes is Merrick's assault on Hari Kumar. In her journal addressed to Lady Manners, Daphne indicates the road from the one to the other, but without a close reading it would be easy to take a wrong turning.[109] All the time wanting Hari, Daphne writes: 'I thought that the whole bloody affair of *us* in India had reached flash point. It was bound to because it was based on a violation.'[110] Much later in her journal she continues:

> *Well, there has been more than one rape.* I can't say, Auntie, that I lay back and enjoyed mine. But Lili was trying to lie back and enjoy what we've done to her country. I don't mean done in malice. Perhaps there was love. Oh, somewhere, in the past, and now, and in the future, love as there was between me and Hari. But the spoilers are always there, aren't they?[111]

These journal musings are supported by other references in the text to the historical record, most notably a nomenclature which ties Daphne's rape to the massacre at Cawnpore in 1857, and the sexual assault on Hari to the slaughter at Amritsar in 1919. The play on words is perhaps too contrived. That it is resorted to at all shows the length to which Scott has to go to ensure that the violations in the *Quartet* are seen in their true perspective in relation to the history of British India.

There is a surety of touch about Scott's use of homosexuality as a political symbol which cannot be said of rape.[112] Allen Boyer has pointed out that characters who are homosexual are given insight into the true nature of imperialism; they understand India and the realities of imperial rule better than the heterosexual characters.[113] The roll-call includes Count Bronowsky, Corporal Dixon, the unnamed 'theatrical' lieutenant who had participated in the action to put down the Mayapore riots, and, of course, Ronald Merrick. The lesson appears to be that not only do these homosexual characters have the keen eye of the outsider, but that having come to terms with themselves in difficult circumstances they are able to pierce through imperialism's deceptions and myths, especially racism. As a result, they are able to see Indians as people and imperialism as a problem of human relations. The position is rather different with Ronald Merrick because it is not until he has made love to Aziz (or so Bronowsky believes) that he grasps the implications of his failure to face up to his homosexual and sado-masochistic tendencies. Bronowsky speaks of the 'revelation of the connection between the homosexuality, the sado-masochism, the sense of social inferiority and the grinding defensive belief in his racial superiority'.[114] Until then Merrick is shown to be a man who largely cuts through the liberal niceties and paternalistic pretensions, but because of his inner fear and self-denial adheres to a code of rigid authoritarianism, his sense of professionalism masking the violence of his methods. Other elements in his make-up are revealed when Sarah tells herself that he is in love with the legends of the Raj, and when he confesses to her that for a moment with Teddy Bingham at Imphal he fell for the dream of man-bap.[115] That Merrick does not entirely conform to a model of all that was wrong with the Raj is a tribute to Scott's commitment to 'Get *at the people*, come up from underneath them if you possibly can.'[116]

The fundamental insight that emerges from all this material is that the Indo-British relationship exists as an idea rather than an actuality. It is an ideal to which homage is paid. It gives rise to codes of conduct. There is an emotional investment built up over time. But it certainly does not express how English and Indians felt towards each other. Nor does it reflect the true measure of the interaction between the two peoples. In the idea of the relationship India at best figures in the abstract; it is always at a distance and can never be experienced in its own terms. Daphne catches something of this when she writes to Lady Manners about Miss Crane. 'She loved India and all Indians but no particular Indian . . . she made friendships in her head most of the time and seldom in her heart.'[117]

Mostly, however, India is not much more than a background and Indians, with occasional exceptions, are the material with which the British in India constructed ideas about themselves. The real relationship with which Scott is concerned is Britain and its idea of itself. This has several facets: there are the differences between the Raj and the society at home; the tension within some Anglo-Indians such as Daphne and Sarah between their sense of self and the requirement to live what Sarah calls 'a received life'; and the differences between the proconsular ethic represented in part by Brigadier Reid and the liberal ideal exemplified by Robin White. The *Quartet* can thus be seen as a case study exploring Said's orientalist thesis, but instead of one dominant idea which subsumes all others, Scott teases from the material a multiplicity of meanings. In place of a simple model of binary opposites, Anglo-India is interposed and becomes a centre containing within it the strains and dilemmas of the colonial connection. And far from the orientalist exercise being functional, at least in terms of power and identity, the *Quartet* leads us to the conclusion that it was profoundly dysfunctional. There is the disintegration of so many of the Anglo-Indian characters, an acute sense of Britain's moral loss and, for India, a legacy of political disorder and psychological disorientation.

The classic statement of Scott's thesis is given by Guy Perron, introduced in the fourth volume of the *Quartet* to weave a pattern from the many and often divergent threads that Scott has laid before us. He writes:

> For at least a hundred years India has formed part of England's idea about herself and for the same period India has been forced into a position of being a reflection

of that idea. Up to say 1900 the part India played in our idea about ourselves was the part played by anything we possessed which we believed it was right to possess (like a special relationship with God). Since 1900, certainly since 1918, the reverse has obtained. The part played since then by India in the English idea of Englishness has been that of something we feel it does us no credit to have. Our idea about ourselves will now not accommodate any idea about India except the idea of returning it to the Indians in order to prove that we are English and have demonstrably English ideas . . . But on either side of that arbitrary date (1900) India itself, as itself, that is to say India as not part of our idea of ourselves, has played no part whatsoever in the lives of Englishmen in general (no part that we are conscious of) and those who came out (those for whom India had to play a real part) became detached both from English life and from the English idea of life. Getting rid of India will cause us at home no qualm of conscience because it will be like getting rid of what is no longer reflected in our mirror of ourselves. The sad thing is that whereas in the English mirror there is now no Indian reflection . . . in the Indian mirror the English reflection may be very hard to get rid of, because in the Indian mind English possession has not been an idea but a reality; often a harsh one.[118]

This passage is central to an understanding of Scott's purpose because of both its evocative power and its concentrated meaning. The way that attention is directed to ideas of the self and the use of the metaphor of reflections in a mirror suggest that, despite the seriousness with which Scott took his role as a historian, as a novelist he aimed to do something more. The task he set himself, it seems to me, was to uncover the essence of what the British experienced in India and, in a more limited, almost incidental way, what some Indians experienced through British rule, and to range these against the parties' innate sense of Englishness or Indianness. Patrick Swinden makes a similar point in more general terms when he asserts: 'Though the surface of his [Scott's] novel is historical, . . . at its core it is metaphysical.'[119]

Seen in this light, *The Raj Quartet* invites comparison with Raja Rao's *The Serpent and the Rope*, though the latter is much less concerned with the empirics of the East–West encounter and carries its inward orientation and metaphysical bent a great deal further. This novel, which hinges on the conflict between illusion and reality (the serpent and the rope respectively), takes as its ostensible subject the marriage between Rama, a South Indian Brahmin, and Madeleine, a French girl with Catholicism 'in her blood', who turns from atheism to Buddhism. The story is told through the musings of Rama, who intertwines the disintegration of the marriage with debates about religious philosophy and the experiences of his travels within and between India and Europe. Two related features of the novel have a relevance here. The first is that the failure of the marriage is due, not to external differences such as colour and nationality or even Madeleine's decision to become a Buddhist nun, but to the philosophical make-up and ingrained values of the two parties which flow from their different religious and cultural backgrounds. There could be no genuine and lasting union between the two individuals because they lived in separate worlds. This was especially true of Rama. Sincerity and understanding were not enough to bridge the gulf created by his Indian sensibility and Vedantist detachment. The second insight offered by the novel, which parallels what I take to be Scott's position, is that the historian cannot penetrate the deeper layers of meaning of certain situations and phenomena. The problem is that the historian comes armed with objectivity and the idea of time-sequence and these may not get to the nub of the matter. This perception is beautifully illustrated by Rama's reflections about the River Cam in Cambridge, which seemed to him never to have grown old: 'for the Cam like us men and women flows right in herself, outside of history . . . The Cam is silent and self-reflective. It teaches you that history is made by others and not by oneself.'[120]

Keeping these ideas in mind, let us return to the picture Perron sketched of the relationship between England and India. He identifies three parties – the English at home, the Anglo-Indians and the Indians – for all of whom the touchstone was their idea of themselves. For the people at home, India did not count in its own right. Earlier Perron had played with the idea that India did not count at all; perhaps it was an illusion that the two peoples had ever coincided. 'If so, then the *raj* was, is, itself an illusion so far as the English are concerned.'[121] Dissatisfied, he crossed this out. No, India mattered in that its possession was an expression of English ideas about moral responsibility. Here we might note that Perron's vignette leaves out of account rather different viewpoints which Scott has presented in other parts of the *Quartet*. Robin White, for example, raises the issue of the relationship between moralism and power which, as he sees it, underlies British attitudes to their 'prize'. From time to time we get suggestions of a pride of possession along the lines of a John Masters novel. Later we are introduced to the idea that Britain's withdrawal proceeded on the basis of ignorance and indifference, or even pragmatism, rather than any ethical conviction that imperialism was immoral. Perron himself observes that it would never have occurred to his Aunt Charlotte to examine her conscience in regard to the quarter of a million deaths in the Punjab at partition.[122]

Perron has much less to say about the position of the English who worked and lived in India – presumably because so much is already clear. India played a real part in their lives. They became detached from English life and the English idea of life. Perron adds a postscript: 'people like the Laytons may now see nothing at all when looking in their mirror. Not even themselves? Not even a mirror?'[123] The problem, we understand, is that, being detached from English life and only involved in a very restricted way in Indian life (for reasons of race and rule), the English in India had to manufacture a sense of identity. Their world had to be shored up, in part by artificial means. The sense of community was carefully cultivated – we are reminded of Kipling's story of the four Englishmen who tried to meet each Sunday though they were not conscious of any special regard for each other.[124] There was the need to have a sense of purpose. Yet it could not be articulated lest it crack or appear hollow. Mrs Smalley broke the code but got to the heart of the matter when she voiced her opinion of Sarah Layton to the ladies of Pankot.

> '. . . the trouble is she doesn't really take it seriously . . .'
> After an appreciable pause Mrs Paynton inquired, 'Take what seriously?'
> 'Any of it,' Mrs Smalley said. 'Us, India. What we're here for.'[125]

Encouraged to continue, Mrs Smalley sums up by saying, 'I think the best way I can describe it is to say that sometimes she looked at me as if I were, well, not a real person.'[126]

Perron's final thought is that the Indians may find it difficult to rid themselves of the experience of English possession. Here Perron ventures beyond the main concerns of the *Quartet*, which are of course the experiences and perspectives of the British, so we cannot evaluate his statement in the context of Scott's narrative as a whole. Accordingly we must look more widely, taking particular account of fiction written by Indians. I want to argue that Perron is persuasive when he says that 'in the Indian mirror the English reflection may be very hard to get rid of', but that his reasoning is much less so. His liberalism has led him to settle for too narrow an approach. It is not so much that English possession had often been harsh (which is undoubtedly true) but that the experience was intense. English possession was certainly a reality in the Indian mind but it was an idea as well. The literature on the psychology of colonialism makes plain the deep ambivalence that so often characterized the response of subject peoples. Perhaps nowhere was the imperial experience more deeply felt than in India, nor the ambivalence sharper. This was not because Indians were more or less brutalized and humiliated than other colonial peoples or because the Raj was more or less beneficent than other imperial administrations. The ambivalence would seem to stem from the very length of the imperial connection – 150 years or more; the unique nature of the Raj with its unparalleled degree of autonomy from the metropole and its distinctive identification with the territory; and India's own cultural traditions which made Indians especially receptive to the internalization of external ideas and values.

There was every reason to expect, therefore, that the experience of British imperialism would endure in the Indian mind and that the images would not simply be negative. The body of Indian fiction in English dealing with the British withdrawal and its aftermath provides confirmation on both counts and in fact goes further. Making allowance for the exceptions and the qualifications, the tendency is for the Raj to be presented in a favourable light, whereas the anti-imperial struggle and the post-independence order it produced are disparaged. The British, who might have been held responsible for much that went wrong with the transfer of power, emerge fairly creditably. Those who risked most in the freedom struggle gain least from the fictional record. In the view of one Indian scholar, the mood of the novels ranges from 'light self-criticism to stark pessimism'.[127]

Before elaborating on these contentions, we should situate the novels of the post-independence period in relation to the terms of inquiry of this chapter. As with so much Indian fiction of the inter-war years, most of the novels we are about to consider are palpably political. It is not a matter of reading between the lines or searching for a hidden meaning, because the texts flag their position with respect to both British rule and the freedom struggle. In large part the politics of the novels are expressed through the lives of Indian protagonists. Some Indian characters are identified with or made representative of the Raj. Others are taken to signify aspects of the anti-imperial struggle. It is in the contrasts and patterns of interaction between the protagonists that the historiography of the text is most likely to emerge. In many of the novels there are also British characters, but usually they have minor parts and their presence is more to elicit Indian responses than to make a substantive contribution in their own right. It is notable, however, that surprisingly often British characters are drawn sympathetically, as if to emphasize the positive aspects of British rule. One thinks of Sergeant Davidson in Chaman Nahal's *Azadi*; Nahal's fictional creation of Kenneth Ashby, the Assistant Commissioner of Amritsar, who is counterpoised to Brigadier-General Dyer in *The Crown and the Loincloth*; Deputy Commissioner Taylor and his wife, Joyce, in Khushwant Singh's *I Shall Not Hear the Nightingale*; Mathieson in R. K. Narayan's *Waiting for the Mahatma*; Richard in Kamala Markandaya's *Some Inner Fury*.

Following the terms of our inquiry thus far, we might expect that a picture of the Indo-British relationship would emerge from the various categories of interpersonal behaviour deployed in the texts. In fact many of the categories form an intrinsic part of the narratives and they have some significance, but they are not the primary means of representation. Manohar Malgonkar makes use of rape as a political symbol in *A Bend in the Ganges*. Debi-dayal's hatred of the British and his resort to terrorism is attributed not to considerations of national politics, but to the attempted rape of his mother by a drunken British soldier. Debi hurled himself at the man, thus enabling his mother to flee. The soldier turned on Debi, dismissing him as 'You damned little squirt!' – a humiliation which rankled for years.[128] However, as a number of critics have observed, Malgonkar subverts the symbolism by suggesting that Debi's mother had not been unwilling; later, in bed with her husband, she whispered her fantasy that he was 'a big, red-faced soldier smelling of drink'.[129]

At the other end of the spectrum, in some of the novels romantic love serves to link the personal lives of the protagonists with the politics of the freedom struggle. In Kamala Markandaya's *Some Inner Fury* it is the impossibility of realizing his love for Premala which leads Govind to turn to terrorism in the struggle against the British. Yet Premala becomes a victim of that very violence and Govind can never be free of guilt. There is also the relationship between Mira, the narrator, and her English friend Richard, which becomes a casualty of the hatred engendered by the 'Quit India' movement. Thus the freedom movement destroys as it advances, and there is a tone of regret in the text not only about the personal losses but also about the Indo-British separation.

A third strategy which locates the political in the personal focuses on relationships within the family unit. This is the approach adopted by Khushwant Singh in *I Shall Not Hear the Nightingale*, a novel that depicts the strains and loyalties within a Sikh family at the time of the 'Quit India' movement. Sher Singh, the only son of a magistrate who is a pragmatic supporter of the Raj, becomes involved with a college terrorist group. His attraction to revolutionary politics is explained in terms of personality problems related to his family situation: Sher Singh was indulged as a child and later made to feel sexually inadequate by his wife. In *The Crown and the Loincloth*, Chaman Nahal makes very different use of the family motif, and the relationship between the personal and the politics is presented with much more subtlety. The novel, which is set in the period 1915 to 1922, tells the story of a large, well-to-do Punjabi family which is taken to be a microcosm of India as a whole. The lives of the patriarch, Thakur Shanti Nath, his wife and their eight children and spouses contain within them all the strands of India's response to British rule over these years. Accommodation and pride, revolutionary violence, and Gandhism and non-cooperation are thus presented in relation to one another and as growing out of India's history and culture.

It is tempting to extend our discussion of interpersonal behaviour and examine the political significance of subcategories such as the father–son or mother–child relationship or even the rather different case of the relationship between officer and man. Fundamentally, however, the point stands that the politics of these novels emerges less from the categories of interpersonal relations than from the qualities of character invested in the protagonists. What requires to be addressed is the tendency for strength of character to be associated with doubts about the liberation struggle, and weakness of character to be run together with the determination to drive the British out of India with all possible speed. What is significant here is that in the texts the qualities of character to be admired are mostly tied to a world-view which purports to be apolitical or even anti-political. By and large, the abnegation of politics is associated with moral rectitude; the pursuit of politics is tainted with corruption and carries the risk of harmful consequences.

In essence, then, the value of the British connection is seen to reside in the distance the Raj kept from politics. That the Raj was intensely political is of course obvious to all of us, but in the narratives recognition recedes because the politics that are elevated are those between Indian protagonists – as, for example, during partition. At this point I want to draw attention to certain features in the literature which powerfully promote the illusion of non-political politics. These are action and adventure, the Army code, and the position of the peasant. It is conceded that all three are extreme cases; they represent the high-water mark of the challenge to nationalist historiography. More usually, the politics of Indian nationalism are questioned rather than rejected; the texts are ambiguous, not declaratory.

Action and adventure are exemplified in the novels of Khushwant Singh and Manohar Malgonkar. Their heroes are men who live by the deed and not the word; they are passionate, direct, violent if need be. In Khushwant Singh's *Train to Pakistan*, Juggut Singh (known as 'Jugga', the scoundrel) saves the train to Pakistan and loses his own life because of his love for a Muslim woman, Nooran, with whom he slept in the fields. Jugga's sturdy independence and resourcefulness are contrasted with the impotence of India's new political leaders and the immobility and inner confusion of Iqbal Singh, the armchair revolutionary, softened by Western education and city life. But if Khushwant Singh prompts us to reconsider the politics of India's independence, Manohar Malgonkar's revisionism is explicit. His commitment to heroic action is more politically directed. His ostensible distaste for politics is a distaste for the new politics, not the old which masquerade as just rule. His fourth novel, *A Bend in the Ganges*, is of particular interest because it sweeps across the great dramas of the 1930s and 1940s, beginning with Gandhi and the freedom movement and ending with the blood-letting of partition. As if to match the breadth of canvas, the brush strokes of Malgonkar's politics are large and obvious. Character after character attests to the honesty of the British and the impartiality of British rule. All too often Indians are shown to be weak, grasping and self-indulgent. Non-violence might have been seen as a sham but it is reviled because it led directly to the violence of partition. The fact that the novel is a story of high adventure only adds to its historiographical impact.

The position of the Army is central to Malgonkar's vision. The Army is above politics: it represents order, integrity and responsibility. In both *Distant Drum* and *Bandicoot Run* Lieutenant-Colonel – later Major-General – Kiran ('call me Jacko, dammit') Garud personifies the code of the regiment which is under threat from the new tendencies in Indian public life.[130] In *Distant Drum* the challenge is represented by the figures of Mr Sonal, a devious senior civil servant, and Lala Vishnu Saran Dev, a small-time political operator. Their types are sufficiently familiar for the distinguished literary scholar Srinivasa Iyengar to write that 'one must still hope that men like Mr Sonal are the exceptions and not the rule', and that although the portrait of Lala is caricature, 'one knows also that there *are* such Lalas all over the country'.[131]

In *A Bend in the Ganges*, Malgonkar directs attention to an even more insidious challenge to the military order – the Indian National Army. Because it represents the intrusion of politics – and the very worst kind of politics – into the military sphere, the INA gets short shrift. Any attempt to understand the motivations of the men who collaborated with the Japanese is debarred by the images in which they are presented. The INA Brigadier was

> soft and fat and dripping with perspiration . . . His proximity brought on a creeping sense of revulsion. He was the embodiment of all that was servile in India . . . How many such creatures did India possess? Thousands upon thousands. Was that why he had looked so familiar – the picture of India's ingrained, traditional servility?[132]

Such heavy-handedness in a writer of very considerable skill must raise the question of whether the text does not contain a sub-text about the author's own sense of identity. Personally as well as for the army collective, the rejection of Indian aspects of self was perhaps a necessary accompaniment to the reassertion of essentially British values and traditions.[133] Generally, however, throughout the novel the die is so loaded that only one viewpoint really emerges. The reader is given little incentive to consider the historical complexity of the issues, let alone to feel the pull of an anti-imperialist position. As critics have observed of this and other Malgonkar novels, those characters who are opposed to the authorial viewpoint never become fully realized.[134] We are more likely to be given entry to the minds of characters favoured by Malgonkar, but even then there is little sense of contending forces or of alternative possibilities.

In several of the novels we have been considering, the peasant speaks in favour of British rule and his voice is given special authority. Through the character of Sunil Kumar in *The Crown and the Loincloth*, Chaman Nahal situates the response of the peasants within their historical experience. Sunil has had little success in mobilizing the Dalits ('untouchables') and other villagers in the Simla Hills to the Gandhian cause. They, like millions of other Indians, were uninterested in any political change. In a lengthy meditation, Sunil reflects on why this was so. All that most of them had known was instability and insecurity. The British, for all their sins, had elevated them to the status of citizens, albeit of the second class. The Dalits were a special case, because they had a barren present as well as a barren past, but for the rest:

> They knew what awaited them if the British left. Anarchy. Of the worst kind. Reversal to primitivism and barbarism, the memories of which were still with them.[135]

This was precisely the response of the villagers of Mano Majra in *Train to Pakistan*. Iqbal's anti-imperialist strictures meant nothing to those Punjabi villagers who held to the view that British rule had at least afforded security and stability – which was more than could be said of the Indian succession.

In *A Bend in the Ganges*, Manohar Malgonkar goes further than this. His peasants do not react to the great issues of the day simply on the basis of their marginalization; their views flow naturally from their very nature and values which are rooted in the soil itself. As such, they speak with an authenticity; they are the voice of the real India. Early in the novel when Gian, one of the two key characters, is drawn to Gandhism, the old family servant, Tukaram asks whether he has joined the cranks who want to send away the sahibs. 'What will we do without the sahibs,' he exclaims, 'they don't take bribes like our people.'[136] Then Gian is told by his brother, Hari: 'We in India can get justice only at British hands – never from our own people.'[137] The key point, however, is that due to his peasant background Gian soon abandons Gandhism and settles for an 'anti-political' stance. We are meant to understand that as a peasant Gian has stability and common sense, whereas his opposite number, Debi-dayal, is rootless and given to political daydreaming. Shed of his Gandhian politics, Gian becomes true to type. In the tradition of British imperial fiction, this leaves him free to admire British rule. At one stage he reflects:

> It was amazing how the Empire worked, held its sway. With a crop of honest selfless officers at the top, and hordes of corrupt, subhuman, minor officials at the bottom. Was that the India of the Indians? What would happen if the steel frame of British officialdom was ever removed, when India became free and her people held full sway?[138]

Mostly, of course, the revisionism of the post-independence texts is more moderate and less explicit. This is the case with R. K. Narayan – though in this respect as in others his work has a distinctive stamp of its own. Narayan's concern is not to proffer an alternative politics to the authorized Indian version of decolonization but to put the politics of the period in the context of ordinary life and everyday affairs. In his view, during the years of nationalist agitation the subject matter of fiction 'became inescapably political . . . the mood of comedy, the sensitivity to atmosphere, the probing of psychological factors, the crisis in the individual soul and its resolution, and above all the detached observation, which constitute the stuff of fiction, were forced into the background.'[139] As if to put the record straight, after independence he wrote *Waiting for the Mahatma*,[140] which revisited the nationalist struggle, and the short story 'Lawley Road', which reassessed the meaning of independence. In both texts the public face of nationalism is shown to mask quite different private concerns and interests. In *Waiting for the Mahatma*, Sriram's attempt to follow the Mahatma is motivated by his infatuation with Bharati. In 'Lawley Road' the Municipal Chairman's determination to get rid of the statue of Sir Frederick Lawley sprang from his listlessness after the independence celebrations, once the processions were over and the bunting was torn off. In both texts it further appears that the British connection is more deeply embedded in Indian life and more likely to endure than the politics of decolonization would indicate. In *Waiting for the Mahatma* the old order – of which the Raj was an integral part – is signified by Sriram's Granny, who does not ask 'why or how and why not' and who does not like the idea of the Mahatma. As Gomathi Narayanan has pointed out, Granny's revival at the cremation ground after her funeral pyre has been lit, attests to the continuance of the old along with the new.[141] In 'Lawley Road' the message is even clearer. The Council finds that a vigorous resolution is not enough to topple the statue of Sir Frederick Lawley because it stood with the firmness of a mountain. 'They realized that Britain, when she was here, had attempted to raise herself on no mean foundation.'[142] More than this, the record establishes that Sir Frederick was a heroic figure in the history of Malgudi, not, as had earlier been surmised, a tyrant who subjugated Indians by the sword. As a result, the Municipal Chairman is required to reinstate the statue as a present to the nation.

In so many respects the themes and representations of Indo-British literature after 1947 cut across the grain of contemporary postcolonial appreciations. The temptation is therefore to pass over the material or simply dismiss it. It is possible to sweep the texts aside as an aberration – the outpouring of those who have lost touch with their culture, who lack a sense of belonging to their national grouping. Hence the view partially endorsed by Pritish Nandy that Indian writing in English is 'a rootless literature, totally alienated from the people, unconcerned with Indian realities'.[143] Travelling along this road, another Indian commentator reaches the extraordinary conclusion that 'Unlike their African brethren, [Indo-English novelists] have not been generally able to create an authentic literature out of their separate experiences.'[144] But the assumption here is surely that there exists a real or essential India, which draws its full quota of meaning from within itself and its own past. Another approach is to take the material with due seriousness but minimize its historiographical significance by interpreting it psychologically. What we are dealing with, it is understood, is the phenomenon of Indian identification with the imperial father and the resultant sense of loss and feeling of guilt once the British are driven out. The relevance of such psychological processes is undoubted, but, as I have suggested much earlier in this chapter, the distinction between the true and the false self can seldom in the end be sustained, and in any case involves political choices. These require open examination, all the more so if they appear to represent the natural order of things.

Even if we accept rootlessness, alienation and dependency as characteristic features of much post-independence fiction in English, all three are tools of political analysis, not simply matters for moral judgement or psycho-social probing. What they reveal is that just as the imperial project was unrealizable, so was the nationalist counter-project. By August 1947 the external had been to some degree internalized. As a result, the old seeped into the new and aspects of the self remained entangled with the other.

To draw together and extend the main themes of this section, we might return to our starting-point, which was the quotation from Naipaul to the effect that politics can only be an extension of ideas about human relationships. As pursued here, three aspects or implications should be singled out: whose relationships and which politics are under discussion; the political as an expression of the personal; and the allegorical role of categories of interpersonal relations. With respect to the first, the narratives with which we have been concerned do not address British and Indian societies as a whole or the full measure of interaction between the two countries. Their focus is more on the upper echelons of both societies and the exchange and interconnection between them, than on the ordinary British man or woman at home or Indians going about their everyday lives. This must be acknowledged as a limitation of our sources. But neither should we marginalize the special relationship of élites in the Indo-British context, after the style of Rushdie's description of the Raj as a pimple on the face of India. Indeed, there has been much here to suggest that concerns and processes at the top often worked their way more broadly into society and that, correspondingly, élite politics were to some degree shaped by what was happening below or at home. Moreover, I would argue that the stories that are told about élites have a powerful bearing on wider and longer-term issues: in the British case, the process of decolonization generally and the difficulties of adjustment to a post-imperial role; in the Indian case, the accommodation with the processes of international in place of imperial exchange, modernity, and the globalization of culture. But to pursue these matters we would need to take account of other source material. Following Said's *Culture and Imperialism*, for example, we might turn to metropolitan culture and narratives not directly concerned with the overseas involvement. With respect to the Indian underclasses it would be necessary to engage with subaltern studies and narratives written in the regional languages.

Implicit in these comments is the awareness that the fictional narratives in English – like all source material – have their elements of in-built bias. To develop a point made a few paragraphs back, their concern with British India and with the British in India would be considered by many to be excessive and their response to the Raj unrepresentative of all shades of opinion (especially Indian). There is no gainsaying that there are problems here, but there is also the compensation that the narratives provide a counter to the romanticization of resistance in some quarters and the selective thematic engagement of much postcolonial discourse. At several points in our discussion, the prescience of the fictional texts has been noted. One aspect which is relevant here is the tendency of the texts to puncture or run together categories that have for a long time structured academic analysis: imperialism and nationalism, collaboration and resistance. Very often the narratives have brought out the ambivalence of the imperial relationship and the extent to which attitudes and action do not bifurcate neatly at the imperial divide. To this extent they have anticipated those contemporary expressions of discontent with the binarism which has left such a mark on historical studies and theoretical postulates.

In his remarkable essay published over forty years ago, Nirad Chaudhuri rejected the relevance of the personal as an exposition of the political. Writing of *A Passage to India*, Chaudhuri took issue with Forster's 'tacit but confident assumption that Indo-British relations presented a problem of personal behaviour and could be tackled on the personal plane'.[145] His commentary is provocative in several respects even as his central contention fails to satisfy. As has been pointed out before, his rejection of the personal is in part couched in personal terms. Chaudhuri differs from Forster with respect to his characterization of British officials – they were not quite so absurd and certainly they had no lack of courage – and he takes strong exception to Forster's depiction of Indians: 'Aziz would not have been allowed to cross my threshold'.[146] Proceeding along these lines, Chaudhuri argues that the ideas and values which lie at the root of historical change cannot be comprehended in terms of personal grievances. Perhaps so, but as we have seen in this section the personal is not limited to humiliation or ingratiation. On the contrary, it can embrace many of the basic issues and processes of which account needs to be taken, including modernization and Westernization (which Chaudhuri sees as pivotal) as well as the complications engendered by rule, race and culture.

More than this, what the fictional narratives establish is that in many respects the personal is political or represents an extension of the political. This applies most obviously to gender and sexuality, but scarcely less so to the geography and sociology of British India – the politics of place and association. To hark back to the formulation of one of the questions posed at the beginning of this chapter, we can say that it is not so much that political and social processes are telescoped into the lives of individuals as that the personalization of issues brings unexpected aspects into focus and hence broadens our conception of what is politics. Of course, given the personal orientation of the texts, there are shortcomings and omissions – with respect to power and economics, for example – and their significance will be addressed in the penultimate chapter.

All of this points in the direction of a challenge to orthodoxy, in that the personalization of the Indo-British connection in the fictional narratives brings to the surface elements of a shared culture between the parties; at various stages sections of each national grouping were implicated in the hopes and designs of the other. In the vocabulary of postcolonialism, there were elements of intimacy in the encounter – though to my mind the word 'intimacy' is suspect because so often the engagement between the parties was cut short, not fully realized, or was more an idea than an actuality. Even accepting these qualifications, the weighting placed on rejection and resistance, both customarily and in a different form in many postcolonial analyses, needs to be lessened to take account of the strands of collusion and complicity. On this basis we might well conclude that the Indo-British relationship was in many of its aspects distinctive, and that the practice of seeing it as reflective of imperial overlordship generally and the process of Third World decolonization needs to be problematized.

Throughout this section I have singled out categories derived from interpersonal behaviour as a characteristic and revealing way of using the personal to probe the political. In this regard, the British and Indian narratives lend no support to Jameson's contention of a fundamental difference between First and Third World texts. With few exceptions, both British and Indian narratives projected a political dimension and their allegorical role was similar. As a broad generalization, categories of interpersonal behaviour tended to be employed when events in the public realm had taken or seemed likely to take an unwelcome turn, the rationale being that resort to the private sphere provided a means of reviewing the situation from a different angle in the hope that it might be changed – though change often related simply to historiographical revision.

Viewed from the perspective of their scholarly contribution, no blanket judgement about the utility of categories of interpersonal relations can do justice to the material we have considered. When such categories are employed literally, as it were, they lack conviction and operate as a form of closure. This is true of the use of love and marriage by our three Indian novelists in the first decade of this century. Of course, in such cases, the way that personal metaphors block out unwanted dimensions tells a story in itself about the public culture and is comparable in a sense to the avoidance of such metaphors on the part of the novelist. With only occasional exceptions, British narratives before the First World War fall into this latter bracket with their studied refusal to personalize relationships across the colour line. Here silence speaks. To open the door to any such possibility threatened to bring down the house of imperialism.

When love, friendship or rape are deployed in a less guarded way, they have within them the capacity to open up an area of experience or thought and to bring new possibilities into focus. In such cases they tap the inwardness of personal life which can then be redirected externally. In this vein they may be suggestive of other ways of reading the public situation, of alternative conceptualizations. Moreover, they serve as devices to link together different writers and different periods, so that the narratives of the colonizer can be read off from the narratives of the colonized and vice versa. Again, what emerges is the points of contact between the two and the areas of commonality.

Reflecting on the whole course of writing on the Indo-British relationship, it appears that the categories of interpersonal behaviour are used in a more politically discriminating manner as we proceed chronologically. Whereas in earlier years the metaphors tended to be employed somewhat mechanically, increasingly they came to represent a means of drawing out the wider possibilities inherent in a situation. In other words, the techniques of deployment became more subtle and adaptive. No doubt this was inevitable as the literary annals swelled with studies of unrequited love, rape and violation and the hopes of friendship, and as later narratives looked back to earlier ones – to Kim as a foundling, to Adela in the Malabar Caves, to the relationship between Raja Rao's Rama and Madeleine. But it mirrors other developments as well. There is the Indian writer's growing confidence in the novel form, and with it the ease of going beyond a formula. And, as the empire slipped steadily into history, there is the British writer's preparedness to use personal relationships as a way of opening up political inquiry rather than closing it down.

Notes

1. V. S. Naipaul, 'The brothels behind the graveyard' in V. S. Naipaul, *The Return of Eva Peron with the Killings in Trinidad* (Penguin, Harmondsworth, 1981), p. 151. Originally published in the *New York Review of Books*, 12 (24 April 1969), 9–16.

2. Sara Suleri, *The Rhetoric of English India* (University of Chicago Press, Chicago and London, 1992), p. 3.

3. Fredric Jameson, 'Third-World literature in the era of multinational capitalism', *Social Text*, 15 (Fall 1986), 65–88 (p. 69).

4. Ibid., p. 79.

5. This judgement is necessarily secondhand and is made on the basis of discussions with U. R. Anantha Murthy and Ashis Nandy, among others. In his reply to Jameson, Aijaz Ahmad provides a measure of corroboration: 'I do not know of *any* fictional narrative in Urdu, in the last roughly two hundred years, which is of any significance and any length . . . and in which the issue of colonialism or the difficulty of a civilizational encounter between the English and the Indian has the same primacy as, for example, Forster's *A Passage to India* or Paul Scott's *The Raj Quartet*' (italics original). Aijaz Ahmad, 'Jameson's rhetoric of otherness and the national allegory', *Social Text* (Fall 1987), 3–25 (p. 21). In a brief note, Sujit Mukherjee writes that novels in Indian languages set during the time of British rule generally ignored English men and women. Sujit Mukherjee, *Forster and Further. The Tradition of Anglo-Indian Fiction* (Orient Longman, Bombay, 1993), p. 20. Looking more broadly, a similar conclusion has been reached about black writing in Rhodesia/Zimbabwe. Taking over 100 novels not translated into English, a researcher found that whites hardly figure at all: 'you can read a couple of dozen such books one after another and not meet one white character'. Doris Lessing, *African Laughter. Four Visits to Zimbabwe* (HarperCollins, London, 1992), p. 161.

6. Three review articles provide an excellent introduction to the debates about nationalism and the difficulty of identifying a core content over time. See Gale Stokes, 'The undeveloped theory of nationalism', *World Politics*, 31:i (October 1978), 150–60; Arthur N. Waldron 'Theories of nationalism and historical explanation', *World Politics*, 37 (April 1985), 416–33; Ernst B. Haas, 'What is nationalism and why should we study it?', *International Organization*,' 40:3 (Summer 1986), 707–44. Inquiry into the meaning of nationalism has, of course, become part of the larger project of explaining the origins and power of the nation-state. Seminal references here are Benedict Anderson, *Imagined Communities. Reflections on the Origin and Spread of Nationalism* (Verso, London, 1983); Ernest Gellner, *Nations and Nationalism* (Blackwell, Oxford, 1983) and *Encounters with Nationalism* (Blackwell, Oxford, 1994).

7. Compare, for example, Corelli Barnett, *The Collapse of British Power* (Eyre Methuen, London, 1972), parts 4 and 5 (p. 164) with John Darwin 'Imperialism in decline? Tendencies in British imperial policy between the wars', *Historical Journal*, xxiii:3 (1980), 657–79, (p. 676).

8. See Hugh Trevor-Roper's remarks in his concluding essay 'History and imagination', pp. 356–69, in Hugh Lloyd-Jones, Valerie Pearl and Blair Warden (eds), *History and Imagination. Essays in Honour of H. R. Trevor-Roper* (Duckworth, London, 1981).

9. For a case in point see Zakia Pathak, Saswati Sengupta and Sharmila Purkayastha, 'The prisonhouse of orientalism', *Textual Practice*, 5:2 (Summer 1991), 195–218.

10. Compare Bhupal Singh, *A Survey of Anglo-Indian Fiction* (Oxford University Press, London, 1934), p. 207: 'The novel seems to have been written for propaganda purposes.'

11. Meenakshi Mukherjee, *The Twice Born Fiction. Themes and Techniques of the Indian Novel in English* (Heinemann, New Delhi and London, 1971), p. 20.

12. S. M. Mitra, *Hindupore. A Peep Behind the Indian Unrest. An Anglo-Indian Romance* (Luzac & Co., London, 1909), p. 223.

13. Ibid., p. 171.

14. S. K. Ghosh, *The Prince of Destiny. The New Krishna* (Rebman, London, 1909).

15. Francis Thompson (1859–1907) dreamt of a regenerated world and for a time saw empire as a possible way forward. He praised Rhodes: 'for that he was/the Visioner of vision in a most sordid day', but 'not the baser things/Wherewith the market and the tavern rings.' His poetry had a mystic quality and a strong ethical concern which perhaps made it especially appealing to some Indians. See Rev. T. H. Wright, *Francis Thompson and his Poetry* (George G. Harrap & Co. Ltd., London, Calcutta, Sydney, 1927), particularly pp. 120–1.

16. Ibid., p. 620.

17. K. E. Ghamat, *My Friend the Barrister* (Ardeshir & Co., Bombay, 1908), p. 168.

18. Ibid., p. 179.

19. Ibid., p. 285.

20. In the view of one Indian scholar, the habit of explaining critical historical events in terms of divine will made the acceptance of British rule easier. Sudhir Chandra, 'Literature and the colonial connection', pp. 145–89 (p. 177) in Sudhir Chandra (ed.), *Social Transformation and Creative Imagination* (issued under the auspices of the Nehru Memorial Museum and Library, Allied Publishers Private Ltd, Navrangpura, Ahmedabad, 1984).

21. K. S. Ramamurti, 'East–West understanding as reflected in British writing on India and Indian writing in English', *Jadavpur Journal of Comparative Literature* (Department of

Comparative Literature, Jadavpur University, Calcutta), 20–21 (1982–3), 59–70 (p. 63). See also Chandra, op. cit., pp. 170 and 173.

22. Albert Memmi, *The Colonizer and the Colonized* (Beacon Press, Boston, 1967; translated by Howard Greenfeld and first published 1957), pp. 121 and 128.

23. See Gouranga P. Chattopadhyay, 'The "Invader in the Mind" in Indian metaculture', *The Economic Times* (Bombay, New Delhi, Calcutta), 21–22 May 1982; and 'The Illusion that was India' (Paper presented at the First International Symposium on Group Relations, Contributions to Social and Political Issues, Oxford, July 1988).

24. Among the many historical accounts of British thinking about India in this period, two are of especial interest: Francis G. Hutchins, *Illusion of Permanence. British Imperialism in India* (Princeton University Press, Princeton NJ, 1967); Kenneth Ballhatchet, *Race, Sex and Class Under the Raj: Imperial Attitudes and Policies and their Critics 1793–1905* (St. Martin's Press, New York, 1980). For an overview see Darby, *Three Faces of Imperialism* (Yale University Press, New Haven CT and London, 1987), pp. 39–49.

25. J. A. Spender, *The Changing East* (Cassell, London, 1926), pp. 153–4.

26. Allen Greenberger, *The British Image of India. A Study in the Literature of Imperialism* (Oxford University Press, London, 1969), p. 56.

27. Benita Parry, *Delusions and Discoveries. Studies on India in the British Imagination* (University of California Press, Berkeley and Los Angeles, 1972), p. 122.

28. Flora Annie Steel, *The Hosts of the Lord* (Thomas Nelson & Sons, Edinburgh and New York, undated; first published 1900), p. 3.

29. Flora Annie Steel, *On the Face of the Waters* (William Heinemann, London, 1897), p. 41.

30. Ibid., p. 37.

31. Maud Diver, *Lilamani* (Blackwood, London, 1910).

32. Maud Diver, *Far to Seek: A Romance of England and India* (Wm. Blackwood & Sons, Edinburgh and London, 1924), pp. 128–9.

33. Janet Montefiore, 'Day and night in Kipling', *Essays in Criticism*, 27:4 (1977), 299–314 (pp. 303–8).

34. Rudyard Kipling, 'Miss Youghal's Sais' in *Plain Tales from the Hills* (Macmillan, London, centenary edn, 1981), p. 27.

35. Rudyard Kipling, 'The Mark of the Beast' in *Life's Handicap*, (Macmillan, London, centenary edn, 1982), p. 244.

36. Rudyard Kipling, 'To Be Filed for Reference' in *Plain Tales from the Hills*, p. 332. A somewhat similar character appears in B. M. Croker's novel *The Company's Servant*. Gojar, the night-watchman at a south Indian railway station, is revealed to be an English gentleman who passed out second at Sandhurst. His addiction to ganja led him to live the life of a native, drifting 'over India like a derelict for twenty long years'. At one stage he boasts that many a tale he could tell Kipling, but judging from what he says in the text, they would be lurid and fanciful – of quite a different order from most of Kipling's own stories. See B. M. Croker, *The Company's Servant* (George Bell & Sons, London, undated; first published 1907), pp. 107–9.

37. John Masters pushes this theme further in *The Deceivers* (Michael Joseph, London, 1952). In order to put down the Thugs, William Savage joins their fraternity in disguise. But to succeed he has to think and feel like one of them – which he does to such a degree that for a time he loses his English identity and kills in honour of Kali.

38. Kipling, 'Miss Youghal's Sais', p. 32.

39. Ibid., p. 29. See also 'The Bronckhorst Divorce Case' in *Plain Tales from the Hills*, p. 251.

40. Gail Ching-Liang Low, 'White skins/Black masks: the pleasures and politics of imperialism', *New Formations*, 9 (Winter 1989), 83–103 (pp. 94 and 98).

41. 'The Story of Muhammad Din' in *Plain Tales from the Hills*.

42. 'Tods' Amendment' in *Plain Tales from the Hills*. The quotation is from p. 198.

43. 'Georgie Porgie' in *Life's Handicap*, pp. 392–3.

44. 'Yoked with an Unbeliever' in *Plain Tales from the Hills*, p. 41.

45. 'Without Benefit of Clergy' in *Life's Handicap*, p. 162.

46. Ibid., p. 150.

47. Ibid., p. 164.

48. Noel Annan, 'Kipling's place in the history of ideas' in Andrew Rutherford (ed.), *Kipling's Mind and Art* (Oliver & Boyd, Edinburgh and London, 1964), pp. 97–125. Reprinted from *Victorian Studies*, 3 (1959–60).

49. 'Namgay Doola' in *Life's Handicap*, p. 291.

50. Mrs Everard Cotes, *The Story of Sonny Sahib* (D. Appleton & Co., New York and London, 1928; first published 1894).

51. See the comments of Subir Ray Choudhuri and also the authorities cited in Subir Ray Choudhuri, 'In search of a parallel: *The Story of Sonny Sahib* (1894) and *Kim* (1901)', *Jadavpur Journal of Comparative Literature* (Department of Comparative Literature, Jadavpur University, Calcutta), 20–21 (1982–3), 137–50 (pp. 141–2).

52. Ibid., p. 148. Here I have paraphrased a quite long paragraph without, I hope, changing its meaning. I am grateful to this critic for first drawing my attention to Mrs Cotes' novel.

53. *The Story of Sonny Sahib*, p. 101.

54. Ibid., p. 23.

55. Ibid., p. 46.

56. Ibid., p. 79.

57. Ibid., p. 107.

58. Mark Kinkead-Weekes, 'Vision in Kipling's novels' in Rutherford, op. cit., pp. 197–234 (p. 217).

59. Rudyard Kipling, *Kim* (Macmillan, London, centenary edn 1981; first published 1901), p. 3.

60. Low, op. cit., p. 83.

61. Satya P. Mohanty 'Drawing the color line: Kipling and the culture of colonial rule' in Dominick LaCapra (ed.), *The Bounds of Race. Perspectives on Hegemony and Resistance* (Cornell University Press, Ithaca NY, 1991), pp. 311–43.

62. Ibid., p. 193.

63. Ibid., p. 104.

64. Nirad C. Chaudhuri, 'The finest story about India in English', *Encounter*, VIII:5 (May 1957), 47–53 (p. 49). But re timelessness see Edward Said, 'Kim: the pleasures of imperialism', *Raritan*, 2 (Fall 1987), p. 29.

65. Jeffrey Myers, *Fiction and the Colonial Experience* (Boydell Press, Ipswich, 1973), p. 24.

66. Parry, op. cit., p. 255.

67. Edward Wilson, 'The Kipling that nobody read' in *The Wound and the Bow. Seven Studies in Literature* (Methuen University Paperbacks, London, 1961; first published 1941), p. 111.

68. *Kim*, p. 386.

69. Suleri, *The Rhetoric of English India*, ch. 5, 'The adolescence of *Kim*'. See especially pp. 111 and 117.

70. Edward Thompson, *Rabindranath Tagore. His Life and Work* (Association Press [YMCA], Calcutta, 2nd edition 1928), p. 36.

71. Rabindranath Tagore, *Gora* (Macmillan, Calcutta, 1969; first published 1924), p. 132.

72. Ibid., p. 405.

73. In an article entitled 'Home', Kipling wrote freely of his love of India. The article records his journey from South India to Lahore in 1891. He did not include it in any of his books. See M. Enamul Karim, 'Kipling's personal vision of India in an uncollected article "Home"', *Journal of Commonwealth Literature*, XIII:1 (August 1978), 19–27.

74. For a more general elaboration see Darby, op. cit., pp. 76 and 114–15.

75. A. Madhaviah, *Clarinda. A Historical Novel* (Cambridge Press, Madras, 1915). Another novel of some interest in this connection is Hasan Ali's *The Changeling*, which depicts in terms of personal relationships the challenge of bridging the worlds of East and West. It tells the story of a young Indian, Rama, and his love for an Indian woman, Shanti, whom he believes is killed in an accident, and his subsequent love for Paula, a Spanish girl, whom he marries. Hasan Ali, *The Changeling* (Herbert Joseph, London, 1933).

76. Mulk Raj Anand, *Coolie* (Arnold-Heinemann, New Delhi, 1984; first published 1936), pp. 296, 316–17.

77. Mulk Raj Anand, *Untouchable* (Allen Lane, Penguin, Harmondsworth, 1940; first published 1935), pp. 125–8.

78. K. R. Srinivasa Iyengar, *Indian Writing in English* (Sterling Publishers, New Dehli, revised and updated edition 1985; first published 1962), p. 271.

79. Raja Rao, *Kanthapura* (Orient Paperbacks, Delhi, 1971; first published 1938).

80. Susie Tharu, 'Reading against the imperial grain: intertextuality, narrative structure and liberal humanism in Mulk Raj Anand's *Untouchable*', *Jadavpur Journal of Comparative Literature*, 24 (1986), 60–71 (p. 63).

81. Stephen Ignatius Hemenway, *The Novel of India vol. 2: The Indo-Anglian Novel* (Writers Workshop, Calcutta, 1975), p. 14.

82. Edmund Candler, *Abdication* (Constable, London, Bombay and Sydney, 1922), p. 22.

83. E. M. Forster, *A Passage to India* (Abinger edition, vol. 6, Edward Arnold, London, 1978; first published 1924).

84. See Barbara Rosecrance, *Forster's Narrative Vision* (Cornell University Press, Ithaca NY and London, 1982), pp. 187–94.

85. Orwell, *Burmese Days*, p. 75.

86. Lionel Trilling, 'A Passage to India' (1942) reprinted in Malcolm Bradbury (ed.), *A Passage to India: A Casebook* (Macmillan, London, 1970), pp. 77–92 (p. 81).

87. This is echoed by Mulk Raj Anand in *Coolie* when Babu Nathoo Ram invites the new officer, Mr England, to tea in the hope that he will write the Babu a recommendation 'before he was influenced by all the other English Officers in the Club and began to hate all Indians, before the kind smile on his lips became a smile of contempt and derision' (*Coolie*, p. 49).

88. *Abdication*, p. 11. See also pp. 23–4.

89. Maud Diver, *The Singer Passes: An Indian Tapestry* (Blackwood, London, 1931), p. 259.

90. *Abdication*, p. 198.

91. Robert Rhodes James (ed.), *Winston S. Churchill: His Complete Speeches 1897–1963*, vol. V, 1928–1935 (Chelsea House Publishers in association with R. R. Bowker Company, New York and London, 1974), p. 4985. The comment was made in a speech to the Council of the West Essex Conservative Association on 23 February 1931.

92. Dennis Kincaid, *Their Ways Divide* (Chatto & Windus, London, 1936).

93. See Suleri, op. cit., ch. 6. This chapter breaks new ground and makes fascinating reading. However, the significance of some points remains obscure.

94. What is of particular interest here is the very different conceptions of the signifiers of friendship between men. Naru wants an easier physicality, whereas this is altogether alien to Edward. The imperial relationship underlines the significance of this difference.

95. Edward Thompson, *An Indian Day* (Alfred A. Knopf, London, 1927), pp. 94–5.

96. Salman Rushdie, *Midnight's Children* (Picador, London, 1982; first published 1981), p. 194.

97. Paul Scott, *The Jewel in the Crown* (Granada Publishing, Frogmore, Herts and London, 1973; first published 1966), p. 133. Reference to all four volumes of the *Quartet* is to the same edition).

98. See, for example, Salman Rushdie, 'Outside the whale', *Granta*, 11 (1983), 124–38.

99. *The Jewel in the Crown*, p. 9.

100. Paul Scott, *A Division of the Spoils* (first published 1975), p. 301.

101. Paul Scott, *The Day of the Scorpion* (first published 1968), p. 279.

102. Paul Scott, *The Towers of Silence* (first published 1971), p. 364.

103. *The Jewel in the Crown*, p. 51.

104. *The Towers of Silence*, p. 30.

105. Robin White in *The Jewel in the Crown*, p. 343.

106. *The Day of the Scorpion*, p. 404.

107. Robin Moore, *Paul Scott's Raj* (Heinemann, London, 1990), p. 62.

108. Sujit Mukherjee suggests that part of Scott's difficulty with regard to Daphne's rape was the problem of making it credible. He therefore took great care in his handling of the incident. See *Forster and Further*, pp. 153 and 155.

109. As Salman Rushdie did in his review in *Granta*, op. cit., p. 127.

110. *The Jewel in the Crown*, p. 427.

111. Ibid., p. 462.

112. This has not prevented some bizarre readings. Consider Jenny Sharpe's argument that by making a sadistic homosexual the agent of Hari's metaphoric rape, 'Scott identifies the decline of the moral ideas of imperialism as the corruption of Victorian manliness.' The novel thus 'safeguards Victorian manliness and the homosocial relations of colonialism'. Jenny Sharpe, *Allegories of Empire. The Figure of Woman in the Colonial Text* (University of Minnesota Press, Minneapolis and London, 1993), p. 155.

113. Allen Boyer, 'Love, sex and history in the *Raj Quartet*', *Modern Language Quarterly* (March 1985), 65–80 (pp. 65 and 71).

114. Paul Scott, *A Division of the Spoils* (first published 1975), p. 571.

115. *The Day of the Scorpion*, pp. 405 and 408.

116. Moore, op. cit., p. 112. It is also relevant to note Scott's comment that Merrick, like all his other characters, came from himself: 'It's all a writer can do – expose himself each time he writes a chapter.' Quoted in Hilary Spurling, *Paul Scott: A Life* (Hutchinson, London, 1990), p. 304.

117. *The Jewel in the Crown*, p. 117.

118. *A Division of the Spoils*, p. 105.

119. Patrick Swinden, *Paul Scott: Images of India* (Macmillan, London, 1980), p. 97.

120. Raja Rao, *The Serpent and the Rope* (abridged edition, Oxford University Press, Delhi, 1978; first published 1960), p. 83.

121. *A Division of the Spoils*, p. 105.

122. Ibid., p. 222.

123. Ibid., p. 105.

124. Rudyard Kipling, 'At the End of the Passage' in *Life's Handicap*.

125. *The Day of the Scorpion*, p. 135.

126. Ibid., p. 136.

127. Gomathi Narayanan, *The Sahibs and the Natives. A Study of Guilt and Pride in Anglo-Indian and Indo-Anglian Novels* (Chanakya Publications, Delhi, 1986), p. 38.

128. Manohar Malgonkar, *A Bend in the Ganges* (Orient Paperbacks, Delhi, 1964), 68–71 (p. 70).

129. Ibid., p. 112. See the comments of Kai Nicholson, *A Presentation of Social Problems in the Indo-Anglian and the Anglo-Indian Novel* (Jaico Publishing House, Bombay, 1972), pp. 138–9 and Narayanan, op. cit., pp. 55–6.

130. Manohar Malgonkar, *Distant Drum* (Orient Paperbacks, Delhi, 1986; first published 1960) and *Bandicoot Run* (Orient Paperbacks, Delhi, 1982).

131. K. R. Srinivasa Iyengar, op. cit., p. 424.

132. *A Bend in the Ganges*, pp. 262–3.

133. This is part of the reason, no doubt, why Malgonkar's treatment of the INA contrasts so sharply with that of his fellow Indian Army officer and personal friend, Paul Scott. It is in line, however, with the position taken by the Indian Army after 1947 – which would make a fascinating story in its own right.

134. See, for example, Meenakshi Mukherjee, *The Twice Born Fiction*, pp. 68–9.

135. Chaman Nahal, *The Crown and the Loincloth* (Vikas Publishing House, Delhi, 1981), p. 227.

136. *A Bend in the Ganges*, p. 25.

137. Ibid., p. 28.

138. Ibid., pp. 124–5.

139. Quoted in Srinivasa Iyengar, op. cit., p. 360.

140. *Waiting for the Mahatma* tells the story of Sriram, a youth from Malgudi, who becomes involved in the 'Quit India' campaign because of his romance with Bharati, a disciple and godchild of Gandhi. With humour and irony (unbecoming in the view of many Indian critics),

it depicts the last phase of the independence struggle as often apolitical and even grubby. R. K. Narayan, *Waiting for the Mahatma* (Indian Thought Publications, Mysore, 1984; first published 1955).

141. Narayanan, op. cit., pp. 47–8.

142. 'Lawley Road' in R. K. Narayan, *Lawley Road and Other Stories* (Orient Paperbacks, Delhi, undated), pp. 7–13 (p. 9).

143. Pritish Nandy, 'Literature of protest' in Suresh Kohli (ed.), *Aspects of Indian Literature* (Vikas Publishing House, Delhi, 1975), pp. 83–9 (p. 86).

144. R. S. Pathak, 'The Indo-English Novelist's Quest for Identity', ch. 1 in R. K. Dhawan (ed.), *Explorations in Modern Indo-English Fiction* (Bahri Publications Private Ltd., New Delhi, 1982), pp. 1–15 (p. 14).

145. Nirad C. Chaudhuri, 'Passage to and from India', *Encounter*, 2:6 (June 1954), 19–24 (p. 23).

146. Ibid., p. 21.

CHAPTER 5

African literature and cultural politics

This chapter addresses Africa's location within the global system and the way in which aspects of that system are reproduced and resisted within Africa. In historical studies there have been profound changes in how Africa is apprehended and, as a result, a transformation in how world history is written.[1] Few comparable initiatives have been taken in contemporary international studies. Hence, analyses of Africa's place in the world remain light years behind analyses of Africa in history. I do not think that anyone would argue that international relations has had much of significance to offer – indeed, in so far as it has been extended to Africa what emerges is the barrenness of disciplinary constructs. Nor can it be said that either postcolonialism or globalization have accorded Africa much space in its own right. In a recent special issue of *Public Culture*, Africa is referred to as 'the sign of the exception in comparative studies', meaning that there is a refusal to make sense of the continent on its own terms, and that it operates as the repository of certain repressions and projections.[2]

My aim in this chapter is to consider whether African novelists writing in English offer a more promising starting-point. It seems axiomatic that as connections are made between different areas and ways of approach increasingly come to diverge, no one province of inquiry can suffice. The questions which lie in the background of our analysis are so wide-ranging that they rule out reliance on source material of a particular kind. What course is to be negotiated between the pressures for international standardization and the claims of cultural distinctiveness? How might the tension be resolved between the constructs and knowledges of international studies, on the one hand, and those of African literary formations, on the other? Who is to be responsible for making postcolonial choices or will the alignment of policy be set by the logic of economic and cultural change? In approaching these questions, I proceed on the assumption that traditional distinctions between the external and internal spheres foreclose inquiry. In the African case, the interpenetration of the two is especially marked. Contemporary proponents of capitalist imperialism recognize the key role of indigenous collaborators in politics and business; in many spheres, social change within African societies is associated with ideas and processes which have their origins outside the continent. Our very understanding of what is internal and what is external is conditioned by time and culture. Is violence essentially an internal phenomenon? Can it be assumed that the West is always located outside the continent?

It is useful to note certain features of the approach adopted in this chapter as compared with the previous chapter. Whereas our inquiry into the Indo-British relationship hinged on the significance of the personal – on the depiction of personal behaviour, feelings and affects and what this might signify politically – here our primary concern is with the cultural. We thus take our lead from African novelists, for whom culture has been the ticket of entry into politics. In following the novelists in this respect, we cannot fail to consider some of the issues of group identity which emerge in postcolonial theory. This will serve to ground the treatment of postcolonialism in the concluding chapter of the book. Whereas our major objective in the last section was to draw on literature to elucidate understanding of a past imperial chapter, our principal purpose here is to consider how far literature might guide thinking about future possibilities, about Africa's place in a postcolonial order. Essentially I have in mind those problems of community and modernity which lie at the intersection of national and international politics.

African literature has come to be regarded as a problematic category, and justifiably so. The long-standing concern about who and what should be regarded as African – which raises issues of skin pigmentation and cultural orientation – has been supplemented by a recognition of the multiple layers of Africanness and the varieties of narrative. It is plainly unlikely that any one formulation will do justice to the relationship between different literatures, in different languages and taking different forms, and be alert to the tensions and compatibilities between them. The category can therefore prove reductionist, ironing out regional, national and other differences because of an assumed continental commonality. Hence, in inquiring into the politics of fiction, we need to be mindful of the diversity of African texts and their cultural particularity. When from time to time reference is made to African literature, this is simply by way of shorthand to mark off writing by Africans from that by non-Africans. At the same time, it will be necessary to look more widely. African texts cannot be read in isolation from the foreign texts that played a significant part in provoking them and shaping their concerns.

It would be instructive to inquire why African literature so quickly established its place not only in literary studies but in the field of politics and society as well. Clearly its acceptance as a distinctive and politically significant body of writing owes much to the challenge it presented to established ways of seeing African societies and received understandings of Africa's history and her relationship with the outside world. Opinion had swung decisively against imperialism. Sociology and even anthropology held a promise which disciplinary politics had lost. Cultural difference retained a special fascination, and with Achebe instead of Cary as guide, it could now be pursued in a way that accorded with changed sensibilities. These considerations go some distance towards explaining why African literature has achieved such prominence, but it remains puzzling why, at least for a time, other Third World literatures trailed behind. Even now, for instance, the politics of Indian writing in English has not received comparable recognition nor spawned a proliferation of special courses. At this point, attention might be directed to publishers and distribution networks and to the singular achievement of Heinemann's African Writers Series.

Viewed both on its own terms and in comparison with other Third World literatures, African writing gives an impression of being set apart. One aspect of the appeal of the texts is the way they convey a sense of another world. Individual works derive some of their force from their relationship to the body of continental writing. It was the Europeans who introduced the politics of difference and thereby provided an impulse for Africans to present their world in shades of otherness. For a time this was related back to the 'master narrative'. We know, for example, that Chinua Achebe's initial reference-point was Joyce Cary's *Mr Johnson* and a determination to set the record straight. But as the number of African novels grew, so, it seems to me, African writing became increasingly inwardly oriented, and the cross-references to other literatures and cultures declined. This process was accompanied – and perhaps encouraged – by the critics' search for a distinctively African stamp on both form and content, and an attempt to develop specifically African standards of literary criticism. For a considerable period, then, until recognition was reluctantly extended to African women's writing, the discourse gave the appearance of having its own characteristic concerns which did not necessarily correspond with those of the outside world. In contrast, recent postcolonial critiques have been anxious to stress the similarities between African and other Third World writing, but very little of this has either emanated from or been taken up in Africa itself.

Associated with what I have described as the inward bent of African literature is the apparently circumscribed nature of political engagement. Now it is true that African writers have been harassed, imprisoned and forced into exile, and that often enough in their fiction there are detailed allusions to political events. The point is rather that the politics of much of the literature has a general oppositional appeal but much less prescriptive edge.[3] Very different views can be taken about this. On a more traditional reading, it might be argued that the tendency is for culture to pass for politics and consolidated vision to displace considerations of social tension and sectional alignment. Relevant here is a debate in African history some years back stemming from William Ochieng's defence of Hugh Trevor-Roper's claim that the emperor of African historiography had no clothes and Terence Ranger's call for a more usable African past.[4] If, however, postcolonialism provides a lead, the contention will surely be that it is only by taking cognizance of a politics which expresses itself in the sphere of the ordinary and the ostensibly non-political that escape can be made from colonial categories. In other words, attention must be directed to those sites which lie outside the arena of politics as laid down by the dominant. It may well be that neither view is wholly convincing. I will attempt to pinpoint some of the issues and weigh the arguments in the sections which follow.

In one way or another, African literature revolves around a concern with identity. Like other postcolonial fictions, it responds to the need to clarify a sense of self in a situation where it is difficult to do so except in terms which refer back to the binary codes of colonial discourse. Yet the African case stands apart because of the intensity of concern and the fact that it searches its way into so many aspects of thought and life. It follows that issues relating to identity provide the backdrop to this section and that much of our discussion will hinge on the pull of the Manichean tradition and the problems associated with it. Identity, however, is too ubiquitous to serve as a core category. Contemporary social theory has exploded the idea of a stable, integrated identity and has pointed to the pitfalls of proceeding on any such assumption. In African studies recent commentaries have been critical of generalized assertions about a 'crisis of identity' or Africans being 'caught between two worlds', arguing that often Africans have adapted remarkably well to the pull of different traditions and the attachment to different affinities.[5] For these reasons, while identity is implicated in almost everything discussed in this section, it does not itself constitute an organizing principle.

Three issues form the basis of our inquiry in this section. The first concerns the politics of the novelist's use of the past. What is relevant here is the recovery or construction of a history and the way that this informs approaches to the present and the future. The second issue addresses ideas about community and draws upon the treatment of pan-Africanism, the practices of everyday life and approaches to the modern nation-state. Third, there is the question of Africa's response to modernity. Is modernity equated with the West? What part have Africans played in its introduction to the continent and the processes of its adaptation? Is the city still seen as basically alien to Africa? By working along these lines, Africa's relationship with the outside world can be seen to be an aspect of Africa's relationship with itself. This provides a further reason why this section takes its cue from the novelists and begins with the people and the culture, not the state and institutional politics, and with the intrusions into Africa of the West and the international system, not the world 'out there'.

Coming to grips with the past

From the beginning the African novel was stamped with the message that the past was a prime concern of politics. For reasons both of personal emancipation and social responsibility, African writers took upon themselves the task of undermining European representations of Africa and establishing new ones. For a century or more Africans had played little part in shaping the dominant ideas about themselves and the continent. It seemed at the time – although this would not be so readily accepted today – that colonial evaluations had deeply permeated African consciousness. European literature, popular culture and political thought – the latter as expressed in national doctrines of trusteeship or in the sacred trust of the League of Nations – interlocked to put Africans at the bottom of the evolutionary ladder.

Little relieved the negativity of assessment. Africans were a people without significant intellectual or cultural attainment. They had no history; 'darkness is not a subject of history', declared Hugh Trevor-Roper, meaning perhaps that there were few indigenous written records and little visible evidence of past achievement (significantly Europeans had dispossessed Africa of Great Zimbabwe by assuming it to be the work of a Mediterranean people). Race continued to provide an explanation of 'backwardness' long after the cruder biological theories had lost credibility. Given this imposed heritage, the African novel became an instrument of correction and a means of self-affirmation. The supposed blankness of the continent resided in the incomprehension of the viewer. Europeans did not understand, and worse, did not want to understand.

Led by Chinua Achebe, the novelists became historians, anthropologists and sociologists in order to reclaim an African identity. Complaints that their fiction veered too much towards cultural history or that their approach was too didactic need to be treated with reserve, given the burden of the past against which the novelists were writing. If novels such as *Things Fall Apart* have about them a touch of nostalgia for precolonial rhythms, was this not functional in the circumstances? That imperialism is at times caricatured and that the dilemmas of colonial rule – so acutely brought out in the writing of Cary – receive scant recognition in African fiction must be understood as part of the rejection of the discourse against which they were writing. Comparing the various expressions of African nationalism, the argument is persuasive that the literary texts went deeper and brought more into question than did the overtly political ones.

No one would turn to African literature to get a 'dates and facts' historical narrative, and they would be disappointed if they did.[6] The nub of our interest lies in the novelist's presentation of history as a space within which to search for meaning, open up new ways of seeing and patterning, and posit suggestive connections between then and now. This may be done by revisiting the past (as was the case in most early African novels). Alternatively, it may take the form of presenting the past in capsule form through symbols, cultural fragments or personal remembrances (as was usual in later novels). Either way, some sensitivity is required to the politics of when the novel was written. If the immediate purpose was to provide a corrective to European distortion, this can hardly be expunged from critical readings.

In the new configurations of knowledge located mainly in the Western academy, the boundaries which once separated past, present and future have been breached. In the prevailing view, the present did not emerge through a kind of progressive unfolding of the past. 'We are', Foucault observes, 'much more recent than we think.'[7] In similar vein, the future is not bounded by being embedded in the here and now. From its earliest days, the approach of African literature was consonant with such precepts, although this owed little to the influence of Western knowledge and much to the immediacy of indigenous culture and the way that African oral traditions were incorporated in the new written narratives. Characteristically, there is a consciousness of the closeness of the past. Invariably, an awareness of the present and the future reverberates through accounts of the past. This fluidity of past, present and future suggests an openness to change and, at the same time, ensures some recognition of the obstacles to change. The issue is not, therefore, one of temporal enclosure but of the politics of the novelists' openness and creativity.

As I see it, this has two aspects. First, what limits might be set to reconstructing the past and do African novelists stay within them? On a postcolonial account, the process of retelling the colonial encounter from a counter-hegemonic standpoint undermines the constructs of Western universalism and creates a space within which previously subordinate peoples can take control of their own destinies. It is precisely the imaginative dimensions of the project that enable the power/knowledge nexus of Western universalism to be broken and the subaltern empowered. Other lines of thought are much less sanguine about the possibilities of political transformation through an imaginative recasting of the past, utilizing myth and invention. Eric Hobsbawm, for example, stresses the need to have regard to historical facts and warns of the dangers of the past being rewritten according to politico-ideological design.[8] Second, there is the question of the openness of the future. Are there not material and structural constraints arising from the past and encoded in the present which foreclose options and contain the possibilities of the subjective? What responsibility do we place on the novelist to engage with these constraints, to temper vision with sober consideration of material conditions and political practices?

Pondering on these questions, I am taken back to Ranger's criticism of African historiography for having a certain 'flabbiness' because African historians were catering for interests that were too easily satisfied and too little demanding. 'African historiography', he continued, 'has been important in Africa for reasons of pride because it could not possibly have been useful for anything else.'[9] Could something of the same be said of African literature? We shall consider this matter in relation to select fictional narratives.

The recasting of the past in furtherance of an Africanist ideology is exemplified in the work of the Ghanaian writer Ayi Kwei Armah. In his novels *Two Thousand Seasons* and *The Healers*, Armah is concerned to provide an alternative mythical history which will help sustain his vision of a regenerated Africa. There are two elements to the politics of these narratives. The first is an interpretation of external intervention in terms of unmitigated violence and exploitation which clearly is intended to release Africans from the psychological bondage of colonialism. The second is a description of pre-colonial values and social patterns which might promote rethinking about the post-imperial order. In *Two Thousand Seasons* Armah has mixed success with his first objective and very little at all with his second. His studied yet furious denunciation of both Arab and European intruders and the destruction they wreaked on Black Africa certainly has a power that sweeps aside ideas of progress and the civilizing mission. Yet, as with Yambo Ouologuem's *Bound to Violence*, the vehemence of the exclusions may work to imprison as well as liberate. There is no reason why the vilification of aliens – the Europeans as 'white maggots', the Arabs as 'predators' – need stop at the Sahara.

As Soyinka remarks, over and above the destruction of alien influences the way forward remains a 'hazy and undefined ideology'.[10] We are given glimpses of an African past in which social life was rooted in a fluid sense of community and egalitarian, non-materialist ethics. An early period of violent patriarchy came to be replaced by the benign rule of women. The moral seems to be that much in the past must be reclaimed but not all. Part of the cause of Africa's downfall, for example, was that in the fertile time 'generosity became our vice'.[11] In *The Healers* Armah attempts to ground his vision by tying it to a particular chapter in Africa's past but in doing so he takes greater historical licence. As in his earlier novel, the future lies with the populace: 'kings and chiefs suck their power from the divisions between our people';[12] 'no single person, however heroic, can bring our whole people together again'.[13] Yet, as has been pointed out, Armah's egalitarianism sits decidedly uneasily alongside his choice of exceptional individuals as heroes.[14]

The way forward in this novel is entrusted to the healers – a group of people who, before colonial occupation, began the task of awakening African communities to their potential. Simply to enumerate the beliefs and qualities of the healers must raise questions about the danger of myth in this context. They are at one with nature; they are committed to non-violence; their strength derives from their belief in natural unities. The healers' way is one of inspiration, not manipulation – a supra-political view of the world which appears to reject compromise and accommodation and has obvious parallels with the philosophy of many post-independence African rulers, especially the military. Armah makes it clear that all remembrance, including his own, is functional. African people forgot many things in order to survive.[15] Now it may be necessary to ask of each piece of the past that we find in our present: 'Will it bear me like a stepping stone, or will I have to bear it, a weight around my neck?'[16]

Armah's departure from the conventions of the European novel and his adaptation of orality to the requirements of the written narrative are by now well recognized. One study of his fiction develops the theme that Armah, building on the tradition of the indigenous African story-teller, has been experimenting with a new narrative form in which myth and metaphor play a central role.[17] As such, his methodology presents a challenge to the 'plodding realism' of mainstream African fiction led by Chinua Achebe.[18] Accepting Armah's literary inventiveness does not, of course, rule out scepticism about the political relevance of his symbolic mode, but are the alternatives as unimaginative as our critic suggests? It is certainly true that few other African writers have been prepared to fashion the past so freely to accord with a political vision. Does this mean that they have foregone the opportunity to open up consideration of what might be done in the present? Let us take the case of Chinua Achebe.

In a much-quoted article Achebe has written of the novelist's responsibility as teacher, arguing specifically that the writer has a duty to help his 'society regain its belief in itself and put away the complexes of the years of denigration and self-denigration'.[19] Yet he has insisted that some bad be shown along with the good: 'We cannot pretend that our past was one long, technicolour idyll.'[20] More recently he has presented African literature as a return to celebration, but, in keeping with Igbo tradition, celebration must include society's problems and imperfections.[21] There can be no doubt that in his own fiction Achebe has taken these responsibilities very seriously, with the result that his novels have been praised for their realistic depiction of the past and criticized because they offer no positive vision of the future. Confronted with the argument that he attaches too much importance to the colonial experience, Achebe gives no ground. In his view, 'it's the most important single thing that has happened to us, after the slave trade', and it must be dealt with.[22] The problem is the lack of 'expertise' at the present time. This can lead a novelist to settle for fantasy. This is what Armah has done in *Two Thousand Seasons*, and in Achebe's opinion the novel is a 'complete failure' – and also 'hideously boring'.[23]

For some years Achebe's writing fell in esteem among the critics, but this process should have been checked with the publication in 1991 of a critical study by Simon Gikandi. Drawing on the work of the Zairean philosopher V. Y. Mudimbe, Gikandi has mounted a powerful defence of Achebe against the charge that he has remained within the traditional paradigms of realism. Gikandi's argument is that Achebe has used the novel as a way of reorganizing African cultures, certain in his belief that narrative could propose an alternative social world to those which had existed or which now exist. Further, not only could narrative represent reality, it could also change it. On this evaluation, Achebe's return to the colonial experience is motivated by the need to imagine a different future, and his texts create a mythical space within which a new social order can be evaluated.[24]

This way of reading Achebe rescues him from being marginalized on the ground that he is trapped by the past and that his nostalgia for earlier values prevents him addressing the way ahead. It is true that Achebe's understanding of the colonial burdens that Africa carries with it, and his depiction of postcolonial uncertainty, mean that he is not prepared to offer the clear sense of direction or speak with the declaratory voice of writers such as Armah or Ngugi. Therein lies part of his strength. His fiction is driven by the twin convictions that there can be no instant liberation of or from the past, and that the disorder and instability of the present do not contain within them a single core of meaning. But Achebe's insistence that it is not the writer's prerogative to set out a kind of social blueprint has other roots which lie in his understanding of the role of narrative and the dangers of absolutism. These concerns are fundamental to *Anthills of the Savannah*, which, of all Achebe's works, most directly addresses the future. As C. L. Innes has pointed out, the scene of action in the novel progressively widens from the cabinet room to the poorer section of the capital, with more and more people having their say.[25] The movement from an authoritative, supposedly objective voice (that of the President) to many voices, is a series of meditations on the significance of story-telling and the power of narrative to effect political change. In an astute reading, Robin Ikegami argues that throughout the novel the potentialities and limits of story-telling are canvassed, but the characters remain confused about how to settle the issue.[26] This Ikegami relates to the uncertainties and insecurities of life in fictional Kangan (read contemporary Nigeria), thus underlining the significance of context to theoretical debates about knowledge and power. Ikem's address to the Students' Union at the University of Bassa becomes the occasion for an engagement with the writer's responsibility and political commitment. When the chairman expressed his view that writers must not stop at documenting social problems, Ikem shouted, 'Writers don't give prescriptions'.[27] Ikem's strictures, taken in conjunction with other passages in the novel about the politics of narrative, make it plain that the most that should be expected of a writer is to sift new ways of thinking and possible points of departure from the heterogeneity of contemporary Nigerian life. The rest is up to the reader as citizen.

At least in his fictional writing, Wole Soyinka does not express himself with Achebe's directness and clarity. We know from his essays that he rejects any wholesale espousal of either traditional African values or a 'Euromodernist' system of thought that repudiates the existence of an African world. This much is scarcely less evident in his plays and novels. The old Africa is shown to have its share of unattractive features. Soyinka does not hesitate to bring out its internal contradictions and even to suggest parallels with new systems of falsity that have been superimposed upon it. On his own admission, *A Dance of the Forests*, written for Nigerian independence, 'takes a jaundiced view of the much-vaunted glorious past of Africa'.[28] At the same time, there is a felt need to draw on the past and show how it infuses the present. Especially in his plays, Soyinka makes much use of traditional African forms and ideas (mostly Yoruba), often adapted or changed in significant ways.[29] This accords with his view that the reference-points for African culture are taken from within the culture itself.[30] I want now to consider how these concerns about the past relate to Soyinka's use of a myth of an ideal social form in his second novel, *Season of Anomy*.

The novel is an allegory of the blood-letting and political manoeuvring which led to Biafra's secession from Nigeria and the civil war which followed. Neocolonialism and widespread violence within the country are the result of an implicit alliance between the military government and a cocoa-producing cartel. Ofeyi, the cartel's promotions executive, attempts to subvert the power of the cartel, joining forces in this ultimately unsuccessful endeavour with the people of Aiyero, a long-isolated, tightly knit society committed to a communal, non-materialist way of life.

At first reading Soyinka might be taken – and has been taken – to hold out Aiyero as an idealization of some kind of traditional social form, an indigenous communalism which could serve as an alternative to Western capitalist models. All property is held in common; there is a sense of harmony both within the community and between the community and the natural environment; the past exercises a strong but unbinding influence on the present. Aiyero's break with its parent community was partly caused by its rejection of Christianity: 'It is time', the Founder said, 'to return to the religion of our fathers.'[31] Yet there are clear indications that Aiyero is not simply a precolonial idyll after the style of Armah which could provide the answer to Africa's contemporary needs. For one thing, Aiyero is in touch with the modern world and draws selectively from it. The Elders of the community send the young men all over the world to gain outside experience. For another, the men of Aiyero are seen as activated by class consciousness rather than tribal bonding. Ofeyi dreams of 'a new concept of labouring hands across artificial frontiers', and he sees this being realized by the men of Aiyero working on projects in other parts of the country: 'New affinities, working-class kinships as opposed to the tribal.'[32] Then there is the paradox that the Dentist, who plays such a key role in the book's politics as dispassionate assassin and ideologue of violence, has from the start been working on behalf of Aiyero. When the truth is finally revealed, Ofeyi is irritated that he has been deceived for so long and the reader is left wondering what he or she is now to make of Aiyero. Clearly Aiyero is not the 'quaint anomaly' – traditional, sentimental, even innocent – that we might have imagined, but Soyinka offers little help in reassessment. As one critic observes: 'After this revelation symbolism takes over and no further clarification of political ideology is attempted in the novel.'[33]

In the end, then, we are uncertain of what Aiyero represents in Soyinka's scheme of values beyond the compatibility of Africa's rural past with an orchestrated campaign for social change, and cultural particularity with universalist idealism. The picture is further complicated because, in an essay attacking his critics, Soyinka has dismissed the idea that Aiyero is a model to be followed, arguing instead that it is only 'an active agent in an endeavour to mobilize the rest of the country'.[34] Presumably he has in mind some kind of mobilization on the basis of class, but he seems decidedly reluctant to be specific about what form this might take.

The reinterpretation of the past is crucial to Nuruddin Farah's purposes in his trilogy *Sweet and Sour Milk* (1979), *Sardines* (1981) and *Close Sesame* (1983), collectively titled *Variations on the Theme of an African Dictatorship*. Unlike Soyinka, there is seldom room for doubt about how we are to understand his country's history or the use to which it should be put. Farah depicts the past both directly through authorial commentary and by means of the remembrances and reflections of his characters; in *Close Sesame*, for example, Deeriye, in the course of a few days, ranges over the history of Somalia from distant legend to the present day, much of it sharpened by recollections of his own involvement in the struggle first against the Italians and later against the regime of the General (the fictional representation of Siyaad Barre who became president in 1969 as a result of a military coup). Even when the latter technique is employed, the history we are given is very directed. Farah himself has stated that the overall theme of his novels is 'Truth versus Untruth'.[35] It is therefore somewhat surprising that chapter 5 of *Close Sesame* is entitled 'History through an unfocused lens' when the history that is narrated is clearly focused. It is an alternative history, a point underlined later when Zeinab reminds her father that he used to say that the history worth studying is one of resistance, not capitulation.[36] This casts doubt on Jacqueline Bardolph's claim that Farah's telling of history in *Close Sesame* creates a space for the reader to make his/her own judgement.[37] As I read the novel (and Farah's other works), there are strict limits to how much the politics of the past are open to argument.

Farah's retelling of the past, then, is highly purposeful and intended to further the cause of Somali liberation – and, by extension, the liberation of all Africa. As he presents it, there is a need to consolidate and bring to the surface the tradition of resistance. This is met, for example, by reviving the memory of martyrs such as the warrior-poet, Sayyid Mohamed Abdulle Hassan (known to the British as 'the mad mullah'), who challenged imperialism in the early part of the century and is Deeriye's inspiration in *Close Sesame*. The significance of such historiographical revisionism is explored in *Sweet and Sour Milk*, a novel about the General's appropriation of the life of a young Somali, Soyaan. Probably poisoned by the General's regime, Soyaan was posthumously proclaimed 'Hero of the Revolution' and his last words were allegedly 'there is no General but our General'. Interrogated by a minister of the regime, Soyaan's brother, Hoyaan, declares:

> Heroes are made, Mr Minister. Hero-worship is a phenomenon as necessary as history itself. Every nation needs heroes in which to invest a past, heroes and legendary figures about whom one tells stories to children and future generations.[38]

Farah is also concerned to highlight elements of the culture received through history which he believes must be swept away if Somalis are ever to be free. His twin targets are patriarchy and tribalism, and the one tends to reinforce the other. As Farah tells it, patriarchy is deeply embedded in Somalia's past. His theme is that the General's rule derives much of its strength from tapping this tradition and exploiting the power structures it has produced in the family, the clan and the tribe. The second part of *Sweet and Sour Milk* is introduced by the epigraph, taken from Wilhelm Reich, 'In the figure of the father the authoritarian state has its representative in every family, so that the family becomes its most important instrument of power.' Deeriye paraphrases these lines in *Close Sesame*, though the name of the author eludes him.[39] Sagal takes their substance and makes it her own in *Sardines*.[40] No less than the family, tribe stands in opposition to personal autonomy and is therefore readily utilized as an instrument of totalitarian rule. Throughout the trilogy Farah shows how the General uses his own tribe as a power base and neutralizes challenges to his rule by making them appear tribally motivated. It is not the younger generation influenced by overseas ideas that the General fears, but the tribal chieftains who represent traditional authority.

Above all else, therefore, Farah's novels are concerned to show that the past is a mixed inheritance that can be deployed in very different ways. More than any other African writer, however, he sees the traditional social structure and cultural patterns as deeply flawed and contributing to the evils of the contemporary order. In this respect, Farah's trilogy is revelatory. Yet on a second reading it does not fully satisfy. Kirsten Holst Petersen has observed that Farah's novels are not concluded, 'they simply fade out mid-plot'.[41] This is perhaps so, but I would locate the problem elsewhere. There are so many themes and they are so overtly presented that the process of relating the past to a desired future is made too easy. Do we not need to wrestle rather more with what to do about those parts of a cultural inheritance which are inimical to development, if they are organic elements of the old society?

A people's history, how it is perceived and used, is the single most important element in V. S. Naipaul's political vision. In *A Bend in the River*, Naipaul pursues this material in the African context and in a way which, understandably, has enraged many Africans. Although the novel is written by a non-African, it is considered here because its treatment of Africa's past runs so counter to the main approaches in African literature, and because it has such resonance with the long-established perceptions of the outside world. In some respects, *A Bend in the River* is firmly in the tradition of the foreign novel of Africa – the Conradian overtones, the sense of the primeval, the political nihilism. But Naipaul's Africa is also informed by his experience of other Third World societies, as is the reader's by a knowledge of his other novels. Hence *A Bend in the River* is part and parcel of Naipaul's post-imperial landscape, in which the psychological damage inflicted by colonialism dooms former subjects to remain 'mimic men' and Third World societies to be for ever 'half-made'.

Though never explicitly stated, the novel is set in Zaire, where everything is rundown in the aftermath of independence and a period of random violence. The Big Man – who does not appear in the novel but who is modelled on Mobutu – dominates the life of the country and presides over a radicalization programme which promises nothing but greater despair and more violence. Salim, the protagonist, comes from an Indian–Muslim family, resident for generations on Africa's east coast. He takes over a store in a town on a bend in the river, and from there we follow his life and the politics of the new state, gaining assorted perspectives on the hopelessness of it all through the activities and reflections of his various friends and acquaintances.

In one form or another we are made aware that the past hangs heavily over the present, narrowing options, conditioning outcomes. The Indians on the coast did not see it that way: 'All that had happened in the past was washed away; there was always only the present.'[42] The Arabs too 'forgot who they were and where they had come from'.[43] But the assumption that things would continue as they always had, that Africa would remain as it had been, was belied and both groups were swept aside. Salim's friend, Indar, was made of sterner stuff and dismissed the past – 'You trample on the past, you crush it' – but he was constantly in flight and unfulfilled.[44] Raymond, the expatriate scholar and adviser to the Big Man, had no true knowledge of Africa and falsified the historical record. For a time he pleased the president and duped himself but eventually he was discarded, a defeated man. Most significant of all, there was the systematic obliteration of the colonial past after independence – houses burnt, monuments knocked down, streets renamed. 'The wish had only been to get rid of the old, to wipe out the memory of the intruder. It was unnerving, the depth of that African rage, the wish to destroy, regardless of the consequences.'[45]

In an essay on Zaire written some four years earlier, which provides much of the material for *A Bend in the River*, Naipaul gives a little more detail and a fuller commentary. 'The Belgian past is being scrubbed out as the Arab past has been scrubbed out.'[46] The history books had been rewritten. Oral accounts were uncommon. As a result few people had much knowledge of their immediate colonial past. And then comes the rub:

> Where so little has changed, where bush and river are so overwhelming, another past is accessible, better answering African bewilderment and African religious beliefs: the past as *le bon vieux temps de nos ancêtres*.[47]

In *A Bend in the River* the Big Man becomes a substitute for Africa's past, the personification of Africa itself. He explains to Raymond that his photograph in African costume 'isn't a picture of me'; 'It is a picture of all Africans.'[48] His words are echoed by a young student at the polytechnic.

At one level Naipaul's message in *A Bend in the River* is crystal clear. It runs through many of his other novels and, for that matter, his observations about his own life. To take control of one's destiny it is necessary to come to terms with one's history. It is the same for a society as for an individual. The past is discarded, forgotten, falsified only at great peril. Not only must it be faced in its entirety but a meaning must be searched out, a coherence found. Only then is it possible to be optimistic about the future – as when Ralph Singh declares in *The Mimic Men*: 'I have cleared the decks, as it were, and prepared myself for fresh action. It will be the action of a free man.'[49] Reflecting on his own personal situation, Naipaul observes:

> I sought to reconstruct my disintegrated society, to impose order on the world, to seek patterns, to tell myself – this is what happens when people are strong; this is what happens when people are weak. I had to find that degree of intellectual comfort, or I would have gone mad.[50]

Yet it is apparent from the tone of much of Naipaul's fiction that all too often the situation is much bleaker than this; optimism of Singh's kind may be misplaced. Some societies, Naipaul suggests, have no history other than that which is imposed on them by outside powers. Imperialism has so warped the society and maimed the spirit that there can be no hope.[51] Nowhere is the scorn of Naipaul's negativity so evident as with respect to Africa. Indeed, it can be said that he appropriates the continent in furtherance of his own highly personalized vision of political redemption. By so doing, he compromises his masterly depiction of how the past is deployed to corrupt the politics of the present. In *A Bend in the River* the history with which Naipaul is concerned is colonial history – that of the Arabs, the Indians and the Europeans. The rest hardly counts. He thus comes perilously close to echoing Trevor-Roper's view that before the intervention of outsiders, all was darkness. This sense of Africa cut off from time is compounded, for Naipaul, by a kind of malaise that seems to seep through from the very continent itself. There are the images of the bush reclaiming what had been valuable real estate; the water hyacinths choking the channels to the villages; the forest and river like presences much more powerful than civilized beings. As Salim journeys into the interior he thinks: 'There can't be a new life at the end of this.'[52] When he is preparing to make his escape, his friend Ferdinand tells him: 'Nobody's going anywhere. We're all going to hell, and every man knows this in his bones.'[53]

Naipaul's narrative starkly depicts the twin dangers of refusing to face the future (although in the particular case it fails to face the fact that Africa had its own past), and of representing the past in the kind of essentialized terms that could be appropriated by a new imperium as bad as the old. Such sympathy as it has, however, is directed to the predicament of the uprooted minority, not to the rooted mass. In this sense, Naipaul's narrative uses Africa but is not addressed to it. By virtue of their commitment, the position of African novelists was altogether different. The problem they faced was how to reclaim the past without foreclosing on the future. And their situation was such that cultural retrieval had to come before political re-visioning.

Given the European narratives against which they wrote and the pull of Manicheanism, it seems to me that the novelists have been less absolutist about Africa's past than there was reason to expect. Armah aside, the temptation to romanticize the precolonial has mostly been resisted – much more so than by many postcolonial theorists who came later. So far as Africa's colonial experience is concerned, the novelists have depicted the internal divisions and patterns of accommodation and in this respect they have often been more penetrating than other opinion-setters. For all the extravagance of Armah's presentation of the imperial encounter, he makes plain the role of kings and chiefs who, for reasons of self-advantage, sold their people into bondage and opened the door to European domination. Likewise Ngugi's depiction of imperialism and nationalism in Kenya takes account of the actions of those Kikuyu who collaborated with the British or who actually enlisted in the Home Guard during the Emergency. For Farah also, collaboration is part of the dynamics of the colonial encounter. Achebe goes much further and problematizes Africa's response to imperialism, continuously raising questions about changing cultural values and patterns of authority within traditional society. As he presents it in *Things Fall Apart*, the coming of the colonial era was not simply a consequence of British strength but also of the weakening of Ibo society from within.

African novelists have been less attentive to the heterogeneous elements within the practices of imperialism – understandably given their focus. Again Achebe is something of an exception here. Always at pains not to distort the historical record, he encourages his readers to see that imperialism spoke with different voices (Mr Brown and the Reverend Smith in *Things Fall Apart*), and that it has its own internal conflicts of interest (Captain Winterbottom, Mr Clarke and Mr Wright in *Arrow of God*). More than this, in the latter novel we understand that Captain Winterbottom's authority is much shallower than either his office or his assurance would suggest, because he misunderstands and misrepresents so much of Ibo culture.

As I read the narratives, there is one particular aspect of the novelist's treatment of the past which signals problems with respect to thinking about the future. This is the tendency to pass too lightly over the attractions of values and beliefs associated with foreign intervention. Despite its profoundly destructive effects, imperialism took root in Africa partly because it was seen by some Africans to offer prospects of a better life. Materialism, Christianity and Western education had a pull because they represented an alternative social order – albeit one that was to be adapted to local circumstances. Although there are obvious exceptions, the historical fiction does not sufficiently bring out the significance of these 'windows of opportunity' associated with imperialism. The ground is thus laid for the reluctance of many novelists to admit the allure of modernity within African societies and the possibilities raised by interaction with the outside world which we will consider in the next sections. In this respect, Ngugi is exceptional. In *The River Between* and *A Grain of Wheat* he shows how powerful was the appeal of Christian doctrine and Western education. For this he has often been criticized by those committed to radical social change and commended for the more overt socialist consciousness of his later novels.[54] I will argue to the opposite effect. *The River Between* and *A Grain of Wheat* provide a better basis for understanding Africa's post-independence course, and what can be done to change it, because they show so clearly the process of internalization of values and beliefs that had once been largely external to Africa.

Grappling with community

In this section I am interested in drawing out some of the ideas about community to be found in African literature and asking about their contemporary political significance. I have chosen to concentrate on three areas of thought and experience which are taken up in many of the novels and which bring culture face to face with politics. The first is concerned with a consciousness of being African which taps a sense of racial affinity or cultural cohesiveness. Can this be harnessed in the management of group relations and how does it relate to ethnic and other particularisms? Second, there is the presentation of material about everyday life and politics of a personal kind. How far do novelists work out from here to engage with politics as traditionally understood and located in the public domain? How far might we, as readers? As a guide, I have in mind the writing of scholars like Achille Mbembe and Allessandro Triulzi on the relationship between the formalities of the official order and the informalities of public initiatives and responses.[55] Third, there is the question of the modern nation-state as a construct for forging new forms of community. What is of interest here is whether the novelist has been prepared to accept the regulatory role of this alien political form. In short, has the modern state been domesticated within African literature? How these and other issues of community are seen is partly a matter of the immediacy and intensity of the colonial experience. The closer and more troubling the colonialism, the more the sense of community in Africa will be defined in opposition to the imperial other – as, for example, in the early Achebe as compared with the later Achebe or East African writing as compared with West African writing. But as the colonial experience recedes, so slippage occurs both with respect to the linkages of Africanness and the potentialities of the postcolonial state. The distancing of colonialism may thus require novelists – along with others – to renegotiate the bonds and limits of African community.

Implicit in this reminder of the historical relativity of thought is an acknowledgement that the very urge to redress colonialist categories prolonged the influence of European thought through its inversion. It was along such lines that so many African writers and intellectuals rejected the Negritude movement. To celebrate the ties that bound together the African world as essentially non-analytical, as matters of feeling and rhythm and intuitive understanding, was to be imprisoned by the Manichean tradition. In Wole Soyinka's terms, the fundamental error was one of procedure: 'Negritude stayed within a pre-set system of Eurocentric intellectual analysis both of man and society and tried to re-define the African and his society in those externalised terms.'[56] The judgement stands. However, recent thinking is more likely to acknowledge the contribution Negritude made to cultural retrieval, and the impossibility, at a particular moment, of breaking completely free of the enclosures of the European model.[57]

'We are all Africans', declared Kwame Nkrumah,[58] and the same sentiment echoes through the pages of many of the first generation of African novels. It is apt that Nkrumah's vision of a united Africa found its foremost fictional embodiment in the writing of a fellow-Ghanaian, Ayi Kwei Armah. For Nkrumah, 'Ghana's freedom would be meaningless if it was not linked with the total liberation of the entire continent of Africa.'[59] For Modin, the central character in Armah's *Why Are We So Blest?*, it is beside the point to declare his nationality: 'I just think of our small states as colonial things. I am African.'[60]

Armah's overriding purpose in *Two Thousand Seasons* and *The Healers* is to promote the unity of Africa – as a natural state, as a political ideal and as something of beauty in itself. On the last page of *Two Thousand Seasons* the message is reiterated: 'There is no beauty but in relationships. Nothing cut off by itself is beautiful.'[61] The narrative voice in both novels is carefully controlled to engage the reader's sympathy. The main ideas are repeated again and again in different contexts. Commentary moves between past, present and future, and we are led to see each in relation to the others. The images – desert, springs, fertility, disease – are chosen to evoke and persuade.

Arguments running counter to Armah's thesis are rebutted or dismissed, often without being explicitly presented. Despite the differences in setting and style, both novels are constructed around the motif of a journey – a journey through time and in self-awareness. Division and falsehood characterize Africa's present and recent past. To have any hope, it is necessary to go back before colonialism to a time when the black people were one – when they 'spread connected over an open land'.[62] In *The Healers* the presentation is more specific. The Fanti, the Asante and other tribal groups were but fragments of the Akan people, and they in turn were just a little piece of the community of all black people.[63] The subsequent disintegration and disease of the spirit was partly a consequence of European penetration and partly an outgrowth of internal splits among black people. Indigenous parasites, interested in privilege not production, became instruments in the hands of the predators from without.

It is evident that Armah's conception of African unity is predicated on pigmentation, not on some geographical sense of the oneness of the continent. Earlier we noted Armah's biting attack on the Arab intrusion into Africa. Other black African writers have portrayed Arabs in similarly negative terms and by implication as outsiders. Arab writers have responded in kind. In one account, 'Arab authors do not invest characters in Black Africa with any form of dignity or heroic status that they can respect.'[64] On both sides the emphasis appears to be on difference rather than similarity – despite the shared experience of Western imperialism. Whereas the historical record of Arab/Black African interaction admits several layers of meaning, most novelists have settled for only one.

If the organizing principle of Armah's history is based on colour, in other respects his history is selective, but less so. The use of myth to advance the pan-African cause is most pronounced with respect to the role of the healers who act as the agents of unification. Yet the vista of African connectedness in precolonial times is less chimerical than might be imagined. In the section on the migration in *Two Thousand Seasons*, Armah writes of 'a line of villages each talking to the next' and 'a chain of granaries and friendships'.[65] Recent historical research suggests that cultural networks linked together the various farming and trading communities; there existed a chain of underground relationships between the villages which, for example, made pilgrimages possible. Even where strong centralized kingdoms such as the Asante held sway, the pattern was not substantially different because the authority of the state was limited and many areas of life were regulated by the customs of the extended village system. Of course the picture is in need of qualification. Often enough the co-operative and integrative strands were broken by competing local interests – as occurs in Elechi Amadi's *The Great Ponds*, which tells of a war between two villages in the Delta region over the ownership of a pond that is rich in fish.[66]

Where the problem sets in, however, is not with Armah's picture of the past but with the ease of its transference to Africa's present. Even if we accept that in the precolonial period the state was largely a fiction and social and political life was rooted in the network of villages overlapping and connecting for specific purposes, its contemporary relevance must be regarded as problematic. The modern state may be suspended above the villages but it is well entrenched; traditional values may be strongly held but expectations and aspirations are different; as a result of material changes, conflicts of interest run deep and are unlikely to fade away. The points of connection with the past should not be allowed to mask the areas of disjunction. These problems of giving pan-Africanism a political imprint are not, of course, peculiar to literature and it is doubtful whether scholars have done any better than writers. Kwame Anthony Appiah has made a guarded attempt, employing contemporary identity theory, but what emerges seems to me fairly thin.[67]

In the writing of other African novelists there are shades of Armah's celebration of a pan-African consciousness but the expression is less direct, the tone more muted. In part this would seem to be a function of when the novels were written. The experience of the independent states has bred a cynicism about visions of political unity. It may also be that Armah's understanding of how much was and might be shared between the various parts of Black Africa reflects elements of a West African literary consciousness – an expansiveness, almost a flamboyance, about Africanism – to which writers in East and Southern Africa could not subscribe because of the immediacy of their political struggles.

The dream of an African political community has therefore given way to more limited expressions of the connectedness of African thought and experience. This does not mean that pan-Africanism has been abandoned; rather, the politics of continentalism have come to be expressed in realms not traditionally associated with governance. In this sense a parallel can be drawn between developments in African literature and the changing concerns of the postcolonial discourse. Three areas carry forward the ideal of an African political consciousness: the commitment to the cultural cohesion of African peoples; the belief in the ordinary African; and the demand that African writing be judged by distinctively African literary criteria.

The idea of the cultural cohesion of African peoples is an antidote to the fear that the house of African politics was built on sand. The grand narrative of African freedom had been punctuated by the growing specificity of interests and ethnicities, the separation of state from society and the failure of politics to renegotiate African economics. By embracing a sense of relatedness, recognizing some elements of a shared past and espousing values taken to be characteristically African – such as extended kinship, respect for age and a love of festivals – the novel could thus serve as a renewed instrument of affirmation.

At least in some quarters this trend to write in favour of cultural integration is seen as consciously shaped. The thinking is that what Africa requires is a 'cultural construct' which could serve as a basis for bringing Africans together, and that writers see themselves as having a crucial contribution to make. Consciously formulated or not, the idea of cultural cohesion has the appeal of the middle ground. It expresses the urge to unity yet avoids the quicksands of African politics or the insubstantiality of the 'African personality'. The latter concept, more contrived and self-consciously employed, caught the imagination for a time but, as Ezekiel Mphahlele observed, in discussion it 'began to recede, to become vaguer and vaguer, and even to seem unreal'.[68]

Something similar may be in the process of happening to cultural cohesion as a literary construct for the continent. Like the African personality, it has most appeal in West Africa, where so much of the literature has a pronounced cultural orientation. In other regions where the anti-colonial struggle has been violent and protracted and the presence of alien groups or outside interests has produced greater bitterness, novelists have been more politicized, less given to philosophical reflection. Two decades back, for example, Mphahlele pointed out that for Southern Africans the 'very bloody struggle helps to determine the shape of their culture'.[69] There is also a sense of distaste – almost resentment – with what appears from certain standpoints to represent West African cultural imperialism. One East African scholar complained to me that Soyinka keeps writing about Yoruba gods as though they were everyone's gods.

Related to this supposed commitment to cultural unity has been the affirmation of the lives and values of ordinary African people. In recent African novels there has been a tendency to acclaim characters seen to be representative of the masses, adhering in large part to traditional ideas and values and often rooted in village life or at least retaining rural ties. In some respects the concern with the subaltern is not new. A 'grass-roots' orientation was characteristic of many of the earliest African novels. Usually this was a commitment to the common people, but its realization very often was in the hands of exceptional individuals who stood apart from the masses and had a clearer vision. The thinker, the artist, the messianic reformer gave voice to the hopes of those who were unable to articulate a different political future.[70] Then, in the novels of many male writers, there was a romanticized depiction of African women, whose fulfilment was seen to reside almost exclusively in marriage and motherhood. This brought its own problems. The argument is persuasive that not only did such representations deprive women of purposeful political action but they also cast them in the role of upholding the traditional order, despite the fact that in substantial measure it operated against their own interests.[71]

Leaving aside for the moment the special case of women writers and women protagonists, for some time the tendency has been to vest agency in ordinary people themselves or at least to close the gap between political action and membership of the community at large. Writers appear to have been reacting against the culture of the big cities, the spread of what they see as foreign norms and values and the alienation of the new élites from society and the soil. There is also the hope that going back to the people will provide an escape from the post-independence spiral of conflict and a secure foundation for some kind of African connectedness.

The keynote is sounded by the narrator in B. Kojo Laing's *Search Sweet Country*: 'All the ordinary people were the real people: they lived beyond the slogans, they outlasted the politicians.'[72] It is only by engaging with the things that fill their lives, with the hold of the past and the pulls of the present, that we can get a bearing on Africa's postcolonial course and how it might be changed. It is notable that Laing's characters are often flawed and that they are presented in a way which shows up their weaknesses and foibles. We are meant to understand their situation rather than admire their qualities. It has been remarked that the epic hero appears to have disappeared from recent African fiction; there has been a democratization of the heroic ideal.[73] Lewis Nkosi has argued in a similar vein. According to his interpretation, history has become the hero. Works by novelists such as Peter Abrahams, Ngugi wa Thiong'o, Sembene Ousmane and Yambo Ouologuem share 'an acute vision of history as a collective working out of a people's destiny'.[74] It is apparent at this point that there are very different conceptions of the position and role of the ordinary African.

In *Search Sweet Country* Laing rejects the monological voice and the predetermined outcome. A number of different characters introduce perspectives which bear on Ghana's future. However strange these individuals may be and however unlikely their politics, they are the makers of Ghana's history, not the political power-brokers cut off from the life of the people. 'One whole country cannot fit under a soldier's cap!'[75] That is why, '[b]y the Chorkor beach Acheampong's Revolution lay exhausted in the sands, being pushed up and down by the damnation of the tides'.[76] The understanding is that building the new Ghana will take time and that in the interim there will be distractions and false starts. This is illustrated by Osofo and his followers' march on the Castle, which is the seat of power in Ghana. Despite the initial euphoria of the crowd – the faces that 'wanted to see the history that ran past them' – the march came to nothing when a group of policemen diverted the marchers by providing them with food in Black Star Square. 'Corned beef politics', Osofo shouted, as his followers flocked to the food.

In contrast to *Search Sweet Country*, where literary politics are distanced by the vibrancy of the characters and the immediacy of the action, the proletarian emphasis in some recent novels is overly deliberate and one can see shades of the Soviet socialist realism of the 1930s. History is given a helping hand to move as it should, and the author's political agenda is evident in the shaping of characters and the management of the plot.

One such novel is Ngugi's *Petals of Blood*.[77] This is certainly a work committed to the ordinary African. Except for Manira, the main characters come from the lower echelons of Kenyan society. They are buffeted by forces over which they have no control. First there is the drought, and then they are faced with the capitalist economic transformation of Ilmorog. Their failings are presented as part and parcel of life, and there is an understanding that it is only by working collectively that they can grow as individuals and improve their lot. Ngugi uses folklore and symbolism to establish that the lives of his principal characters remained linked to the traditional village culture of the Kikuyu: Mwathi's hut, the rain-spirit that possesses Wanja, the millet drink Theng'eta which 'gave seers their tongues; poets and Gichandi players their words'. The old woman, Nyakinyua, plays a key role in bringing an awareness of the communal past into a present which, in Wanja's words, knows only one law: 'You eat somebody or you are eaten.'[78]

Yet superimposed on this picture of ordinary but dislocated life is another text about the evils of imperialism and neo-colonialism in Kenya and what must be done to make the society whole again. Because of its rehearsed nature, the political argument is often at one remove from the lives we are following. In any case it has a reductionist, doctrinaire quality which makes it not easily digestible in a novel about people in their everyday affairs. One result is the lack of consistency in the characters of Manira and Karega. Manira's conversion to religious extremism carries little conviction, while Karega's cast of mind gives the impression of being 'touched up' as an afterthought.

I would argue, however, that the tension in the novel between life and politics produces a more fundamental weakness. No reader can have any doubt about the economic and social costs of an externally imposed, and to some extent externally propelled, capitalism. Nor about the need for workers and peasants to take collective action to cut down black magnates such as Chuzi, Mzigu and Kimeria, expose religious oppression and resist the appeals of the tribalism promoted by the new élites. But Ngugi is vague and ambivalent about what is to replace the neo-colonial system. From what Karega says, it appears that a new political order would build upon something of Africa's past; he reflects that 'Africa, after all, did not have one but several pasts which were in perpetual struggle'. Moreover, it would also take advantage of modern industry and technology.[79] Elsewhere in the novel the viewpoint is much simpler and more romantic. There is a nostalgia for precolonial Ilmorog with its communal rhythms and primitive socialism, free from the conflicts of interest introduced by imperialism. If there are utopian elements in this picture of the past, then they are enormously magnified in so far as the old Ilmorog offers a pointer to a post-imperial future. Eustace Palmer has advanced a similar criticism with respect to the treatment of education in the novel. It is one thing to demand the diseuropeanization of education but quite another for Karega and his fellow-students to call for a new philosophy and approach which they cannot spell out but only signify by invoking the phrase 'African populism'. Palmer comments that Karega does not seem to know what he wants, 'But Ngugi ought to know.'[80]

It is instructive to compare *Petals of Blood* with another novel 'of the people', Marjorie Oludhe Macgoye's *Coming to Birth*. Published nine years later, and also set in Kenya, it covers the end of the colonial period and the first decade and a half of independence. It tells the story of a young Luo woman, Pauline, who leaves her village to live with her husband Martin in a shanty dwelling in Nairobi. The marriage falters, partly because of Pauline's failure to have a child. Striking out for herself, she joins a homecraft training school in Kusumu, where she learns new skills and gains self-assurance. After a period as a homecraft club leader, Pauline moves back to Nairobi, a more independent and fulfilled person. The latter part of the novel records her *modus vivendi* with Martin, her working life as a privileged domestic, and her response to Nairobi life.

What is significant about this work – and it is indicative of the approach of other writers of the past decade or so – is that Pauline is shown coming to terms with her lot, little engaged by the public sphere. Her life and growth are presented with a directness which seems in keeping with both her personality and the society to which she belongs. There is no attempt to idealize traditional Luo values nor to dramatize the process of adjustment and change: 'You took from custom what suited you, and so it had always been.'[81] Unlike *Petals of Blood*, politics remain in the background – in some respects conditioning the life of the main characters, in other respects scarcely intruding at all. Although Pauline never becomes especially politicized, her personal development is accompanied by an increased political awareness: 'Kenya was a hard enough idea to get hold of. Africa, to Pauline, was a name on a map. But perhaps before she went to Nairobi she would not even have recognised the map.'[82] According to one critic, Macgoye is least convincing when she attempts to make the changing relationships between the characters carry the burden of postcolonial politics.[83] In my view, this is exactly what the author does not do. Politics and personal relations are related spheres, but the message of the novel is that in this transitional Third World society the one does not neatly determine the other.

These comments on Macgoye direct attention to other novels written by women and about women. Can it be said that there is a similar tendency in women's writing to focus on the lives and values of ordinary Africans? Without wishing to draw too sharp a distinction between the two bodies of writing, it appears that women writers have struck out in directions of their own. Although most of their protagonists have been 'ordinary' in terms of their socio-economic situation and the difficulties they confront, the emphasis has been on their strength of character and personal development. Very often they are portrayed as more open to social change than men and more determined in their everyday lives to bring it about. In her analysis of the writing of Flora Nwapa and Buchi Emecheta, Florence Stratton points out that the city, for all its perils and unpleasantness, is seen as providing new opportunities for women, as being a space for challenging traditional practices.[84] In general there is much less propensity to celebrate the village or write nostalgically about old ways. There is also a strong sense that change and development at the personal level are part and parcel of the process of creating a new political culture. In this respect, Macgoye's *Coming to Birth* does not articulate the kind of connectedness that we see in the novels of Grace Ogot, Flora Nwapa, or, even more, Bessie Head. Lloyd Brown makes the pertinent point that in recognizing the importance of personal growth to social change, many of the women writers show a realism which precludes the kind of easy optimism about social transformation often found in protest literature.[85] Taking this further, it could be suggested that the women writers start with the personal and are thus led to engage with broader political issues, whereas much of the established male writing appears to adjust the personal to preferred conceptions of cultural politics. If this is so, it underlines a central contention of this book, that literature is most rewarding to the student of politics when it works from the personal to the political.

The other line of thinking which promotes the ideal of an African political consciousness derives primarily from secondary literary sources rather than from the novels themselves. This is the demand that African writing should have an African content, an African form and be judged by distinctively African criteria. In addition, it is sometimes argued that for a work to come within the canon of African literature it must be written by an African, be committed to a political vision – even a particular vision – of Africa's future, and, looking to the years ahead, be written in an African language. It is indicative of this approach that Ngugi prefaces his case for writing in the vernacular by characterizing contemporary Africa as a struggle between an imperialist tradition and a resistance tradition.[86] For him, literature can only be relevant and have 'a correct perspective' if it embraces the resistance tradition; there is no middle ground. Although disagreeing with Ngugi on the issue of language, the authors of *Toward the Decolonization of African Literature* are even more categorical. They declare that: 'African literature *is* an autonomous entity separate and apart from all other literatures. It has its own traditions, models and norms.'[87] It follows 'that genuinely autonomous criteria would have to be applied in judging African literature'.[88]

Such views, although extreme, suggest a tendency in African texts to cultivate the distinctively African and insulate the African experience from overseas developments. As was suggested at the beginning of this chapter but now needs fuller development, much African fiction inclines to look inward and draw strength from its own corpus, giving the impression that Africa's problems and how they are approached fall into a category of their own. Compared with Indian writing in English, for example, there is a much greater predictability about themes, the characters show much less ambivalence, the viewpoints are more alike. We do not need to search far for the explanation. India was never deprived of a history. Even in the high noon of empire, India was seen as having a rich and fascinating past. Hinduism cushioned large sections of Indian society from the psychological and cultural impact of imperialism, whereas in Africa there was the disturbance to traditional religion and thought occasioned by the extraordinary advance of Christianity (and Islam). Partly because they were written, Indian indigenous languages did not experience the decline suffered by their African counterparts. For all these reasons, the African need to build bulwarks to protect the self was that much more acute. Ali Mazrui once declared that Africans are not the poorest, nor the most brutalized, but the most humiliated people. 'No people in human history have for so long been regarded as so inferior. The range of humiliation is from the slave trade to *apartheid*.'[89]

These words of Mazrui make understandable the urge to assert difference from the European or external other and the desire to accentuate the alikeness of Africans and the commonalities of the African experience. But however understandable, the processes which we perhaps glibly describe in terms of modernization and globalization have redrawn the axes of African community. Resistance to the outside, commonality on the inside, simply do not begin to address the diversity of contemporary Africa. On this reckoning, each of the three expressions of an African consciousness represents an attempt to freeze African cultural and literary politics at the beginning of the postcolonial journey. The case is most graphically put by Dambudzo Marechera, drawing on the fractured vision of one who is both an insider and an outsider.

What is significant about Marechera is that, unlike other African writers of the 1970s and '80s, he had a deep antipathy to the urge to find some unity of spirit among his fellow-Africans. It was not only that his own experience made him antagonistic to the idea of the oneness of Africa. It was also a matter of his belief that the writer's responsibility was to strip away the deceits and pretences of cultural propriety. He was thus led to dismiss the promotion of an ideal which, as he saw it, was shaped in conscious opposition to the pattern of life of family, friends and the new élites. 'We are what we are not, is the paradox of fiction' he wrote, [90] but not for a moment did he endorse such a paradox with respect to the relationship between African literature and African life. What is uppermost in his writing is the acute sense of contradiction within African thought and life, and his own ambivalence towards Africanness. This sense of fracture marks Marechera as Black Africa's first postmodernist writer and derives from the fact that so much of what he wrote about contemporary literature and politics came from within, from a highly personalized understanding of Africa and the outside world. In one respect there is a similarity between Marechera and V. S. Naipaul: the conviction that the historical and cultural experience of colonialism had so dislocated the spirit that it was no longer possible to cling to the old adhesions of traditional community or embrace the new libations of national and continental liberation.

Marechera's understanding of postcolonial politics and culture and the role of literature is most fully articulated in *The Black Insider*. Written in 1978, though not published until 1990, some of Marechera's concerns may now appear as those of an earlier era, but in fact the burden of his argument has a direct contemporary relevance. Developing a critique of the African image, his target is romanticized notions of Africanness which deflect attention from the failures and false starts of recent history. This is witnessed by references in the body of the text to the mirage of a snug mud-hut, the agreement about the need to be silent in the interests of unity about the pragmatism of the leaders of the front-line states, and the recognition that the OAU had become the maintenance man of the black *anciens régimes* instead of the protector of the people's liberties. Hence literature is diverted from its proper role of unlocking the mind and laying out new possibilities, untrammelled by the enclosures of race, culture and nation. Marechera's narrative method – personal reminiscences interlaced with vignettes of colonialism and anticolonialism and reflections on writers drawn from different continents and different traditions – seems calculated to force the reader to think at different levels and wrestle with connections. There is thus a danger of smoothing out the wrinkles and settling for a single core of meaning. As I read the text, however, Marechera is expressing his disillusionment with the failure of African intellectuals to expose the dead-ends and the circularities of the postcolonial condition. It is only when those with an education, who are in touch with the outside world, face up to the brutality of personal relations, the intolerance born of alienation, the disappearance of a sense of home and the demoralization of exile, that the process of change can begin. Instead, however, refuge is taken in a false sense of belonging, in mimicking white culture or parading a shallow radicalism.

Marechera pays his dues to Gabriel Okara, Aye Kwei Armah (*The Beautiful Ones Are Not Yet Born*), Christopher Okigbo, Soyinka and Ngugi, but what strikes him most acutely is African literature's unrealized possibilities. They are unrealized because too often writers have confined themselves to one province of literature, and within that province they have papered over the cracks and opted for comforting clichés.[91] The opportunity to show the emperor as he really is has been passed up because writers have been taken in by the psychology of clothes. Hence the culture of conformity, the myth of rootedness, the cult of mediocrity. The African image becomes a symbol of literature's failure. It is an 'obscene idol'.[92] It has – shades of Naipaul – given rise to a 'new kind of fascism'.[93] It is 'such a good advertising and public relations stunt' that it blinds us to tribalism, materialism and social class.[94]

Predictably, readers of the *The Black Insider* in various manuscript forms found the work too élitist, insufficiently 'African', and hence not suitable for publication in Heinemann's African Writers Series. Similar points were made in reviews of his published work. Though wounded by such criticisms, Marechera viewed them as symptomatic of the state of African literature and its associated political culture. In line with his practice of infusing the personal into the political, he wrote episodes in several of his works which responded to his critics and at the same time related their arguments back to the culture of African literature as he saw it. In *The Black Insider* he quotes directly from a reader's report on *The House of Hunger* but leaves the material to speak for itself.[95]

In *The House of Hunger* and *Black Sunlight*, on the other hand, Marechera injects the substance of the critics' complaints into the narrative and then proceeds to show their wider political and cultural ramifications. In *The House of Hunger* he tells of a fight at school between Edmund, the lonely swot, and Stephen, the class bully, in which Edmund is mercilessly beaten and left in a pool of blood. Edmund loves Russian literature and wants to be a writer. He is also interested in European music and painting. Stephen is an avid reader of the Heinemann African Writers Series and firmly believes that European tools of criticism should not be used in the analysis of African literature. Yet it is Edmund who becomes a guerrilla and is captured by Smith's security forces.[96] In *Black Sunlight* we are introduced to Blanche and Nick, an *alter ego* of the author. Blanche insists that a cultural system must shape the behaviour of individuals in the interests of a consistent whole, favourable to the survival of the society. The narrator comments that he 'returned from Oxford to find the culture and the society of my country broken down, replaced by manufactured images, fiction and fantasy'.[97] Nick has intellectual similarities to Blanche but he believes that the individual must take a stand when faced with an unsympathetic or mindless culture. Nick is a poet who is denounced for his 'modernistic European manner', and held to be conservative because he writes in English in spite of his revolutionary subjects. Attacked by students at his first public poetry reading, he responds by castigating them and their low cultural level. Marechera clearly endorses Nick's sense of self against the herd and his intellectual openness which puts him at odds with what he takes to be the canon.

We can expect more in the way of strident expressions of dissociation from established culture as writers engage with the horrific aspects of 'everyday life' in Africa, especially the situation of the urban poor. It also seems likely that, after the manner of contemporary cultural studies, estrangement will be presented as having a positive side, as holding some promise of new forms of community and new kinds of political action. I am thinking here of the practices which have developed in the unofficial economy, the protests of gangs of embittered youths, and what Triulzi has called the 'street buzz' of cities like Lagos and Nairobi, where a new politics appears to be emerging involving graffiti, street talk, pavement radio and the like.[98] In some respects this might represent an extension of existing literary concerns – for example, Achebe's depiction of the ordinariness of African life which might not have appeared so to his readers, or Farah's reference to rumour and its possibilities in the context of the silence of the regime and what he calls its 'politics of mystification'. But there will also be the difference that popular culture rather than ordinary life will constitute the frame of reference and there will be greater emphasis on subaltern empowerment.

Although not as yet much pursued in the literature, such developments have international aspects – for instance, connections in fashion, popular music and the culture of sport – and they could have ramifications for non-governmental aid programmes, tourism and other exchanges. We would be wise to keep in mind, however, that analyses along these lines usually put much faith in agency and show a considerable measure of social optimism. Agency is hardly a new category in African studies. If one thing is clear by now, it is that Africans have long acted to enhance their own identities and pursue their own interests but very often their actions did not produce sufficient dividends; their agency failed to transform their economic and political environment. Here account needs to be taken of those fictional narratives which give sobering accounts of African urban life. In Meja Mwangi's *Going Down River Road*, set in the slums and shanty towns of Nairobi, poverty maims the spirit. Ben, the main character, reflects: 'Nobody seems aware of where they are going.'[99] In his latest novel, *Dangerous Love*, Ben Okri introduces the reader to some of the ugliness of life for the poor in

Lagos of the 1970s. Although the protagonist, Omovo, struggles against demoralization and tries to see openings for change, there is little in the narrative to relieve the images of loss and victimhood.[100] Interestingly, both writers take the struggle to board a bus and how passengers behave towards each other as a symbol of social disintegration. For good measure, Mwangi adds a description of how drivers never give way at pedestrian crossings: 'They fear losing forever their right of way.'[101]

I now turn to the final issue raised at the beginning of this section: whether the modern state has been tacitly underwritten within African literature. Putting the issue in this way is not perhaps circumspect because it invites broad generalizations of a political kind at the expense of more nuanced readings in which the political cannot neatly be extracted from the literary. It should also be said that until a few years back it was unlikely that the question would have been posed in these terms because the nation-state was taken to be an instrument for releasing African societies from continued external domination and delivering the promises of social change.[102] If the pairing of nation and literature had accomplished so much in Europe, why should it not be a positive force in Africa also? Inevitably, looking back involves carrying back something of the perspective of the present but we need to be mindful of the distortions which can result from unreflective transposition.

Taking these considerations very seriously, it is my view that the construct of the nation-state is so interrelated with ideas about modernity and centralized rule and is of such far-reaching significance, that it must be raised directly. I do so, not to pass judgement on what was written earlier, but to indicate the space for alternative lines of approach and new readings of the texts. The coupling of the state with the cultural politics of Africa has never been a happy or productive union, and it must be at least two decades since anyone has argued to the contrary. We have now reached a stage where it is possible to write not merely of an intellectual failure to grapple with the problems of authority and community, but of the spectre of anarchy on the continent.[103] Choosing his words more judiciously, Basil Davidson expresses the contemporary disillusionment with the record of the state in Africa when he writes of the 'curse of the nation-state' and the cultural misery it has caused throughout the continent.[104] The issue now is not so much the strength or weakness of the state, or even whether it is good or bad, but the very construct itself. As a result, we have seen the emergence of new discourses devoted to re-imagining the state and rethinking the political.

Clearly, African fictional narratives have not gone this far and we would hardly have expected them to. Attention has very largely been concentrated on the state in action, as expressed through the behaviour of its leadership and the processes of rule, rather than the state as political design. There is much more exposure of its malfunctioning than questioning of its underlying assumptions. Excepting the early days, when African unity could be a hope as well as a dream, the tendency has been for the nation-state to be taken as a given in African fiction. The political geography of borders has received considerable censure. The literature of the Nigerian civil war has touched on some of the problems congruent with the state being the supposed expression of community and deemed the guarantor of security. It is possible that new readings of this literature may draw out critiques of the state from novels focused on the implications of the war for its victims (as, for example, Isidore Okpewho's *The Last Duty*) or from those which examine the behaviour of the leadership and associated élites (as in Eddie Iroh's *Forty-eight Guns for the General* or Chukwuemeka Ike's *Sunset at Dawn*). At one time or another, nearly all African novelists have been concerned with the state's violence and repression, its distance from the people and the culture of ruling regimes – the role of the military, the misuse of power, the significance of international economic and political links.

What is more problematical, however, is the novelists' approach to the nation-state itself: can it be made to fit Africa's cultural inheritance, might it be useful to imagine alternative formations?[105] Now there is certainly an argument that in Africa the state is virtually indistinguishable from the culture of its ruling élites; the personalization of power is such that state and regime are to all intents and purposes one and the same thing. Yet even following this line of thinking, fundamental issues remain to be addressed. The most important of these is that the nation-state was an import from Europe, in large part imposed on Africa. Of course it came and was received with high hopes, but it brought with it a high degree of centralization, an urban bias and certain presumptions about organic solidarity which bore little relation to the experience of most African societies. As we have seen, African literature was forthright in its resistance to external imposition but for the most part the nation-state proved to be an exception. This is less remarkable than it might seem when account is taken of the close association between literature and the nation-state in Europe and, more pertinently, in other parts of the former colonial empires as well. Indeed, viewed in comparison with other Third World literatures, what is striking is the critical edge characteristic of African narratives.

Approaching the fictional texts in this spirit, let us consider the positions taken by some of the novelists most concerned with the trajectory of the African state. For Chinua Achebe, rewriting the decline of Igbo culture led inexorably to the challenge of writing what should stand in its stead. For most of his adult life, as brought out in *No Longer at Ease, A Man of the People* and *Anthills of the Savannah*, this meant Nigeria as a nation – a dream that had been with him since before independence.[106] Yet given the turbulence of the times, Nigeria as a nation was clearly a problem that could be apprehended in various ways. Not unreasonably, Achebe chose to present it by articulating a new consciousness of community with a territorial base. As argued earlier, he used the novel as a means of redressing, not simply representing, the existing order of things. And as Gikandi has pointed out, the difficulty he faced was that both his characters and the symbols of his political ideal resisted easy incorporation in the text.[107] It is a measure of Achebe's achievement that he is able to proffer hope when his narratives are mostly studies in pessimism. Achebe coupled his commitment to territorial nationalism with an increasingly biting critique of the political leadership, which he saw as isolated from the people and unresponsive to the participatory traditions of indigenous social organization. His understanding unquestionably linked the personalization of power with the political culture but it did not, to my mind, seriously address the construct of the nation-state itself – the theoretical frame with which the political culture had to mesh, the ideational receptacle into which the sense of community had to flow. His position appears to be that the state is not open to deconstruction because there is no alternative in the offing.

Both Farah and Soyinka have deep doubts about the nation-state, Farah writing more about the practice, Soyinka more about the ideal. There is a case to be made that each has made a substantial contribution to rethinking the African state, so long as one does not take an instrumentalist view of the politics of literary narratives. Farah's primary contribution is to direct attention to the exclusory implications of the nationalist credo and the human suffering that this entails. Writing as a critic from within, he starts with the idea that Somalis see themselves as unique; as legend has it, Somalia is the only country in Africa that qualifies to be called a nation.[108] Farah goes on to suggest that this promiscuous idea (as he terms it) may have something to do with the lack of a centrally organized opposition or front of resistance – presumably because of the difficulty of inventing alternative national symbols. His indictment of the politics of national consciousness is one of the distinctive features of his 1986 novel, *Maps*. There are the horrors of war and personal violence perpetrated in the name of a people. There is the problem of refugees. There is the tragedy of those groups, such as the Somalis in the Ogaden and in Kenya, who cannot satisfy the criteria of national identity and who become 'unpersons'. Clearly, Farah has made an impressive start in piercing through the mystique of the nation-state but – to extend a point made in our first section – I wonder if it is really followed through.

Soyinka's field of vision is of unparalleled breadth and the problems associated with community and authority are never far from view. The fundamental theme in his work is the conflict between individual freedom and the workings of organized society, with Soyinka committed to the largest possible measure of individual freedom. His scepticism about the state is manifest in his depiction of the tendency of organized society to authoritarianism and in his championing of individuals who challenge the collective will and offer some prospect of social renewal. Alongside this overriding concern with the individual in society, Soyinka offers a number of more directed perspectives on the modern nation-state in Africa. For all his concern about African reference-points, he expresses a profound pessimism about African culture and history containing within itself anything which might enable the continent to strike a distinctive course with its adoption of the nation-state. In his play *A Dance of the Forests*, written for Nigerian independence in 1960, we are told: 'Nations live by strength; nothing else has meaning' and that '[w]ar is the only consistency'.[109]

Moreover, 'the direct descendants of our great forefathers' who might offer hope, when found and brought for 'the gathering of the tribes', turn out to be no better than the rest.[110]

Then there is Soyinka's depiction of those occasions – in, for example, *Opera Wonyosi* – when government is a charade; where, despite the public face, the business of rule is an exercise in conspiracy on the part of the privileged few. This theme is given a particular twist in *Season of Anomy*, where the interests of the Cartel and its need to meet the challenge presented by the Aiyero reformers are seen as the *raison d'être* of the state. The Commander-in-Chief 'represented the fourth arm of the Cartel'; he was 'a tool, a mere representative symbol'.[111] There was nothing accidental about the actions of the soldiers who destroyed the town of Gborolu, seemingly immune to the blandishments of the cartel. 'They were after the men of Aiyero everywhere. But they have to disguise it by unleashing death on a far wider scale.'[112] Soyinka takes a different tack in *The Interpreters*, which traces the search of five young men attempting to come to terms with themselves in the rapidly changing Nigeria of the 1960s. On one reading, the role of the Afro-American homosexual, Joe Golder, helps in a minor way to establish the novel's problematic of how much is lost once a case has to be stated and a name given. In over-simplified terms, the artificiality of Golder's attempt to define himself on the basis of his own sexuality is not unlike the artificiality of the situation of the interpreters, which requires them to define themselves on the basis of being Nigerian. The problem is one of imported categories and social inscription.[113]

The difficulty, both here and with respect to Soyinka's other discursions into the politics of the nation-state, is to know how far to take them and the extent to which one line of thinking relates to another. This is partly a consequence of the multiplicity of angles that Soyinka brings into view. Ideas tumble through the texts and very often Soyinka leaves it to the reader to select and order them. It is sometimes said that his fundamental concern is with individual consciousness and that this involves a tendency to retreat from politics. I would make the point somewhat differently, emphasizing the parallels that can be drawn between his work and contemporary writing on identity and cultural politics. Either way, however, Soyinka's narrative style – his heavy reliance on metaphor, the importance he places on allusion, his condensed language and economy of expression – makes for difficulties.[114] The result is that much of Soyinka's politics is not readily accessible.

Sharper critiques of the exclusions and compulsions of the nation-state punctuate the narratives of women writers which are now receiving critical attention after an extended period of neglect. As in other continents, African women novelists and, more so perhaps, associated feminist critical commentaries have broken with the canonical orthodoxies which have kept nationalism and the state, on the one hand, and gender and sexuality, on the other, as discrete and autonomous categories.[115] They have been concerned to show that in (many) male-authored texts, women have served as sex objects (thus confirming the masculinity of the modern state) or as symbols of traditional values (thus legitimizing the state through an implied association with a much older cultural heritage. Proceeding in this way, Grace Ogot from Kenya and the Nigerian writers Flora Nwapa and Buchi Emecheta have broken new ground.[116] Reacting against the tradition in which women have been denied significant agency in the nationalist struggle and excluded from political power after independence, these writers have portrayed women as powerful in their own right and often as more radical than men. Gender thus becomes a partial explanation for the conservatism of the nationalist movements and the failure of postcolonial politics. Yet the narratives are not without problems of their own. For example, Ogot's novel *The Graduate* too easily endorses the ideal of the Kenyan nation and through the appointment of a woman to the Public Affairs portfolio ensures that all will be well.[117] At this stage, despite the often suggestive allusions, I do not think it can be said that African women writers have extended their critiques of the politics of nationhood much beyond finding a space for women. Bessie Head is the one exception.

As Head saw it, the nation was another of those categories, like society and tribe, which stripped individuals of their vision and creativity and deprived marginalized social groups such as the Basarwa of their humanity. Elizabeth, in *A Question of Power*, sums up Bessie Head's position when she reflects that the surface reality of African society 'had a strong theme of power-worship running through it, and power people needed small, narrow, shut-in worlds. They never felt secure in the big wide flexible universe where there were too many cross-currents of opposing thought.'[118] Head has less to say about the state as a bureaucratic structure but it is a background presence in her novels – oppressive, proprietary, sinister. In *Maru* and *A Question of Power* there is much to be read about the enclosures of social order from the circumstances and qualities of the main characters. Margaret Cadmore, who in her quiet way challenges the conventions of Dilepe village, had absorbed from her missionary foster-mother 'a type of personality that would be unable to fit into a definition of something as narrow as tribe or race or nation'.[119] Her brilliance as a student, we are told, was based entirely on social isolation. Being unwanted in society had created in her 'an attraction for the unpredictable . . . and for all forms of vigour and growth outside the normal patterns'.[120] Maru and Sello are extraordinary individuals who stand apart from their fellows. Despite their very different life-experiences, they share a consciousness of inner power, they have feminine traits as well as masculine, and they have a visionary or prophetic aura. For these very reasons, and in a sense paradoxically, they express something of Bessie Head's dream of a universalism based on the wish to be ordinary.[121]

Bessie Head's belief in the importance of individuals who do not fit the orthodoxies of the postcolonial order is shared by Dambudzo Marechera, the writer who is probably the most vehement in his rejection of the nation-state project. Reflecting on the Zimbabwean experience, he recalls the bitter feeling that nation and people had lost each other. This prompts him to wonder whether there had ever been a nation at all. Taking account of Zimbabwe's origins – 'the pirate's right to booty' – he thinks not. And the new brand name after independence made no difference – except that the machinery of the nation-state gave the citizens a prefabricated identity.[122] But Marechera's dissatisfaction runs much deeper than this; it is not simply the brand name but the product itself which is fundamentally flawed. The problem is that 'nation-making moves only through a single groove'. The obsession is such that '[i]t is not enough to be in power but to be power itself'.[123]

Here Marechera makes common cause with Bessie Head. An intellectual alliance is struck between two writers who, for all their differences, share the sense of being outsiders and whose writing shows the marks of their inability to cope with society as they found it. Both novelists may now have been received into the body of African literature, but they also stand apart.

Responding to modernity

Modernity is a loaded word and, in much contemporary discourse such as postcolonialism, it is seen to connote a project that is fundamentally flawed. Nevertheless, few would doubt that modernity has taken root and developed in various forms in Africa. The debate is rather about how central and how Western is modernity in African social change. The idea of the modern, as contrasting or interacting with the traditional, is firmly embedded in African literature and widely employed in critical discourse. My use of the modern here is intended to signify the contemporary processes of cultural and economic change which represent a break with or an adaptation of traditional values and forms of social organization, and which are often perceived as related to the intrusion of the external world. Understood in this sense, our concern is with the novelist's approach to the modern and whether it has been seen as tied to the West, international agencies and the processes of global exchange.

Probably the most telling index of the writer's approach to the modern is provided by characterization and the relationship of the characters to societal patterns. Yet this has not proved to be particularly safe ground for generalization. Despite some well-recognized trends, critical commentary on characterization in African literature is strewn with propositions which, with the advantage of hindsight, appear questionable. We can confidently observe, however, that there has been a movement away from the sociological, or what has been called the 'situational' novel,[124] which attempts to mirror the communal nature of traditional life, to writing which etches more sharply the lived experience of particular individuals. This is illustrated by a comparison between, say, A Man of the People and Anthills of the Savannah. It is also evidenced by recent novels addressing the culture clash during the colonial period, for example Timothy Wangusa's Upon this Mountain.[125] In this work – which has been described as a Ugandan Things Fall Apart written in a minor key – the collision of Western values with traditional rituals is depicted through tracing the development and experiences of a Ugandan adolescent, Mwambu. In some instances the elevation of the individual has been accompanied by a new interest in the psychological – dramatically so in the works of Head and Marechera. Another noticeable trend is that particular characters are less likely to be the personification of the polarities of cultural authenticity and the rejection of traditional communalism. Indeed, characters that are pulled both ways have become stock-in-trade. More open to differing interpretation, but certainly a development of considerable interest, are the increasing number of exceptionally powerful figures which set the tone of some African fiction. Earlier I drew attention to Head's Maru and Sello, but we also find extraordinary individuals in the novels of Marechera and Farah – in the latter case especially women – and in Soyinka's drama. It is possible to see some of these figures as carrying forward the tradition of the epic hero of the early days of African literature. However, with the obvious exception of Ngugi's Matigari, a more persuasive interpretation might emphasize the extent to which their individualism cuts across the grain of traditional values.

The significance of these developments lies in the pivotal position of the individual as a signifier of the core of ideas relating to modernity. This is not to suggest that the individual in an African context is a re-enactment of the individual in Western society. It may well be the case that in Africa the individual will retain much closer ties to his or her community and will serve more as a focal point of the community's expectations than would be expected in the West. None the less, the very affirmation of individuality both reflects and facilitates the transformation of other values relating, for example, to materialism, social mobility and economic change. The changes with respect to characterization are thus expressive of the writer's general orientation to the extent to which the traditional has been permeated by the modern. It must be said, of course, that the novel is hardly a neutral medium in this regard. As a Western literary form, the novel was shaped by the material and ideational changes associated with the rise of capitalism and it privileged the individual over society. Yet in the hands of pioneering African novelists such as Achebe and Amos Tutuola it proved adaptable enough to the needs of presenting a different consciousness, and it is difficult to see why, years later, the form itself should be held responsible for fixing the relationship between the individual and society.

By no means all African novelists have welcomed the emergence of a new sense of personal autonomy, but let us for a moment consider a writer who has, and sketch some of the manifestations of this new autonomy. I will take Nuruddin Farah, not because he is representative even of the critics of traditionalism, but because he is expressive of a sensibility which is gaining ground. As written into the lives of so many of his characters, Farah's commitment is to expanding the freedom of the individual. This he sees as a societal good as well as a matter of personal fulfilment, inasmuch as the traditional culture not only oppresses people directly – and here he singles out the position of women – but also underwrites the structure of authoritarian rule. Ebla, the illiterate nomadic heroine of *From a Crooked Rib*, is determined 'to break the ropes society had wrapped around her' and the only course open to her is to escape the rural encampment, first to a provincial town and then to the capital. In *Sardines* Farah challenges Somali patterns of socialization and upbringing which produce cultural conformity. Medina, the chief protagonist, is determined that her daughter, Ubax, will have a very different start in life. As a very young child, Ubax is encouraged to question, challenge, even to interrogate her mother. Medina remembers that her own father had once said: ' You must leave breathing-space in the architecture of your love; you must leave enough room for little Ubax to exercise her growing mind.'[126] *Close Sesame* introduces us to the potentialities of friendship, through Deeriye's musings on his son, Mursal, and his contemporaries. 'Friendship is an organizational concept of self-definition', Deeriye reflects, but a clan-based society has no respect for relationships of this kind.[127] Mursal takes up the theme when he speaks of a healthy autonomy, 'one of self-definition or self-destruction; and away from familial (tribal) dependence.'[128]

What does Farah tell us of the influences behind these breaks with Somali orthodoxy? What is it that pushes his characters to assert a spirit of individualism? Farah gives no clear answers but he suggests some possibilities. In *From a Crooked Rib* the immediate cause of Ebla's flight to the city is to escape a forced marriage to an old man. All we are offered to explain Ebla's defiance of tradition, however, is that her father and mother had died when she was very young and that her only tie to the community was her love for her grandfather – 'but maybe she mistook pity for love'. Farah is aware there is a problem here and he inserts the line: 'She thought of many things a woman of her background would never think of.'[129] We are told a great deal about the thinking and background of the wise and humane patriarch, Deeriye, but it is hard to get a sense of what gave rise to his belief in personal autonomy. There is his involvement in the Somali nationalist struggle and his years of imprisonment by the Italians; from an early age there is his consciousness of the past and its relevance to contemporary life; there is his admiration for great historical figures driven by a commitment to resistance. No one aspect of his experiences or mental make-up stands out as an explanation of why Deeriye is both such a fierce critic of his culture and yet is empowered by it – but perhaps that is as it should be. Medina's case is quite different. Cosmopolitan and unconventional, her outlook has been shaped by being brought up in the capital cities of Europe and Africa, having money sent when it was needed, and being given a privileged education, including time at an Italian university. The difference in the strength of character of Deeriye and Medina is perhaps an indication of the different weighting that Farah attaches to internal and external formative influences.

Extending this last comment to relate to other writers, the elevation of the individual need not involve any wholesale rejection of traditional kinship patterns or a continued communal consciousness. There is reason to think that in some areas the communitarian nature of many African societies offers more scope for individualism than Western scholars often imagine. Be that as it may, we should not simply assume that African individualism will follow Western precedents – although often it may.[130] In fact, some fictional narratives, which interestingly include a number written by women, depict an individualism which accommodates itself to many strands of the traditional cultural inheritance. In his reading of Nwapa's *Efuru*, Brown draws attention to how Efuru's individualism coexists with her 'deep loyalty to those communal traditions which do not seem irrelevant or restrictive to her'.[131] Sekai Nzenza argues similarly with respect to women's writings about patriarchy, polygamy and motherhood, and points to the importance placed on female solidarity.[132] She goes on to stress the dangers of cultural misunderstanding which accompany insensitive attempts to transplant Western feminist perspectives and scholarly paradigms. Nzenza's warning serves to point to a postcolonial theme of general applicability: in the interaction between and the merging of the traditional and modern, new hybrid forms may be emerging which hold the promise of different futures.

In beginning this subsection with the rise of African individualism and fleshing this out by considering the writing of Nuruddin Farah, I have emphasized an openness to modernity. But personal politics do not always run in parallel with public politics and a conservatism with respect to the latter can rebound on the former. I now want to suggest that the literary response to other manifestations of modernity has been more divided and involved considerable hesitancy and ambivalence.

In fiction, as in disciplinary discourses about politics, modernization and dependency, the city has been the symbol of the modern. The capital in particular has been represented as the connecting rod between the old Africa and the world outside; according to one's perspective, as the hub of those processes of change concerned with commodity and cultural exchange, or as the primary site of infection of the barren, exploitative and depersonalized nature of modern life. Mostly the city has been counterpoised to village Africa with its old-established rhythms and customs. This dichotomy is evident, for example, in Ngugi's novels, where Nairobi and Ilmorog are directly linked to materialism as symbolized by the 'wa Benzi' (owners of Mercedes Benz), the degeneration of women through prostitution, and the culture of 'parrotry'.[133] Rural Africa, on the other hand, remains a storehouse of indigenous spiritual and socialist sensibilities and traditional communalism. Something of the same binary mode is apparent in Achebe's writing, although its influence is muted by the recognition of other oppositional polarities within the city, in the rural landscape, and between the neglected north and the relatively prosperous south of the country. Moreover, unlike Ngugi, Achebe does not see the city as alien to contemporary Africa; over time it has taken root and it is now an integral part of Nigerian culture.[134]

Recognition of the city as a fact of contemporary African life does not necessarily involve an emotional acceptance or a willingness to incorporate it in thinking about the future. And in fact many of the narratives are resistant. Time and time again we find a preference for the individual who has clung to his or her cultural roots, who is at home or yearns to be at home in the village, and whose strength is derived from connectedness with the past. If there is some duality in a character's make-up – elements of the traditional and elements of the modern, of the simple and the sophisticated, of the country and the city – invariably it is the former which are privileged. In this respect the contemporary African writer is not so different from many of the earlier colonial writers and administrators who so clearly favoured the 'pagan' over the 'accultured' African.[135]

The continuing resistance to the city and the values it inculcates is epitomized by the prize-winning Zimbabwean novelist, Chenjerai Hove. His novel, *Bones*, tells the story of Marita, a powerful traditional woman, who goes to the city to establish whether her son who became a freedom fighter is still alive. According to Marita: 'The city is a wild place where many things lose purpose . . . People of the city are strange. A lot has gone into their heads. So much has gone into their heads that to clean them is very difficult.'[136] After Marita dies as a result of torture inflicted by the security forces, her young friend Janifer reflects: 'the city is like the throat of a crocodile; it swallows both the dirty and the clean'.[137] The power of these indictments of city life is greatly enhanced because the reader cannot help but be moved by Marita's compassion and drawn by her strength of character. Hove's second novel, *Shadows*, traces the impact of settler colonialism and the war of independence on a Zimbabwean rural community, and it develops similar themes to *Bones*. There is the sense of a peasant people in communion with its past and with nature, the role of the spiritual, and a consciousness of belonging. The richness of this life is contrasted with the anonymity of 'the city of cotton' where Johana's father is alone, unknown and 'deaf to any voices flowering around him'.[138]

Hove's commitment to rural life and traditional values is a far cry from the approach of his compatriot and contemporary, Marechera. Although it expresses a sensibility which is shared by many other African writers, it cannot be said to reflect some distinctive Zimbabwean experience. Marechera's rejection of the African village – 'bask[ing] in the sun, waiting for death' – is as heartfelt as Hove's celebration. Not that he held any brief for Harare or the new towns: they 'are only the new dunghills from which will emerge iron flies in a cloud to scatter all over the hills'. Why stress rootedness, Marechera asks, when we are a continent of refugees? 'There is no sense of home any more, no feeling of being at one with any specific portion of the earth.' Until this uprootedness is confronted, until the wounds and scars are conceded, there is no possibility of making a fresh start.[139]

As gender politics has become an issue in its own right, the difference in the approach of male and female writers to the city and the country has attracted the interest of critics. What emerges here is that even if male writers are responsive to the place of the city in African life and the possibilities it offers for individual fulfilment, they have relegated women to the village. The woman's role is to be a good mother and the custodian of traditional values. The ideal is thus for her to remain in the village. If she comes to the city with her husband, as does Mrs Nanga in Achebe's *A Man of the People*, then she must at least know her place. Often, of course, there are problems about this. In the case of Mrs Nanga, the reader infers that, for all her traditionalism, as time passed she became resentful of being confined to the role of a 'bush wife'. Cypian Ekwensi's *Jagua Nana* offers a variation on this theme: the protagonist experiences the high life of Lagos, only to be consigned back to the village to fulfil her destiny.[140] Brown comments that 'Ekwensi's handling of Jagua Nana is ultimately shaped by a certain limited, and limiting, idealism about women and their traditional roles.'[141] While I accept Brown's basic point, the account of Jagua as a 'Lagos woman', as vibrant as the city itself, is so compelling that her conversion to traditional values lacks conviction. Significantly, on the last page we find that she wants to go to Onitsha to become a merchant princess.

If some women characters in male-authored novels appear too strong to be contained by the narrative structure, in female-authored novels women characters are usually given the space to show their strength and independence of spirit. Often, perhaps usually, this space is provided by the city. Instead of the city being presented as threatening to women and likely to bring shame upon them, it is shown to offer opportunities for independent action and personal development. This is most likely to be pursued by tracing the lives of female characters who have unusual freedom in their marriages, choose to remain single, or exploit their sexuality to establish or assert this independence. The picture is not unrelieved, however. City life has its difficulties, as Emecheta shows in *The Joys of Motherhood*.[142] Escape from the village can involve terrible losses, as in Tsitsi Dangarembga's *Nervous Conditions*, where two children sent to mission school die and a third only belatedly and painfully comes to realize the costs.[143] It has, I think, now been established that the distinction between the city and rural Africa is in many respects artificial and that in each the values of the other are present.[144] In this respect, women writers have probably done better than men.

When we turn to development, which has traditionally been seen as the economic dimension of modernity, it must be doubtful whether African literary narratives offer much help in guiding thinking about future choices – and perhaps we should not expect them to do so. In chapter 6 it will be argued that fiction has generally contributed less to rethinking in the economic sphere than it has in other areas of life. The proposition holds true for African literature. From the earliest days most writers have concentrated on cultural politics: colonial denigration, the assertion of African history and culture, the problem of arriving at some balance between Western and indigenous values. The treatment of questions of development and underdevelopment and matters of international economic exchange has been altogether more cursory. Of course economic processes are depicted and winners and losers are identified. For the most part, however, the narratives proceed on the basis of generalized assumptions about the exploitative nature of overseas involvement and the personal and cultural costs of economic change. Seldom is it possible to extract from the texts any clear sense of options and alternatives.

Ngugi, Armah and Okot p'Bitek are of a different stamp, because they develop economic themes and present them boldly. It is therefore appropriate to ask whether our understanding of the politics of modernity is enhanced by their treatment of the economics of exploitation. I want to suggest that while the force of their radicalism may move the reader to think very seriously about dependency and neo-colonialism, it helps very little when it comes to rethinking what kind of development might be appropriate to contemporary African societies. Let us briefly consider the case of Ngugi. As his non-fictional works make clear, Ngugi is not opposed to modernity as such; indeed, he envisages a key role for modernity in the reclamation of those positive aspects of the traditional culture which may make it possible to lift Africa out of the imperialist quagmire.[145] What Ngugi is emphatically opposed to is modernization along Western lines or on Western terms. *Matigari* expresses the basis of his thinking in fictional form by celebrating the communal tradition and casting down the Western ethic of individualism. Coming out of the mountains, Matigari resolves to call up his people: 'We shall all gather, go home together, light the fire together and build our home together. Those who eat alone, die alone.'[146] John Boy Junior enunciates a very different creed:

> Our country has remained in darkness because of the ignorance of our people. They don't know the importance of the word 'individual', as opposed to the word 'masses'. White people are advanced because they respect that word, and therefore honour the *freedom of the individual*.[147]

Essentially, *Matigari* leaves the matter of development and modernization there. Looking to the future, the politics of the novel thus reside in the power of its rejection of Western economic intervention and of Westernization as expressed in the collaboration and consumption of the new élites. Parallel with what I argued earlier was the failure of *Petals of Blood* to consider the constituent elements of a new political and educational order, in *Matigari* no serious attempt is made to envisage the constituent elements of a new economic order. In neither novel is any clear distinction made between Westernization and modernization. Nor is there any consideration of how and in what way a merger could be negotiated between the traditional and the modern. Although Ngugi has outlined what has become a central theme in progressive development thinking, he does not pursue the possibilities in his fiction. Now it could be said, following the lines Achebe's approach considered earlier, that this is not appropriate in a work of fiction. The difference, to my mind, is that Ngugi hardly leaves space for the reader to reflect along her or his own lines.

Isidore Okpewho's novel, *Tides*, published in 1993, is perhaps indicative of a new cast of writing which wrestles with the politics of economic development in a non-doctrinaire way.[148] Written as a series of letters between two friends starting from different political premisses, it addresses the social and environmental costs of oil drilling in the delta region of Nigeria. A wide range of related issues are debated, including the ethnic character of the opposition movement in the context of the claims of national well-being; the relationship between military rule, tribal chiefs and overseas oil interests;

and the role of violence both on the part of the ruling élite and those who oppose such violence. Interest in the novel is heightened because it foreshadowed the international publicity given to the subject following the execution of the playwright Ken Saro-Wiwa and his fellow Ogoni activists who had been campaigning against the oil drilling in the Niger delta. Yet its more enduring value lies in the way that matters of national and international policies are transposed to the personal level and explored as problems of individual consciousness. Many of the issues of Third World development and environmental degradation are treated in an ordered and informed way – although in places there is so much data and detail that the pages resemble a technical manual. But it is when politics is confronted in terms of personal choice, involving where and how to live and having to balance responsibilities to family, ethnic group and nation, that the novel makes its distinctive contribution.

Concern about external economic involvement prompts the question of the novelist's response to foreign aid. How has the aid project been tackled in fiction and what of the role of international agencies and aid workers? To date, treatment has been limited. There are good reasons for thinking that aid will become an issue, and a revealing one at that (especially in a country such as Uganda where aid is changing the face of the capital and the culture of those who live there). But as yet it has been little probed in fiction. Only occasionally do aid workers find a place in the texts. In Farah's *A Naked Needle*, for instance, aid personnel are referred to derisively, but they do not appear as characters. Kuschin, taking his English girl-friend Nancy on a tour of Mogadishu, gives thumbnail sketches of the various national groups supposedly involved in assistance of one kind or another. In place of the expelled Peace Corpse (*sic*), there are the Italians, 'semi-nude, loose hair in hippie style, hipsters in dandy tradition, in no way superior to the American bastards. And I wonder if we should still be married to an idea of such inferior denomination.'[149] At the university the Italian instructors 'rove in and out like rabbits in an experimental maze'. They come for four months, which is a vacation in Africa for them.[150] Then there are the Russian peasants – 'friends of the people, representatives from their people' – who enjoy being in a position to buy American and Italian manufactured goods. 'The Ruskis go in flocks like cattle-egrets . . . [m]aybe their number one commandment outside the Soviet Union is: never go around anywhere in groups of less than three.'[151]

Nearly two decades later, Farah returns to develop these asides and confront the question of international aid in a more sustained manner. In *Gifts*[152] he employs a twin strategy of telling the story of a woman wrestling with her reluctance to accept gifts because of her fear of dependence, and presenting a collage of the politics of international aid by appending extracts from newspaper accounts of the diplomacy of aid-giving, mostly to the ends of chapters. I do not think the strategy succeeds, however, because the relationship between the personal and the political is left obscure. The story turns on Duniya's acceptance of Bosaaso as her lover. Gifts of various kinds serve as milestones in her thinking. There is a hopefulness about the narrative and it conveys a sense of the triumph of human feeling over cynicism and calculation. Quite the reverse is true of the capsules about giving and receiving between nations. The lines of argument here are heavily influenced by Marcel Mauss' *The Gift*, to which Farah acknowledges his indebtedness: every gift involves an obligation to reciprocity; much depends on understandings on each side; there are differences between traditions in pre-capitalist societies and contemporary expectations. For the moment, it seems aid does more harm than good. Perhaps given a different power relationship, the political might follow the personal with gifts becoming mutually enriching. It is not at all clear – much less how it could happen.

The most suggestive depiction of aid at work is given by Bessie Head in *When Rain Clouds Gather* and *A Question of Power*. *When Rain Clouds Gather* tells the story of agricultural development in a Botswana village, initiated by an Englishman, Gilbert Balfour, assisted by a Black South African refugee named Makhaya.[153] A range of developmental ideas and schemes are set out ably and in some detail – though at times the tone is somewhat didactic. Gilbert and Makhaya are attuned to the rhythms of village life and they quickly win enthusiastic support for their various initiatives. There is one potential difficulty and that is the opposition of the local chief. He sees Gilbert's agenda, backed as it is by voluntary organizations in England prepared to provide finance, as improving the lot of the poor and thereby threatening his power and wealth. This aside, however, the novel displays an optimism about the acceptance of change on the part of the villagers and about what can be accomplished. Only once does Gilbert ponder on the dilemmas of development and even then his thinking does not cut deep.

Although aid and development are incidental to Head's main themes in *A Question of Power*, this novel does begin to engage with some of the issues taken for granted in *When Rain Clouds Gather*. The question of the effectiveness of aid is raised, and especially as seen through the eyes of the novel's principal protagonist, Elizabeth, the motives and nature of the aid workers are shown to require scrutiny. The setting is again a village in Botswana where a developmental project has been established. This time, however, the venture is much larger and more institutionalized than in the earlier novel. It comprises a school, an experimental farm and a local industries shop, and we are introduced to an assorted cast of volunteers from several overseas countries. There are of course the freaks and misfits, but also a number of dedicated individuals who have a rapport with the villagers. The creativity and potential benefits of the project are stressed but there are problems as well. These include overbearing and racist volunteers, a reluctance to establish a second vanguard of local teaching instructors, and the scepticism of the villagers about co-operative undertakings. At one stage we are told of the villagers: 'Not one person had walked home with money after all this labour, and that was what they wanted to know about.'[154] All the same, there is rather less resistance to change than might have been expected – although it needs to be remembered that Elizabeth (like the author) was an outsider and did not have the same identification with the traditional as the locals. There is also the feeling that there is moral value in bringing together people from different backgrounds, and that this enabled the locals especially to comprehend another world. Despite the problems, therefore, the novel is a vote for development and for the aid project as a way of realizing it.

A very different treatment of development is to be found in popular fiction which depicts contemporary urban life in Africa. This literature has not yet received much scholarly recognition and has generally been dismissed as pulp writing. Yet the genre is of particular interest to those concerned with the response to economic change in Africa because of its wide readership and its grass-roots exposé of the seamy side of life in the capitals and their conurbations. It also has a frankness often missing in other writing, a consequence of having escaped the screening and censorship which is directed to publications both in the social sciences and fiction by well-recognized authors, which might find their way overseas and into domestic political debate.

The urban novel of Nairobi, which dates from the early 1970s, is a flourishing illustration of the genre and Meja Mwangi may be taken as its paradigmatic writer. The picture which emerges from the novels is not so much a portrait of development as a collage of the conditions of urban life created by the rapid development of certain sectors of the economy linked to the international system, the migration of large numbers of people from rural areas, extensive unemployment and so on. The representations of the breakdown of traditional values and social units, the human dislocation of structural change and the high incidence of personal violence is a corrective to the view from the top. When these novels are examined as a genre and their themes categorized, we can expect to get a biting commentary on modernization which may well interlock with, and even extend, the radical critiques of development advanced by scholars such as Arturo Escobar.[155] Some of these novels can be read as recording and helping to shape the making of a new urban culture. In this respect we might note that writers like David Maillu are incorporating 'street' dialects into their works, particularly 'Sheng', which is a fusion of English and Swahili spoken predominantly by youths in urban areas.

Accepting that several African novelists with international readerships have written into their fiction perspectives on the economics of development, and that there is a growing popular literature which records the lived consequences of urban growth, the fact remains that recent fictional narratives disappoint when it comes to weighing up the broader costs and benefits of economic modernization and wrestling with conflicting conceptions of social good. In these respects, Joyce Cary's African novels remain an impressive achievement. Understandably, Cary's writing has lost favour in the postcolonial era because of its ethnocentrism and its imperial biases, but *An American Visitor* and *Mr Johnson* still stand as instructive studies of the moral and political dilemmas of development policies. If we widen our focus from material progress – building roads and bridges, and opening mines – to matters of education and religion, *Aissa Saved* and *The African Witch* also become relevant. Taken collectively, then, Cary's four African novels can be said to represent an inquiry into the modernity project generally.[156]

Returning to African writing, I want to sum up this section by examining one novel which incorporates many of the threads about modernity and development which we have been discussing and brings them together in an original and highly relevant way. This novel is B. Kojo Laing's *Search Sweet Country*. As we noted earlier, this is a work about 'ordinary' people, meaning that they are in the mainstream of Ghanaian life; but they are also extraordinary in the sense that their dreams and supernatural beliefs are part of the reality of their world. The cast is sprinkled with eccentrics, escapists and visionaries searching for their private utopias and ideal social forms. There is Beni Baidoo with his obsession to found a village; the cleric Osofo, who married Christ and the herbs and powders of juju and made his bishop defensive about his silks, his perfume and his rings; 1/2-Allotey who was hoping to find in the hills 'a way of living, a way of thinking'. The imaginative context of the novel is complemented by an artful use of language. The author creates powerful, expressive images by objectifying emotions and ideas and wrenching things in the material world from their context so that they express a feeling or a mood. Thus a mouth is left on the floor for someone else to pick up, laughter is carried off in a pocket, and tongues of rumour lie cut in the streets 'still desperately mongering, much like worms halved and still writhing'.

The joy and technical virtuosity of this novel should not obscure its importance as a reflective and sustained inquiry into the limits and possibilities of modernity in Africa. It has been suggested that the need for and the difficulty of change are inseparable from Laing's linguistic project and that in some respects there is a kind of 'linguistic idealism'.[157] I am not persuaded that this is so, but the point is debatable. Bearing it in mind, let us consider some of the novel's key elements and themes. Significantly, the novel is carried forward by individuals, each with his or her distinctive quirks and ambitions. Nearly all of these individuals, however, embody aspects of the collective, and we are meant to understand that whatever form the new Ghana takes, it will allow space for the individual as well as reflect a collective consciousness.

There is a similar stress on the need to find a bridge between the traditional and the modern. Despite Ghana's long association with foreigners, despite the fascination with the new, we are constantly made aware of the strength of the culture and the pull of traditional ways. 1/2-Allotey asserts that Ghana has been very stubborn:

> we have kept our basic rhythms, we know our languages and have assimilated so much into them, we laugh the way we used to laugh if you take away the bitterness here and there.[158]

Professor Sackey has no doubt that this is so: 'we love the past, pounded right into the middle of our fufu!'[159] The problem, as he sees it, is that 'the weight of our past seems to be crushing the present . . . and the future will not be born!'[160] This is an extreme position but there is no question of the text's commitment to a considerable degree of modernization. Some characters speak for more; others less. Papa Erzuah is probably in the former category, but he expresses the spirit of the novel when he says:

> we must continue to modernise faster . . . look at an old man like me talking about something like modernising. But there's been so much change already in my life that I want more and more! Change everything except the roots that do the changing!'[161]

The novel thus endorses a modern future but at the same time insists that the past must not be discarded, forced out by the 'deadness' of modern gadgets and processes. 1/2-Allotey takes Professor Sackey to task when he asks: 'Are you angry that I come from a long line of fetish priests, and that I want to make alive my own type of farmer-priest? Sir, how many herbs have you analysed in your long sociological life?'[162] He is convinced – as is the author – that a choice does not have to be made between the modern and the traditional: 'There must be a middle way somewhere . . . I want to find this balance!'[163]

There are two further aspects of Laing's vision which should be singled out. First, modernization does not mean Westernization. Nor should it take place under the tutelage of the West. At one point, Ebo the Food exclaims: 'Let's have a little machine life, yes; but I hate the type that we see in other lands.'[164] Second, the city is not viewed as alien to Africa. Although criticisms are voiced of life in the capital, the novel is a celebration of Accra; the city is a blend of the diverse and is original, something different from the elements that went into its making.

Here, in fictional form, is a study of the main features of hybridity as it was subsequently developed within the postcolonial discourse. The traditional and the modern are not seen as binary opposites but as shading into each other, even organically linked. Nor are they seen as separated in time but as existing contemporaneously. The clash between the indigenous and the overseas worlds is present, but so is the idea of a conversation between cultures.[165] In venturing so far beyond the conventions of most African narratives in these respects it may be significant that the novel is set in Accra, the most open of African cities, and its author is Ghanaian – as is Kwame Anthony Appiah, a leading exponent of hybridity in academic circles.

Laing holds out no blueprint of the future and it is enough in this first novel that he lays out the way in which one should be drawn up. It is of some regret, however, that his two later novels do not take his vision further. Perhaps new readings will indicate that the possibilities are there.

Any appraisal of the political contribution of African literature must be attentive to the historical circumstances of when it was written, and dependent upon presumptions about its purposes and possibilities. From its earliest days much has been claimed for African literature and its status remains high today. Yet perhaps to a degree without parallel elsewhere, it has been subject to competing demands and expectations. Literature has been seen as a way of recovering a sense of self, expressing the hopes of decolonization, and imagining alternative futures. Writers have been called upon to defend Africa from external denigration and act as critics and conscience on the inside. At the same time, they have had to negotiate between different conceptions of the writer's role: the individual consciousness of the artist; collective responsibility and political commitment; openness to external forms and ideas; an Afrocentric particularism. In many respects, therefore, the difficulties faced by African literature have reflected the politics of the continent.

Now that colonialism's historical moment has passed, it is more than ever necessary to acknowledge literature's achievement of African affirmation. It would be difficult to exaggerate the importance of fiction's insistence on rewriting the colonial account, recovering a history and culture, and asserting the dignity and creativity of Africans. And even though colonialism as a formal system has been brought to an end, it has left an ideational residue which continues to influence perceptions and politics. Consider, for example, the representations of Africans and their condition by international aid agencies and Western newspaper reporting of atavistic violence and tribalism. Thus while new tasks have claimed the attention of novelists, they have not been entirely relieved of the old. Literature has not, of course, been alone in challenging the politics of overseas representation but situated as it is between the brokers of day-to-day power and those in the academic world, its role has been of special importance. In all this, Achebe has been a towering figure and his influence has remained substantial while that of opinion-setters in politics fluctuated (Nkrumah) or faded (Kenyatta).

I will set out in summary fashion the main lines of argument canvassed in this section before indicating their limitations and commenting on their significance. The remarkable strength of African literature – its commitment to reaffirmation – has contributed to an unevenness of treatment which has ramifications for understanding Africa's place in a postcolonial world. The novelists' commitment to rewriting the past has tended to inhibit approaches to the future. Their elevation of culture has mitigated against direct engagement with structural politics. Their cultivation of African distinctiveness has stood in the way of fully coming to terms with hybridity. If this assessment seems rather too negative, a reminder is appropriate that literature needs to be positioned alongside other discourses. On almost any comparative reckoning, the novelist emerges very creditably indeed.

The point is well taken that for a society to determine its own future it must come to terms with its past. Nowhere in the world has the need to reconceive the past been felt more acutely than in Africa. Literature's role here has been crucial and the past that has been brought forward is by no means simply laudatory. Think of Achebe, and even more of Farah. But the immediate need to counter the racial and cultural slurs involved an implicit selectivity. Little was said about the significance of the organizational, economic and technological imbalances which made such humiliation possible. In the interests of resistance, the tendency has been to discount what some Africans saw as the attractions and opportunities presented by external intervention. The very ambivalence of the response to colonialism has contributed to the reshaping of identity and the strengthening of connections with the outside world. This has not, perhaps, been sufficiently brought out in fiction. It should also be said that the relevance of the past to Africa's postcolonial situation needs to be mediated by a recognition of very different contemporary needs and expectations with respect to material benefits and social opportunities. Regarding the former, women writers have played a significant part in redressing the privileging of male voices. By way of illustrating the latter, consider the evident reluctance of writers to engage with issues of food production and distribution, despite their political importance.

The cultural orientation which from the beginning characterized African literature was refreshingly innovative and foreshadowed a similar movement in other discourses. Looking beyond the formal structures of power to the politics of everyday affairs has been a corrective to the Western scholarly preoccupation with the state, Westminster models and the intervention of the military which, it is now only too apparent, skid across the surface of African life. So also the way that fiction gave expression to hopes for broadening the bounds of community through drawing on racial consciousness, ideas about continentalism and a sense of the cultural cohesion of African peoples has been an antidote to the narrow purview of realist analyses. But despite the many positive aspects of literature's cultural expansiveness, at times there is insufficient connection with public politics. Not infrequently, culture seems to be a way of escaping from, rather than engaging with, political structures and material life. Addressing different conceptions of the literary project, Appiah appears to express a similar concern when he observes that the African writer's problem 'is finding a public role, not a private self'.[166] At some point everyday practices have to be related to institutions and procedures at the centre; commonalities of culture have to come to terms with factions, contradictions and specific interests. Otherwise writers run the risk of their narratives either losing relevance or coming to internalize, almost unconsciously, the dominant constructs of the time. It seems to me, on the first count, that African writers have only hesitantly faced up to the challenge of economic change and development. On the second, what Basil Davidson has called the 'nation-statist paradigm' has not been as searchingly confronted as might have been hoped. A fuller endorsement of contemporary identity politics would of course produce less qualified assessments. More economic assumptions would then be read into accounts of cultural change and mobile identities. The trope of madness would be interpreted as a blow against the modern state – for after all, as deployed by Head, Marechera and Farah, dementia is a form of defiance.

No one would question the appropriateness of the novelists' search for distinctively African reference-points, especially in the immediate aftermath of the colonial experience. But the concern that has been expressed from time to time in this section is that a continuing commitment to resistance and recovery impedes recognition of the extent to which Africans have been touched and changed by global processes and external influences. The traditional has been brought into dialogue with the modern. Increasingly the village is linked to the city, and thence to the international economy and communications network. In short, the established distinction between what is internal and what is external, between what is African and what is international, has lost much of its meaning. My argument has been that these developments, which work to promote the growth of a syncretic culture and encourage the emergence of hybridity in various forms, have not received enough acknowledgement within African literature. This can be attributed to a continuing pattern within the narratives to differentiate the African self from a range of invasive others. But it may also reflect something of how the narratives are read, especially by outsiders attracted by the idea of cultural difference.

Put another way, what I am pointing to is the emergence of multiple identities and the reluctance in some, though not all, of the fiction to explore the possibilities of the situation. In his eloquent study of what it means to be an African today, Kwame Anthony Appiah has called for recognition of the enriching potential of this freeing-up of identity and he sets out the very positive experience of his own family.[167] But cross-cultural exposure may not always be so happy, especially in the first instance. The fictional narratives record decidedly mixed responses. Amos Tutuola finds no difficulty in bringing different worlds together: Yoruba gods coexist with Christian influences; Cowrie shells are used alongside English pounds.[168] Dambudzo Marechera rails against cultural and national enclosures, yet testifies to the personal dislocation of bringing different systems and ways of thinking into relation with each other. Another Zimbabwean novelist, Tsitsi Dangarembga, writes to similar effect. *Nervous Conditions* tells of the difficulty of attempting to negotiate hybridity. One of the main protagonists, Nyasha, suffers a breakdown because of her exclusion from the traditional culture. The other, Tambu, at the time saw her missionary education as a way to freedom, an escape from the flies, the fields, the poverty and lethargy of the village. Only slowly and painfully does Tambu come to gain some perspective on her dual inheritance.

I have attempted to establish how much African literature has contributed to a sense of an African self, especially in historical and cultural terms. However, bearing in mind the growth of interaction between Africa and the outside world, there is a certain disappointment that the international aspects and implications of Africanness have not been addressed more fully. From the wider perspective of international studies, this concern that the literary narratives are too rooted in African particularity needs to be tempered by the recognition with which I began this section: namely, that international relations, globalization and postcolonialism have made little attempt to engage with the specifically indigenous or continental dimensions of Africa's problems and possibilities.

Notes

1. See, for example, Steven Feierman, 'Africa in history: the end of universal narratives', ch. 2 in Gyan Prakash (ed.), *After Colonialism. Imperial Histories and Postcolonial Displacements* (Princeton University Press, Princeton NJ, 1995).

2 . Editor's comments, 'More on writing the postcolony', *Public Culture*, 5:1 (Fall 1992), 46.

3. Chinweizu has made a broadly similar judgement, although his argument heads in a different direction. See Chinweizu, *Decolonizing the African Mind* (Pero Press, Lagos, 1987), 'Literature and national building in Africa', pp. 211–30.

4. See William Ochieng, 'Undercivilisation in Black Africa', *Kenya Historical Review*, 2:1 (1974) and T. O. Ranger, 'Towards a usable African past' in Christopher Fyfe (ed.), *African Studies Since 1945. A Tribute to Basil Davidson* (Longman, London, for the Centre for African Studies, Edinburgh, 1976), pp. 17–30.

5. See, for example, Terence Ranger, 'Concluding summary: religion, development and identity' in Kirsten Holst Petersen (ed.), *Religion, Development and Identity* (Seminar Proceedings, no. 17, Scandinavian Institute of African Studies, Uppsala, 1987), pp. 145–62 (pp. 145–7); Kwame Anthony Appiah, *In My Father's House. Africa in the Philosophy of Culture* (Methuen, London, 1992), pp. vii–ix and 9–11.

6. Stanlake Samkange's *On Trial for My Country* (Heinemann, London, Ibadan, Nairobi, 1966) has elements of such an approach and it disappoints as a result.

7. Michel Foucault, *Politics, Philosphy, Culture. Interviews and Other Writings 1977–1984*, edited with an introduction by Lawrence D. Kritzman, translated by Alan Sheridan and others (Routledge, New York and London, 1988), p. 156.

8. Eric J. Hobsbawm, 'The new threat to history', *New York Review of Books*, 16 December 1993, p. 63.

9. Ranger, in Fyfe, op. cit., p. 23.

10 . Wole Soyinka, *Myth, Literature and the African World* (Cambridge University Press, Cambridge, 1976), p. 112.

11. Ayi Kwei Armah, *Two Thousand Seasons* (East African Publishing House, Nairobi, 1973), p. 8.

12. Ayi Kwei Armah, *The Healers* (Heinemann, London and Ibadan, 1979; first published 1978), p. 269.

13. Ibid., p. 270.

14. See, for example, Derek Wright, *Ayi Kwei Armah's Africa. The Sources of His Fiction* (New Perspectives on African Literature, no. 1, Hans Zell, London, Munich, New York, 1989), pp. 263–4. For similar comments on *Two Thousand Seasons*, see pp. 239–41.

15. Armah, *The Healers*, p. 83.

16. Ibid., p. 172.

17. Wright, op. cit., especially pp. 7 and 222–7. See also Derek Wright, 'Orality in the African historical novel: Yambo Ouologuem's *Bound to Violence* and Ayi Kwei Armah's *Two Thousand Seasons*', *Journal of Commonwealth Literature*, xxiii:1 (1988), 91–101.

18. Wright, *Ayi Kwei Armah's Africa*, p. 3.

19. Chinua Achebe, 'The novelist as teacher', *New Statesman*, 29 January 1965; reprinted in William Walsh (ed.), *Readings in Commonwealth Literature* (Clarendon Press, Oxford, 1973), pp. 181–5 (p. 184).

20. Chinua Achebe, 'The role of the writer in a new nation', *Nigeria Magazine*, 81 (1964); reproduced in G. D. Killam (ed.), *African Writers on African Writing* (Heinemann, London, 1973), p. 9.

21. Chinua Achebe, 'African literature as celebration', *Dissent* (New York); Special Issue, 'Africa: Crisis and Change' (Summer 1992), 344–9.

22. 'An Interview with Chinua Achebe', *Times Literary Supplement*, 26 February 1982, p. 209.

23. Ibid.

24. Simon Gikandi, *Reading Chinua Achebe* (Studies in African Literature, New Series, James Currey, London; Heinemann, Portsmouth NH; Heinemann Kenya, Nairobi, 1991), pp. 3 and 4.

25. C. L. Innes, *Chinua Achebe* (Cambridge University Press, Cambridge, 1990), pp. 160–1.

26. Robin Ikegami, 'Knowledge and power, the story and the storyteller: Achebe's *Anthills of the Savannah*', *Modern Fiction Studies*, 37:3 (Autumn 1991), 493–507.

27. Chinua Achebe, *Anthills of the Savannah* (Picador in association with William Heinemann, London, 1988; first published 1987), p. 161.

28. Wole Soyinka, *Six Plays* (The Master Playwrights, Methuen, London, 1984), p. xiii.

29. See Oyin Ogumba, 'Traditional content of the plays of Wole Soyinka', *African Literature Today*, 4, 2–18.

30. Soyinka, *Myth, Literature and the African World*, p. viii.

31 Wole Soyinka, *Season of Anomy* (Rex Collings, London, 1973), p. 10.

32. Ibid., pp. 27 and 170.

33. James Booth, *Writers and Politics in Nigeria* (Hodder & Stoughton, London, 1981), p. 156.

34. Wole Soyinka, 'The critic and society: Barthes, leftocracy and other mythologies' in Henry Louis Gates (ed.), *Black Literature and Literary Theory* (Methuen, New York and London, 1984), pp. 27–57 (p. 46).

35. Nuruddin Farah, 'Why I write', *Third World Quarterly*, 10:4 (1988), 1591–9 (p. 1599).

36. Nuruddin Farah, *Close Sesame* (Allison & Busby, London and New York, 1983), p. 147.

37. Jacqueline Bardolph, 'Time and History in Nuruddin Farah's *Close Sesame*', *The Journal of Commonwealth Literature*, xxiv:1 (1989) (A symposium on the work of Nuruddin Farah), 193–206 (p. 204).

38. Nuruddin Farah, *Sweet and Sour Milk* (African Writers Series, Heinemann, London, 1980; first published 1979), p. 183. See also the discussion between Segal and Ebla on the meaning of Soyaan's death in *Sardines* (African Writers Series, Heinemann, London, Ibadan, Nairobi, 1982; first published 1981), pp. 40 and 41.

39. Farah, *Close Sesame*, p. 94.

40. Farah, *Sardines*, p. 62.

41. Kirsten Holst Petersen, 'The personal as political: the case of Nuruddin Farah', *Ariel*, 12:3 (July 1981), 93–110 (p. 94).

42. V. S. Naipaul, *A Bend in the River* (Penguin, Harmondsworth, 1980; first published 1979), p. 18.

43. Ibid., p. 20.

44. Ibid., p. 120.

45. Ibid., p. 32.

46. V. S. Naipaul, 'A new king for the Congo: Mobutu and the nihilism of Africa', originally published in *The New York Review of Books* and republished in V. S. Naipaul, *The Return of Eva Peron with The Killings in Trinidad* (Penguin, Harmondsworth, 1981; first published 1980), pp. 165–96 (p. 182).

47. Ibid., p. 184.

48. Naipaul, *A Bend in the River*, p. 141.

49. V. S. Naipaul, *The Mimic Men* (Penguin, Harmondsworth, 1980; first published 1967), p. 251.

50. Adrian Rowe-Evans, 'Interview with V. S. Naipaul', *Transition*, 8:40 (1971), 59–62 (p. 59).

51. On this point see Michael Neill, 'Guerrillas and gangs: Frantz Fanon and V. S. Naipaul', *Ariel*, 13:4 (October 1982), 21–62 (p. 51).

52. Naipaul, *A Bend in the River*, p. 10.

53. Ibid., p. 281.

54. See, for example, David Maughan-Brown, *Land, Freedom and Fiction. History and Ideology in Kenya* (Zed Books, London, 1985), p. 234.

55. See, for example, Achille Mbembe, 'The banality of power and the aesthetics of vulgarity in the postcolony', *Public Culture*, 4:2 (Spring 1992), 1–30; Allessandro Triulzi, 'African cities, historical memory and street buzz', ch. 6 in Iain Chambers and Lidia Curti (eds), *The Post-Colonial Question. Common Skies, Divided Horizons* (Routledge, London and New York, 1996).

56. Soyinka, *Myth, Literature and the African World*, p. 136.

57. See V. Y. Mudimbe (ed.), *The Surreptitious Speech. Présence Africaine and the Politics of Otherness 1947–1987* (University of Chicago Press, Chicago and London, 1992), especially V. Y. Mudimbe, 'Finale', pp. 435–45.

58. Kwame Nkrumah, *I Speak of Freedom* (Mercury Books, London 1961), p. xiii.

59. Ibid., p. 133. For a similar statement see *The Autobiography of Kwame Nkrumah* (Thomas Nelson & Sons, Edinburgh, 1957), p. 290.

60. Ayi Kwei Armah, *Why Are We So Blest?* (Heinemann, London, 1972), p. 176.

61. Armah, *Two Thousand Seasons*, p. 321.

62. Ibid., p. 7.

63. Armah, *The Healers*, p. 84.

64. See Kole Omotoso, 'Trans-Saharan views: mutually negative portrayals' in Eldred D. Jones (ed.), *African Literature Today 14: Insiders and Outsiders* (Heinemann, London, 1984), pp. 111–17 (p. 116).

65. Armah, *Two Thousand Seasons*, pp. 76 and 77.

66. Elechi Amadi, *The Great Ponds* (Heinemann, London and Ibadan, 1969).

67. See Appiah, op. cit., ch. 9 (pp. 286 and 292–3).

68. Ezekiel Mphahlele, *The African Image* (Faber & Faber, London, 1962), p. 19.

69. Ibid. (2nd revised edition 1974), p. 23.

70. See Richard Peck, 'Hermits and saviors, osagyefos and healers: artists and intellectuals in the works of Ngugi and Armah', *Research in African Literatures*, 20:1 (Spring 1989), 26–43.

71. The major secondary works here are Lloyd W. Brown, *Women Writers in Black Africa* (Contributions in Women's Studies 21, Greenwood Press, Westport CT and London, 1981); Florence Stratton, *Contemporary African Literature and the Politics of Gender* (Routledge, London and New York, 1994).

72. B. Kojo Laing, *Search Sweet Country* (Heinemann, London, 1986), p. 244.

73. Dan Izevbaye, 'Issues in the reassessment of the African novel' in Eldred D. Jones (ed.), *African Literature Today 10: Retrospect and Prospect* (Heinemann, London, 1979), pp. 7–31 (p. 20).

74. Lewis Nkosi, *Tasks and Masks. Themes and Styles of African Literature* (Longman, London, 1981) p. 31.

75. Laing, op. cit., p. 222.

76. Ibid., p. 244.

77. Ngugi wa Thiong'o, *Petals of Blood* (Heinemann, London, 1977).

78. Ibid., p. 291.

79. Ibid., pp. 214 and 323.

80. Eustace Palmer, 'Ngugi's *Petals of Blood*' in Eldred D. Jones (ed.), *African Literature Today 10: Retrospect and Prospect*, pp. 153–66 (p. 164). For the key passages in the novel dealing with the issue of education, see *Petals of Blood*, pp. 168–74.

81. Marjorie Oludhe Macgoye, *Coming to Birth* (Heinemann, London, 1986), p. 65.

82. Ibid., p. 72.

83. Adewale Maja-Pearce, *Times Literary Supplement*, 5 September 1986.

84. Stratton, op. cit., pp. 100–1 and 118.

85. Brown, op. cit., pp. 180–1.

86. Ngugi wa Thiong'o, *Decolonising the Mind. The Politics of Language in African Literature* (James Currey, London, 1986), pp. 2 and 3.

87. Chinweizu, Onwuchekwa Jemie and Ihechukwu Madubuike, *Toward the Decolonization of African Literature*, vol. 1 (Howard University Press, Washington DC, 1983), p. 4.

88. Ibid., p. 10.

89. In the first of two Dyason Memorial Lectures to the Australian Institute of International Affairs in 1972, 'Africa, the West and the world', *Australian Outlook*, 26:2 (August 1972), 115–36 (p. 115). Mazrui developed this theme in his 1979 Reith Lectures, the second of which was entitled 'The cross of humiliation'. See Ali A. Mazrui, *The African Condition* (Heinemann, London, 1980).

90. Dambudzo Marechera, *The Black Insider*, compiled and edited by Flora Veit-Wild (Baobab Books, Harare, 1990), p. 32.

91. These themes are developed in D. Marechera, 'The African writer's experience of European literature', *Zambezia* (The Journal of the University of Zimbabwe, Mount Pleasant, Harare) xiv:ii (1987), 99–105, and D. Marechera, 'Soyinka, Dostoevsky: the writer on trial for his time', *Zambezia* xiv:ii (1987), 106–11. Both essays are reprinted, along with some of Marechera's previously unpublished writing, in Flora Veit-Wild, *Dambudzo Marechera: A Sourcebook on His Life and Work* (Hans Zell, London, Melbourne, Munich, New York, 1992).

92. Marechera, *The Black Insider*, p. 106.

93. Ibid., p. 82

94. Ibid., p. 84

95. Ibid., p. 109. And see Flora Veit-Wild's comment in her introduction, p. 12.

96. Dambudzo Marechera, *The House of Hunger* (Heinemann Educational Books, London, Ibadan, Nairobi, 1978; reprinted 1984), pp. 60–6.

97. Dambudzo Marechera, *Black Sunlight* (Heinemann Educational Books, London, Ibadan, Nairobi, Exeter, 1980), p. 110.

98. Triulzi, op. cit.

99. Meja Mwangi, *Going Down River Road* (Heinemann Educational, London, 1976), p. 92.

100. Ben Okri, *Dangerous Love* (Phoenix, London, 1996).

101. Mwangi, op. cit., p. 39.

102. See Appiah, op. cit., ch. 3.

103. See Aristide R. Zolberg, 'The specter of anarchy', *Dissent* (New York), 39:3 (Summer 1992), 303–11.

104. Basil Davidson, *The Black Man's Burden. Africa and the Curse of the Nation-State* (James Currey, London, 1992). See, for example, p. 97.

105. For a very positive assessment of the contribution of the African writer – though one that does not directly address the issues I am raising here – see K. E. Agovi, 'The African writer and the phenomenon of the nation state in Africa', *Ufahamu*, 18 (1990), 41–62.

106. It is significant that for a period in the late 1960s Achebe was able to substitute Biafra for Nigeria without disturbing the basic structure of his thought.

107. Gikandi, *Reading Chinua Achebe*, pp. 80 and 81.

108. See Farah, 'Why I write', op. cit., pp. 1597–8. Uncle Hilaal gives voice to this pattern of thinking in Nuruddin Farah, *Maps* (Picador, London, 1986) pp. 148–9 and 166.

109. Wole Soyinka, *Five Plays* (Oxford University Press, London, 1964), p. 57.

110. Soyinka's pessimism is not entirely unrelieved. Forest Head, the leader of the gods, admits the possibility of 'new beginnings', but, judging from the play as a whole, the prospect seems remote.

111. Soyinka, *Season of Anomy*, p. 138.

112. Ibid., p. 159.

113. Chris Dunton, 'Wheyting be Dat? The treatment of homosexuality in African literature', *Research in African Literatures*, 20:3 (Fall 1989), 422–48 (pp. 440–4).

114. See here Niyi Osundare 'Words of iron, sentences of thunder: Soyinka's prose style' in Eldred D. Jones (ed.), *African Literature Today 13: Recent Trends in the Novel* (Heinemann, London, Ibadan, Nairobi; Africana Publishing Company, New York, 1983), pp. 24–37.

115. See, for example, Andrew Parker, Mary Russo, Doris Sommer and Patricia Yaeger (eds), *Nationalisms and Sexualities* (Routledge, New York and London, 1992).

116. Here I would cite especially Grace Ogot's *The Graduate* (Uzima Press, Nairobi, 1980), Flora Nwapa's *Efuru* (Heinemann, London, 1978; first published 1966) and Buchi Emecheta's *Destination Biafra* (Fontana Paperbacks, London, 1983). Emecheta has for many years lived in London.

117. For an analysis along these lines see Ify Achufusi, 'Problems of nationhood in Grace Ogot's fiction', *Journal of Commonwealth Literature*, xxvi:i (1991), 179–87.

118. Bessie Head, *A Question of Power* (Heinemann, London, Nairobi, Ibadan, Lusaka, 1974), p. 38.

119. Bessie Head, *Maru* (Zimbabwe Publishing House, Harare, 1987; first published 1971), p. 16.

120. Ibid., p. 94.

121. See Bessie Head's comments in Randolph Vigne (ed.), *A Gesture of Belonging. Letters from Bessie Head, 1965–1970* (SA Writers, London; Heinemann, Portsmouth NH, 1991) pp. 124, 151 and 168.

122. Marechera, *The Black Insider*, p. 105.

123. Ibid., p. 37.

124. Charles R. Larson, *The Emergence of African Fiction* (Indiana University Press, Bloomington and London, 1972; revised edition), pp. 116–17.

125. Timothy Wangusa, *Upon this Mountain* (Heinemann, Oxford and Portsmouth NH, 1989).

126. Farah, *Sardines*, p. 14.

127. Farah, *Close Sesame*, p. 109.

128. Ibid., p. 114.

129. Nuruddin Farah, *From a Crooked Rib* (Heinemann, London, Ibadan, Nairobi, 1970), p. 8.

130. I am thinking here of the celebrated S. M. Otieno case in which the Westernized widow of Otieno, living in Nairobi, unsuccessfully brought legal action to secure the right to bury her late husband's body, against the claims, based on tribal custom, of his rural-based Luo clan. See J. B. Ojwang and J. N. K. Mugambi (eds), *The S. M. Otieno Case. Death and Burial in Modern Kenya* (Nairobi University Press, Nairobi, 1989).

131. Brown, op. cit., p. 147.

132. Sekai Nzenza, 'Women in postcolonial Africa: between African men and Western feminists', ch. 10 in Phillip Darby, *At The Edge of International Relations* (Pinter, London, 1997), pp. 222–33.

133. 'Parrotry' is the term borrowed from Daniel Arap Moi to describe the cult of following in the leader's footsteps. In September 1984 Moi declared: 'I call on all ministers, assistant ministers and every other person to sing like parrots . . . you ought to sing the song I sing. If I put a full stop, you should also put a full stop. This is how the country will move forward.' Quoted in Ngugi wa Thiong'o, *Decolonising the Mind*, p. 86.

134. For a rather different interpretation which stresses the recent convergence of Ngugi and Achebe's approach to the past, see Leonard A. Podis and Yakubu Saaka, 'Anthills of the Savannah and Petals of Blood. The creation of a usable past', *Journal of Black Studies*, 22:1 (September 1991), 104–22.

135. The similarity in perspective of the colonial writer and the African writer in this area casts doubt on the argument advanced by JanMohamed (*Manichean Aesthetics*, p. 35), among others, that the preference for the 'pagan' was an imperative of colonialist ideology.

136. Chenjerai Hove, *Bones* (Baobab Books, Harare, 1988), p. 89.

137. Ibid., p. 13.

138. Chenjerai Hove, *Shadows* (Baobab Books, Harare, 1991), p. 22.

139. See Marechera, *The Black Insider*, pp. 79–80. The quotations are from these pages.

140. Cyprian Ekwensi, *Jagua Nana* (Heinemann International, Oxford, 1987; first published 1961).

141. Brown, op. cit., p. 7.

142. Buchi Emecheta, *The Joys of Motherhood* (Allison & Busby, London, 1979).

143. Tsitsi Dangarembga, *Nervous Conditions* (Zimbabwe Publishing House, Harare, 1988).

144. See, for example, R. A. Obudho and G. O. Aduwo, 'The rural bias of Kenya's urbanisation', ch. 5 in Ojwang and Mugambi, op. cit.

145. See Ngugi wa Thiong'o, *Barrel of a Pen. Resistance to Repression in Neo-Colonial Kenya* (New Beacon Books, London, 1983), pp. 78–9.

146. Ngugi wa Thiong'o, *Matigari* (Heinemann International, Oxford, 1987), p. 6.

147. Ibid., pp. 48–9.

148. Isidore Okpewho, *Tides* (Longman, Harlow, 1993).

149. Nuruddin Farah, *A Naked Needle* (Heinemann, London, 1976), pp. 107–8.

150. Ibid., pp. 108–9.

151. Ibid., p. 111.

152. Nuruddin Farah, *Gifts* (Serif, London, 1993).

153. Bessie Head, *When Rain Clouds Gather* (Bantam Books, New York, 1970; first published 1968).

154. Bessie Head, *A Question of Power*, pp. 153–4.

155. See, for example, Arturo Escobar, 'Imagining a post-development era? Critical thought, development and social movements', *Social Text*, 31/32, 10:2 and 3 (1992), 20–56. J. Roger Kurtz of the Department of Comparative Literature, University of Iowa, has done extensive work on the representation of Nairobi in the Kenyan novel. I am indebted to his help in writing this section.

156. For critical analyses along these lines, two older studies of Cary's African fiction still repay close attention. These are M. M. Mahood, *Joyce Cary's Africa* (Methuen, London, 1964) and Michael J. C. Echeruo, *Joyce Cary and the Novel of Africa* (Longman, London, 1973).

157. M. E. Kropp Dakubu, '*Search Sweet Country* and the language of authentic being', *Research in African Literatures*, 24:i (1993), 19–35 (pp. 33–4).

158. Laing, *Search Sweet Country*, p. 77.

159. Ibid., p. 79.

160. Ibid., p. 241.

161. Ibid., p. 189.

162. Ibid., p. 149.

163. Ibid., p. 80.

164. Ibid., p. 188.

165. The potential overseas gains from cultural interaction are not really explored but they are suggested by the transformation wrought in Sally Soon, 'the English witch'. She was sent over on a secret assignment against Ghana, but fell in love with Ghanaians and settled to do a doctorate on 'Development and the informed Ghanaian psyche'.

166. Appiah, op. cit., p. 121.

167. Ibid., see especially preface and ch. 9.

168. Mineke Schipper, *Beyond the Boundaries. African Literature and Literary Theory* (W. H. Allen & Co., London, 1989), p. 76.

— Part III —

Reframing Issues

CHAPTER 6

Fiction's silences and relocations?

To this point my argument has been that fiction offers new ways of seeing the relationship between the West and the Third World and of engaging our emotions. In Part 1 of the book the disciplinary enclosures of politics, history and especially international relations were contrasted with the more open and evidently subjective practices of novelists, in support of the claim that very often fiction broke new ground, provided a corrective to, or was more prescient than, conventional source material. In the context of British rule of India, chapter 4 addressed the tendency of fictional narratives to privilege the individual and it set out some of the ways in which Indo-British politics could be explored through or telescoped into the personal. Chapter 5 took as its theme the relationship between culture and politics in contemporary Africa and argued that the cultural orientation of fiction provided an entry into foundational issues of African national and international politics.

In this penultimate chapter I want to consider the other side of the ledger: to ask about fiction's apparent blind spots and consider whether novelists have made allowance for systemic and structural factors which, according to orthodoxy, proscribe the nature of the interaction between North and South. On the face of it, those two warhorses which guard the flanks of mainstream approaches to the determinants of action in international affairs – power politics and the processes of exchange set in train by economic forces – have had a low profile in fictional narratives. In the case of power politics we need to consider how far novelists have depicted the workings of *realpolitik*, perhaps in other terms, or whether their narratives give no credence to the idea of Africa and Asia as an extended chessboard. Over the past few years the power-politics pattern of thinking has come under vigorous challenge by voices from the margins of international relations – influenced, for example, by feminist perspectives, the ecological imperative and ideas taken from post-structural theory. Might literature and literary discourse contribute to this debate? Regarding the role of economic forces, I have in mind the claims of political economy that the mode of production and/or the processes of exchange structure the conditions of international life, and that they do so profoundly unequally. Notable bases of reference here are the classic theories of the imperialism of trade and the imperialism of capital and, drawing upon them, the more recent discourses about dependency and arrested development. What is at issue here is how far fictional narratives contain material which bears upon these theoretical elaborations and perhaps provides glimpses of their workings or ramifications in ordinary life.

The pertinence of inquiring along these lines is not only that we are led to think about ways in which imaginative literature might extend our understanding but also that we are confronted with the possibility that it might mislead. Presumably, when the matter is put bluntly, no one would imagine that it is possible through literature to plot the influence of power and economics on Western involvement in the Third World. But what is at issue is seldom spelt out clearly and the tendency is to settle for a well-rounded picture. With respect to the structural and the systemic, as well as in other areas, silence in the text requires interrogation. There is a strong case to be argued that often where novelists have shown little interest in *realpolitik*, race, culture or gender are unduly elevated, sometimes in a way which suggests that the sources of behaviour are different in North and South. In turn, postcolonial theorists, influenced partly by fictional narratives, have by omission discounted power politics, opting instead for a self/other category of explanation which, although containing elements of a similar mechanistic logic, escapes close scrutiny because it accords with contemporary sensibilities. It can further be argued – and this bears on the question of the global economic system – that there is a tendency for subalternity to become a 'hold-all' category, a rather woolly substitute for class.

There is one other issue which I propose to raise along the way. Most of the novels that we have considered in the earlier sections are about empire or reflect back on the imperial experience. This, I would argue, is in line with contemporary postcolonial literary practice – notwithstanding the curious claim of Laura Chrisman that 'recent critical interest has centred mostly on issues of Post-World War Two'.[1] The richness of the novel of or against empire is undoubted and its continuing relevance should by now be plain. But are there not significant issues in the contemporary international politics of the North/South engagement which extend far beyond the historical experience of formal imperialism, even if they have roots there? Is fiction much of a guide here?

For those looking for some direct engagement with power and economics, fictional texts will disappoint. It is uncommon for works of fiction to intervene in these domains and when they do so the results are rarely thematic. Generalizations about the modern novel are rightly suspect but it is, I think, apparent that fiction's personal and social orientation has meant that the state and the economy have been second-order concerns, if they have featured at all. Moreover, the tendency has been for narratives to be anchored within particular contexts – local, regional, national – and only occasionally and usually incidentally to relate different contexts to each other or to extend out to the global. As a consequence, the operation of systemic factors has to be read into rather than drawn from the action of the novel. Very often the main characters are taken from some way down the social scale so that we are unlikely to be given direct access to the calculations of statespersons or taken into the boardrooms of powerful corporations. In sum, the novel of the East/West encounter is likely to privilege society over the state and culture over political economy or geopolitics. Its spatial reach tends to be limited and grounded in the particular and its point of view and level of analysis emblematic of the middle or lower echelons of society rather than of those at its apex. As I will argue in the final chapter, these characterizations very largely hold good for postcolonial theory as well.

These comments require to be referenced to literary sources. In this chapter, as in the book as a whole, our primary concern is with fiction which at least to some degree looks beyond a national or colonial setting, or situates the national or colonial in relation to external forces or other cultures. In other words our focus, to employ the traditional phraseology, is on novels of the East/West encounter. Now it may be that novels of domestic life, novels which have no obvious imperial or international aspect, also tell a story about the world outside. The distinction I have made within the body of literature is of course an artificial one; it is intended simply as a rule-of-thumb guide, not to preclude inquiry into domestic novels when this looks promising, but simply to restrict sources to manageable proportions on the basis of likely utility. Writing some years back on the need for reassurance which seemed to animate much of America's overseas policy in the cold war era, I argued that a potentially revealing but largely neglected source might be those fictional works set in the United States which developed themes relating to personal insecurity and alienation.[2] Although not itself directly related to external policies, such fiction might provide material for a study of the subconscious manifestations of L. B. Johnson's dictum that '[o]ur safest guide to what to do abroad is always what we do at home'.[3] With respect to the Vietnam War, Norman Mailer and Michael Herr have written along these lines, specifically drawing the linkages between American culture and the source of the conflict. For all its insights, however, the limitation of so much of this kind of writing about intervention in Vietnam is that the external world and international politics are deprived of significance. American culture and the individual consciousness tend to become the only referents.

The position is not dissimilar when we examine British fiction and the overseas experience. In his influential study *Rule of Darkness*, Patrick Brantlinger rejects the traditional distinction between domestic or courtship novels and narratives of empire.[4] On his reading, imperialist ideology and romanticism found expression in domestic realism extending back to early and mid-Victorian times. Edward Said argues likewise in *Culture and Imperialism*, stressing that we need to change our ways of looking at the canonical works of nineteenth- and twentieth-century European culture.[5] In the British novel especially, he notes allusions to the facts of empire which he calls a structure of attitude and reference that supported and sustained the imperial vision. Empire functions, he continues, 'as a codified, if only marginally visible, presence in fiction'.[6] Said is unquestionably right to regard 'imperial concerns as constitutively significant to the culture of the modern West'[7], but the relationship of the culture at home to the imperial project overseas seems to me more ambiguous. Certainly in many respects they came together – think of the public schools, muscular Christianity, the code of manliness – but empire also had its apartness which was rooted in the practices of rule, personal contact and a different temporality. Allusions and references in the domestic novel tell us something about the place of empire in the metropole but much less about empire itself. Said's reading of Jane Austen's *Mansfield Park*, with its six references to Antigua and one to slavery, merely confirms this. And part of the reason we find out so little about empire is that the culture in which it was enmeshed is altogether more fractured than Said allows for. As I have suggested in several places in this book, there was the sphere of polite society, the hearth and domestic values, and there was the escape into the past, to a world of action and the romance of the outward life. This was so despite the connections between them and almost regardless of who benefited. The tensions between the novel of empire or adventure and that of the Great Tradition is a measure of the difference.

The significance of the heterogeneous elements in the imperial culture becomes further apparent when we consider the reticence of the fiction of empire about economics. By way of explanation it is often observed that the novelists of empire avoided or repressed the issues of who paid and who benefited because of the rapacious nature of the exchange, preferring instead to concentrate on the 'redeeming' aspects of the project. Clearly there is much to be said for this view of the functionality of the silences in the texts. Yet the imperial novel was anchored in the overseas experience and in the British case we know from the various studies of the background and ideologies of those who ruled the empire that their cast of mind was largely anti-commercial and in a sense pre-capitalist – as exemplified by the way that in India those involved in commerce were looked down upon as 'boxwallahs'.[8] Proceeding along these lines, it might be more productive to see the literary narratives as expressing one side of a divided imperial culture. In any case, until late in the day the economic critics of empire were very much in a minority, faced as they were with the deeply entrenched orthodoxies of classical political economy. More often than not, such arguments as were advanced against empire were couched in terms of the costs to the metropole rather than the exploitation of the periphery. In this context we are reminded of the extent of opposition to African expansion, the resistance to a second oriental empire in the East, and the continuing commitment, even in the difficult conditions of the 1930s, to the Great Commercial Republic of the World as against imperial economic enclosure.

American novels set in Asia show a similar reluctance to concern themselves with matters of trade and investment – scarcely surprisingly since until the 1970s America's direct economic interests in the area were modest. Especially in the earlier period – until well into the cold war in fact – there are the expected references to the economic ravages of European imperialism (as for example in Louis Bromfield's *The Rains Came*[9]). Overwhelmingly, however, when these novels have an economic slant, it relates to development. And in nearly all cases development is seen to be dependent upon culture and technology, plus what could be achieved through American intervention both in terms of example and aid. Only rarely – as in James Ullman's *Windom's Way*[10] – is there any suggestion that development might require rethinking the role of external capitalism. Again, this is not surprising given that for most of the cold war period economic backwardness was seen as arising from the internal environment and quite unrelated to the international economic system.

Third World texts likewise have been oriented much more to the cultural and political ramifications of the nexus with the West than to its economic dimensions. The qualification must be added, however, that very often there has been some recognition of economic dependency or exploitation by way of background assumption or authorial commentary. Such texts thus have a distinctive tone and point of view. Of course there is a minority tradition of Afro-Asian novels which fly a flag signalling their radical economic stamp. The best known of such works are those by Ngugi wa Thiong'o and Mulk Raj Anand. Earlier in this book I argued that Ngugi's transposition of a post-Leninist critique of economic imperialism into fiction does nothing to advance the theoretical postulates of that body of writing and cramps the imaginative side of his work. On the other hand, Ngugi's didactic fiction contributes to a changing popular consciousness and constitutes a powerful intervention in the contemporary political debate. Much the same observations can be made about Anand's novels, which expose the costs and more general consequences of capitalist penetration of India through characterization, setting, plot and authorial narrative. Although Anand rehearses a familiar politics, he extends our thinking by depicting the way imperialism intersects with indigenous social differentiations and demarcations of economic privilege, maintained particularly by caste and popular Hinduism. If, as recent critics have maintained,[11] in novels such as *Untouchable* Anand erases the voice of the subaltern and denies that subaltern political agency, in his later works imperialism is presented as triggering the possibilities of defiant thought and action. The 'Lalu' trilogy records the steps in the process.[12]

The skeleton of my argument about economics and the East/West novel is now in place and I want to give it some flesh by looking in a little detail at particular novels and narrative devices. First I will consider a novel which stays close to the established scholarly material, then take a novel which meditates about the political choices associated with economic processes, and finally direct attention to certain ways of rendering economic issues in fiction which cast them in a new light. In the first category I have chosen J. G. Farrell's *The Singapore Grip*, a historical novel which has been widely commended for the breadth of its canvas and its evocation of the last days of the closed world of an old colonial society.[13]

The novel is set in Singapore from 1937 to the fall of the city to the Japanese in 1942 and its main characters are associated with a great merchant and agency house, Blackett and Webb. Walter Blackett, the chairman of the firm, is determined to arrange a marriage for his daughter which will advance the interests of the company. His first choice is Mathew Webb, the only son of the founder of the firm, who is knowledgeably idealistic, having worked for a time for the Committee for International Understanding in Geneva, an organization vaguely connected to the League of Nations. Around this seemingly unpromising story-line, Farrell has constructed a multi-layered narrative which explores – among other things – the economics of empire, the play of power politics and the British response to the Japanese threat and subsequent invasion.

Our analysis here will be restricted to the economics of the novel (though some of my observations apply to the treatment of power politics as well). In Mathew Webb's musings on colonial economic orthodoxies and their shortcomings, in his exchanges with Blackett, and in various other dialogues and asides, the major issues of economic imperialism and colonial development in the Far East are aired and debated. An inventory would run like this: the cartel arrangements following the Stevenson plan of the 1920s to restrict the production of rubber; the relationship between rubber producers and manufacturers; the plantation economy versus peasant production and the associated problem of the creation of a landless proletariat; the export of British capital to the colonies for the construction of bridges and railways; the collusion between colonial officials on the spot and planters to the detriment of native producers; metropolitan resistance to colonial industrialization.

Clearly there are risks in introducing so much economic material but Farrell manages to do so in a way which is neither dry nor superficial. If, because of the prominence given to Mathew's viewpoint, the exploitative nature of colonial capitalism is uppermost, counter-arguments are canvassed and we are made aware that any reckoning must be broadly based. The colonial question has been carefully researched – a bibliography is even provided. Yet Farrell has succeeded in integrating academic economic considerations into the plot and characterization, with the result that the reader becomes personally involved in seemingly impersonal issues – though no more so, I would assert, than is the case with Sir Keith Hancock's magisterial survey of imperial economic policy.[14] Farrell also brings to our attention episodes in imperial economic history which have a wider pertinence – for example the schemes to restrict rubber production which anticipated Third World attempts to establish commodity cartels in the 1970s.

For all these strengths, however, I do not think that the novel goes beyond the existing literature or that it reassembles what we already know and presents it in a fresh light. This is another way of saying that the novel stays too close to its historical sources and the material is presented in essentially the same terms as academic discourse – assertion and contestation. One other observation is appropriate and it relates not to the narrative as it is written but to how it may be construed. In the case before us there is a problem in working from the particular (colonial capitalism in Malaya) to the general (the economics of empire) in that, with respect to the plantation economy and peasant production, Malaya was something of a special case. Almost surely a novel set in West Africa would have taken a different tack because there the Colonial Office and successive governors successfully resisted planter interests.[15]

Joyce Cary was a writer of a very different stamp from J. G. Farrell. His four African novels, reflecting on, rather than simply working up, his experiences in the Nigerian Political Service from 1913 to 1919, are less realistic and they have little of the breadth of scope of *The Singapore Grip*. Yet they are more searching about those aspects of the economics of imperialism that they take up. Two or three decades ago Cary was held to be a significant novelist of the colonial encounter but his status has fallen in contemporary criticism, partly as a result of the readings of his work by critics such as Chinua Achebe and Abdul JanMohamed, which emphasize his cultural condescension and implicit racism.[16] That Cary's novels are deeply imbued with an imperial sensibility is of course true. But Cary's proconsular paternalism is engaged in a constant battle with his commitment to liberalism, and it is this dialectic which gives his novels much of their value to the student of politics. This is so, I would argue, with respect not only to the dilemmas of imperialism – as encapsulated for instance, in the debates about indirect rule and the preparation for independence – but also to contemporary issues of Western involvement in Africa and Asia.

Molly Mahood points us in the right direction when she observes that Cary found relief from guilt 'in developing an historical perspective that allowed him to see the colonial intrusion as an inevitable disturbance in a world of continual change'.[17] For our purposes this thought can be taken up by looking at *An American Visitor*, not Cary's best African novel, but the one which most directly addresses the problematic of the economics of imperialism. On the one side, there is Marie Hasluck, the American anthropologist, initially committed to resisting all encroachments of Western materialism and culture on Birri society; on the other, the tin-mining party, of which Cottee is the spokesman, arguing for the inevitability and desirability of opening up Birri society to Western civilization, but in the immediate instance standing for the expropriation of tribal land by metropolitan fiat in the form of an Exclusive Prospecting Licence. Firmly placed at the centre is Bewsher, the District Officer, intent on warding off the miners until such time as the Birri people (under his tutelage) could develop a federation, native courts and evolve 'some sort of agreement about the laws affecting strangers – they practically haven't got any at present'.[18] Then economic development could come – would need to come – but in a controlled and responsible manner.

This bald outline of the ideational structure of *An American Visitor* does not bring out the more subtle interplay between economic forces and political action that is built into the action and dialogue of the novel. In his attempt to keep out the miners, Bewsher is shown to be motivated by a strong sense of moral responsibility. Whatever the imperial government authorized in its *Gazette*, Bewsher was not going to have Birri turned into a slum. His ideal would resonate with much progressive thinking today: 'to preserve and develop the rich kind of local life which is the essence and the only justification of nationalism'.[19] At the same time, however, there is more than a streak of self-indulgence about his romanticization of primitivism.[20] One of the miners often describes officials like Bewsher as 'playboys' and Bewsher himself reveals the proprietary side of his vision when he says that the miners could just as well make their money in Kamchatka or South America. 'There's no reason on earth why they should come to Birri and smash up my whole show.'[21]

The miners as individuals are of little interest – but then we are given not much more than silhouettes. It is enough to know that they are out to make a quick profit and are indifferent to the social costs of their violent intrusion into Birri society. Their role is essentially a 'walk-on' one to present the case for change. This Cottee does forcefully, if in the circumstances disingenuously. At one point Marie finds it difficult to counter Cottee's logic and draws heart from the thought that Cottee was wrong in himself whereas Bewsher would always be more right than Cottee because he felt and cared deeply. We are thus invited to reflect on the meaning of moral action in the face of historical determinism. The old order was doomed – and not simply because of the profit motive of a few. As Cottee saw it:

> even if civilization meant for the Birri a meaner, shallower kind of life, how could any man hope to fight against it when it came with the whole drive of the world behind it, bringing every kind of gaudy toy and easy satisfaction?[22]

In the context of the novel, the world is not simply external. The narrative makes clear that within Birri society there are also pressures for change. For some, European intrusion offered material benefits and social recognition. Henry, having learnt to despise his tribe, became Marie's servant. Later he made large profits from the war and opened a shop near the mine, 'doing a splendid trade in condemned tinned meats slightly blown, second-hand caps and trousers, aphrodisiacs and smuggled gin. Abortions sixpence' (p. 233).

I want now to draw attention to certain textual practices, which while bringing matters of economic interest (or political design) to the foreground of the narrative, at the same time have the effect of removing them from economic (or political) discourse. In other words, the very elevation of the economic (or the political) is accompanied by a process of relocating what is at issue from the realm of the economic (or the political) to the realms of the private, the philosophical or the metaphysical. The first such strategy involves taking some material object as a symbol of capitalism or imperialism. The most celebrated case is silver in *Nostromo*, but there is also the ivory in *Heart of Darkness* and the treasure in *King Solomon's Mines*. The second is the process of dehistoricizing and thereby depoliticizing the narrative so that the forces which drive individuals or classes and shape events cannot be located in a particular spatio-temporal frame or tied to the workings of a particular socio-economic system. Let us elaborate for a moment on these ideas, acknowledging that their wider implications cannot be pursued or we would be caught in theoretical debates tied to contesting readings of canonical narratives beyond the scope of this book.

Most commodities carry with them social associations and through these associations they have a power to direct our thinking along particular lines and engage our sympathies in particular ways. This is especially the case with precious metals such as silver and gold, which have an allure associated with wealth, status and power and thereby conjure up images of avarice, corruption and materialism. When employed in a fictional narrative they therefore come with certain resonances, they are taken to have certain implications. One might even say that when drawn upon by the novelist critical of imperialism, half the job of undermining the imperial ethic has already been done. But the politics of signification is not as clear-cut as this. The very power of such symbols may leave unclear precisely what is being signified. And here we need to take into account the manner and frequency of their usage in the text. Thus in *Nostromo* silver is emblematic, but emblematic of what? Certainly silver is synonymous with material interest, and it diminishes and enslaves, but whether it speaks directly of capitalist imperialism is quite another matter. The effect of the reification of silver – and of the mine itself – may be to write off the possibility of political agency because it invests in material objects a power beyond human control. Again, the centrality of silver in the text and its multifarious contextualizations may be understood as a parable about the debasing influence of materialism which is rooted not in the political economy of imperialism but in the nature of humankind. To my mind, the most incisive readings of *Nostromo* are along these lines, notwithstanding the remarkable and often prescient treatment of the politics of imperialism – for instance, the position of the colonial state, the shift of foreign capital from Britain to the United States, the significance of the construction of the railway and the secession of Sulaco. On Said's account, '*Nostromo* is a novel about political history that is reduced, over the course of several hundred pages, to a condition of mind, an inner state.'[23] As Michael Wilding reads the text, what we have 'is less any modern analysis of politics and society than a moral fable, a fable whose moral is to suggest a disgusted withdrawal from political and social life'.[24]

Shades of these warnings (not to read too much economics into the fictional text) extend to *King Solomon's Mines* – or more particularly to a recent intervention about the significance of the treasure of the mines. On its surface, *King Solomon's Mines* is hardly a promising text for the student of the material practices of imperialism because, unlike *Nostromo*, there are few references to economic motivations or processes and little sense of historical context. Moreover, the idea of treasure captures nothing characteristic of the second expansion, being more expressive of the spirit of the first. In contrast to the silver in *Nostromo*, the treasure stands at a distance from production; it is something 'found' not extracted; it connotes quest rather than enterprise. According to Laura Chrisman, however, *King Solomon's Mines* engages directly with political economy but in its silences and relocations the text places the treasure, and the activities of those who take it, beyond the sphere of capitalist economics.[25] Chrisman's thought-provoking reading of – or reading into – the narrative may stimulate productive inquiry into other texts which touch on material practices. As it stands, however, while *King*

Solomon's Mines perhaps holds out clues as to why and how economic issues are repressed, it tells us nothing about imperial economic issues themselves.

The dehistoricizing process to which I referred earlier has elements of overlap with the practice of reification, in that events and relationships are detached from their socio-economic context and construed in other, less immediately or palpably political, terms. Dehistoricization may show in the fracturing of chronology, the interpenetration of different historical epochs or the presentation of characters in such a way that they stand for some moral attribute regardless of their material environment. Its effect is to privilege the abstract over the situational and set up a presupposition that social causality is universal in time and space. In the case of *Nostromo*, Said's argument is that the historical discursiveness of the narrative masks its psychological and intensely personal understanding of the impossibility of genuine social change, but that the novel's greatness lies in its recognition of its self-referential nature.[26]

It is instructive at this point – and will serve to link our discussion of material interest and *realpolitik* – to refer to a contemporary writer, J. M. Coetzee, who is more concerned with questions of politics than of economics. Coetzee's practice of dehistoricizing his narratives has become something of a trade mark. His reluctance to engage with the specificity of the South African context in which he is writing, and mostly about which he is writing, has generated a debate which rehearses many of the issues we have touched upon, often in suggestive ways. In the view of some critics he has failed the test of political commitment but there are also the more modulated arguments that his tendency to universalize, to erase a sense of boundaries, runs the risk of his narratives being taken as bland reflections on the human condition and that, despite his critique of the rhetoric of imperialism, his refusal to give voice to non-European peoples works to sustain a Eurocentric world-view.[27] Bearing these arguments in mind, I want to make two interpretative comments about Coetzee's approach which have a general relevance to the issues we have been discussing. The first relates specifically to *Waiting for the Barbarians*. I argued in chapter 3 that the novel is a study of the limits of dominance. But it is more than this. By deliberately obscuring reality, by putting the narrative outside history and beyond geography, Coetzee is able to confront the question of power in the abstract; to reflect on the logic and justification of empire, the meaning and place of the enemy, uninhibited by the politics of particularity. One might say that *Waiting for the Barbarians* comes very close to being a literary theory of imperialism, and as such its strengths and weaknesses are of an altogether different kind from, say, those of *Burmese Days*. The point is not that the text turns its back on politics and history but that it invites us to consider them from a standpoint outside themselves. This leads into my second comment, which is that in so much of his fiction Coetzee, flying his postmodernist colours, attests to the limits and duplicities of representation. Hence his texts maintain a studied distance from the world of realism and from those discourses – such as politics – which attempt to unravel it on that plane. In a revealing interview some years back,

Coetzee declared: 'what I am now resisting is the attempt to swallow my novels into a political discourse . . . because, frankly, my allegiances lie with the discourse of the novels and not with the discourse of politics'.[28]

We are now in a position to make some kind of interim assessment of the significance of the narrative practices we have been discussing for our understanding of the treatment in fiction of economic interest and power politics.[29] Clearly there is a loss of realism when texts address issues of economics and power through the idiom of metaphysics or a highly personalized psychology, and therefore the literary cannot directly be translated into the political. To put it another way, it is more difficult to establish the political relevance (if any) of narratives that vacate the authorized ground of politics and history and require one to read off an inner consciousness or a defamiliarized external world – where sunglasses have been invented but the horse remains the means of transportation – or in the science fiction of Doris Lessing.[30] However, if we accept that what is familiar is the result of our cognitive mapping and that this is often culturally and even disciplinary specific, there is much to be said for the role of texts which unsettle and provoke through defamiliarization. If the text draws attention to the question of the fidelity of its own story-telling, so much the better. The importance of considering other stories and indeed the meaning of stories is underlined by the extent to which mainstream scholarly treatment of the issues of our immediate interest is set by nineteenth-century European thought. I am referring here to materialist conceptions of history and the reification of the nation-state. In critical discourse novels which stand at a distance from reality are often described as fables or parables, but is not much of international relations and even history of a similar nature? Of course the methods are regularized, scholarly conventions imply some sort of authoritativeness, and conclusions are costumed differently but we need to be alert to the similarities as well. I am not suggesting that literary approaches should be privileged in some way, but rather that when literary and non-literary narratives are examined in relation to each other, the process of mutual interrogation, the critical exchanges which will surely result, may be highly productive. Such seems clearly to be the case with the debate about the significance of *Nostromo*.

In the course of our discussion so far, we have considered certain texts which can be construed as relating to the workings of power in international relations and certain lines of argument about the pursuit of economic interest which can be extended to the pursuit of national interest – which is what power politics is about. I now want to turn specifically to the issue of power in international relations and inquire whether our general proposition at the outset, namely that the fictional texts seldom address power politics or significantly advance our thinking in this area, is in need of qualification.

With respect to the period of empire, one writer stands in need of close study and that is Kipling. As has been argued in previous chapters, Kipling had an acute sense of the political and his vision of empire was shaped in sober awareness of the weaknesses within and the threatening nature of external forces. His pessimism about the way of the world – which was deepened by the Boer War and later the Great War – made his politics essentially Hobbesian, but this is often masked in his fiction by his sense of delight in the immediate and the particular. Critics such as Annan have revealed the sophistication of his social theory and there have been occasional pieces which touch on its external manifestations. In a thought-provoking essay, Richard Cronin, for example, has argued that in *Kim* enlightenment and war, knowledge and power, are mutually supporting.[31] But Kipling is more knowing than this and as I read the text he is very careful to avoid any such treatment of the issues involved. More than perhaps any other writer, Kipling was convinced that power and knowledge did not always run together and, particularly in some of his short stories, he reveals how substantially they diverge. 'The Bridge-Builders' is perhaps the classic statement to this effect. The fact remains, however, that as yet there has been no serious interrogation of his international politics (which corroborates my argument about the limited reach of international relations and the selective politics of literary criticism and – as I will contend in the next chapter – postcolonialism). Such a study would necessarily have recourse to Kipling's newspaper commentaries and poetry as well as his fiction. It could be expected to embrace his celebration of the ordinary soldier, his masculine construction of power and status, his treatment of the Great Game, and his often highly personalized approach to the struggle between the Great Powers. It would be surprising if a study of this kind did not reveal another dimension of Kipling's political thought.

Apart from Kipling, our attention in the texts about empire is only rarely drawn to the international context of imperial issues and the pursuit of national power. When it is, the references are mostly made in passing and are incidental or ancillary to the main lines of the narrative. Think, for example, of the passages in Conrad and Buchan about the competition between the Powers which are invariably directed to showing, not the similarities in *realpolitik*, but the exceptionalism of British idealism. A similar point can be made with respect to the Great Game, where the agents of German or Russian espionage are characteristically portrayed as having some abnormality or lack of moral fibre to contrast them with their British counterparts. Interestingly this seems less true of Indian narratives, presumably because there is detachment from or opposition to the imperial viewpoint. In one Indian text, Dhan Gopal Mukerji's *The Secret Listeners of the East*, the Great Game provides the substance of the plot and the politics of espionage are confronted directly if unimaginatively.[32] The narrator, a Bengali doctor turned scoutmaster, is engaged in tracking down the assassins of a British general who was a leader of the Scout Movement of British India. This unlikely scenario provides the basis for Kiplingesque episodes in disguise and signalling and an account of political intrigue in the Muslim states on India's northern border. The Great Game is given an extra-European dimension because the espionage and killings are the work of Jehadis or Crusaders of Mohammedanism, who in fact committed themselves against the British towards the end of the First World War and formed a secret order called 'the Invisible Listeners of the East' to assassinate British officers and to undermine Britain's position in the East. Significantly, the surviving assassin is sympathetically drawn. He is a man of courage and moral purpose who had once been a soldier in the Indian Army, but who had been converted to the Muslim cause by killing a Turk and fellow-Muslim at Gallipoli and by General Dyer's action at Amritsar in 1919.

In a few early Indian narratives, issues of international power and status are introduced with the clear purpose of providing a warning that unless some accommodation is reached with Indian nationalism, geopolitics will mesh with domestic grievances to bring down the Indian Empire. This is true, as we have seen, of S. M. Mitra's *Hindupore*, which invokes but does not pursue the significance of Japan's emergence as a Great Power.[33] A more sustained *realpolitik* intervention is to be found in S. K. Ghosh's *The Prince of Destiny*,[34] which reflects on the significance of the defeat of the Italians at Adowa in 1896 and that of Russia at the hands of the Japanese in 1904–5.

Although it was not so seen by Europeans at the time, Adowa is presented as a landmark in relations between East and West and is treated at length. The issue is raised during the hero's voyage to England, when news is had at Aden of Italy's defeat in a preliminary battle with the Abyssinians. In the Suez Canal eight Italian transports carrying troops to Massowah steam past Barath's ship. The British passengers are strangely reserved, their thinking being that a 'European power had no business going to war with an Oriental foe without immediate and signal victory'.[35] This minor episode provides the occasion for a chapter entitled 'The lesson of Adowah', which has elements of a political essay. The author's message is threefold. First, Adowa contributed to Japan's resolve to develop the material means to be independent of Europe. Second, in India the government was determined to strengthen its hold over the native states, diminish the status of the princes and elevate considerations of prestige over those of friendship and sentiment. Third, Italy's defeat at the hands of a non-European army led to a new assertiveness and sense of common destiny on the part of Asian peoples. Adowa, not the passage of the Yalu in the Russo-Japanese war eight years later, marked the beginning of a new epoch in the relations between Asia and Europe.

It must be said that there appears to be little historical support for these challenging themes. Adowa does not seem to have been a significant influence on Japan's military posture or its general approach to international politics. So far as India is concerned, Adowa was not a subject which attracted much attention in political speeches or the press – certainly it did not burn itself into the public mind as did the Japanese defeat of Russia in 1905. Nor is the argument persuasive that in the aftermath of Adowa the position of the princes was downgraded. If Adowa represents the real watershed in relations between Europe and Afro-Asia, it does so with the advantage of hindsight, not on the basis of how people thought at the time.

The novel proceeds on firmer ground when it turns to the rise of Japan and the response in India. We are told that in the early years of the century, Japan's military and economic development attracted close attention in India. The Anglo-Japanese Alliance was regarded as a confession of England's inability to hold India against Russia without Japanese aid. Moreover, a Japanese victory over Russia would be welcomed as the defeat of Europe by Asia. When the first successes fell to Japan, 'there were whispers in the very bazaars of India; and when the successes continued, the whisper became spoken words. The East sees quickly the hand of Fate.'[36] Those observations are given added bite by the activities and arguments of Naren, a young Bengali revolutionary. Addressing a public meeting in Barathpur, Naren speaks of the follies of the English and the strengths of the Japanese. The British today admire only physical force, and the possibility is canvassed that the Bengalis may become '[t]he Japanese of India'. The West is no match for a resurgent Asia: 'It is the eternal law of the survival of the fittest.'[37] This last reference is only one illustration of the way European maxims and assumptions of power politics are drawn on in the novel to make the case that the balance of economic and military power is shifting in favour of the East. In his speech to the people of Barathpur, Barath foresees the time, forty years on, when Britain's population will be half that of Germany and a third that of the United States. '*She will then be under sentence of death as a great Power* – unless she appeals to India.'[38] In such ways, by invoking *realpolitik* and the prospect of pan-Asianism, the author adds a dimension of threat to his appeal for closer Indo-British relations on the basis of sentiment and affinity.

Turning to fiction which depicts the closing stages of imperial rule or which considers the politics of the new states in the light of the imperial inheritance, again we find that the pursuit of power in international diplomacy receives only occasional and incidental treatment. In a few texts there are imaginative asides or novel perspectives which warrant the attention of the student of international politics, but this is a far cry from suggesting that they have within them the capacity to challenge or substantially supplement disciplinary orthodoxies. In Lawrence Durrell's *Mountolive*, for instance, there is much rich material about the changing nature of Great Power diplomacy in the Middle East in the years before the Second World War and the pressures building up at the grass-roots. In a letter to the Ambassador Designate to Egypt, Pursewarden, writer, cynic and 'first political', dismisses British policies of accommodation with Arab nationalism unaccompanied by the power to use the poison-cup. The Victorians who fathered the dream of the Arabian nights

> were people who believed in fighting for the value of their currency; they knew that the world of politics was a jungle. Today the Foreign Office appears to believe that the best way to deal with the jungle is to turn Nudist and conquer the wild beast by the sight of one's nakedness . . . why are we thinking up these absurd constructs to add to our own discomfiture – specially as it is clear to me that we

have lost the basic power to act which alone would ensure that our influence remained paramount here?[39]

Powerful evocative passages of this kind repay close reading but they are not pursued in a consistent way because the politics of the novel is essentially supportive of the study of the artist's relationship to society and the portrait of the city of Alexandria.

Rather different issues are raised when we think about Salman Rushdie and his two novels about the Indian subcontinent after independence, where the political is entwined with the personal and the new is seen to grow out of the old. For a time I considered whether *Midnight's Children* and *Shame* might be read as representing the beginnings of a critique of the extension of reasons of state to the politics of decolonization and after. Rushdie sets the scene with Mountbatten's 'soldier's knife that could cut subcontinents in three' and his description of Pakistan (or 'not quite' Pakistan) as a 'country so impossible that it could almost exist'. Many of the features we might expect of such a critique are present: the nation and the national interest as a ruse to divert attention from the self-serving actions of society's power-brokers; the similarities, almost collusion, of national élites – after the war the commanders on opposing sides drinking together and reminiscing; the regional illogic of war strategies and the drive for territory – the capture of Aansu which nobody knew what to do with, 'and a few years later there were ski-lodges up there and scheduled air flights'. There are also those more fundamental moves – characteristic of Rushdie's narratives – such as the focus on the story that is told (which takes in not only communications and media propaganda but fiction itself) and the challenge to Western modes of historical categorization and political representation. But for all the promise that these novels hold of breaking new ground by working out from the domestic political culture as captured through the personal to the geopolitics of the subcontinent, I do not think they succeed. There are simply too many threads and allusions; the potential of the fabulous and the extraordinary to liberate and redirect thinking has not been much exploited with respect to the international; too often the virtuosity of the writing inhibits the full development of the politics of the narrative.

One could discuss other novels of empire or its immediate aftermath which bear obliquely on the problem of power in international relations, but it is more fruitful to ask why the broad pattern is as it is, why *realpolitik* so seldom intrudes into the narrative. Part of the explanation might lie with the depersonalized nature of the subject and the novelist's discomfort with constructions such as the state and power in the abstract. It may also be that the imperial and the international are seen as worlds in their own right, with little connection being made between them. This is certainly characteristic of international relations as a discipline, which has taken remarkable little interest in the processes of nineteenth-century imperialism or the problems of imperial relations in the twentieth century. A more fundamental reason for the neglect of considerations of power would seem to lie in the assumption of difference, both between the various imperial actors and even more between colonizer and colonized. Whereas ideas about power politics are mostly predicated on commonalities of thought and action, so much of the mythology of empire was impregnated with the idea of difference – difference relating to culture, history and, above all, race. This is vividly illustrated by what have been called nightmares about the threat posed to the 'civilized world' or the international order by the Afro-Asian masses. The idea of the 'black peril' or the 'yellow hordes' was deeply embedded in the imperial psyche and reflected in the narratives of the time. Its echoes are caught in later fiction of a variety of kinds: in Jean Raspail's *Le Camp des Saints*, where the white world is overwhelmed by the peoples of Afro-Asia and its own migrant workers; in the portrait of Laval in David Caute's *The Decline of the West* – a man committed to an orgy of violence in Africa in the name of Western civilization, who sees himself as '[t]he warrior of France who faithfully serves his mistress . . . [t]he last Roman legionary at Pompeii'; and in popular novels of the Korean War which depict the enemy as shades of Genghis Khan advancing in 'human waves'.[40]

It can confidently be asserted that post-imperial fiction is much less reticent about developing themes relating to international power and economics than was the fiction of the imperial period. It also seems to be true that even where issues of power and economics are not taken up directly, often they can be seen to lie in the background or be read into processes or issues under another name. Think, for example, of First World narratives dealing with the cold war or Third World narratives raising questions about development. Let us consider why fiction now accords a higher visibility to international leverage and exchange than before and why this can be expected to continue.

Central to the explanation must be the end of formal empire itself. Imperial rule both unleashed and held back processes of global change and exchange. In the former category would come the incorporation of Asia and Africa into the international economic system; in the latter, the status, power and, arguably, internal stability of the metropoles. On almost any reckoning, therefore, decolonization as a historical process was of far-reaching significance for the changes it brought about or unmasked. What we would emphasize today, however, is different from what seemed important at the time. From a contemporary perspective, the grand politics of the collision between imperialism and nationalism no longer satisfies and the focus has shifted to more nuanced and often culturally oriented lines of argument. For instance, account must be taken of the longer-term repercussions in the First World of the wars of national liberation and the loss of position involved in consensual disengagement; of the linkage between imperial defeat and retreat and the Falklands War, Operation 'Desert Storm' and the French stand in Africa and the Pacific. Then there is the diaspora, the movement of migrant workers, the mixing of peoples and cultures which has been seen as a mark of the postcolonial era and has worked to consolidate the West as the centre. And flowing into the Third World, along the channels cut by the old imperialism, are the artefacts and symbols of modernity: arms and technology, aid packages and relief programmes of many kinds. Independence also brought new possibilities for the South and new fears for the North – resource diplomacy, nuclear proliferation, political challenge in the name of the Newly Emerging Forces or Islamic fundamentalism. Upon this mosaic of themes the cold war imposed a design of its own for much of the period. International geopolitics thus ensured a degree of interest and often alarm which could hardly have been generated by a Third World decoupled from the dramas at the centre.

Emerging variously in the latter stages of what we might call the first moment of the postcolonial era were fundamental changes in thinking about how to apprehend the external world and address the significance of the relocations of the period. I am referring here especially to conceptions of the political and geographical. Because of the need to take account of issues such as gender and conservation and the pressure to recontextualize, say, the movement of refugees or the approach to natural disasters, the ambit of the political has been broadened, often in ways of which we are hardly aware. So there has also been a growing sense of the connectedness over time and space between developments which were once compartmentalized and kept in different worlds – 'international' terrorism, the position of women in Pakistan or Muslims in the West. The effect of this rethinking has been to diminish the sense of Asia and Africa as 'out there' and to some degree link international processes to daily life. Along with other forms of art and scholarship, the novel of the postcolonial period has reflected, and reflected upon, these changes and it is therefore a primary imaginative source and part of the archival record of the decolonization era.

Much of what I have been discussing in the last two paragraphs relates to the processes of globalization. Increasingly, not only issues of culture, but also considerations of power and economics as they reveal themselves in contemporary international life, come under the rubric of globalization. We may therefore find that they receive closer attention in that discourse than in disciplinary international relations – although naturally the terms of reference will be different. Despite extravagant formulations that the world is becoming one, there are countervailing tendencies. As Arjun Appadurai has so effectively demonstrated, at the centre of contemporary global interaction is the tension between cultural homogenization and cultural heterogenization.[41] Some of this tension is concentrated at those points where global forces, and the resistance they engender, intersect with the claims of the nation-state – hence the calls to rethink the nation-state.[42] In this, as in other respects, there are parallels between globalization and imperialism. This is hardly surprising since in the Third World context the global so often followed the route pioneered by the imperial. And just as imperialism needs to be understood in terms of its impact on ordinary people and everyday life, so also does globalization. This is why fiction is such a valuable source in charting the appeal and limits of the global. In chapter 2, I drew attention to the relevance of Thomas Akare's *The Slums* and Shashi Tharoor's *Show Business* to debates about the internationalization of culture. It is scarcely an exaggeration to claim that most contemporary novels with a North/South aspect contain material that bears upon the relationship between the local and the global – which is, after all, what globalization is about.

The fact that globalization and international relations are adjacent discourses and that their concerns overlap provides strong support for the argument that there should be more dialogue between them than presently takes place. Literary sources could play an important role in the translation of ideas between the two – a role, moreover, that could help combat their shared Eurocentrism. But for all the commonalities between them, the two formations still have their own agendas and will inevitably continue to privilege different kinds of source material. So far as disciplinary international relations is concerned, power politics is sure to remain a major area of study. Here also fictional narratives can stimulate rethinking along imaginative lines.

I am not suggesting that the tendency in recent fiction is to engage directly with questions of *realpolitik* and the state. Some writers do, for example Frederick Forsyth in *The Dogs of War* and *The Fist of God*. Others do not. Think of narratives as expressive of the era as V. S. Naipual's *Finding the Centre* and *The Enigma of Arrival* or Salman Rushdie's *The Satanic Verses* (although the novel itself became an episode in contemporary international politics). What I am saying is that on both sides of the divide – which is no longer such a divide – fiction is more likely to have an international aspect or be seen as resonating with questions about the global system than was formerly the case. Nor is there any implication that fictional narratives which address international relations on its own terms and in its own language are likely to be more instructive than those which do not. Indeed, in line with the approach adopted throughout this book, I would assert the reverse. No fictional text could be more directly relevant to our project than William Clark's *Cataclysm*, which signals its purpose with the subtitle, 'The North–South Conflict of 1987'.[43] Written by the former Director of Britain's Overseas Development Institute and later Vice-President of the World Bank, with the help of a team of advisers which included Robert McNamara, it is virtually a textbook on international relations in fictional form. All the expected topics such as Third World debt, the role of the World Bank/IMF, the diplomacy of threat and reliance on military force are presented in an extremely informed manner, and there is even an index for easy reference. However, its realism is to a large extent unrealistic and its characterization controlled by its politics. The notes on the dust-jacket state that it is written 'with authority', but it is the kind of authority that stultifies thought in the interests of generating a sense of crisis. If the book succeeds at all, it can only be in this respect and even then by staying within the existing paradigms of international relations.

With this warning about what not to look for, let us consider more fruitful possibilities. I want to conclude by illustrating some of the ways in which a reading of fiction of the post-imperial era can open up our thinking about power and the international politics of the Third World. I propose first to direct attention to the conclusions of a study of popular fiction about Asia and comment on their significance for our purposes. Then I will indicate the potential of two particular texts, written later and concerned with different aspects of postcolonial international relations. In this way we will have broached the significance of a generic body of popular fiction as well as taken account of the potentialities of individual narratives.

A major gap in scholarly analysis of Western fiction about the Third World exists in that period after the Second World War but before the Vietnam War when the brokerage of power shifted from Britain to the United States. In a study which makes a notable contribution to redressing this neglect, Richard Fuller has charted the changing representations of Asia in American bestsellers of the cold war period.[44] His thesis is that from the late 1940s to the early 1960s there was a dramatic recasting of the image of Asia under the ideological imperative of competing with communism in this crucial theatre of geopolitics. A short summary of Fuller's argument will make clear the extent to which fictional appreciations were overhauled and the significance of the revised representations. It was characteristic of American novels written in the inter-war years and during the Second World War that Asian peoples and societies were approached in terms of difference from the West. The narratives of this time were in fact stamped with familiar orientalist inscriptions. With the advent of the cold war and the imposition of the global conflict between the communist powers and the United States, however, Asians became like Americans and they were invested with the same virtues and failings – drawn, of course, from the liberal democratic lexicon. As characters, Asians were given an internal life, whereas before they had been little more than plot devices. Economic development was thus naturalized into Asian society (though always with the caveat of an American catalyst); the peasant (once detached from corrupt ideologues) was enlisted as an ally in the global struggle; and Asian nationalism (purged of élite excesses) claimed for the West. In short, cultural similarity became the condition of the time and it was driven by the power politics of the cold war. But once the Vietnam War took its toll and America began to falter, novelists reverted to traditional stereotypes. Asian difference then became the explanation of America's difficulties.

Even this heavily abbreviated outline of the issues involved is enough to establish the significance of the fictional narratives for our present inquiry. Although for the most part the texts do not probe the mindset of power politics, they indicate the way such thinking spilled over from its declared political domain and shaped popular conceptions of Asian societies and people. That Asia could be rewritten according to American design, and that Asians could be invested with American qualities of character through a process of universalization, testifies to the capacity of ideas about power and strategy to generate a complementary cultural consciousness. It is no exaggeration to claim that, taken collectively, the novels of the period tell a story about America's approach to Asia which extends established accounts based on conventional sources. It also needs to be said that Fuller's account of thematic change in the narratives provides a case study of the way that representations of the other are adjusted in the interests of protecting the self. Asians became like Americans in order to preserve America's understanding of the universalism of its ideology and its role as a great power. Herein lies a warning that self/other politics do not always correspond to the North/South division. Again we see that Said's thesis of the invariable difference of the Orient from the West is overdrawn, as are those lines of postcolonial theory which assume an orientalist mystique endlessly reproducing itself over time. The logic (or illogic) of the power calculations of the central balance, at least in the years of the cold war, cut orientalism down to size and changed its expression.

To close on a very different note, let us consider two recent novels that can hardly fail to induce the reader to reflect on constructions of power in international politics and the human costs involved. These novels are Timothy Mo's *The Redundancy of Courage* and Amitav Ghosh's *The Shadow Lines*. Published three years apart, one a record of action, the other a study in remembrance, both narratives succeed in showing how extraordinary is the ordinary in international life.

The Redundancy of Courage is a fictional re-creation of the impact of the Indonesian invasion of East Timor on Timorese life and the subsequent guerrilla struggle in the mountains. It does not primarily concern itself with the international aspects of the episode, although some are astutely touched upon. For example, there is the importance of the international press – even if it directed only '[h]alf an eye . . . for the duration of a blink' – and the recognition that '*if it doesn't get on to TV in the West, it hasn't happened*'.[45] And there is the treatment of the Australian Government's response: 'The government behaved like a government.'[46] Fundamentally, however, the novel focuses on how the conflict appeared to the victims and what consequences it had for them. In place of the realist view of Indonesian action as a surgical exercise contained within a narrow time-frame, we are given a perspective of the invasion itself as a cancer which continues to afflict over time – although inevitably there had to be some acceptance. Consider the following passage:

> In the end normalcy resumed. It's not, in fact, normalcy. Not under our kind of circumstances. But the psyche can only take so much abnormality. It rebels in the end, fails to register, refuses to endure. In the unusual it discerns only the usual. It habituates itself to the grossest of existences. From an unplanned string of horrors it extracts a timetable of the banal. (p. 109)

For my own part, I was led to reconsider my earlier appreciation of the conflict, which was essentially in geopolitical terms along the lines of the general reflection of George Ball, Under-Secretary of State in the Kennedy and Johnson administrations that 'the disintegration of empire created new states to complicate the peace'.[47] Mo's personalization and brutalization of the realist account adds a vital dimension and brings to mind Ken Booth's call to people 'strategic discourse with real nations rather than stereotypes . . .

and with individuals affected by a distinctive cultural heredity as opposed to individuals supposedly driven by a universal political and strategic logic'.[48]

There are similarities between the themes and point of view of *The Redundancy of Courage* and those of Amitav Ghosh's brilliant second novel, *The Shadow Lines*. In Ghosh's narrative, however, the critique of accustomed ways of political thinking is more comprehensive and searching, and entirely at one with the story. The unnamed narrator traces the lives of members of his Bengali family and those of the Prices, their English friends, from Calcutta before the Second World War, through the England of the 1940s and 1950s, to the riots and wars on the Indian subcontinent in the 1960s. All the time we are made aware of how personal connection cuts deeper than political borders, how the present picks up on the past, and how private turmoil intersects with public drama. The novel's title signifies both the power of the border between nations which is so often the source of war and violence and the absurdity of the boundary between peoples across which so much life and death flows.

A few extracts from the narrative will convey something of the novel's politics, although taken by themselves they can hardly catch the way the writing draws in the reader or brings out the connectedness of the whole text. The narrator, still grieving over his cousin Tridib's death in the communal riots in Dhaka in 1964, agonizes over the connection between the tragic events in different parts of the subcontinent and why some were reported and some were not. What is it, he asks, 'that makes all those things called "politics" so eloquent and these others unnameable things so silent?'[49] A few pages on, he provides part of the answer: 'The theatre of war . . . is the stage on which states disport themselves; they have no use for memories of riots.' Certainly, once the riots had started in Dhaka and Calcutta, both governments put a stop to them as quickly as possible.

> In this they were subject to a logic larger than themselves, for the madness of a riot is a pathological inversion, but also therefore a reminder, of that indivisible sanity that binds people to each other independently of their governments. And that prior, independent relationship is the natural enemy of government, for it is in the logic of states that to exist at all they must claim the monopoly of all relationships between peoples.[50]

And so the threads wind back to earlier fragments in the novel. To the narrator's cousin, Ila, a product of international schooling, who belonged to a cosmopolitan set in London and told the narrator that he would not understand the exhilaration of the great events of the time because nothing really important ever happens in Calcutta or Delhi.

> Well of course there are famines and riots and disasters, she said. But those are local things after all – not like revolutions or anti-fascist wars, nothing that sets a political example to the world, nothing that's really remembered. (p. 104)

And to the narrator's grandmother, Mayadebi, who could not understand about borders and wanted to know whether she would be able to see the one between India and East Pakistan from the plane. The narrator's father explained: '[t]he border isn't on the frontier: it's right inside the airport' (p. 151). And to the fear on the streets of Calcutta before the riots exploded and the disarrangement of the narrator's universe which could be read into 'the perfectly ordinary angle of an abandoned rickshaw' (p. 203).

> That particular fear has a texture you can neither forget nor describe . . . It is a fear that comes of the knowledge that normalcy is utterly contingent, that the spaces that surround one, the streets that one inhabits, can become, suddenly and without warning, as hostile as a desert in a flash flood. It is this that sets apart the thousand million people who inhabit the subcontinent from the rest of the world – not language, not food, not music – it is the special quality of loneliness that grows out of the fear of the war between oneself and one's image in the mirror. (p. 204)

Ghosh's narrative stands on its own as a powerful statement of the need to reconceptualize basic issues of contemporary international politics. It also serves as an exemplification of the way the dissolution of empire has expanded the meaning of the political and the role that literature can play in bringing this to our attention. In different ways, Coetzee, Mo and Ghosh lead us to reconsider the nature and implications of power in international relations, which traditional disciplinary practices have codified as outside the province of the literary. That power politics is rendered in more personal, psychological or metaphysical terms enables us to see it differently and bring other perspectives to bear. Account must still be taken of literature's silences and it is obvious that there will be much that is given only partial or selective treatment. More and more, however, we can expect to emphasize fiction's relocations rather than its silences. I do not think that we can yet say the same about economic interest, but in the light of the processes of globalization it will be surprising if the movement is not in this direction.

A coda should be added that this chapter can be read in a different way. The accent in the foregoing paragraph is on the insights and elusions of fiction when considered in relation to what have long been regarded as systemic features of international politics and economic exchange. Emphasis might instead be placed on the potentiality of fiction to stimulate engagement between old and new discourses in such a way that both would benefit. Implicit in this chapter is the view that reconceptualization along postcolonial lines offers exciting possibilities for disciplinary formations such as international relations to broaden their horizons. One of the tasks of the concluding chapter is to establish that the new formations of knowledge need to reckon with the impediments to change at the international level, as recounted by disciplinary international relations and associated schools of thought like dependency, if their theorizing is to be translated into practice.

Notes

1. Laura Chrisman, 'The imperial unconscious? Representations of imperial discourse', *Critical Quarterly*, 32:3 (Autumn, 1990), 38–58 (p. 38).

2. Phillip Darby, *Three Faces of Imperialism* (Yale University Press, New Haven CT and London, 1987), p. 188.

3. Quoted in Robert Dallek, *The American Style of Foreign Policy: Cultural Politics and Foreign Affairs* (Mentor, New American Library, New York, 1983), p. 216.

4. Patrick Brantlinger, *Rule of Darkness. British Literature and Imperialism 1830–1914* (Cornell University Press, Ithaca NY and London, 1988). See especially the introduction.

5. Edward Said, *Culture and Imperialism* (Chatto & Windus, London, 1993), pp. 73–88. Considerable recent work has been done on the contribution of colonialism to metropolitan culture. See for instance Vron Ware, *Beyond the Pale. White Woman, Rascism and History* (Verso, New York, 1992); Bill Schwarz (ed.), *The Expansion of England. Race, Ethnicity and Cultural History* (Routledge, New York, 1996).

6. Said, op. cit., p. 75.

7. Ibid., p. 78.

8. See, for example, L. H. Gann and Peter Duignan, *The Rulers of British Africa 1870–1914* (Hoover Institution Publications, Croom Helm, London, 1978), pp. 5 and 43; Charles Allen (ed.), *Plain Tales from the Raj* (Futura, Macdonald & Co., London, 1976; first published 1975), pp. 103–4 and 227–8.

9. In the early part of this novel, which is set in India, British imperialism is depicted as the principal cause of economic backwardness. Later pride of place is given to the bondage of Hinduism. Louis Bromfield, *The Rains Came* (Penguin Books, Harmondsworth, 1959; first published 1937).

10. This novel, which is set in an unnamed south-east Asian country, which is presumably the Philippines, locates the causes of a local insurgency in the exploitative activities of a multinational plantation company backed by the United States Government. Very quickly, however, the narrative changes direction and becomes an indictment of communist penetration. James Ramsey Ullman, *Windom's Way* (Herald-Sun Reader's Bookclub in association with the Companion Book Club, London and Melbourne, 1954; first published 1952).

11. See Susie Tharu, 'Reading against the imperial grain', *Jadavpur Journal of Comparative Literature*, 24 (1986), 60–71; Arun P. Mukherjee, 'The exclusions of postcolonial theory and Mulk Raj Anand's *Untouchable*: a case study', *Ariel*, 22:3 (July 1991), 27–48.

12. Mulk Raj Anand, *The Village* (Cape, London, 1939); *Across the Black Waters* (Cape, London, 1940); *The Sword and the Sickle* (Cape, London, 1942).

13. J. G. Farrell, *The Singapore Grip* (Fontana Paperbacks, London, 1979; first published 1978). After various false leads, we learn that the title relates to the hold of local prostitutes but it also serves as a metaphor for colonial capitalism.

14. W. K. Hancock, *Survey of British Commonwealth Affairs*, vol. 2, *Problems of Economic Policy* (Oxford University Press for RIIA, London, Part 1, 1940, Part 2, 1942).

15. See Darby, op. cit., pp. 137–8 and Hancock, op.cit., Part 2, pp. 188–200.

16. With respect to the former, two excellent studies are: M. M. Mahood, *Joyce Cary's Africa* (Methuen, London, 1964); Michael J. C. Echeruo, *Joyce Cary and the Novel of Africa* (Longman, London, 1973). For a more recent and less complimentary study see Abdul JanMohamed, *Manichean Aesthetic, The Politics of Literature in Colonial Africa* (University of Massachusetts Press, Amherst, 1983), ch. 2.

17. M. M. Mahood, *The Colonial Encounter* (Rex Collings, London, 1977), p. 168.

18. Joyce Cary, *An American Visitor* (Michael Joseph, London, 1949; first published 1933), p. 47.

19. Ibid., p. 133.

20. M. M. Mahood has an interesting discussion of the identification of many colonial officials with their tribes. Her chapter on *An American Visitor* is entitled 'A pagan man'. Cary wrote an unpublished sketch on the same theme and gave it the same title. See Mahood, *Joyce Cary's Africa*, pp. 130–3.

21. Cary, *An American Visitor*, p. 42.

22. Ibid., p. 234.

23. Edward W. Said, *Beginnings: Intention and Method* (Basic Books, New York, 1975), p. 110.

24. Michael Wilding, 'The politics of *Nostromo*', *Essays in Criticism*, 16:4 (1966), 441–56 (p. 455).

25. Chrisman, op. cit., especially pp. 49, 55 and 56.

26. Said, *Beginnings: Intention and Method*, pp. 118, 136 and 137. See also Fredric Jameson, *The Political Unconscious: Narrative as a Socially Symbolic Act* (Methuen, London, 1981), p. 279.

27. With respect to the former argument see, for example, Irving Howe's review of *Waiting for the Barbarians* in *New York Times Book Review*, 18 April 1982, pp. 1 and 36 (p. 36). On the latter see Benita Parry 'Speech and silence in the fictions of J. M. Coetzee', *New Formations*, 21 (Winter 1994), 1–20.

28. Quoted in Parry, ibid., p. 20.

29. The use of the word 'interim' here involves more than the usual disclaimer because we can expect other interventions, following the example of Laura Chrisman, and there will be studies of new texts using symbols such as oil, rather than silver or treasure, which are of the currency of contemporary international relations.

30. See her five novels published between 1979 and 1983 under the overall title *Canopus in Argos: Archives*.

31. Richard Cronin,'The Indian English novel: *Kim* and *Midnight's Children*', *Modern Fiction Studies*, 33:2 (Summer 1987), 201–13 (p. 208).

32. Dhan Gopal Mukerji, *The Secret Listeners of the East* (E. P. Dutton & Co., New York, undated but apparently published in 1926).

33. See ch. 4, p. 84–5.

34. For the context of this intervention, see ch. 4, pp. 85–7.

35. S.K. Ghosh, *The Prince of Destiny. The New Krishna* (Rebman, London, 1909), p. 132.

36. Ibid., p. 507.

37. Ibid., pp. 563–4.

38. Ibid., p. 596. Italics in the original.

39. Lawrence Durrell, *Mountolive* (Faber & Faber, London, 1958), pp. 93–4.

40. See, for example, Pat Frank's *Hold Back the Night* (J. B. Lippincott, Philadelphia and New York, 1952).

41. Arjun Appadurai, 'Disjunction and difference in the global cultural economy', *Public Culture*, 2:2 (Spring 1990), 1–24. See also Jonathan Friedman, 'Being in the world: globalization and localization', *Theory, Culture and Society*, 7 (1990), 311–28.

42. On the key issue of territoriality see Michael J. Shapiro, 'Moral geographies and the ethics of post-sovereignty', *Public Culture*, 6:3 (1994), 479–502; Arjun Appadurai, 'Sovereignty without territoriality: notes for a postnational geography' in Patricia Yaeger (ed.), *The Geography of Identity* (University of Michigan Press, Ann Arbor, 1996), pp. 40–58.

43. William Clark, *Cataclysm* (Sidgwick & Jackson, London, 1984).

44. Richard Fuller, The Image of Asia in American Bestsellers of the Cold War, 1947–1965, unpublished PhD thesis, University of Melbourne, 1989.

45. Timothy Mo, *The Redundancy of Courage* (Vintage, London, 1991), pp. 72 and 91. Italics in the original.

46. Ibid., p. 93.

47. George W. Ball, *The Past Has Another Pattern. Memoirs* (W. W. Norton & Co., New York, 1982), p. 176.

48. Ken Booth, *Strategy and Ethnocentrism* (Croom Helm, London, 1979), pp. 135–6.

49. Amitav Ghosh, *The Shadow Lines* (Ravi Dayal Publisher, Delhi, 1988), p. 288.

50. Ibid., p. 230.

CHAPTER 7

A postcolonial retrospect

This book has addressed the question of the contribution of fiction to an understanding of the relationship between colonizer and colonized, North and South. But this formulation of the book's problematic is deceptively simple. Very different views are held as to what constitutes the relationship and hence the kind of issues that are pertinent. In the traditional understanding, what matters is public and mostly high politics – except that from very early on, imperial studies was led to inquire into social and cultural questions closer to the ground. In marked contrast, some contemporary lines of analysis approach the relationship through the medium of identity politics. The stage is set by the processes of othering, in which the discursive plays a primary role. The potentialities of fiction necessarily depend upon which presumptions are brought to bear. That is to say, what we learn from fiction must be related to who is the reader.

The argument of this book has been forthright when the 'we' is taken to be students of international relations and adjacent discourses. For such a readership, fiction can provide an entry to other worlds: culture in being and in the making; people going about their ordinary – and often extraordinary – lives; the subjectivity of experiences; the actuality of moral consciousness. Clearly, at any one time, or with respect to specific aspects of the engagement, not all of these realms will connect with North/South politics; but what has been rejected is the notion that the more formalized processes of interaction operate in a domain of their own and constitute a world apart. Systems of exchange must be mediated by lived experience. It is here that fiction, by looking inward and reaching outward, extends our understanding.

Inward and outward are of course closely placed, two sides of a single coin. By inward we might think first of the societal and the cultural as opposed to the state and the regulation of diplomacy or international political economy. Or a start might be made with the personal, embracing modes of behaviour, emotions and affects, gender and sexuality. And hence to the subjective – identity, the imaginary, the political unconscious. What bears emphasis is that none of these ways of proceeding stops short at the international. More often than not, 'out there' and 'in here' are entangled. One of the characters in Amitav Ghosh's novel *The Circle of Reason* is described as having had her heart colonized by her Singer sewing machine.[1] R. B. J. Walker writes in similar vein when he observes: 'The state is within us as much as we are within it.'[2]

That fiction usually works from the inside outward is not in itself a reason for valorizing the novel. But having regard for the fact that what we might call the grand narratives of the international work from the top down (the change in the spatial metaphor is significant), the novel's orientation serves to redress and complement. International relations, globalization and dependency all draw their foundational paradigms from the global and the systemic and they have been reluctant to allow the orthodoxies thus established to be unsettled from below. This is quintessentially the case with international relations, where designs for the regional and the local have long been read off understandings of the centre. Even globalization and dependency theorists only turned to the periphery and the particular after hypotheses about the dynamic of the centre failed to hold.

One of the principal contentions of this book has been that fiction brings out how often the North/South encounter as it manifests itself on the ground does not conform to the story as told from above. All too often, disciplinary theorizing discounts the cultural and spatial influence of site, downgrades the agency of subordinate peoples and privileges the centre. The short-comings associated with unrelieved reliance on conventional sources are therefore politically disabling for those who seek international change. Especially with regard to modes of reading, fiction holds out possibilities of empowerment. As a rule, literary narratives are attentive to the particularities of time and place. Frequently they provide material about daily life which directs attention to ways of seeing and forms of action which fall outside the models of domination and subordination or collaboration and resistance. Partly for those reasons, Third World literary narratives constitute a primary source for challenging the ethnocentrism, charged with self-interest, which persuades many established knowledge formations. If provincializing Europe is an impossibility,[3] then at least the novel has emerged as an effective instrument for puncturing Western universalism. It might further be said that although fictional treatment of the politics of international linkages is often oblique, tentative and uneven, this stands in salutary contrast to the sense of certitude about disciplinary analyses and their completeness. Impressions, vignettes and fragments may contribute to a greater awareness of the constructed nature of academic narratives and their provisionality.

Readers who engage with the new discourses are unlikely to need convincing about the need to break with disciplinary orthodoxies. Thinking afresh is, after all, the *raison d'être* of the new formations of knowledge. But this has by no means always been accompanied by an openness of mind, much less a familiarity with what is being rejected. Often the ground on which discourse proceeds has been secured by developing concepts and a language which deter, even debar, the outsider. (Disciplinary policing comes in a variety of forms, some more subtle than others.) The likelihood is therefore that readers versed in these new approaches will readily accept the political relevance of literary narratives, but that they will read them in ways consonant with their particular discourse, probably emphasizing the subjectivity of experience and putting a premium on agency. Yet might it not be productive to read against the grain of contemporary theorizing? Might not alternative readings work to provoke conversations between different scholarly formations?

Accordingly, there is a need to consider the significance for this book of the challenge to traditional approaches to North/South international politics mounted by colonial discourse analysis and postcolonial theory. The question before us, then, is how the themes developed in this book stand up when considered in relation to the contentions of postcolonialism. By addressing the relationship between the approach adopted here and the perspectives of postcolonialism, it should be possible to contribute to our inquiry in various ways. For one thing, by working along these lines we can review the main arguments of the book and draw them together from a different vantage-point. Of more consequence, it will help to situate this inquiry in relation to other ways of examining the narration of the North/South encounter. In a period of growing specialization, involving a proliferation of new disciplinary studies, it is important that one approach be positioned *vis-à-vis* another so that the points of actual or potential engagement can be determined and some sense gained of the space between them. This argument has a particular pertinence with respect to postcolonial discourse because of its self-referential nature and the need to translate some of its critical procedures so that we can better assess how far they are different from what went before and in which ways. There is also the possibility that it may be thought that postcolonialism does the job undertaken by this book and that an analysis of imaginative literature as in practice representing a province of narrative has been rendered unnecessary by the emergence of this new discourse. The conclusion drawn here is that any such view is mistaken. In the course of argument there will be a need to direct attention to some of the shortcomings of postcolonialism. Although it is not intended to attempt a general evaluation of the discourse, a recognition of certain of its weaknesses constitutes an endorsement of the value of fictional narratives to an understanding of the cultural politics of imperialism and its legacies in Africa and Asia.

Before addressing these various concerns, it is necessary briefly to review postcolonial discourse, set out what it attempts to do and outline some of its basic themes. For our purposes this is best done with a broad brush, yet this is where the difficulty lies because it is an exercise largely avoided within the discourse itself. Postcolonial theorists have shown a decided reluctance to spell out the aims and ambit of the discourse, preferring to make a virtue out of being free-floating and open-ended. The problem is compounded by postcolonialism's changing frames of reference over time. More than is true of traditional disciplines the subjects and source materials of discourse at any particular moment are set in the course of dialogue and by the concerns of the principal protagonists.

On some accounts, postcolonialism represents a set of conceptual tools which enable the experience of colonial domination to be understood in new and diverse ways. In this view, postcolonialism is taken to be a broad church, encompassing a range of theoretical questions, and as such it cannot be contained within geographical parameters or delimited in terms of set political groupings. Whatever the merits of this understanding, it is of limited utility for our present inquiry. I will therefore proceed with a more grounded formulation which relates forms of knowledge to political practice and anchors the discourse in the historical experience of European imperialism and its cultural and psychological aftermath. Accordingly, the nub of postcolonialism is taken to be located in its concern to open up a space for Third World peoples to plot a course for themselves, free from the domination of outside forces. Its frame of reference is international because the major processes which circumscribe freedom of action and thought are seen to be located externally – in the West and the global system created and maintained by the West. A heavy emphasis is placed on historical inquiry because the contemporary subordination of the Third World is understood to derive from nineteenth-century imperialism and its intellectual and cultural constructs. The development of an alternative historiography is therefore a necessary first step towards envisaging a liberated future. In rewriting the historical record – and indeed generally – representation is invested with a power in its own right. From Fanon to Achebe and through to Bhabha, a connecting theme is the way Western representations construct meaning and 'reality' for the Third World. According to this understanding, the text is not simply a way of recording but also a means of determining the relations between North and South. The innovativeness of postcolonialism's epistemology is paralleled by the radicalism of its politics in that the discourse is directed to challenging the subordination of the Third World to external designs. Thus postcolonialism is not simply a mode of intellectual inquiry; it represents an attempt to generate strategies of political change.

There is some debate about the origins of the discourse and a case can be put that the writings of Fanon, Foucault and Said provided the basis upon which others built. But, in my opinion, this view involves a very selective reading of the texts and a good deal of hindsight. A much stronger claim can be mounted that postcolonialism grew out of the study of fiction written in ex-colonial countries and the search to discern commonalities both in content and form. Initially it was directed primarily to writing in Commonwealth countries, especially India and the former colonial territories in Africa and the Caribbean. The British connection provided a linkage-point between the different regional and national literatures and facilitated scholarly exchange through established networks and fora. The project then broadened out to survey Third World literature generally, the assumption being that the imperial experience provided a sufficient basis of commonality and the British nexus was unnecessarily restricting. From such beginnings, essentially of a comparative nature and located within a single discipline, postcolonialism branched out to become more theoretical and less concerned with imaginative literature.

In this process two stages can be distinguished, which for convenience we will call postcolonialism's second and third phases. In the second phase of its development, the idea of resistance became the hallmark of the discourse and various ancillary concepts such as subversion and appropriation took their place alongside it. By such means, the initiative could be wrested from the metropoles and a start made with the process of self-recovery. The fictional texts elevated to the counter-canon were mainly selected on the basis of their oppositional stance towards imperialism and their positive portrayal or advocacy of precolonial culture. As it happened, however, reliance was increasingly placed on the non-fictional writings of Third World intellectuals such as Fanon, Said and Spivak, and fictional texts became of secondary importance. Thus it might be said that the distinctiveness of the discourse no longer resided in its source material but in its thematic presuppositions.

During this second phase, the discourse broadened its approach to resistance by tapping other ways of conceptualizing the imperial experience and striking implicit alliances with more specialized schools of inquiry. Significant here are the works of Third World scholars such as Albert Memmi, Octavio Mannoni and, especially, Frantz Fanon, who utilized Freudian and other psychoanalytic perspectives to interpret the colonizer/colonized relationship and on this basis, posited the necessity of release through rejection. At the hands of JanMohamed, Fanon became the principal inspiration for an exploration of the Manichean dialectic and a fundamental rejection of imperialist categories of thought which involved going beyond the categories themselves.[4] At the same time, other postcolonialists – most notably Spivak – reached out to subaltern studies, a project devoted to challenging Eurocentric conceptions of Indian history which 'wished away the phenomenon of resistance' and hence misrepresented the power relations under imperialism.[5] By giving voice to the so-called 'subaltern', writers in this endeavour have sought to overturn the élitist categories of established Indo-British scholarship. Although distinct from postcolonialism *per se*, subaltern studies was held up as a form of postcolonial criticism to which reference might be made for historical and theoretical insights.

Developing alongside the broader conceptual reach of the discourse was a sharper and more ideologically driven debate about some of post-colonialism's key categories and stratagems. It was as if the declining authority of the novelist gave the postcolonial critic freer rein to determine the terms on which the discourse went forward. Differences in conception, hitherto in the background, were now openly articulated and ranged against each other. A fundamental site of contention concerned the nature and possibilities of resistance. On the one side, Said and JanMohamed were held to postulate the unmitigated antagonism of colonizer and colonized, and it followed that postcolonial opposition needed to be total and unproblematic. On the other side, there was the position of Spivak and Bhabha, who were critical of a simple model of binary oppositions and for whom resistance had to proceed in a more differentiated manner.[6] A related matter of debate concerned the indigenous cultural ideal. The notion of recovering an authentic native voice/identity and returning to precolonial culture had a strong appeal to those who embraced a thoroughgoing strategy of resistance. As we have noted, the Nigerian critic Chinweizu argued vigorously along such lines, and the tendency to see the way forward in terms of a retrieval of the past was prevalent in the writings of many postcolonial theorists. Even at that stage, however, there were expressions of dissent, most notably from Bhabha and less directly from Said. Although during this phase of postcolonialism Manicheanism heavily influenced thinking about the cultural politics of the Third World, there were also those who rejected both the possibility and desirability of a monocultural future.

It is this more moderated oppositional stance which has come to characterize the third and contemporary phase of postcolonialism. Following the lead of Bhabha and Spivak, the colonial encounter is seen as involving ambivalence both on the part of the colonizer and the colonized. Similarly, in the postcolonial context, difference and otherness are understood to involve more than the external and the adversarial; they are located within the parties as well as outside them, and even between them there are moments of intimacy and elements of complicity. There has also been a continuing tendency to expand the understanding of the political, with the result that the discourse has extended its purview into areas previously considered peripheral to the politics of imperialism. In this respect, the most important initiatives relate to gender and sexuality, but the significance of space and place has also become more prominent. Overall, the direction of movement has been to reposition the colonial and postcolonial relationships along less essentialist lines and bring out its heterogeneous and syncretic features.

With a few significant exceptions, imaginative literature has slid further into the background of the discourse. When literary texts are considered, they are more likely to be deconstructed to bring to the surface their representational attributes than examined for their ideational content. In other words, theory has broken free from its secondary status and now speaks through the literary text. There has thus been a decisive shift from the early days when postcolonialism was tied to the study of the novel; now it is the critical essay which is the staple of the discourse and determines the issues and method-ology for debate. Postmodernism has been the crucial influence here and it pervades this third movement of postcolonialism. The focus on the particular and the marginal; the heterogenity of meaning and narrative; the questioning of Eurocentric positivism and universalism; the ambiguity towards modernity; the critique of Western individualism; the interest in the constructions of self and other – all bear the trade mark of recent critical social theory.

Two points can be singled out from the various accents and tendencies in recent postcolonial theory which highlight the magnitude of the shift in postcolonialism's claims and the challenge it presents to traditional modes of analysis. First, the marginal is now posited as the primary source of systemic change and the repository of the most creative ways of thinking about social futures. Whether it be the Third World intellectual in Western academic circles, the subaltern in colonial society, or the diaspora, the impetus for radical and subversive change is seen as coming from those at the margin. Second, in the course of attempting to open up alternative sites of enunciation for the significance of postcolonial agency, the discourse has expanded its understanding of the meaning and significance of culture. In so doing, postcolonialism has broken into what were once the territorial preserves of established disciplines – including politics and history as well as literature – and conceptualized the familiar in new ways. The point has been reached where it is even possible to claim that we are witnessing the emergence of a 'new discourse of global cultural relations'.[7]

Throughout this book I have been concerned to show that fiction opens up very different vistas from studies in disciplinary international relations, even if, from the vantage-ground of narratology, both travel down the same road. The same point stands in relation to postcolonialism. The material which follows mainly emphasizes the differences in perspective which depend on whether we take fictional texts or postcolonial discourse as our starting-point. However, it is necessary to bear in mind that there is considerable overlap between the two and that at times they merge. Postcolonialism is not opposed to the literary text. It began with literature and although it has since taken a course of its own, it continues to draw on literary sources. Moreover, the province of literature has not been sealed off from the intrusion of contemporary theory. Novelists may incorporate in their fiction ideas taken from theoretical disquisition – think of Rushdie and Marechera, to name two. Equally, how we evaluate bodies of literature and read individual texts may be influenced by postcolonial theory – in some cases heavily. It is difficult to pin down many such borrowings but illustrations would include those readings of Third World literature which interrogate the treatment of modernity and the nation-state.

Of more direct significance, this book makes common cause with postcolonialism in that its import is to reconceptualize the imperial relationship. Postcolonialism's strength – and to my mind its weakness also – resides in the sweep of its imaginative recasting of the politics of imperialism and the resistance it engendered. It is partly because of the free-floating nature of the discourse that it has been able to discount or pass over so much established thought. Here, in partial contrast, I have attempted to stay close to the literary texts and relate them throughout to the concerns of international relations and, to a lesser extent, those of other bodies of disciplinary thought. Despite this difference in approach, one of the fundamental conclusions of this book corresponds with a major theme of postcolonialism in its third phase. This is that the relationship between the West and the Third World cannot be encapsulated within a binary schematic.

I will now review the case as it has been developed in this book for rejecting binarism as an organizing principle, indicating where it converges with postcolonialism and where it diverges. I will then add a caveat to the effect that postcolonialism has gone too far in its cultivation of the middle ground and its privileging of the 'in-between'. It is evident that paradigms of binarism have long enclosed analysis of the imperial relationship. One thinks immediately of how they are enshrined in Marxist theories of imperialism and emerge in different if more veiled forms in the logic of power politics, with its zero-sum connotations and its emphasis on winners and losers. More recently they have been reinscribed by the critiques of orientalism and by major strands of postcolonialism. Fiction pays its dues to each of these traditions of thought, but the argument advanced here is that it leads us beyond all of them. Many of the most celebrated fictional narratives cry out to be read as challenging the established conventions about the difference between North and South and the necessarily conflictual nature of their engagement. Whole bodies of fiction of less renown – early Indian writing about the imperial relationship, British post-imperial narratives tinged with lament about what might have been – can only be read in this way. Even when the fictional narratives follow the contours of orthodoxy, their silences and indications of strain often invite doubts about how much has been omitted from the story of domination or their utility in providing guide-lines as to how to proceed afterwards. In this bracket I would put most of the early British narratives set in India and many of the African texts of cultural affirmation.

No one would deny that lying behind First World/Third World relations there were and are basic structures of division embedded in power and race and, many would add, in economics and gender as well. The argument is rather that the fictional narratives bring out counter-movements and cross-trading and introduce elements of change. The very expression of power usually signifies some incapacity or sense of absence; it is seldom exercised without augmenting or bringing into being capabilities of resistance on the part of those who experience it. Confirmation is given that the modern and the traditional are not locked in a relationship of mutual antagonism. Remembering the appeal of the primitive and the fascination with the past of Rider Haggard's heroes, and the old man in Kojo Laing's *Search Sweet Country* who insists that Ghana 'must continue to modernise faster', who would any longer imagine that modernity and pre-modernity confront each other incomprehensibly across the imperial divide? It is now well recognized that the lines of racial division are drawn at least partly by vulnerability and desire. Fiction makes plain the masculinity of empire by holding out the figure of woman as the trope of Africa and by feminizing some Third World peoples, but it then puts it at a slant by revealing the pull of the homoerotic which extends across the colour-line. Contrary to what Salman Rushdie would have us believe, implicit in many of the narratives is not fear of, but fascination with, 'big brown cocks'.[8]

More than this, our reading of the fictional texts has disclosed elements of a symbiotic culture between colonizer and colonized, arrived at either by borrowings of the one from the other which are domesticated in various ways, or emerging from the inevitable collusions of the colonial moment. Kipling's epigraph about the thankfulness of the man with two separate sides to his head points in this direction, although Kipling himself took good care to confine any actual crossing and meshing to the margin. The novel itself is a powerful testament to shared formations in the making, inasmuch as it came from the West and was implicated in Western expansion, was taken up and developed to serve the supposed interests of Third World peoples and states, and then returned to the West in forms which challenged traditional thinking. The novel is thus both partisan – it extends the representations of the dominant and serves as an instrument of subversion on the part of the dominated – and bipartisan in the sense that it establishes areas of congruence and commonality. In almost every area of cultural contact we can trace movement and accommodation across the divide. Consider, for instance, the depiction of the role of women. The marginalization of women at the hands of imperial novelists such as Conrad and Cary was reinscribed in the narratives of many of the first generation of African writers; it was the story of Mr Johnson which had to be set straight, not that of Bamu. Yet at a later stage Western feminist narratives surely played a part in giving women a voice in the making of a new Africa – notwithstanding the dismissive authorial treatment of Lou Cranford, the American journalist, in *Anthills of the Savannah* and the Afro-American Atta in *Sardines*.

Approached through the agency of self/other politics, the hybridity which emerges in the narratives of the colonized looks suspiciously like an ideological rationalization of collaboration. In some quarters the very fact that the narratives are written in English ties them prima facie to the culture of the metropole. Any departure from postcolonial orthodoxies thus leaves writers open to the charge that they have 'sold out' or squandered their authority as Third World intellectuals. The result is that writers as different as V. S. Naipual and R. K. Narayan – the one whose narratives are driven by the anxieties and strains of the imperial inheritance, and the other whose accounts of small-town Indian life are contingent upon their equanimity about the legacies of the Raj – are read not with an eye to their disclosures about cultural interpenetration but as lessons in the politics of inclusion and exclusion.

This revisionism is significant not simply for thinking about the past but for envisaging the future. At various points in this book the argument has been developed that the key categories which encase our analysis of the encounter between the West and Asia and Africa – imperialism and nationalism, collaboration and resistance – distort historical understanding because they appropriate to their own design those processes linking the one to the other, and leave out of account those shared anxieties and desires which are intrinsic to the cultural exchange. What now needs to be stressed is that these processes of linkage and the areas of overlapping fear and hope are crucial to any consideration of post-imperial futures. The great failure of binarism lies in its inability to give a lead as to what might come next. The reworking of the traditional categories of reference which has been accomplished by and incorporated into postcolonialism makes less difference than at first appears. On most readings, domination and subordination, the self and the other, only hold out the prospect of more of the same.

Most of what postcolonialism offers for the future is not laid out before us but needs to be teased from its readings of the past and its strategies of resistance. In its second and predominant phase the possibilities of change are strictly circumscribed by the insistence on boundaries, difference and mutual opposition. For the North, despite some recognition of new perspectives and some significant departures from the ranks, the outlook is that conceptions of selfhood will remain intact and the culture of domination will soldier on. For the South – shades of dependency theory but with a postmodernist twist – the prospect is endless opposition, allowing only that its forms will change and new subalterns will emerge. More possibilities are opened up by the recent turn of some postcolonial theorists to the tensions and ambivalences within and between the worlds of the colonizer and the colonized. There is still, however, an evident reluctance to break from fixed anchorages. Even Homi Bhabha, whose work represents an exciting new chapter in exploring the potentialities of hybridity and cultural change, is unable to dispense with the innate oppositions of the grand narrative. Lurking beneath the surface of his project to redirect postcolonial discourse is a binarism of Bhabha's own, located in the challenge of the marginal, the migrant and the indeterminate to the more shadowy forces of the centre, the emplaced and the referenced.

Without wanting to imply too sharp a distinction between a reading of the fictional texts and the elaborations of postcolonial theory, it can still be said that many, though certainly not all, of the fictional narratives lead into a consideration of alternative futures rather than foreclose the possibility. Often the ground is prepared by the depiction of things that were shared in a period when supposedly they were not, and by showing processes which worked counter to the politics of difference. From here a move can be made – one sometimes taken by the novelists and sometimes not – to contemplating more sustained dialogue between cultures. The recognition that there were meeting places and processes of exchange between colonizer and colonized can thus lead to some dislocation of the notional worlds of North and South. It may be countered that this is too positive a scenario; ambivalence and overlap need not lead to a 'world in creolisation'.[9] Quite so, but what is important is to allow the cross-currents of cultural interaction to come to the surface for debate, rather than have them immediately appropriated or rejected by the logic of a single theoretical paradigm.

There are other texts which can hardly be read in this way and which offer little hope of a better world emerging from the dialectics of contact and commerce. Narratives by Marxist writers such as Mulk Raj Anand and Ngugi, the treatment of exile and identity in Naipaul and Marechera, even the feminist realism of Flora Nwapa and Buchi Emecheta appear largely resistant to postcolonial revision. The instabilities and vulnerabilities of established power, the possibilities of displacement and appropriation on the part of subject peoples, the exploitation of new sources of knowledge and inventive forms of agency must be imposed on the texts, citing closures of various kinds. Seldom can they be grafted on to what is already there because of its inhospitability. The entrenched nature of economic and social barriers to change, the disabling psychological legacies of colonialism, the insistence on the connections between personal choice and political reform – all make weak stock for such heady scions.

The root of the problem is that postcolonial stratagems are often too removed from the actual conditions under which people live their lives. As several critics have suggested, the postcolonial model is essentially discursive, it does not sufficiently look beyond language and text.[10] The centrality of '[t]he work of the word'[11] in Homi Bhabha's writings, for example, has led Benita Parry to counter that what Bhabha offers is '[t]he World according to the Word'.[12] But 'the word' in fact derives much more from literary theory and psychoanalysis than from the fictional text. In so many of the narratives considered here, 'the word' (and the subjectivity of self) is situated in the social and the material; the impediments to change are contextualized and there is a strong sense of the conflictual aspects of personal and group interaction, gains and losses, and the relationship between action and returns. It is for this reason that the scope for agency is very often more narrowly construed than in postcolonial theory. If one thing emerges clearly it is that African and Asians acted to change their situation and advance their own interests, but in so many instances their action did not produce substantial dividends; their agency failed to transform their economic and political environment. There were blockages and barriers that hemmed them in and corralled their futures. The conclusion follows that hybridity cannot stand alone. It must be brought into dialogue with those accounts of political behaviour which proceed on the basis of fundamental conflicts of interest within and between societies and in the processes of international exchange.

Having plotted the trajectories of the literary texts and postcolonial discourse with respect to the broad configurations of the North/South encounter, we are now in a position to review some of the contributory themes of this book and address their relationship to postcolonialism. I propose first to examine the treatment of the Third World, then to consider the treatment of the First World, and finally to assess the relevance for all the issues raised here of the constructs of international relations as a discipline.

Grounded as they are in the particularities of local and sometimes regional settings, the fictional narratives give little sense of the Third World as such. The nation is invariably present or at least implicit. In many of the African texts there is a continental dimension as prescribed by Chinweizu et al., or a racial inclusiveness as in the fiction of Ayi Kwei Armah. In remarkably few of the texts are there cross-references to the writings of other Third World authors or the experience of other Third World peoples; conversations with other cultures are mostly restricted to the former metropoles. In order to trace links with other postcolonial literatures or gain a generalized Third World perspective, it is necessary to extrapolate from the approaches within the texts or read them in conjunction with non-fictional writings – such as is commonly done in the case of Ngugi wa Thiong'o.

Even more significantly, our analysis of Third Word fiction has emphasized the heterogeneity of the texts' politics and the variety of voices which are projected. Although there was broad agreement about the centrality of the imperial experience, there were substantial differences in the way it was represented and what it was understood to mean for indigenous social groups or cultural formations. Very often these differences in approach were projected back into the past and shaped contrasting images of precolonial societies, and they were carried forward, usually by way of subtext and asides about tradition and modernity, into glimpses of preferred futures. At the most obvious level, difference was manifest between writing in different time periods and from different regions. Working from the material considered here, the depiction of the North/South engagement and its ramifications could be expected to become still more variegated if the range of texts written (and read) by people with different class, ethnic and gender backgrounds were to be expanded, and account taken of oral narratives and those written in indigenous languages.

What I have been arguing is pre-eminently true of Indian narratives in English. Leaving to one side the years between the wars when there was a considerable measure of congruence between writers that the Raj had run its course and there was a need for social change to accompany the transfer of power to Indian hands, what stands out is the diversity of viewpoints about the imperial project and its nationalist successor. Certainly one cannot speak of representative texts without reference to others which contest them, and even the notion that the literature evinces a distinctive Indian sensibility runs into the problem of the hybridity of content and style that pervades significant parts of it.

In the case of African literature there is less heterodoxy and not the same sense of casting around to get alternative bearings on the intrusion of the external and its meaning for African culture and politics. This is not to deny the very considerable internal differences. With notable exceptions, West African fiction has been less declaratory in its resistance to external intervention than much of the writing by East and Southern Africans, influenced by the violence of their anti-colonial struggles and the presence of white settlers. Then there are such writers as Nuruddin Farah, Bessie Head and Dambudzo Marechera, whose work cuts distinctive paths. Increasingly it is also recognized that women's writing challenges received understandings. Even so, the corpus of African writing in English has a kindred quality; there is a consistency about its orientation to the politics of othering. In part this must be attributed to the monumental influence of Chinua Achebe, though characteristically his own narratives left more possibilities open than did those of writers who followed him. Account must also be taken of the cultural climate which probably predisposed readers and critics to find thematic commonalities.

To argue thus is not to privilege Indian literature over African on the basis of its wider reach or prepare the ground for some argument *à la* Pritish Nandy that African writers have been more progressive than Indian. Instead, it is to recognize that to some degree the configurations of the literatures reflect the different historical experiences and material circumstances of Indian and African societies. That the Indian narratives have such points of convergence with imperial ones shows the extent to which the external had been internalized at certain levels of Indian society – and often recognized as such.

What this suggests is that if resistance is to be articulated more decisively it is probably necessary to look to narratives in the regional languages, even though this might pull against the national axis of politics. That African writing has been so deeply opposed to the other, and that difference has been relegated to the outside, catches something of the extraordinary destructiveness of imperial penetration and the dependencies perpetuated by the contemporary international processes in that continent. This in turn must be related to the nature of metropolitan interests, the forms of imperial rule and the characteristic patterns of indigenous social organization and religion. It has been the norm in several discourses to present the processes of imperial intervention and decolonization as of a kind. Very often India is taken as the model and other parts of the Third World are assumed to conform or made to fit. The conclusion to be drawn from our comparative analysis of the fictional narratives is that India was a special – perhaps unique – case, and that the circumstances and consequences of Africa's interaction with the outside were in many respects different.

Postcolonialism sets its sights in the opposite direction. The discourse is built on the need to take a holistic view and in large part the urge to generalize overtakes recognition of the differences between sectional interests, national formations, continents and even historical periods. Its tendency is thus to essentialize, universalize and dehistoricize. In its most extravagant conception it produces, through the workings of the logic of its 'worlding', assumptions about the cultural and literary commonality of African and Asian countries, on the one hand, and settler societies such as Australia and Canada, on the other.[13] In so far as it proceeds on the basis of fictional texts, it is highly selective about those it brings within its purview. Naipaul is mostly declaimed for having crossed to the other side, the status of Soyinka and Narayan is seen as problematical, and writers of the ilk of Malgonkar are simply left out of account.

These tendencies are most pronounced in postcolonialism's second movement. Aijaz Ahmad has remarked on the paradox that so many of the strictures of postmodernism are suspended in the face of postcolonialism's elevation of the Third World text and its solidification as counter-canon.[14] Arun Mukherjee has drawn attention to the homogenizing functions of its categories and subcategories and its essentializing terminology and vocabulary.[15] The centre-piece is the canonization of resistance, flanked on one side by constructs such as the 'native' and the 'subaltern', and on the other by ideas of recovery and retrieval and strategies of subversion and appropriation. Reductionism of this kind is hardly characteristic of postcolonialism's third and often consciously postmodern phase, but even here the more discriminating privileging procedures imply a reordering of earlier categories rather than their dismemberment. Resisters are now those who 'revise and initiate'; suffering brings (and keeps?) them together; difference is visited upon the rest. Such would seem the case with the enunciation of the margin as the site of creative thinking and new ways of seeing. Minorities, migrants, refugees, Third World *émigrés* in the Western academy become akin to a flock of birds flying together – notwithstanding (or so it seems to me) Bhabha's disclaimer in the name of the indeterminate.[16]

It is hardly necessary to stress again the contiguities of First World and Third World texts. In reviewing our analysis of literary narratives written from the centre, therefore, I will concentrate on what I consider to be their distinctive characteristics and then comment briefly on their treatment in the postcolonial discourse. We have read First World texts set in the Third World primarily to gain an understanding of the construction and reconstruction of the imperial self in its encounter with foreign peoples and distant places, but also to get insights into the processes of change initiated by overseas involvement. It has been of the essence of this book to argue that the literary narratives, more than other source materials, bring out the tensions and cross-purposes within the imperial project. Underlying and indeed impelling the drive for domination, the strong sense of moral absolutism, and the characteristic rejection of the lives of other peoples and the ways of other cultures, were insecurity and uncertainty. There was also a latent fascination with the other because of its elements of difference and its elements of similarity with times past. It is the existence of these other dimensions which enables the narratives to be read as a partial counter to, and a correction of, earlier and contemporary political orthodoxies. There are two aspects here. The first is the prescience of many of the texts in showing that imperialism was not working out as intended and that its days were numbered. One thinks immediately of Kipling, who was writing the elegy of empire alongside his promotion of its cause at the very time when it was coming to be thought that British rule would last for ever. The second is the propensity of the texts to disclose the vulnerabilities of imperial rule and the disabling effects of possession which accompanied the expansion of material capability and overseas territory. Orwell's 'Shooting an Elephant' is a classic statement of the hollowness of domination. Although less widely read in this way, Conrad's *Heart of Darkness* is another. When writers looked to the years ahead, as some did, the prognosis was likely to be even more sobering.

In the instances I have cited above, the texts function more or less directly as a commentary on the fragility and the transitory nature of Western overlordship. There are others, however, where the closures are so overt, where any possibility of change is countermanded even before it is aired, that they point in the same direction when read against the grain. Such is often the case, I have argued, with the refusal to countenance relationships across the colour line or entertain the idea that the children of empire could ever grow up. A similar kind of closure lies behind the conventions of behaviour, dress and speech: Orwell's 'unbreakable system of taboos'; Cary's 'a thousand rules . . . that are not needed in more civilized places'; the refusal of Paul Scott's ladies of Pankot to enunciate their sense of purpose lest it evaporate by being put into words.

These comments invite a more general reflection about the politics of literature, which is that personalization in the fictional narratives works to reveal political process. Almost inevitably the narration of individual lives, of how people feel and plan and act, involves reckoning with aspects of culture and socio-economic forces which empower and constrain them. It is not, as is often thought, that the concentration on the personal binds the narrative to the immediate and the particular. Rather, the focus on the personal directs attention to broader societal conditions and to change over time because of the way they enframe the lives of men and women and establish the patterns of personal interaction.

Proceeding on this basis, my argument is that the literary narratives play a crucial part in reconceptualizing the phenomenon of imperialism. For too long, though for understandable reasons, so much of the discussion of imperialism has been about assumed or alleged motives and this has laid ground rules for analyses of outcomes. Thus the story as it is usually told has a political plot and the key characters are villains and victims. But there is another story which needs to be told about the internationalization of systems, techniques and values for a time located in Europe, about how deeply changes have taken root in the Third World and about the processes of adaptation and hybridization. In several respects Samir Amin has pointed the way here,[17] and the discourse on globalization has extended the debate. The story of global exchange has its political aspects but the economic and cultural are of greater import – as was argued very early in this book by contrasting the longer-term influence of European missionaries in Africa with that of the statesmen assembled in Berlin in 1884–5. Moreover, in considering outcomes or relating the past to the present, the processes at work are of much greater consequence than the intentions of the parties. Certainly by now we should be extremely wary of any notion that the processes of change are controlled by élites at either end. There is the further point that the impact of imperialism on Third World societies has been more varied and often different in kind from that which was envisaged by nineteenth-century publicists and theorists. It would be difficult, for example, to explain the hybridity which has developed on the Indian subcontinent by reference to the debate 150 years ago between the orientalists and the anglicists.

First World texts have had a varied status in postcolonial theory and criticism, but the main approaches correspond to the three phases identified earlier. Initially there was little incentive to probe imperial literary productions – or, for that matter, political purposes – because the task in hand was to codify the initiatives of postcolonial societies. The position of the First World was virtually a foundational assumption of the discourse, and if more were needed it could be read off the narratives of Third World writers. Then a powerful movement developed which was concerned to reread some of the classic imperial texts with a view to laying bare their political presuppositions and challenging their literary standing. A variety of discursive strategies were employed to this end, most of which were indebted to post-structuralism. The texts were scoured for omissions and repressions which, once brought to the surface, made plain their complicity in the imperial project and directed attention to its rapacious aspects – for instance, the economic drives which underlay the civilizing mission. Other studies addressed the power of literary representations and sought to establish their functionality in an imperial design in which cultural productions became a mechanism of colonial control. Gauri Viswanathan's *Masks of Conquest*, which examines the adaptation of the content of English literary education to the needs of the Raj, became a landmark for studies of this kind.[18] More generally, at the hands of critics such as JanMohamed, the magisterial style and authority of imperial transcripts of other peoples and cultures were punctured to expose ignorance and ethnocentrism.

These new ways of reading First World texts and seeing expansionism as ingrained in culture enabled a fuller understanding of how deeply rooted imperialism was within metropolitan societies and why it went forward so readily overseas. But it was a partial reading (in both senses of that word) and it followed the lines already drawn by the binarism of postcolonialism's second phase and a Manicheanism which remained influential even after it had been disclaimed. The deconstruction of First World texts had an invigorating effect on thinking about Third World cultural reclamation, but it also had its costs in that very often it misrepresented the solidity of imperialism and the impact of imperial processes on Third World societies.

Consider, for instance, the way imperialism has been equated with an unremitting modernity and an unproblematic masculinity. With respect to the former, I have argued that First World narratives catch something of Joseph Schumpeter's dialectic with their evident tension between espousing the modern and romanticizing the pre-modern. As Joyce Cary's African novels suggest, and the politics of indirect rule confirm, there was always a deep ambivalence in imperial practice about the virtues and possibilities of modernity. A rather different version of the pull of the pre-modern finds expression in American fictional narratives of the cold war which drew on the frontier tradition. The mental make-up of Homer Atkins, 'the ugly American', and the heroes of the fiction of the Vietnam War, asserted the relevance of the values of the frontier to modern American life. Such characters are expressive of an ethos of cultural destruction which can hardly be compared with the mindset of Cary's Rudbeck and Bewsher or the Burtons and Turtons of the Raj. When we turn to masculinity, the reading of male domination magnified the significance of the symbols of power and penetration, and largely cast to one side the insecurity implicit in the bonding of brothers and the fear of woman. The extent to which this reading is identified with certain lines of feminist theory perhaps provides one reason for its continuing currency in contemporary postcolonial criticism.

But there is a larger and more general issue here. In postcolonialism's third and most recent phase, practice has so far fallen short of theory. As a result of the reconceptualization of imperial othering led by Bhabha, Spivak and S. P. Mohanty, and the revisionism of Said, the imperial text is now firmly back on the agenda, the dangers of a reductionist reading have been well rehearsed, and the initial steps have been taken towards breaking down the totalizing imperatives of the discourses about First and Third Worlds. Bhabha pointed the way when, in attempting to negotiate a path between/across

Said and Fanon, he argued to the effect that colonial discourse was shot through with fantasy and desire.[19] Said took the lesson, and in *Culture and Imperialism* he goes some distance towards acknowledging the limitations of his insistence in *Orientalism* on the closure and coherence of occidental discourse. But this opening up of interpretative possibilities, this recognition of the articulation of the unconscious alongside the instrumentalist transcription of power and knowledge, has not, I suggest, been carried through very much in the veritable deluge of essays deconstructing the imperial text. The informing assumptions of this body of writing remain very largely indebted to the theoretical constructs of postcolonialism's second phase. One cannot help but wonder whether the new accent on the margin and the 'migratory quality of experience' has inhibited the process of apprehending counter-movements and self-contestation in the literary culture of empire. Sara Suleri's *The Rhetoric of English India* is exceptional in this regard with its claim that the fiction of nineteenth-century Anglo-India is 'a narrative of perpetual longing and perpetual loss'.[20] This work may well transform postcolonial readings of imperial texts, but as yet its influence can only be detected in occasional essays. One such case is a recent study of Paul Scott – drawing as much on psychoanalytical insights as literary analysis – which tentatively raises the possibility that Scott may be white England's first novelist of decolonization. The argument is that Scott offered, from within English culture, a critique of its own racism and ethnocentrism.[21]

In this postcolonial retrospect I have reaffirmed the claims of the literary narratives to be accorded the status of a primary and revelatory source for rethinking the terms of the North/South engagement. I have rejected the notion that the fictional texts have been displaced by the emergence of colonial discourse analysis and postcolonial theory which speak through them – and at times for them. In so doing, the shortcomings of post-colonialism have been underlined, whereas, in a different context, it would have been appropriate to highlight the degree to which the discourse has enlivened debate by its radicalism, originality and conceptual vigour.[22] It remains to draw together the threads of my argument about the relevance of the concerns of international relations and those other formations of thought directed to the structural and the systemic. This book began with the argument that there is a need to develop a broader conception of international relations; it must close with the argument that the discipline has a leavening role to play with respect both to the characteristic concerns of fiction and the perspectives of postcolonialism.

At a time when the new formations of knowledge are extending their reach and there has been some realignment of traditional knowledge formations, the walls of international relations remain disturbingly solid. The very frequency with which the word 'discipline' is invoked in the literature of international relations – even on the part of critics of conventional thought – is indicative of a mindset which believes that somehow the 'international' stands apart. To be sure, over the past decade the way international relations has been constructed has been challenged by feminists, postmodernists and critical theorists. More recently, ecologists have joined the battle,[23] while at the same time increasing attention has been paid to normative questions which have been neglected for so long.[24] Despite the differences between these approaches, what is shared is the rejection of foundationalism, a determination to expose the hegemonic nature of disciplinary narrative – which follows in part from the nexus between a problem-solving orientation and established power interests – and a concern to engage with the possibilities of change residing in people who traditionally have not had standing in the affairs of state. That all this represents a break with earlier scholarship is undoubted. What has been argued, however, is that so far the influence of the critics has been limited; rethinking with respect to (say) territoriality or identity and subjectivity has been restricted to the margins of the international relations project. What is more, the canonical orthodoxies and even the contestations of those seeking change have been tied to essentially Western experience. In the former case, one notes the way universals have been extrapolated from a reading of the history of the great powers, thus aligning the discipline with the interests of the dominant. With regard to the latter, Krishna has been forthright in his censure of the Eurocentrism of much postmodernist writing and its insensitivity to the history of others.[25] Given this record, the temptation to dismiss the discipline is understandable. Yet it needs to be resisted. Despite its inadequacies, international relations addresses key determinants of North/South relations through its longstanding and forceful articulation of *realpolitik* and its more recent elaboration of the politics of global economic exchange.

Neither the main body of fictional narratives nor the postcolonial discourse seriously concern themselves with these systemic impediments to Third World change. International behaviour is shaped both by influences from within societies and by what might be called the culture of international society – multilateral pressures to conform to established ways of seeing and acting in international politics. Novelists and postcolonial theorists have had much to say about the former but very little about the latter. Presumably no one would go to fiction to pursue the way in which the behaviour of collectivities – most particularly the state – is conditioned by the nature of the global system and the interaction of its constituent parts. Clearly, the interests of the novelists have been mainly elsewhere. There is no implication here that the strictures of international relations should be taken on their own terms; there are, in fact, very good reasons for not doing so. What is more, it is crucial to my argument that writers such as Ghosh and Coetzee have expanded our thinking by taking issue with aspects of power politics through processes of defamiliarization and relocation. I do not think that similar fictional initiatives have as yet been taken with regard to the international economic system. But here also we must be open to the possibility that fiction may bring out the shortcomings of disciplinary constructs and suggest alternative lines of approach.

Postcolonialism's claims are larger and the risks of taking the discourse as a compendium of global relations are correspondingly greater. In so far as its paradigms of self–other politics can be understood to encapsulate the major processes of interaction between North and South, an engagement with the disciplinary orthodoxies of international relations is critical. As an overtly committed body of theory and criticism, the range of positions canvassed has been limited and, until lately, scholarly contestation has been largely 'in-house'. Consider, for example, the easy acceptance of postcolonialism's key reference-points – the power and functionality of representation and knowledge. There is an evident need for the ascendancy of the discursive to be pitted against an instrumental reading of power, an analysis of structural determinants, and a much fuller consideration of where representation and knowledge can be counterproductive. Aijaz Ahmad has sharply criticized the discourse for its 'diminution of politics as such'.[26] I have argued elsewhere that resistance has been resituated so that it now lies largely outside the arena we have traditionally regarded as the political.[27] Finding resistance in new places (such as everyday life) and identifying new forms (in gestures, the symbolic and the practice of unsettling meaning) holds much promise. Even so, we still have to reckon with old barriers to change, both within Third World societies and in the processes of international exchange. The problem about overdoing the emphasis on culture, identity and subjectivity in that conflict is too easily wished away. As I read it, what emerges from some of the writing in contemporary postcolonialism is the 'unnaturalness' of so much cultural difference. This accords with the shift in focus from political aggregates, most notably the state, to people in their everyday lives, with particular attention being paid to gender, sexuality and the body. Yet little of this writing seriously addresses what have long been taken to be the fundamental questions of politics – the location of politics within and between societies; and it is, after all, the changing power relations which work to reinscribe cultural differences in some spheres and dismantle them in others. As Chantal Mouffe has observed, the different forms of identity are the stake of a power struggle.[28]

There has been a similar neglect to confront economic interest, especially as manifested in the international order. The tendency has been for postcolonial analysis to proceed on the basis of generalized assumptions about underlying economic forces, the nature of which is not so much examined as taken to be reflected in the cultural realm. Attention must be directed to the relevance of postcolonial strategies to the transfer of resources and technologies around the globe and what this means for economic practices within societies. How might subversion and appropriation be related to the processes of economic exchange? Should we be thinking in terms of hybrid economics? The existing literature provides few leads to questions of this kind. Writing in *Critical Inquiry*, Masao Miyoshi censures postcolonial theorists for failing to broach key issues of contemporary international capitalism such as the transnational corporation, focusing instead on matters of history and culture which are at one remove from economic and political actuality.[29] Miyoshi's critique repays close reading and it has been cited in some of the literature, yet the material with which he builds his case would be familiar to most students of international political economy. I make this point simply to highlight the degree to which postcolonial analysis has isolated itself from the writing on dependency, world systems theory and the economics of globalization.

In summary, and not to put too fine a point on it, postcolonialism is able to hold high the torch of radicalism precisely because it distances itself from mainstream political and economic material. If account were taken of some of the contentions of international relations and the writing on global economic exchange, postcolonialism's radical edge might not have the same sharpness but the discourse would bear more directly on the barriers to change between the First and Third Worlds and within the Third World itself.

Relating this back to the main body of argument in this book, my principal claim is that imaginative literature can help bridge the gulf between established approaches to North/South relations and new discourses directed to culture, identity and subjectivity. Although fiction can hardly be regarded as a neutral medium, it is more or less outside the zones of proprietorship implicitly claimed and variously policed by the contending knowledge formations. Its diversity and, within limits, its openness to interpretation allows connections to be made with analyses on both sides. As such, literature can encourage different bodies of knowledge to talk to each other across the lines of demarcation. Not for a moment, however, am I suggesting that literature's role is essentially instrumental. On the contrary, I believe that in many ways fiction can contribute more to an understanding of cross-cultural relations than either disciplinary knowledge or newly emergent bodies of theory.

Notes

1. Toru-debi wrestled with her love for the machine and her concern for her husband's nephew whom she was suddenly called upon to bring up. But 'the Singer had been part of her dowry . . . it was her child in a way her husband's nephew could never be'. Amitav Ghosh, *The Circle of Reason* (Hamish Hamilton, London, 1986), p. 6.

2. R. B. J. Walker, 'From IR to world politics', ch. 2 in Joseph A. Camilleri, Anthony P. Jarvis and Albert J. Paolini (eds), *The State in Transition. Reimagining Political Space* (Lynne Rienner, London, 1995), p. 23.

3. See Dipesh Chakrabarty, 'Postcoloniality and the articifice of history: Who speaks for Indian pasts?', *Representations*, 37 (Winter 1992), 1–26.

4. Abdul JanMohamed, *Manichean Aesthetics: The Politics of Literature in Colonial Africa* (University of Massachusetts Press, Amherst, 1983).

5. Ranajit Guha, 'Dominance without hegemony and its historiography' in *Subaltern Studies VI* (Oxford University Press, Delhi, 1989), p. 299.

6. See Benita Parry, 'Problems in current theories of colonial discourse', *Oxford Literary Review*, 9:1–2 (1987), 27–59. Whether Parry has done justice to the various critics she discusses is arguable, but what is relevant here is the way she breaks anti-colonialist criticism into opposing schools of thought.

7. John McClure and Aamir Mufti in their introduction to a special issue of *Social Text* on postcolonialism. See *Social Text*, 31/32 (1992), p. 3.

8. Salman Rushdie, 'Outside the whale', *Granta*, 11 (1983), 124–38 (p.129).

9. I borrow the phrase from Ulf Hannerz, 'The world in creolisation', *Africa*, 57:4 (1987), 546–59.

10. See Benita Parry, 'Signs of our times. Discussion of Homi Bhabha's *The Location of Culture*', *Third Text*, 28/29 (Autumn/Winter 1994), 5–24; Russell Jacoby, 'Marginal returns. The trouble with post-colonial theory', *Linguafranca* (Sept./Oct. 1995), 30–7; Alex Callinicos, 'Wonders taken for signs: Homi Bhabha's postcolonialism', *Transformations*, 1 (Spring 1995), 98–112.

11. Homi K. Bhabha, *The Location of Culture* (Routledge, London and New York, 1994), p. 125.

12. Parry, 'Signs of our times', p. 9.

13. See Bill Ashcroft, Gareth Griffiths and Helen Tiffin, *The Empire Writes Back: Theory and Practice in Post-colonial Literatures* (Routledge, London and New York, 1989), p. 2. The authors go so far as to state: 'The literature of the USA should also be placed in this [postcolonial] category.'

14. Aijaz Ahmad, 'Disciplinary English: theory, Third Worldism and literary study in India', *Occasional Paper on History and Society no. XLIII* (Centre for Contemporary Studies, Nehru Memorial Museum and Library, New Delhi, September 1991), p. 57.

15. Arun P. Mukherjee, 'The exclusions of postcolonial theory and Mulk Raj Anand's *Untouchable*: a case study', *Ariel*, 22:3 (July 1991), 27–48 (p. 29).

16. Homi K. Bhabha, 'Freedom's basis in the indeterminate', *October*, 61 (Summer 1992), 46–57 (pp. 46–7).

17. See in particular Samir Amin, *Eurocentrism*, translated by Russell Moore (Zed Books, London, 1989).

18. Gauri Viswanathan, *Masks of Conquest: Literary Study and British Rule in India* (Columbia University Press, New York, 1989).

19. Homi K. Bhabha, 'The other question . . .', *Screen*, 24:6 (Nov./Dec. 1983), 18–36.

20. Sara Suleri, *The Rhetoric of English India* (University of Chicago Press, Chicago and London, 1992), p. 10.

21. Bill Schwarz, 'An Englishman abroad . . . and at home: the case of Paul Scott', *New Formations*, 17 (Summer 1992), 95–105.

22. See, for example, Phillip Darby and A. J. Paolini, 'Bridging international relations and postcolonialism', *Alternatives*, 19:2 (1994), 371–97.

23. See for instance Eric Laferriere, 'Emancipating international relations theory: an ecological perspective', *Millennium*, 25:1 (1996), 53–75.

24. Andrew Linklater has been prominent in this regard. See his *Beyond Realism and Marxism: Critical Theory and International Relations* (Macmillan, London, 1990) and 'The question of the next stage in international relations theory: a critical–theoretical point of view', *Millennium*, 21:1 (1992), 77–98.

25. Sankaran Krishna, 'The importance of being ironic', *Alternatives*, 18 (1993), 385–417, pp. 405–6.

26. Ahmad, op. cit., p. 42.

27. Phillip Darby, *At the Edge of International Relations* (Pinter, London, 1997), p. 27.

28. Chantal Mouffe, 'For a politics of nomadic identity' in George Robertson, Melinda Nash, Lisa Tickner, Jon Bird, Barry Curtis and Tim Putnam (eds), *Travellers' Tales. Narratives of Home and Displacement* (Routledge, London and New York, 1994), p. 106.

29. Masao Miyoshi, 'A borderless world? From colonialism to transnationalism and the decline of the nation-state', *Critical Inquiry*, 19 (Summer 1993), 726–51.

Bibliography

Literary texts

Achebe, Chinua, *No Longer at Ease* (Heinemann Educational Books, London, 1963; first published 1960).

Achebe, Chinua, *Anthills of the Savannah* (Picador in association with William Heinemann, London, 1988; first published 1987).

Akare, Thomas, *The Slums* (Heinemann, London, 1981).

Ali, Ahmed, *Twilight in Delhi* (Oxford University Press, Bombay, 1966; first published in 1940).

Ali, Hasan, *The Changeling* (Herbert Joseph, London, 1933).

Amadi, Elechi, *The Great Ponds* (Heinemann, London and Ibadan, 1969).

Anand, Mulk Raj, *Untouchable* (Allen Lane, Penguin, Harmondsworth, 1940; first published 1935).

Anand, Mulk Raj, *Coolie* (Arnold-Heinemann, New Delhi, 1984; first published 1936).

Anand, Mulk Raj, *The Village* (Cape, London, 1939).

Anand, Mulk Raj, *Across the Black Waters* (Cape, London, 1940).

Anand, Mulk Raj, *The Sword and the Sickle* (Cape, London, 1942).

Armah, Ayi Kwei, *Why Are We So Blest?* (Heinemann, London, 1972).

Armah, Ayi Kwei, *Two Thousand Seasons* (East African Publishing House, Nairobi, 1973).

Armah, Ayi Kwei, *The Healers* (Heinemann, London and Ibadan, 1979; first published 1978).

Bhattacharya, Bhabani, *So Many Hungers* (Orient Paperbacks, Delhi, 1984; first published 1947).

Bromfield, Louis, *The Rains Came* (Penguin, Harmondsworth, 1959; first published 1937).

Buchan, John, *A Lodge in the Wilderness* (Wm. Blackwood & Sons, Edinburgh and London,1906).

Burgess, Anthony, *Devil of a State* (Heinemann, London, 1961).

Burgess, Anthony, *The Long Day Wanes. A Malayan Trilogy* (Penguin, Harmondsworth, 1972).

Candler, Edmund, *Abdication* (Constable, London, Bombay and Sydney, 1922).

Cary, Joyce, *An American Visitor* (Michael Joseph, London, 1949; first published 1933).

Caute, David, *At Fever Pitch* (André Deutsch, London, 1959).

Caute, David, *The Decline of the West* (Panther Books, London, 1968).

Clark, William, *Cataclysm. The North–South Conflict of 1987* (Sidgwick & Jackson, London, 1984).

Coetzee, J. M., *Waiting for the Barbarians* (King Penguin, Harmondsworth, 1982; first published 1980).

Conrad, Joseph, *Heart of Darkness* (Penguin, Harmondsworth, 1983; first published 1902).

Conrad, Joseph, *Nostromo* (Penguin, Harmondsworth, 1983; first published 1904).

Cotes, Everard, *The Story of Sonny Sahib* (D. Appleton & Co., London, 1928; first published 1894).

Croker, B. M., *The Company's Servant* (George Bell & Sons, London, undated; first published 1907).

Dangarembga, Tsitsi, *Nervous Conditions* (Zimbabwean Publishing House, Harare, 1988).

Desai, Anita, *Clear Light of Day* (Penguin, Harmondsworth, 1980).

Diver, Maud, *Lilamani* (Blackwood, London, 1910).

Diver, Maud, *Far to Seek: A Romance of England and India* (Wm. Blackwood & Sons, Edinburgh and London, 1924).

Diver, Maud, *The Singer Passes: An Indian Tapestry* (Blackwood, London, 1931).

Durrell, Lawrence, *Mountolive* (Faber & Faber, London, 1958).

Ekwensi, Cyprian, *Jagua Nana* (Heinemann International, Oxford, 1987; first published 1961).

Emecheta, Buchi, *The Joys of Motherhood* (Allison & Busby, London, 1979).

Farah, Nuruddin, *From a Crooked Rib* (Heinemann, London, Ibadan, Nairobi, 1970).

Farah, Nuruddin, *A Naked Needle* (Heinemann, London, 1976).

Farah, Nuruddin, *Sweet and Sour Milk* (African Writers Series, Heinemann, London, 1980; first published 1979).

Farah, Nuruddin, *Sardines* (African Writers Series, Heinemann, London, Ibadan, Nairobi, 1982; first published 1981).

Farah, Nuruddin, *Close Sesame* (Allison & Busby, London and New York, 1983).

Farah, Nuruddin, *Maps* (Picador, London, 1986).

Farah, Nuruddin, *Gifts* (Serif, London, 1993).

Farrell, J. G., *The Singapore Grip* (Fontana Paperbacks, London, 1979; first published 1978).

Forster, E. M., *A Passage to India* (Abinger edition, vol. 6, Edward Arnold, London, 1978; first published 1924).

Forsyth, Frederick, *The Dogs of War* (Corgi, London, 1976).

Forsyth, Frederick, *The Fist of God* (Bantam, London, 1994).

Frank, Pat, *Hold Back the Night* (J. B. Lippincott, Philadelphia and New York, 1952).

Ghamat, K. E., *My Friend the Barrister* (Ardeshir & Co., Bombay, 1908).

Ghosh, Amitav, *The Circle of Reason* (Hamish Hamilton, London, 1986).

Ghosh, Amitav, *The Shadow Lines* (Ravi Dayal Publisher, Delhi, 1988).

Ghosh, S. K., *The Prince of Destiny. The New Krishna* (Rebman, London, 1909).

Greene, Graham, *The Heart of the Matter* (Penguin, Harmondsworth, 1962; first published 1948).

Greene, Graham, *The Quiet American* (Penguin, Harmondsworth, 1971; first published 1955).

Haggard, H. Rider, *King Solomon's Mines, She, Allan Quartermain* (Octopus Books, London, 1979).

Haggard, H. Rider, *Nada the Lily* (Macdonald, London, 1932; first published 1892).

Head, Bessie, *When Rain Clouds Gather* (Bantam Books, New York, 1970; first published 1968).

Head, Bessie, *Maru* (Zimbabwe Publishing House, Harare, 1987; first published 1971).

Head, Bessie, *A Question of Power* (Heinemann, London, Nairobi, Ibadan, Lusaka, 1974).

Hobart, A. T., *Yang and Yin: A Novel of a Doctor in China* (Cassell, London, Toronto, Melbourne, Sydney, 1937).

Hove, Chenjerai, *Bones* (Baobab Books, Harare, 1988).

Hove, Chenjerai, *Shadows* (Baobab Books, Harare, 1991).

Kincaid, Dennis, *Their Ways Divide* (Chatto & Windus, London, 1936).

Kipling, Rudyard, *Plain Tales from the Hills* (Macmillan, London, 1982; first published 1888).

Kipling, Rudyard, *Life's Handicap* (Macmillan, London, 1982; first published 1891).

Kipling, Rudyard, *Wee Willie Winkie* (Macmillan, London, 1982; first published 1895).

Kipling, Rudyard, *The Day's Work* (Macmillan, London, 1982; first published 1898).

Kipling, Rudyard, *Kim* (Macmillan, London, Centenary edition 1981; first published 1901).

Laing, B. Kojo, *Search Sweet Country* (Heinemann, London, 1986).

Laing, B. Kojo, *Major Gentl and the Achimota Wars* (Heinemann, Oxford, 1992).

Lederer, William J. and Burdick, Eugene, *The Ugly American* (Corgi Books, London, 1960; first published 1958).

Lessing, Doris, *The Grass is Singing* (Heinemann, London, Ibadan, Nairobi, 1973; first published 1950).

Macgoye, Marjorie Oludhe, *Coming to Birth* (Heinemann, London, 1986).

Madhaviah, A., *Clarinda. A Historical Novel* (Cambridge Press, Madras, 1915).

Mailer, Norman, *Why Are We in Vietnam?* (Oxford University Press, Oxford, 1988; first published 1967).

Mailer, Norman, *The Armies of the Night* (Penguin, Harmondsworth, 1968).

Malgonkar, Manohar, *A Bend in the Ganges* (Orient Paperbacks, Delhi, 1964).

Malgonkar, Manohar, *Bandicoot Run* (Orient Paperbacks, Delhi, 1982).

Malgonkar, Manohar, *Distant Drum* (Orient Paperbacks, Delhi, 1986; first published 1960).

Marechera, Dambudzo, *The House of Hunger* (Heinemann Educational Books, London, Ibadan, Nairobi, 1978; reprinted 1984).

Marechera, Dambudzo, *Black Sunlight* (Heinemann Educational Books, London, Ibadan, Nairobi, Exeter, 1980).

Marechera, Dambudzo, *The Black Insider* compiled and edited by Flora Veit-Wild (Baobab Books, Harare, 1990).

Masters, John, *The Deceivers* (Michael Joseph, London, 1952).

Mitra, S. M., *Hindupore. A Peep Behind the Indian Unrest. An Anglo-Indian Romance* (Luzac & Co., London, 1909).

Mo, Timothy, *The Redundancy of Courage* (Vintage, London, 1991).

Moore, Robin, *The Green Berets* (Avon Books, New York, 1965).

Mukerji, Dhan Gopal, *The Secret Listeners of the East* (E. P. Dutton & Co., New York, undated but apparently published in 1926).

Mwangi, Meja, *Going Down River Road* (Heinemann Educational Books, London, 1976).

Nahal, Chaman, *The Crown and the Loincloth* (Vikas Publishing House, Delhi, 1981).

Naipaul, V. S., *The Mimic Men* (Penguin, Harmondsworth, 1980; first published 1967).

Naipaul, V. S., *A Bend in the River* (Penguin, Harmondsworth, 1980; first published 1979).

Naipaul, V. S., *The Enigma of Arrival* (Penguin, London, 1987).

Naipaul, V. S., *A Way in the World. A Sequence* (Heinemann, London, 1994).

Narayan, R. K., *Lawley Road and Other Stories* (Orient Paperbacks, Delhi, undated).

Narayan, R. K., *Waiting for the Mahatma* (Indian Thought Publications, Mysore, 1984; first published 1955).

Ngugi wa Thiong'o, *The River Between* (Heinemann, London, 1978; first published 1965).

Ngugi wa Thiong'o, *Petals of Blood* (Heinemann, London, 1977).

Ngugi wa Thiong'o, *Matigari* (Heinemann International, Oxford, 1987).

Nwapa, Flora, *Efuru* (Heinemann, London, 1978; first published 1966).

Ogot, Grace, *The Graduate* (Uzima Press, Nairobi, 1980).

Okpewho, Isidore, *Tides* (Longman, Harlow, 1993).

Okri, Ben, *Dangerous Love* (Phoenix, London, 1996).

Orwell, George, *Burmese Days* (Penguin, Harmondsworth, 1967; first published 1934).

Rao, Raja, *Kanthapura* (Orient Paperbacks, Delhi, 1971; first published 1938).

Rao, Raja, *The Serpent and the Rope* (abridged edition, Oxford University Press, Delhi, 1978; first published 1960).

Rushdie, Salman, *Midnight's Children* (Picador, London, 1982; first published 1981).

Rushdie, Salman, *Shame* (Picador, London, 1984; first published 1983).

Samkange, Stanlake, *On Trial for My Country* (Heinemann, London, Ibadan, Nairobi, 1966).

Scott, Paul, *The Raj Quartet* (Granada Publishing, London, 1973).

Seth, Vikram, *A Suitable Boy* (Phoenix House, London, 1993).

Soyinka, Wole, *Five Plays* (Oxford University Press, London, 1964).

Soyinka, Wole, *The Interpreters* (Fontana Paperbacks, London, 1972; first published 1965).

Soyinka, Wole, *Season of Anomy* (Rex Collings, London, 1973).

Soyinka, Wole, *Six Plays* (The Master Playwrights, Methuen, London, 1984).

Steel, Flora Annie, *On the Face of the Waters* (William Heinemann, London, 1897).

Steel, Flora Annie, *The Hosts of the Lord*, (Thomas Nelson & Sons, Edinburgh and New York, undated; first published 1900).

Steen, Marguerite, *The Sun is My Undoing* (Collins, London, 1941).

Tagore, Rabindranath, *Gora* (Macmillan, Calcutta, 1969; first published 1924).

Tharoor, Shashi, *Show Business* (Picador, London, 1994; first published 1992).

Thompson, Edward, *An Indian Day* (Alfred A. Knopf, London, 1927).

Thompson, Edward, *An End of the Hours* (Macmillan, London, 1938).

Ullman, James Ramsey, *Windom's Way* (Herald-Sun Reader's Bookclub in association with the Companion Book Club, London and Melbourne, 1954; first published 1952).

Updike, John, *The Coup* (University of Queensland Press, St. Lucia, Queensland, 1979; first published 1978).

Vassanji, M. G., *The Book of Secrets* (Macmillan, London, 1995; first published 1994).

Wangusa, Timothy, *Upon this Mountain* (Heinemann, Oxford and Portsmouth NH, 1989).

Waugh, Evelyn, *Black Mischief* (The Folio Society, London, 1980; first published 1932).

Woolf, Leonard, *The Village in the Jungle* (Hogarth Press, London, 1931; first published 1913).

General references

Achebe, Chinua, 'The role of the writer in a new nation', *Nigeria Magazine*, 81 (1964); reproduced in G. D. Killam (ed.), *African Writers on African Writing* (Heinemann, London, 1973).

Achebe, Chinua, 'The novelist as teacher', *New Statesman*, 29 January 1965; reprinted in William Walsh (ed.), *Readings in Commonwealth Literature* (Clarendon Press, Oxford, 1973).

Achebe, Chinua, 'African literature as celebration', *Dissent* (New York); Special Issue, 'Africa: Crisis and Change' (Summer 1992), 344–9.

Achufusi, Ify, 'Problems of nationhood in Grace Ogot's fiction', *Journal of Commonwealth Literature*, xxvii:i (1991), 179–87.

Acton, Lord, *Essays in the Liberal Interpretation of History*, edited and with an introduction by William H. McNeill (University of Chicago Press, Chicago and London, 1967).

Agovi, Kofi, 'The African writer and the phenomenon of the nation state in Africa', *Ufahamu* 18 (1990), 41–62.

Ahmad, Aijaz, 'Jameson's rhetoric of otherness and the national allegory', *Social Text*, 7 (Fall 1987), 3–25.

Ahmad, Aijaz, 'Disciplinary English: theory, Third Worldism and literary study in India', *Occasional Paper on History and Society no. XLIII* (Centre for Contemporary Studies, Nehru Memorial Museum and Library, New Delhi, September 1991).

Allen, Charles, (ed.), *Plain Tales from the Raj* (Futura, Macdonald & Co., London, 1976; first published 1975).

Amin, Samir, *Eurocentrism*, translated by Russell Moore (Zed Books, London, 1989).

Annan, Noel, 'Kipling's place in the history of ideas' in Andrew Rutherford (ed.), *Kipling's Mind and Art* (Oliver & Boyd, Edinburgh and London, 1964); reprinted from *Victorian Studies*, 3 (1959–60).

Appadurai, Arjun, 'Disjunction and difference in the global cultural economy', *Public Culture*, 2:2 (Spring 1990), 1–24.

Appadurai, Arjun, 'Sovereignty without territoriality: notes for a postnational geography' in Patricia Yaeger (ed.), *The Geography of Identity* (University of Michigan Press, Ann Arbor, 1996), pp. 40–58.

Appiah, Kwame Anthony, *In My Father's House. Africa in the Philosophy of Culture* (Methuen, London, 1992).

Ashcroft, Bill, Gareth Griffiths and Helen Tiffin, *The Empire Writes Back: Theory and Practice in Post-colonial Literatures* (Routledge, London and New York, 1989).

Ashley, Richard and Walker, R. B. J., 'Introduction: speaking the language of exile: dissident thought in international studies', *International Studies Quarterly*, 34:3 (1990), 259–68.

Ashley, Richard and Walker, R. B. J., 'Conclusion: reading dissidence/writing the discipline: crisis and the question of sovereignty in international studies', *International Studies Quarterly*, 34:3 (1990), 367–416.

Ballhatchet, Kenneth, *Race, Sex and Class Under the Raj: Imperial Attitudes and Policies and their Critics 1793–1905* (St. Martin's Press, New York, 1980).

Bardolph, Jacqueline, 'Time and history in Nuruddin Farah's *Close Sesame*', *The Journal of Commonwealth Literature*, xxiv:1, 1989 (A Symposium on the Work of Nuruddin Farah), 193–206.

Barnett, Corelli, *The Collapse of British Power* (Eyre Methuen, London, 1972).

Benjamin, Walter, 'Theory of history as a state of siege', *Social Text*, 23 (Fall/Winter 1989).

Bhabha, Homi K., 'The other question. . .', *Screen*, 24:6 (Nov./Dec. 1983), 18–36.

Bhabha, Homi K., 'Freedom's basis in the indeterminate', *October*, 61 (Summer 1992), 46–57.

Bhabha, Homi, *The Location of Culture* (Routledge, London and New York, 1994).

Blake, Susan, 'A women's trek. What a difference does gender make?' in N. Chaudhuri and M. Strobel (eds), *Western Women and Imperialism. Complicity and Resistance* (Indiana University Press, Bloomington, 1992), pp. 19–34.

Booth, James, *Writers and Politics in Nigeria* (Hodder & Stoughton, London, 1981).

Booth, Ken, *Strategy and Ethnocentrism* (Croom Helm, London, 1979).

Boyer, Allen, 'Love, sex and history in the *Raj Quartet*', *Modern Language Quarterly* (March 1985), 65–80.

Brantlinger, Patrick, *Rule of Darkness. British Literature and Imperialism 1830–1914* (Cornell University Press, Ithaca NY and London, 1988).

Brown, Lloyd W., *Women Writers in Black Africa* (Contributions in Women's Studies, 21, Greenwood Press, Westport CT and London, 1981).

Busia, Abena P. A., 'Miscegenation as metonymy: sexuality and power in the colonial novel', *Ethnic and Racial Studies*, 9:3 (3 July 1986), 360–72.

Butterfield, Herbert, *History and Human Relations* (Collins, London, 1951).

Buttinger, Joseph, 'Fact and fiction on foreign aid. A critique of *The Ugly American*', *Dissent*, 6 (1959), 317–67.

Callaway, Helen, *Gender, Culture and Empire: European Women in Colonial Nigeria* (Macmillan in association with St. Antony's College, Oxford, Basingstoke, 1987).

Callinicos, Alex, 'Wonders taken for signs: Homi Bhabha's postcolonialism', *Transformations*, 1 (Spring 1995), 98–112.

Chakrabarty, Dipesh, 'Postcoloniality and the artifice of history: Who speaks for Indian pasts?', *Representations*, 37 (Winter 1992), 1–26.

Chandra, Sudhir, (ed.), *Social Transformation and Creative Imagination* (issued under the auspices of the Nehru Memorial Museum and Library, Allied Publishers Private Ltd., Navrangpura, Ahmedabad, 1984).

Chatterjee, Partha, *Nationalist Thought and the Colonial World – A Derivative Discourse* (Zed Books for The United Nations University, Bath Press, Avon, 1986).

Chattopadhyay, Gouranga P., 'The "Invader in the Mind" in Indian metaculture', *The Economic Times* (Bombay, New Delhi, Calcutta) 21–22 May 1982.

Chattopadhyay, Gouranga P., 'The Illusion that was India' (Paper presented at the First International Symposium on Group Relations, Contributions to Social and Political Issues, Oxford, July 1988).

Chaudhuri, Nirad C., 'Passage to and from India', *Encounter*, 2:6 (June 1954), 19–24.

Chaudhuri, Nirad C., 'The finest story about India in English', *Encounter*, 8:5 (May 1957), 47–53.

Chennells, Anthony John, Settler myths and the Southern Rhodesian novel (unpublished PhD thesis, University of Zimbabwe, Harare, August 1982).

Chinweizu, *Decolonizing the African Mind* (Pero Press, Lagos, 1987).

Chinweizu, Onwuchekwa Jemie and Ihechukwu Madubuike, *Toward the*

Decolonization of African Literature, vol. 1 (Howard University Press, Washington, DC, 1983).

Choudhuri, Subir Ray, 'In search of a parallel: *The Story of Sonny Sahib* (1894) and *Kim* (1901)', *Jadavpur Journal of Comparative Literature*, (Department of Comparative Literature, Jadavpur University, Calcutta), 20–21 (1982–3), 137–50.

Chow, Rey, *Women and Chinese Modernity. The Politics of Reading Between West and East* (Theory and History of Literature, Vol. 75, University of Minnesota Press, Minnesota and Oxford, 1991).

Chrisman, Laura, 'The imperial unconscious? Representations of imperial discourse', *Critical Quarterly*, 32:3 (Autumn 1990), 38–58.

Crick, Bernard, *George Orwell: A Life* (Secker & Warburg, London, 1980).

Cronin, Richard, 'The Indian English novel: *Kim* and *Midnight's Children'*, *Modern Fiction Studies*, 33:2 (Summer 1987), 201–13.

Curtin, Philip D., *The Image of Africa. British Ideas and Actions, 1780–1850* (Macmillan, London, 1965).

Dakubu, M. E. Kropp, 'Search Sweet Country and the language of authentic being', *Research in Africa Literatures*, 24:i (1993), 19–35.

Dallek, Robert, *The American Style of Foreign Policy: Cultural Politics and Foreign Affairs* (Mentor, New American Library, New York, 1983).

Darby, Phillip, *Three Faces of Imperialism. British and American Approaches to Asia and Africa* (Yale University Press, New Haven CT and London, 1987).

Darby, Phillip (ed.), *At the Edge of International Relations. Postcolonialism, Gender, Dependency* (Pinter, London, 1997).

Darby, Phillip and Fuller, Richard, 'Western domination and Western literature' *Melbourne Journal of Politics*, 14 (1982–3), 5–18.

Darby, Phillip and Paolini, A. J., 'Bridging international relations and postcolonialism' *Alternatives*, 19:2 (1994), 371–97.

Darwin, John, 'Imperialism in decline? Tendencies in British imperial policy between the wars', *Historical Journal*, xxiii:3 (1980), 657–79.

Davidson, Basil, *The Black Man's Burden. Africa and the Curse of the Nation-State* (James Currey, London, 1992).

Davidson, James F., 'Political science and political fiction', *American Political Science Review*, 55:4 (December 1961), 851–60.

Davies, A. F., *Skills, Outlooks and Passions. A Psychoanalytic Contribution to the Study of Politics* (Cambridge University Press, Cambridge, 1980).

Der Derian, James and Shapiro, Michael, (eds), *International/Intertextual Relations:*

Postmodern Readings of World Politics (Lexington Books, Lexington MA, 1989).

Devetak, Richard, 'The Project of Modernity and International Relations Theory', *Millennium*, 24:1 (1995), 27–51.

Dhawan, R. K. (ed.), *Explorations in Modern Indo-English Fiction* (Bahri Publications Private Ltd., New Delhi, 1982).

Dunton, Chris, 'Wheyting be Dat? The treatment of homosexuality in African literature', *Research in African Literatures*, 20:3 (Fall 1989), 422–48.

Eagleton, Terry, *Literary Theory. An Introduction* (Blackwell, Oxford, 1983).

Echeruo, Michael J. C., *Joyce Cary and the Novel of Africa* (Longman, London, 1973).

Erikson, Erik H., *Gandhi's Truth. On the Origins of Militant Nonviolence* (Faber & Faber, London, 1970).

Erikson, Erik H., *Life History and the Historical Moment* (W. W. Norton & Co., New York, 1975).

Escobar, Arturo, 'Imagining a post-development era? Critical thought, development and social movements', *Social Text*, 31/32, 10:2 and 3 (1992), 20–56.

Farah, Nuruddin, 'Why I write', *Third World Quarterly*, 10:4 (1988), 1591–9.

Farah, Nuruddin, 'Childhood of my schizophrenia', *Times Literary Supplement*, 23–29 November 1990, p. 1264.

Featherstone, Mike, (ed.), *Global Culture. Nationalism, Globalisation and Modernity* (Sage Publications, London, Newbury Park and New Delhi, 1990).

Feierman, Steven, 'Africa in history: the end of universal narratives', ch. 2 in Gyan Prakesh (ed.), *After Colonialism. Imperial Histories and Postcolonial Displacements* (Princeton University Press, Princeton NJ, 1995).

Foster-Carter, Aidan, 'From Rostow to Gunder Frank: conflicting paradigms in the analysis of underdevelopment', *World Development*, 4:3 (March 1976), 167–80.

Foucault, Michel, *The Archaeology of Knowledge and the Discourse of Language* (Pantheon Books, New York, 1982; first published 1971).

Foucault, Michel, *Politics, Philosophy, Culture. Interviews and Other Writings 1977–1984*, edited with an introduction by Lawrence D. Kritzman, translated by Alan Sheridan and others (Routledge, New York and London, 1988).

Foucault, Michel, *The History of Sexuality, Vol. 1: An Introduction* (Penguin, Harmondsworth, 1990).

Frederiksen, Bodil Folke, 'City life and city texts: popular knowledge and articulation in the slums of Nairobi' in Preben Karsholm (ed.), *Cultural Struggle and Development in Southern Africa* (Baobab Books, Harare; James Currey, London; Heinemann, Portsmouth NH, 1991).

Friedman, Jonathan, 'Being in the world: globalization and localization', *Theory, Culture and Society*, 7 (1990), 311–28.

Fuller, Richard, The Image of Asia in American Bestsellers of the Cold War, 1947–1965, unpublished PhD thesis, University of Melbourne, 1989.

Fyfe, Christopher (ed.), *African Studies Since 1945. A Tribute to Basil Davidson* (Longman, London, for the Centre for African Studies, Edinburgh, 1976).

Gann, L. H. and Duignan, Peter, *The Rulers of British Africa 1870–1914* (Hoover Institution Publications, Croom Helm, London, 1978).

Gikandi, Simon, *Reading Chinua Achebe* (Studies in African Literature, New Series, James Currey, London; Heinemann, Portsmouth NH; Heinemann Kenya, Nairobi, 1991).

Gladstone, W. E., 'Aggression on Egypt and freedom in the East', *Nineteenth Century* (London), 2 (Aug.–Dec. 1877).

Grant, Rebecca and Newland, Kathleen (eds), *Gender and International Relations* (Oxford University Press, London, 1991).

Green, Martin, *The English Novel in the Twentieth Century* (Routledge & Kegan Paul, London, 1984).

Green, Philip and Walzer, Michael (eds), *The Political Imagination in Literature: A Reader* (The Free Press, New York, 1969).

Greenberger, Allen J., *The British Image of India. A Study in the Literature of Imperialism* (Oxford University Press, London, 1969).

Guha, Ranajit, 'Dominance without hegemony and its historiography', *Subaltern Studies VI* (Oxford University Press, Delhi, 1989).

Gusdorf, Georges, 'Conditions and limits of autobiography' in James Olney (ed.), *Autobiography: Essays Theoretical and Critical* (Princeton University Press, Princeton NJ, 1980), pp. 28–48.

Hancock, W. K., *Survey of British Commonwealth Affairs*, vol. 2, *Problems of Economic Policy* (Oxford University Press for RIIA, Part 1, 1940, Part 2, 1942).

Hannerz, Ulf, 'The world in creolisation', *Africa*, 57:4 (1987), 546–59.

Harlow, Barbara, *Resistance Literature* (Methuen, New York and London, 1987).

Hart, Donn V., 'Overseas Americans in Southeast Asia: fact in fiction', *Far Eastern Survey* 30:i (January 1961), 1–15.

Hawthorn, Jeremy, 'Individuality and characterization in the modernist novel' in Douglas Jefferson and Graham Martin, *The Uses of Fiction. Essays on the Modern Novel in Honour of Arnold Kettle* (Open University Press, Milton Keynes, 1982), pp. 41–58.

Hellman, John, *American Myth and the Legacy of Vietnam* (Columbia University Press, New York, 1986).

Hemenway, Stephen Ignatius, *The Novel of India vol. 2: The Indo-Anglian Novel* (Writers Workshop, Calcutta, 1975).

Hoffman, Mark, 'Restructuring, reconstruction, reinscription, rearticulation: four voices in critical international theory', *Millennium*, 20:2 (Summer 1991), 169–85.

Howe, Irving, *Politics and the Novel* (Books for Libraries Press, Freeport, New York, 1970; Essay Index Reprint Series).

Huntington, Samuel P., 'The clash of civilizations?', *Foreign Affairs*, 72:3 (Summer 1993), 22–49.

Hutchins, Francis G., *Illusion of Permanence. British Imperialism in India* (Princeton University Press, Princeton NJ, 1967).

Hyam, Ronald, *Britain's Imperial Century 1815–1914: A Study of Empire and Expansionism* (Batsford, London, 1976).

Hyam, Ronald, *Empire and Sexuality: The British Experience* (Manchester University Press, Manchester and New York, 1990).

Ikegami, Robin, 'Knowledge and power, the story and the storyteller: Achebe's *Anthills of the Savannah*', *Modern Fiction Studies*, 37:3 (Autumn 1991), 493–507.

Innes, C. L., *Chinua Achebe* (Cambridge University Press, Cambridge 1990).

Isaacs, Harold R., *Scratches on Our Minds. American Views of China and India* (M. E. Sharpe, Inc., White Plains NY, 1980; first published 1958).

Iyengar, K. R. Srinivasa, *Indian Writing in English* (Sterling Publishers, New Dehli, revised and updated edition 1985; first published 1962).

Iyer, Raghavan, (ed.), *The Glass Curtain Between Asia and Europe* (Oxford University Press, London, 1965).

Izevbaye, Dan, 'Issues in the reassessment of the African novel' in Eldred D. Jones (ed.), *African Literature Today 10: Retrospect and Prospect* (Heinemann, London, 1979), pp. 7–31.

Jacoby, Russell, 'Marginal returns. The trouble with post-colonial theory', *Linguafranca* (Sept./Oct. 1995), 30–7.

Jameson, Fredric, *The Political Unconscious: Narrative as a Socially Symbolic Act* (Methuen, London, 1981).

Jameson, Fredric, 'Third-World literature in the era of multinational capitalism', *Social Text*, 15 (Fall 1986), 65–88.

JanMohamed, Abdul, *Manichean Aesthetics: The Politics of Literature in Colonial Africa* (University of Massachusetts Press, Amherst, 1983).

Karim, M. Enamul, 'Kipling's personal vision of India in an uncollected article "Home"', *Journal of Commonwealth Literature*, XIII:1 (August 1978), 19–27.

Kennedy, Dane, 'Imperial history and post-colonial theory', *The Journal of Imperial and Commonwealth History*, 24:3 (September 1996), 345–63.

Kennedy, Paul, *The Rise and Fall of the Great Powers: Economic Change and Military Conflict from 1500 to 2000* (Fontana Press, London, 1989).

Kermode, Frank, 'Secrets and narrative sequence' in W. J. T. Mitchell (ed.), *On Narrative* (University of Chicago Press, Chicago and London, 1981).

Ki-Zerbo, J. (ed.), *General History of Africa, vol. I* (UNESCO; Heinemann Educational Books, London; University of California Press, Berkeley, 1981).

Kinkead-Weekes, Mark, 'Vision in Kipling's novels' in Andrew Rutherford (ed.), *Kipling's Mind and Art* (Oliver & Boyd, Edinburgh and London, 1964).

Knapman, Claudia, *White Women in Fiji 1835–1930: The Ruin of Empire?* (Allen & Unwin, Sydney, 1986).

Krishna, Sankaran, 'The importance of being ironic: a postcolonial view of critical international relations theory', *Alternatives*, 18 (1993), 385–417.

LaCapra, Dominick, *History and Criticism* (Cornell University Press, Ithaca NY and London, 1985).

Laferriere, Eric, 'Emancipating international relations theory: an ecological perspective', *Millennium*, 25:1 (1996), 53–75.

Lapid, Yosef, 'The third debate: on the prospects of international theory in a post-positivist era', *International Studies Quarterly*, 33:3 (September 1989), 235–54.

Larson, Charles R., *The Emergence of African Fiction* (Indiana University Press, Bloomington and London, 1972; revised edition).

Lechner, Frank J., 'Cultural aspects of the modern world system' in William H. Swatos Jr. (ed.), *Religious Politics in Global and Comparative Perspective* (Greenwood Press, Westport CT, 1989).

Lessing, Doris, *African Laughter. Four Visits to Zimbabwe* (HarperCollins, London, 1992).

Levine, George, *The Realistic Imagination* (University of Chicago Press, Chicago and London, 1981).

Linklater, Andrew, *Beyond Realism and Marxism. Critical Theory and International Relations* (Macmillan, London, 1990).

Linklater, Andrew, 'The question of the next stage in international relations theory: a critical–theoretical point of view', *Millennium*, 21:1 (1992), 77–98.

Little, Richard and Smith, Steve (eds), *Belief Systems and International Relations* (Blackwell in association with the British International Studies Association, Oxford, 1988).

Llosa, Mario Vargas, 'Is fiction the art of lying?', *New York Times Book Review*, 7 October 1984, pp. 1 and 40.

Loescher, G. and Monahan, L. (eds), *Refugees and International Relations* (Oxford University Press, London, 1989).

London, Bette, 'Reading race and gender in Conrad's Dark Continent', *Criticism*, XXXI:3 (Summer 1989), 235–52.

Louis, William Roger (ed.), *Imperialism: The Robinson and Gallagher Controversy* (New Viewpoints, New York, 1976).

Low, Gail Ching-Liang, 'White skins/black masks: the pleasures and politics of imperialism', *New Formations*, 9 (Winter 1989), 83–103.

Lukács, Georg, *The Historical Novel*, translated by Hannah and Stanley Mitchell (Penguin, Harmondsworth, 1969; first published in Russian 1938).

Lukács, Georg, *The Theory of the Novel* (Merlin Press, London, 1971; first published 1920).

Mahood, M. M., *Joyce Cary's Africa* (Methuen, London, 1964).

Mahood, M. M., *The Colonial Encounter* (Rex Collings, London, 1977).

Mandel, Barett J., 'Full of life now' in James Olney (ed.), *Autobiography: Essays Theoretical and Critical* (Princeton University Press, Princeton NJ, 1980), pp. 49–72.

Manzoni, Alessandro, *On the Historical Novel*, translated with an introduction by Sandra Berman (University of Nebraska Press, Lincoln and London, 1984; first published in Italian 1850).

Marechera, Dambudzo, 'The African writer's experience of European literature', *Zambezia* (The Journal of the University of Zimbabwe, Mount Pleasant, Harare), xiv:ii (1987), 99–105.

Marechera, Dambudzo, 'Soyinka, Dostoevsky: the writer on trial for his time', *Zambezia*, xiv:ii (1987), 106–11.

Marrouchi, Mustapha Ben T., 'The critic as dis/placed intelligence: the case of Edward Said', *Diacritics*, 21:1 (Spring 1991), 63–74.

Marrouchi, Mustapha Ben T., 'Literature is dead, long live theory', *Queen's Quarterly*, 98:4 (Winter 1991), 775–801.

Martin, Wallace, *Recent Theories of Narrative* (Cornell University Press, Ithaca NY, 1986).

Mason, Philip, *Prospero's Magic* (Oxford University Press, London, 1962).

Mason, Philip, *Patterns of Dominance* (Institute of Race Relations, Oxford University Press, London, 1970).

Maughan-Brown, David, *Land, Freedom and Fiction. History and Ideology in Kenya* (Zed Books, London, 1985).

Mazrui, Ali A., *The African Condition* (Heinemann, London, 1980).

Mazrui, Ali A., *Cultural Forces in World Politics* (James Currey, London, 1990; Heinemann, Kenya and Portsmouth NH, 1990).

Mbembe, Achille, 'The banality of power and the aesthetics of vulgarity in the postcolony', *Public Culture*, 4:2 (Spring 1992), 1–30.

McCarthy, Mary, 'The lasting power of the political novel', *New York Times Book Review*, 1 January 1984, pp. 1, 27 and 29.

McClure, John and Mufti, Aamir, Introduction, *Social Text*, 31/32 (1992).

Memmi, Albert, *The Colonizer and the Colonized* (Beacon Press, Boston, 1967; translated by Howard Greenfeld and first published 1957).

Miyoshi, Masao, 'A borderless world? From colonialism to transnationalism and the decline of the nation-state', *Critical Inquiry*, 19 (Summer 1993), 726–51.

Mohanty, Satya P., 'Drawing the color line: Kipling and the culture of colonial rule' in Dominick LaCapra, (ed.), *The Bounds of Race. Perspectives on Hegemony and Resistance* (Cornell University Press, Ithaca NY, 1991), pp. 311–43.

Montefiore, Janet, 'Day and night in Kipling', *Essays in Criticism*, 27:4 (1977), 299–314.

Moore, Robin, *Paul Scott's Raj* (Heinemann, London, 1990).

Morgenthau, Hans J., *Politics Among Nations* (Alfred A. Knopf, New York, 3rd edition 1963).

Mouffe, Chantal, 'For a politics of nomadic identity' in George Robertson, Melinda Nash, Lisa Tickner, Jon Bird, Barry Curtis and Tim Putnam (eds), *Travellers' Tales. Narratives of Home and Displacement* (Routledge, London and New York, 1994).

Mphahlele, Ezekiel, *The African Image* (Faber & Faber, London, 1962).

Mudimbe, V. Y., (ed.), *The Surreptitious Speech. Présence Africaine and the Politics of Otherness 1947–1987* (University of Chicago Press, Chicago and London, 1992).

Mukherjee, Arun P., 'The exclusions of postcolonial theory and Mulk Raj Anand's *Untouchable*: A case study', *Ariel*, 22:3 (July 1991), 27–48.

Mukherjee, Meenakshi, *The Twice Born Fiction. Themes and Techniques of the Indian Novel in English* (Heinemann, New Delhi and London, 1971).

Mukherjee, Sujit, *Forster and Further. The Tradition of Anglo-Indian Fiction* (Orient Longman, Bombay, 1993).

Murdoch, Iris, *Metaphysics as a Guide to Morals* (Chatto & Windus, London, 1992).

Murray, Gilbert, *Humanist Essays* (Unwin Books, London, 1964).

Myers, Jeffrey, *Fiction and the Colonial Experience* (Boydell Press, Ipswich, 1973).

Naipaul, V. S., 'A new king for the Congo: Mobutu and the nihilism of Africa' and 'The brothels behind the graveyard' in *The Return of Eva Peron with the Killings in Trinidad* (Penguin, Harmondsworth, 1981; first published 1980).

Nandy, Ashis, *At the Edge of Psychology. Essay in Politics and Culture* (Oxford University Press, Delhi, 1980).

Nandy, Ashis, *The Intimate Enemy. Loss and Recovery of Self Under Colonialism* (Oxford University Press, London, 1983).

Nandy, Pritish, 'Literature of protest' in Suresh Kohli (ed.), *Aspects of Indian Literature* (Vikas Publishing House, Delhi, 1975), pp. 83–9.

Narasimhaiah, C. D. (ed.), *Awakened Conscience. Studies in Commonwealth Literature* (Sterling Publishers, New Delhi, 1978).

Narayanan, Gomathi, *The Sahibs and the Natives. A Study of Guilt and Pride in Anglo-Indian and Indo-Anglian Novels* (Chanakya Publications, Delhi, 1986).

Neill, Michael, 'Guerrillas and gangs: Frantz Fanon and V. S. Naipaul', *Ariel*, 13:4 (October 1982), 21–62.

Ngugi wa Thiong'o, *Barrel of a Pen. Resistance to Repression in Neo-Colonial Kenya* (New Beacon Books, London, 1983).

Ngugi wa Thiong'o, *Decolonising the Mind. The Politics of Language in African Literature* (James Currey, London, 1986).

Nicholson, Kai, *A Presentation of Social Problems in the Indo-Anglian and the Anglo-Indian Novel* (Jaico Publishing House, Bombay, 1972).

Nkosi, Lewis, *Tasks and Masks. Themes and Styles of African Literature* (Longman, London, 1981).

Nkrumah, Kwame, *I Speak of Freedom* (Mercury Books, London, 1961).

Ochieng, William, 'Undercivilisation in Black Africa', *Kenya Historical Review*, 2:1 (1974).

Ogumba, Oyin, 'Traditional content of the plays of Wole Soyinka', *African Literature Today*, 4, 2–18.

Ojwang, J. B. and Mugambi, J. N. K. (eds), *The S. M. Otieno Case. Death and Burial in Modern Kenya* (Nairobi University Press, Nairobi, 1989).

Omotoso, Kole, 'Trans-Saharan views: mutually negative portrayals', in Eldred D. Jones (ed.), *African Literature Today 14: Insiders and Outsiders* (Heinemann, London, 1984), pp. 111–17.

Orwell, George, 'Shooting an Elephant' in Sonia Orwell and Ian Angus (eds), *The Collected Essays, Journalism and Letters of Orwell vol. 1, An Age Like This* (Secker & Warburg, London, 1968).

Osundare, Niyi, 'Words of iron, sentences of thunder: Soyinka's prose style' in Eldred D. Jones (ed.), *African Literature Today, 13: Recent Trends in the Novel* (Heinemann, London, Ibadan, Nairobi; Africana Publishing Co., New York, 1983), pp. 24–37.

Palmer, Eustace, 'Ngugi's *Petals of Blood*' in Eldred D. Jones, (ed.), *African Literature Today, 10: Retrospect and Prospect* (Heinemann, London, 1979), pp. 153–66.

Pannikar, K. M., *Asia and Western Dominance. A Survey of the Vasco Da Gama Epoch of*

Asian History 1498–1945 (Allen & Unwin, London, 1953).

Paolini, Albert, 'Foucault, realism and the power discourse in international relations', *Australian Journal of Political Science,* 28:1 (March 1993), 98–117.

Parekh, Bhikhu, *Gandhi's Political Philosophy: A Critical Examination* (Macmillan, London, 1989).

Parker, Andrew, Mary Russo, Doris Sommer and Patricia Yaeger (eds), *Nationalisms and Sexualities* (Routledge, New York and London, 1992).

Parry, Benita, *Delusions and Discoveries. Studies on India in the British Imagination* (University of California Press, Berkeley and Los Angeles, 1972).

Parry, Benita, *Conrad and Imperialism. Ideological Boundaries and Visionary Frontiers* (Macmillan, London, 1983).

Parry, Benita, 'Problems in current theories of colonial discourse', *Oxford Literary Review,* 9:1–2 (1987), 27–59.

Parry, Benita, 'Signs of our times. Discussion of Homi Bhabha's *The Location of Culture'*, *Third Text,* 28/29 (Autumn/Winter 1994), 5–24.

Parry, Benita, 'Speech and silence in the fictions of J. M. Coetzee', *New Formations,* 21, (Winter 1994), 1–20.

Parsons, Grant, 'Another India: imagining escape from the masculine self', in Phillip Darby (ed.), *At the Edge of International Relations. Postcolonialism, Gender and Dependency* (Pinter, London, 1996).

Pathak, Zakia, Sengupta, Saswati and Sharmila Purkayastha, 'The prisonhouse of orientalism', *Textual Practice,* 5:2 (Summer 1991), 195–218.

Patteson, Richard F., 'Manhood and misogyny in the imperialist romance', *Rocky Mountain Review of Language and Literature,* 31:1 (1981), 3–12.

Peck, Richard, 'Hermits and saviors, osagyefos and healers: artists and intellectuals in the works of Ngugi and Armah', *Research in African Literatures,* 20:1 (Spring 1989), 26–43.

Petersen, Kirsten Holst, 'The personal as political: the case of Nuruddin Farah', *Ariel,* 12:3 (July 1981), 93–110.

Petersen, Kirsten Holst (ed.), *Religion, Development and Identity* (Seminar Proceedings, no. 17, Scandinavian Institute of African Studies, Uppsala, 1987).

Peterson, V. Spike (ed.), *Gendered States: Feminist, (Re)Visions of International Relations Theory* (Lynne Rienner, Boulder CO, 1992).

Pettman, Ralph, *Human Behaviour and World Politics. A Transdisciplinary Introduction* (Macmillan, London, 1975).

Podis, Leonard A. and Saaka, Yakubu, 'Anthills of the Savannah and Petals of Blood. The creation of a usable past', *Journal of Black Studies,* 22:1 (September 1991), 104–22.

Ramamurti, K. S., 'East–West understanding as reflected in British writing on India and Indian writing in English', *Jadavpur Journal of Comparative Literature* (Department of Comparative Literature, Jadavpur University, Calcutta), 20–21 (1982–3), 59–70.

Ramamurti, K. S., *Rise of the Indian Novel in English* (Sterling Publishers Private Ltd., New Delhi, 1987).

Rimmon-Kenan, Shlomith, *Narrative Fiction: Contemporary Poetics* (Methuen, London, 1983).

Robinson, Ronald and Gallagher, John, with Alice Denny, *Africa and the Victorians: The Official Mind of Imperialism* (Macmillan, London, 1961).

Rockwell, Joan, *Fact in Fiction. The Use of Literature in the Systematic Study of Society* (Routledge & Kegan Paul, London, 1974).

Rosecrance, Barbara, *Forster's Narrative Vision* (Cornell University Press, Ithaca NY and London, 1982).

Rothstein, Robert A. and LeCron Foster, Mary (eds), *The Social Dynamics of Peace and Conflict. Culture in International Security* (Westview Press, Boulder CO and London, 1988).

Ruggie, John Gerard, 'Territoriality and beyond: problematizing modernity in international relations', *International Organization,* 47:1 (Winter 1993), 139–74.

Runyan, Anne Sisson and Peterson, V. Spike, 'The radical future of realism: feminist subversions of international relations theory', *Alternatives,* 16:1 (Winter 1991), 67–106.

Rushdie, Salman, 'Outside the whale', *Granta,* 11 (1983), 124–38.

Ryle, Martin, 'Long live literature? Englit, radical criticism and cultural studies', *Radical Philosophy,* 67 (Summer 1994), 21–7.

Said, Edward W., *Beginnings: Intention and Method* (Basic Books, New York, 1975).

Said, Edward W., *Orientalism* (Routledge & Kegan Paul, London, 1980; first published 1978).

Said, Edward W., 'Identify, negation and violence', *New Left Review,* 171 (1988), 46–60.

Said, Edward W., *Culture and Imperialism* (Chatto & Windus, London, 1993).

Said, Edward W., 'Orientalism and after: an interview with Edward Said', *Radical Philosophy,* 63 (Spring 1993), 22–32.

Sarma, Gobinda Prasad, *Nationalism in Indo-Anglian Fiction* (Sterling Publishers, New Delhi, 1978).

Schafer, Roy, 'Narration in the psychoanalytic dialogue' in W. J. T. Mitchell (ed.), *On Narrative* (University of Chicago Press, Chicago and London, 1981), pp. 25–49.

Schipper, Mineke, *Beyond the Boundaries. African Literature and Literary Theory* (W. H. Allen and Co., London, 1989).

Scholes, Robert and Kellogg, Robert, *The Nature of Narrative* (Oxford University Press, London, 1966; reprinted 1978).

Schwarz, Bill, 'An Englishman abroad . . . and at home: the case of Paul Scott', *New Formations*, 17 (Summer 1992), 95–105.

Scott, James, *Weapons of the Weak. Everyday Forms of Peasant Resistance* (Yale University Press, New Haven CT and London, 1985).

Shapiro, Michael J., 'Moral geographies and the ethics of post-sovereignty', *Public Culture*, 6:3 (1994), 479–502.

Sharpe, Jenny, *Allegories of Empire. The Figure of Woman in the Colonial Text* (University of Minnesota Press, Minneapolis and London, 1993).

Shohat, Ella, 'Notes on the post-colonial', *Social Text*, 31/32 (1992), 99–113.

Singh, Bhupal, *A Survey of Anglo-Indian Fiction* (Oxford University Press, London, 1934).

Smith, Tony, 'Requiem or new agenda for Third World studies?', *World Politics*, 37:4 (July 1985), 532–61.

Soyinka, Wole, *Myth, Literature and the African World* (Cambridge University Press, Cambridge, 1976).

Soyinka, Wole, 'The critic and society: Barthes, leftocracy and other mythologies' in Henry Louis Gates (ed.), *Black Literature and Literary Theory* (Methuen, New York and London, 1984).

Spence, Donald P., *Narrative Truth and Historical Truth. Meaning and Interpretation in Psychoanalysis* (Norton, New York, 1982).

Spender, J. A., *The Changing East* (Cassell, London, 1926).

Spivak, Gayatri Chakravorty, 'Can the subaltern speak?' in Cary Nelson and Lawrence Grossberg (eds), *Marxism and the Interpretation of Culture* (University of Illinois Press, Chicago, 1988).

Spurling, Hilary, *Paul Scott: A Life* (Hutchinson, London, 1990).

Stokes, Eric, *The English Utilitarians and India* (Clarendon Press, Oxford, 1959).

Stoler, Ann, 'Rethinking colonial categories: European communities and the boundaries of rule', *Comparative Studies in Society and History*, 31:1 (1989), 134–61.

Stott, Rebecca, 'The Dark Continent: Africa as female body in Haggard's adventure fiction', *Feminist Review*, 32 (Summer 1989), 69–89.

Stratton, Florence, *Contemporary African Literature and the Politics of Gender* (Routledge, London and New York, 1994).

Street, Brian V., *The Savage in Literature. Representations of 'Primitive' Society in English Fiction 1858–1920* (Routledge & Kegan Paul, London and Boston, 1975).

Suleri, Sara, *The Rhetoric of English India* (University of Chicago Press, Chicago and London, 1992).

Sylvester, Christine, *Zimbabwe: The Terrain of Contradictory Development* (Westview Press, Boulder CO, San Francisco and Oxford, 1991).

Sylvester, Christine, 'Urban women's cooperatives, "progress", and "African feminism" in Zimbabwe', *Differences*, 3:1 (1991), 29–62.

Sylvester, Christine, *Feminist Theory and International Relations in a Postmodern Era* (Cambridge University Press, Cambridge, 1993).

Swinden, Patrick, *Paul Scott: Images of India* (Macmillan, London, 1980).

Taussig, Michael, *Shamanism, Colonialism and the Wild Man. A Study in Terror and Healing* (University of Chicago Press, Chicago and London, 1987).

Tharu, Susie, 'Reading against the imperial grain: intertextuality, narrative structure and liberal humanism in Mulk Raj Anand's *Untouchable*', *Jadavpur Journal of Comparative Literature*, 24 (1986), 60–71.

Thompson, Edward, *Rabindranath Tagore. His Life and Work* (Association Press [YMCA], Calcutta, 2nd edition 1928).

Trevor-Roper, Hugh, 'History and imagination' in Hugh Lloyd-Jones, Valerie Pearl and Blair Warden (eds), *History and Imagination. Essays in Honour of H. R. Trevor-Roper* (Duckworth, London, 1981).

Trilling, Lionel, *The Liberal Imagination. Essays on Literature and Society* (Secker & Warburg, London, 1951).

Trilling, Lionel, 'A Passage to India', (1942) reprinted in Malcolm Bradbury (ed.), *A Passage to India: A Casebook* (Macmillan, London, 1970), pp. 77–92.

Triulzi, Allessandro, 'African cities, historical memory and street buzz', in Iain Chambers and Lidia Curti (eds), *The Post-Colonial Question. Common Skies, Divided Horizons* (Routledge, London and New York, 1996).

Veit-Wild, Flora, *Dambudzo Marechera: A Sourcebook on his Life and Work* (Hans Zell, London, Melbourne, Munich, New York, 1992).

Vigne, Randolph (ed.), *A Gesture of Belonging. Letters from Bessie Head, 1965–1970* (SA Writers, London; Heinemann, Portsmouth NH, 1991).

Viswanathan, Gauri, *Masks of Conquest: Literary Study and British Rule in India* (Columbia University Press, New York, 1989).

Walker, R. B. J., 'Culture, discourse, insecurity', *Alternatives*, 11:4 (October 1986), 485–504.

Walker, R. B. J., 'The concept of culture in the theory of international relations' in Jongsuk Chay (ed.), *Culture and*

International Relations (Praeger, New York, 1990).

Walker, R. B. J., 'From IR to world politics', in Joseph A. Camilleri, Anthony P. Jarvis and Albert Paolini (eds), *The State in Transition. Reimagining Political Spaces* (Lynne Rienner, London, 1995).

Wallerstein, Immanuel, 'Culture as the ideological battleground of the modern world-system' in Mike Featherstone (ed.), *Global Culture. Nationalism, Globalization and Modernity* (Sage, London and Newbury Park, New Delhi, 1990).

Walsh, William (ed.), *Readings in Commonwealth Literature* (Clarendon Press, Oxford 1973).

White, Hayden, *Tropics of Discourse* (Johns Hopkins University Press, Baltimore, 1978).

White, Hayden, 'The value of narrativity in the representation of reality' in W. J. T. Mitchell (ed.), *On Narrative* (University of Chicago Press, Chicago and London, 1981), pp. 1–24.

White, Hayden, 'Historical pluralism', *Critical Enquiry*, 12 (Spring 1986), 480–493.

White, Hayden, *The Content of the Form: Narrative Discourse and Historical Representation* (Johns Hopkins University Press, Baltimore, 1987).

Wilding, Michael, 'The politics of *Nostromo*', *Essays in Criticism*, 16:4 (1966), 441–56.

Williams, Raymond, *Culture and Society 1780–1950* (Chatto & Windus, London, 1958).

Williams, Raymond (ed.), *George Orwell. A Collection of Critical Essays* (Prentice-Hall Inc., Englewood Cliffs NJ, 1974).

Williams, Raymond, *Politics and Letters. Interviews with New Left Review* (Verso, London, 1981; 1st edition 1979).

Wilson, Edward, 'The Kipling that nobody read' in *The Wound and the Bow. Seven Studies in Literature* (Methuen University Paperbacks, London, 1961; first published 1941).

Woolf, Leonard, *Growing: Vol. II of His Autobiography* (Hogarth Press, London, 1961).

Worsley, Peter, *The Three Worlds. Culture and the World Development* (Weidenfeld & Nicolson, London, 1984).

Wright, Derek, 'Orality in the African historical novel: Yambo Ouologuem's *Bound to Violence* and Ayi Kwei Armah's *Two Thousand Seasons*', *Journal of Commonwealth Literature*, XXIII:1 (1988), 91–101.

Wright, Derek, *Ayi Kwei Armah's Africa. The Sources of His Fiction* (New Perspectives on African Literature, no. 1, Hans Zell, London, Munich, New York, 1989).

Wright, Rev. T. H., *Francis Thompson and his Poetry* (George G. Harrap & Co. Ltd., London, Calcutta, Sydney, 1927).

Young, Robert, *Colonial Desire. Hybridity in Theory, Culture and Race* (Routledge, London and New York, 1995).

Young, Wayland, *Eros Denied* (Weidenfeld & Nicolson, London, 1965).

Zolberg, Aristide R., 'The Specter of Anarchy', *Dissent* (New York), 39:3 (Summer 1992), 303–11.

Index

Abdication 104, 105, 108, 109
Achebe, Chinua 28, 41, 143–4, 163–4, 170, 171–2
Acton, Lord 20
Adowa, Italian defeat at 203
Africa 136, 139–40, 179–81
  pasts in fiction 139–50, 152–3, 156
  women's writing 157–8
African Witch, The 71, 177
agency 55, 154, 216, 225
Ahmad, Aijaz 227, 233
aid 174–6
Aissa Saved 71, 177
Akare, Thomas 47
Ali, Ahmed 49
Allan Quartermain 68
Almayer's Folly 71
Amadi, Elechi 152
ambivalence 127
  of colonized 83, 89, 120, 125–6, 180
  of colonizer 59, 228, 230
America 17, 26, 35–6, 53
  culture 69–70, 193
  novels of Asia 26–7, 46, 194–5, 209–10
American Visitor, An 176, 197–8
Amin, Samir 229
Anand, Mulk Raj 101, 102, 103–4, 195, 224
Angola 17
Anthawar House 102
Anthills of the Savannah 143–4
Appadurai, Arjun 207
Appiah, Kwame Anthony 153, 181
Armah, Ayi Kwei 141–3, 151–2
Asia 53–4, 58
  feminization of 72–3
At Fever Pitch 69
'At the End of the Passage' 62
Australia 210, 227

Bangladesh (East Pakistan) 210–11
Bend in the Ganges, A 121, 123–4
Bend in the River, A 147–9
Berlin Conference (1884–85) 15, 229
Bhabha, Homi 219, 224, 230
Bhattacharya, Bhabani 43
binary oppositions 117, 127, 221–4
Black Insider, The 159
Black Mischief 59
Black Sunlight 160–1
Blake, Susan 42
body, the 110, 233
Bones 171
Book of Secrets, The 15
Booth, Ken 210–11
borders, national 15, 162–3, 211–12
Botswana 175
Bound to Violence 141–2
Brantlinger, Patrick 193
'Bridge-Builders, The' 56–7
Britain 53, 55, 58
  culture 193–4, 231
  in India 79, 83, 100–1, 103, 104
  withdrawal from India 112–13
Bromfield, Louis 194
Brown, Lloyd 157
Buchan, John 70
Buck, Pearl 26, 46
Burdick, Eugene 27
Burgess, Anthony 60, 113
Burma 60, 63
Burmese Days 60, 63, 105–6, 128

Camp des Saints, Le 206
Candler, Edmund 104, 108, 109
Cary, Joyce 46, 71, 176–7, 197–8
Cataclysm 208
Caute, David 69, 206

Chaudhuri, Nirad 26, 127–8
Chennells, Anthony 38
China 72
Chinweizu 219, 225
Chow, Rey 72
Chrisman, Laura 193, 199
Christianity 145, 150, 158, 177, 193
Churchill, Winston 110
Circle of Reason, The 215
city life 47, 157, 161–2, 170–2, 176
Clarinda 101
Clark, William 208
class 49, 97, 182
Clear Light of Day 48
Close Sesame 42, 145–6, 169
Coates, Everard 96
Coetzee, J. M. 64, 200–1
colonial dependence 89
colonialism 66, 89, 120, 151, 224
  see also imperialism
Coming to Birth 156–7
commodities, representations of 198–200
Conrad, Joseph 61–2, 71, 199
Coolie 101, 102
Coup, The 60
cultural difference 45–6, 109–10, 137, 233
  in Africa 158–61
cultural intimacy 126, 222
cultural similarity 210
Curtin, Philip 25

Dance of the Forests, A 144, 164–5
Dangarembga, Tsitsi 171, 181
Dangerous Love 161–2
Davidson, Basil 162
Davies, A. F. 14
Decline of the West, The 206
decolonization 11, 26, 127, 206
dependency theory 36, 216

Desai, Anita   48
development   172–4, 194–5
Devil of a State   60
disciplines
   boundaries   3, 9, 81, 191,
      216, 223, 231
   dialogue between   1, 37,
      234
disguise   93, 97
Diver, Maud   72, 92, 110
domination   53–5, 73
Durrell, Lawrence   204–5

East Timor   210–11
economic interest   191,
   194–201, 233–4
   in fiction   192–201, 212
'Education of Otis Yeere,
   The'   56
Egypt   55, 204
Ekwensi, Cyprian   172
Emecheta, Buchi   172
Erikson, Erik   23
everyday life   14, 48, 49,
   154–5, 177, 180, 207–8

Farah, Nuruddin   28, 42,
   145–7, 164, 168–9, 174–5
Farrell, J. G.   195–6
feminism   17–18, 170, 223,
   230
fiction
   compared with non-
      fiction   2, 20–4, 34–6
   engagement with culture
      45–7
   personal orientation
      39–44
   reader involvement
      28–30, 37–8, 48–50
   status of   2
   see also the novel
Forster, E. M.   46, 105, 108–9,
   110–11
*Forty-eight Guns for the
   General*   163
Foucault, Michel   20, 54, 140
France   42, 206
Frank, Andre Gunder   36,
From a Crooked Rib   168–9
Fuller, Richard   209–10

Gandhi, Mohandas K.   23,
   43, 44, 110
Gandhism   103
gender   66
   representations of
      women   70–1, 171–2
'Georgie Porgie'   94
Ghamat, K. E.   87–8
Ghana   151, 155, 177–8

Ghosh, Amitav   211–12, 215
Ghosh, S. K.   85–7, 203–4
Gifts   174–5
Gikandi, Simon   143
Gladstone W. E.   55
globalization   46–7, 207–8,
   216, 229
Going Down River Road   161
Good Earth, The   46
Gora   99
Graduate, The   166
Grain of Wheat, A   150
Great Ponds, The   152
Green Berets, The   27
Green, Martin   59
Greenberger, Allen   56, 91
Greene, Graham   26–7, 67

Haggard, H. Rider   67, 68,
   71
Hancock, W. K.   196
Head, Bessie   166–7, 175–6
Healers, The   142, 152
Heart of Darkness   61–2
Heart of the Matter, The   67
Hegel   54
Hemenway, Stephen   104
Henty, G. A.   68
Hinduism   57, 84, 86, 89,
   99–100, 158
Hindupore   83–5, 223
Hobart, Tisdale   72
Hobsbawn, Eric   141
Hosts of the Lord, The   92
House of the Hunger, The   160
Hove, Chenjerai   171
Howe, Irving   29
Huntington, Samuel   47
Hyam, Ronald   66–7
hybridity   83, 178, 179, 181,
   222–5, 229, 233

*I Shall Not Hear the
   Nightingale*   122
identity   119–20, 139, 180,
   181, 233
identity politics   13, 180, 215
Ike, Chukwuemeka   163
Ikegami, Robin   144
imperialism   11, 25, 53, 79,
   81, 105, 108, 193, 194,
   199, 223, 225, 228, 229,
   230
   limited impact   26, 56–61,
      63–4
   as modernization   59–60
   vulnerability of   61–3
   see also colonialism
India   56, 211–12, 217
   pasts in fiction   82–90
   see also nationalism, Indian

Indian Day, An   106, 111–12
Indian National Army   123,
   134 n.133
Innes, C. L.   143
insecurity   55–7, 228, 230
international relations   36,
   191, 216
   contribution of   231–4
   depersonalization   13–14,
      42–3
   disciplinary isolation
      17–18, 231–2
   Eurocentrism   10–11
   limitations of politics
      15–16
   neglect of culture   11–13
   positivism   16–17
   'third debate'   18–19
Interpreters, The   165
Iroh, Eddie   163
Islam   47, 158
Issacs, Harold   26
Italy   87
Iyengar, K. R. S.   103

Jagua Nana   172
Jameson, Frederic   80
JanMohamed, Abdul   197,
   219
Japan   84, 87, 203, 204
Joys of Motherhood, The   172

Kanthapura   103
Kennedy, Paul   53, 54, 56–7
Kenya   149, 155, 156–7, 164,
   166
Kermode, Frank   38, 39
Kim   97–100
Kincaid, Dennis   106
King Solomon's Mines   67, 71,
   199–200
Kipling, Rudyard   45–6, 55,
   62, 92–100, 201–2
Krishna, Sakaran   232

LaCapra, Dominick   21, 24
Laing, B. Kojo   155, 177–8
Lawley Road   125
Lechner, Frank   47
Lederer, William J.   27
Lessing, Doris   64–5
Lilamani   92
Little Tobrah   94
Lodge in the Wilderness, A   70
Long Day Names, The   60
Low, Gai Ching-Liang   93
Lukács, Georg   39–40, 44

McCarthy, Mary   29
Macgoye, Marjorie Oludhe
   156–7

Madhaviah, A. 101
Mahood, Molly 197
Mailer, Norman 48, 69–70
Malaya 60
Malgonkar, Manohar 121, 123–4
Man of the People, A 171–2
'Man Who Was, The' 58
Manzoni, Alessandro 29
Maps 164
Marechera, Dambudzo 159–61, 166–7, 171, 181
'Mark of the Beast, The' 93
Markandaya, Kamala 121
Maru 166
masculinity 67, 73, 123, 230
  see also sexuality
Mason, Philip 55
Matigari 173
Mazuri, Ali 13, 158
Mbembe, Achille 44
Memmi, Albert 89
Midnight's Children 44–5, 205
Mimic Men, The 148
missionaries 15, 25
Mitra, S. M. 83–5, 203
Miyoshi, Masao 233
Mo, Timothy 210
modernity 167–78, 230
Mouffe, Chantal 233
Mountbatten, Lord 12
Mountolive 204–5
Mphahlele, Ezekiel 154
Mr Johnson 67, 196
Mukerji, Dhan Gopal 202–3
Mukherjee, Arun 227
Murdoch, Iris 50
Murray, Gilbert 30, 34
Murugan the Tiller 102
Mwangi, Meja 161, 176
My Friend the Barrister 87–8

Nada the Lily 68
Nagarajan, K. 102
Nahal, Chaman 122, 124
Naipaul, V. S. 79, 147–9
Naked Needle, A 174
Nandy, Ashis 3, 43–4
Nandy, Pritish 126
Narayan, R. K. 125, 223
narratology 21–4, 221
nation-state 12, 13, 90, 151, 153, 207, 215
  in African literature 162–7, 180
nationalism 81, 223
  Indian 49, 88–9, 122
Negritude 151
Nervous Conditions 172, 181
Ngugi wa Thiong'o 28, 150, 155–6, 158, 170, 173, 195
Nigeria 144, 152, 163, 164, 165, 166, 170
civil war 144–5, 163, 173
Nkrumah, Kwame 151
No Longer At Ease 41
North/South relations 9, 13, 46, 191, 215, 216, 217, 222
Nostromo 199
novel, the
  adaptability of 168, 222–3
  changing forms 40–1, 83
  domestic/overseas 193–4
  moral agency of 49–50
  in politics 24–8
Nzenza, Sekai 170

Ogot, Grace 166
Okpewho, Isidore 173–4
Okri, Ben 161–2
On the Face of the Waters 91, 92
Opera Wonyosi 165
Orientalism 45, 117, 210, 222
Orwell, George 60, 63–4, 105, 108
Ouologuem, Yambo 141–2
Outcast of the Islands 71

Pakistan 205
pan-Africanism 151–3
  cultural cohesion 153–4
Panikkar, K. M. 53, 54
Parry, Benita 25–6, 91, 98, 225
Passage to India, A 105, 108–11, 127
peasant, the 124
  see also subalternity
personal as political 79–80, 113–15, 122, 128–9, 228–9
  foundlings 95–100
  friendship 101, 105–12, 169
  love 83–8, 90, 121
  rape 115–16, 121
Petals of Blood 155–6
Petersen, Kirsten Holst 147
place and space 108, 128, 220
postcolonialism 3, 46, 138, 217–21
  alternative futures 223–4
  nature of 217–18
  phases in development 218–21
  weaknesses of 225, 227–8, 231–4
postmodernism 18–19, 24
power politics
  in fiction 98–9, 191, 192–4, 201–12
in international relations 11–14
Prince of Destiny, The 85–7, 203–4
psychoanalysis 23–4

Question of Power, A 166, 175–6
Quiet American, The 26–7

race 47–8, 49, 55, 97, 152
Rains Came, The 194
Raj Quartet, The 113–20
Ranger, Terence 138, 141
Rao, Raja 103
Raspail, Jean 206
Redundancy of Courage, The 210
refugees 14
representations 25–6, 230, 233
resistance 28, 127, 181, 227, 233
riots 211–12
River Between, The 150
Robinson and Gallaghar controversy 35
Ruggie, John Gerard 18
Rushdie, Salman 44–5, 205
Russo–Japanese war 203–4

Said, Edward 1, 24, 39, 193, 199, 231
Sardines 146, 169
satyagraha 23
Scott, James 54
Scott, Paul 112, 113–20, 231
Search Sweet Country 155, 177–8
Season of Anomy 144–5, 165
Secret Listeners of the East, The 202–3
self–other politics 93, 210, 233
Seth, Vikram 48
sexuality 66–7, 71–2
  homosexuality 55, 68–70, 110–11, 116–17, 165
Shadow Lines, The 211–12
Shadows 171
Shame 205
She 71
'Shooting an Elephant' 63
Show Business 47
Singapore Grip, The 195–6
Singer Passes, The 110
Singh, Khushwant 122, 123
Slums, The 47
So Many Hungers 43
social distance 90–2, 105,

122

Somalia   145–6, 164, 169

Some Inner Fury   121

Soyinka, Wole   142, 144–5, 151, 164–5

Spence, Donald   23

Spender, J. A.   91

Spivak, Gayatri Chakravorty   219

Sri Lanka (Ceylon)   58

Steel, Flora Anne   71, 91

Steen, Marguerite   72

'Story of Mohammad Din, The'   94

Story of Sonny Sahib, The   96–7

'Strange Ride of Morrowbie Jukes, The'   62

Stratton, Florence   157

subalternity   154, 182, 219, 220, 224, 227

subjectivity   44, 215, 233, 234

Suitable Boy, A   48

Suleri, Sara   79, 98, 110–11, 231

Sun is My Undoing, The   72

Sunset at Dawn   163

Sweet and Sour Milk   146

Sylvester, Christine   14, 17

Tagore, Rabindranath   99

Taussig, Michael   44

Tharo, Susie   103

Tharoor, Shashi   47

Their Ways Divide   106

Things Fall Apart   41

Thompson, Edward   106, 108, 111–12

'To Be Filed for Reference'   93

'Tods' Amendment'   94

Train to Pakistan   123

Trilling, Lionel   39, 107

Trotsky, Leon   43

Twilight in Delhi   49

Two Leaves and a Bud   101

Two Thousand Seasons   141–2, 143, 151, 152

Uganda   167

Ugly American, The   27

Ullman, James   194

Untouchable   102

Updike, John   60

Upon this Mountain   167

Vassanji, M. G.   15

Venkataramani, K. S.   102

Vietnam   17, 48, 69–70

Village in the Jungle, The   58–9

Viswanathan, Gauri   230

Waiting for the Barbarians   64, 200

Waiting for the Mahatma   125

Walker, R. B. J.   13, 215

Wallerstein, Immanuel   13

Wangusa, Timothy   167

Waugh, Evelyn   59

When Rain Clouds Gather   175

White, Hayden   22, 24, 35

Why Are We in Vietnam?   69–70

Why Are We So Blest?   151

Wilding, Michael   199

Williams, Raymond   16

Wilson, Edmund   98

Windom's Way   194

'Without Benefit of Clergy'   94

women
    in African fiction   154
    and social change   42
    in Western fiction   70–1

Woolf, Leonard   58–9

Worsley, Peter   13

Yang and Yin   72

'Yoked With an Unbeliever'   94

Zaire   147–8

Zimbabwe (Rhodesia)   14, 38, 66, 160–1, 166–7, 171, 181